DATE DUE	
MAY 2 6 1999	12-19-2019
	200091760
11/05/99 Inet	
MAY 0 8 2000	
11-02-00 IL: 2567740	
NOV 0 3 2002	
OCT 0 6 2003	
4/3/2009 IL:	50562974
9/1/2010	IL 67032387

COUNSELING THE
GIFTED AND TALENTED

Edited by Linda Kreger Silverman

A Keystone Consortium Book

Contributing Authors

Leland Baska
Nicholas Colangelo
Kathy M. Evans
John F. Feldhusen
Dan Holt
Fathi Jarwan
Deirdre V. Lovecky
Sal Mendaglio
Jean Sunde Peterson
Kenneth Seeley
Linda Kreger Silverman
Joyce VanTassel-Baska

LOVE PUBLISHING COMPANY®
Denver, Colorado 80222

Photographs by Caryn Boddie and Ron Forsberg.
Courtesy of the Rocky Mountain School for the Gifted and the Gifted Child Development
Center.

Library of Congress Catalog Card Number 92-74350

Copyright ©1993 Love Publishing Company
Printed in the U.S.A.
ISBN 0-89108-227-1

Contents

6 Counseling Gifted Learning Disabled: Individual and Group Counseling Techniques   131

Sal Mendaglio
University of Calgary, Alberta, Canada

7 Counseling Families   151

Linda Kreger Silverman
Gifted Child Development Center, Denver, Colorado

11 **Assessment Tools for Counselors** 239
John F. Feldhusen
Fathi Jarwan
Dan Holt
Purdue University, Indiana

PART IV   SPECIAL ISSUES 261

12 **Gifted Students at Risk** 263
Ken Seeley
Piton Foundation, Denver, Colorado

13 **Multicultural Counseling** 277
Kathy Evans
College of William and Mary, Williamsburg, Virginia

Preface

Linda Kreger Silverman

Counseling the Gifted and Talented has been designed as a textbook for
graduate courses in gifted education and counseling psychology. It should also
prove helpful to therapists, counselors, school psychologists, coordinators of
gifted programs, teachers of the gifted, support personnel, administrators and
parents who wish to have a better understanding of the social and emotional
needs of gifted children and youth. Gifted adults have many of the same issues
as gifted children; therefore, psychologists and counselors will find strategies
in these chapters applicable to many of their adult clients, and grown-up gifted
children will gain self-awareness and self-acceptance as they see themselves
described in these pages.

The book is organized in four parts: *understanding giftedness, the counseling process, counseling in the schools* and *special issues*. The first part
provides a new definition of giftedness, a rationale for counseling services
focused on the gifted population, a theoretical basis for understanding the
emotional intensity of the gifted, a clinical perspective of five traits of
giftedness, and a developmental model that serves as a basis for counseling
interventions. The second part contains specific techniques for individual
counseling, group counseling, counseling with families, bibliotherapy, and
stress reduction. This section instructs teacher/counselors about the basic
strategies of individual and group counseling and informs seasoned professionals about some of the unique issues involved in counseling the gifted.
Chapter 5 invites teacher/counselors to conduct "discussion" groups with
gifted students on a variety of issues, while chapter 6 includes tapescripts of
actual group counseling sessions with gifted/learning disabled students. Part
III describes the roles of school psychologists, teachers of the gifted, counselors, and administrators in meeting the affective needs of the gifted; outlines an
effective method of academic counseling; includes a blueprint for translating

assessment information into curricular strategies; provides a comprehensive discussion of career development; and concludes with a detailed analysis of the most widely used assessment instruments. Part IV covers underachievers and other gifted students at risk, multicultural counseling, and gender issues related to social development and leadership. The book ends with a list of strategies for developing moral leadership.

Counseling the Gifted and Talented includes an annotated resource guide to assist parents and school districts in locating counseling and assessment services; an up-to-date bibliography for parents; a list of excellent children's literature that feature gifted children as protagonists; biographies for gifted students; and an annotated description of the major publications in the field. These special features make this an excellent reference book for libraries, educational service centers, and other agencies that serve gifted children and their families.

The focus of this book is on prevention rather than remediation, seeing the counseling process as a means of facilitating self-actualization in gifted students. All individuals who interact with gifted children need to develop some counseling expertise. With this in mind, much of the book has been devoted to providing concrete strategies for the noncounselor. We present new conceptualizations and a thorough, up-to-date review of the literature, intermingled with rich anecdotal material from case files. Our aim was to make a scholarly treatment of this subject accessible to a broad range of readers. It is hoped that the reader will gain a deeper appreciation of the inner struggles of gifted students and learn concrete strategies for meeting the social and emotional needs of this population.

Special thanks to Elizabeth Maxwell for expert editorial assistance and for her constant support throughout this project. Thanks also to my family for their patience and love.

This book is dedicated in loving memory of
Dr. Leta Hollingworth (1886–1939),
the first counselor of gifted children,
who devoted her life to furthering our
understanding of the emotional needs of the gifted.
It is also dedicated to my cousin,
Dr. Louis Gerstman (1931–1992),
who won fame for teaching the computer to talk,
yet considered his greatest accomplishment the more
than three hundred doctoral candidates he mentored
through neuropsychology and related fields at
City University of New York.

PART I

Understanding Giftedness

1

The Gifted Individual

Linda Kreger Silverman

EMOTIONAL ASPECTS OF GIFTEDNESS

To the uninformed, giftedness may seem a sort of special privilege, but to the gifted individual, often it feels like a distinct disadvantage. It is painful to be different in a society that derides differences. Pain may also come from internal sources—from a finely tuned psychological structure that experiences all of life more intensely. Giftedness has an emotional as well as a cognitive substructure: cognitive complexity gives rise to emotional depth. Thus, gifted children not only *think* differently from their peers, they also *feel* differently.

> One of the basic characteristics of the gifted is their intensity and an expanded field of their subjective experience. The intensity, in particular, must be understood as a *qualitatively distinct characteristic*. It is not a matter of degree but of a different quality of experiencing: vivid, absorbing, penetrating, encompassing, complex, commanding—a way of being quiveringly alive. (Piechowski, 1991b, p. 2, emphasis added)

Dr. Annemarie Roeper (1982) has defined the term *giftedness* in a way that encompasses its emotional side: "Giftedness is a greater awareness, a greater sensitivity, and a greater ability to understand and transform perceptions into intellectual and emotional experiences" (p. 21). Another new definition that highlights the internal experience of the gifted may be particularly helpful to counselors:

> Giftedness is *asynchronous development* in which advanced cognitive abilities and heightened intensity combine to create inner experiences and awareness that are qualitatively different from the norm. This asynchrony increases with higher intellectual capacity. The uniqueness of the gifted renders them particularly vulnerable and requires modifications in parenting, teaching and counseling in order for them to develop optimally. (The Columbus Group, 1991, p. 1)

3

Asynchrony in the gifted means "a lack of synchronicity in the rates of their cognitive, emotional and physical development" (Morelock, 1992b, p. 11). Lack of synchronicity creates greater inner tension, as when a five-year-old child perceives a horse through eight-year-old eyes but cannot replicate the horse in clay with her five-year-old fingers and so screams in frustration. Internal asynchrony is mirrored in external adjustment difficulties because the child feels "different," "out of place"—*out of sync*—with others. Uneven development of gifted children has been noted by numerous clinicians and researchers (Altman, 1983; Delisle, 1990; Gowan, 1974; Hollingworth, 1942; Kerr, 1991; Kline & Meckstroth, 1985; Munger, 1990; Roedell, 1989; Schetky, 1981; Sebring, 1983; Terrassier, 1985; Webb, Meckstroth, & Tolan, 1982). Manaster and Powell (1983) suggested that gifted adolescents are in psychosocial jeopardy if they are *out of stage* ("dealing with concepts and goals far beyond the reach of those around them"), *out of phase* ("*alienated* and distant from or *without a peer group* with which to interact"), or *out of sync* ("feel that they are different...and feel they do not, should not or cannot fit in") (p. 71). Their framework is based on the assumption that everyone needs a sense of belonging in order to experience psychological well-being. Unfortunately, the authors erroneously concluded that "in all other ways the gifted are typical, common, ordinary, regular and normal and able to healthily fit in with others. ...[They] must have...*the courage to be average* in order to be psychosocially adjusted" (p. 73).

A more comprehensive precursor to the Columbus Group definition is Terrassier's (1985) "dyssynchrony," which has both internal and external aspects. Internal dyssynchrony implies the disparate rates of development of various capacities of the child. Manifestations of external dyssynchrony include a lack of goodness-of-fit between the school curriculum and the child's needs, a lack of conformity to cultural expectations based upon the chronological age of the child, problems relating to age peers, and preference for older companions.

Child development books usually contain charts showing the interaction between stages of psychosexual, psychosocial, and cognitive development according to chronological age (which presumably correlates with physical development). The basic premise is that these stages all occur in concert with each other. Uniform progression in all areas is rare, but discrepancies are more exaggerated in the gifted (Schetky, 1981), particularly the highly gifted [above 145 IQ], whose development is the most uneven. Despite various concerns about intelligence testing, *the intelligence quotient* does provide valuable information about the rate at which cognitive development outstrips physical development and therefore *is an index of the degree of asynchrony*. Tolan (1989) offers a clear example of asynchronous development and the difficulties it presents:

In terms of development chronological age may be the least relevant piece of information to consider. Kate, with an IQ score of 170, may be six, but she has a "mental age" of ten and a half.... Unfortunately, Kate, like every highly gifted child, is an amalgam of many developmental ages. She may be six while riding a bike, thirteen while playing the piano or chess, nine while debating rules, eight while choosing hobbies and books, five (or three) when asked to sit still. How can such a child be expected to fit into a classroom designed around norms for six year olds? (p. 7)

There are more questions than answers about the developmental paths of gifted children and a discouraging lack of research to answer these questions. We do know that their development takes an altered course. "With the gifted individual we are often looking not only at precocious development but unique developmental characteristics so that the normal developmental path is less effective as a prospective guide" (Horowitz, 1987, p. 165). Altman (1983) maintains that "the gifted child may achieve stages of emotional and physical development in alternative patterns [from age peers] and/or at varying times chronologically," and may progress through the stages more rapidly, with shorter intervals of "relative stability within stages and between periods of change" (p. 66). According to Altman, unusually rapid development may be a source of emotional trauma, with little emotional support from peers whose developmental changes are more consistent with each other. Even the various developmental stage theories, then, need to be adapted in order to understand the atypical development of the gifted. Asynchronous development results in unusual "awareness, perceptions, emotional responses and life experiences" throughout the life span (Morelock, 1992b, p. 14).

This new definition goes beyond Terrassier's dyssynchrony and other definitions focusing on uneven development in that it incorporates the emotional dimension, emphasizing the interrelationship of cognitive complexity and emotional intensity. Although the emotional sensitivity of the gifted has been reported frequently (Clark, 1992; Genshaft & Broyles, 1991; Jacobs, 1971; Manaster & Powell, 1983; Roedell, 1984; Webb, Meckstroth, & Tolan, 1982; Whitmore, 1980), many seem to be unaware that intense emotions attend giftedness. The term *emotion* is conspicuously absent in the indexes of most books on the gifted and talented, indicating how little attention is paid to this component of giftedness. Historically, the expression of intense feelings has been perceived as a sign of emotional instability (Lombroso, 1905) rather than as evidence of a rich inner life. Neglect of the emotional aspects of giftedness can be traced to the traditional Western view of emotion and cognition as separate, contradictory phenomena. Only recently have we become aware of the inextricable link between emotion and cognition and their combined impact on individuals of high intelligence.

The picture of the more emotional person, as it is emerging from this research, stands in significant contrast to the traditional dominant view. This picture reveals that a high level of emotional responsiveness may be associated with advanced cognitive organization. All of the cognitive skills that were found to be related to the ability to respond with more emotions are marks of a highly organized awareness—an awareness that might be governed by a well-structured system of values, oughts, and beliefs, but not by momentary excitements. (Sommers, 1981, p. 560)

Sommers (1981) found that college students who evidenced advanced cognitive organization had a wider "emotional range" (p. 555), a term she used to denote variety of emotional response. Sommers's concept of emotional range may shed light on one of the age-old mysteries in teaching and raising gifted children: How can an eight-year-old talk like a forty-year-old one minute and act like a four-year-old the next? Apparently the child's cognitive complexity enables a much wider range of emotional response than is found in the average child. As a firstborn in a household of adults, for example, the child learns adult emotional responses, and when a new baby enters the family, regressive behavior often appears. "Act your age!" is not a simple directive to a child whose mental age, physical age, and emotional age are not well integrated. This explains the apparent discrepancy in the literature between those who find gifted children emotionally advanced (Robinson & Noble, 1991) and those who see them as emotionally immature. Actually, they are both, depending on the moment at which one catches them.

The Columbus Group definition further indicates that cognitive complexity and emotional intensity leave the gifted emotionally vulnerable and therefore in need of modifications in parenting, teaching, and counseling. This definition may be the first to acknowledge the emotional vulnerability of the gifted child and the importance of the counselor's role in the child's emotional development. Roedell (1984) suggests that even moderately gifted children [130–145 IQ] are "vulnerable to a variety of adjustment difficulties" (p. 127) and that social adjustment, emotional maturity, and healthy self-concepts depend to a great extent on environmental support. She found the degree of vulnerability directly related to the degree of developmental difference.

> As the degree of intellectual advancement increases, so does the child's risk of social maladjustment and unhappiness....there is general agreement that highly gifted children are more susceptible to some types of developmental difficulties than are moderately gifted or average children. Areas of vulnerability include uneven development, perfectionism, adult expectations, intense sensitivity, self-definition, alienation, inappropriate environments, and role conflicts. (Roedell, 1984, p. 127)

Hollingworth (1931) suggested that gifted children are particularly vulnerable between the ages of four and nine:

> To have the intelligence of an adult and the emotions of a child combined in a childish body is to encounter certain difficulties. It follows that (after babyhood) the younger the child, the greater the difficulties, and the adjustment becomes easier with every additional year of age. The years between four and nine are probably the most likely to be beset with the problems mentioned. (p. 13)

Vulnerability is to be expected when advanced cognition brings information into awareness for which there is insufficient emotional maturity. Gowan

(1974) likened precocious cognitive awareness to premature rupturing of the protective placental shell during the prenatal period. Too early exposure to environmental realities can be as precarious in postuterine as in prenatal development. This phenomenon is apparent in an excellent case study presented by Morelock (1992a) of a highly gifted four-year-old girl who experienced intense emotional turmoil during a period of rapid cognitive development:

> As Jennie grappled with the sudden onslaught of increased abstract capacity, she was forced to deal with the emotional repercussions of her own thought. Thus, in Jennie's mind at the age of four, God could not possibly be a loving God if He would refuse Heaven to anyone. And the terrible realization of her own mortality could not be softened by her mother's reassurances, because "Nobody knows for sure; *children* die sometimes." In spite of her impressive capacity for abstract thought, Jennie *was* only four. Her emotional needs, like those of other four-year-olds, included a trust in the strength and reliability of her parents and the predictability of a secure world. However, her advanced cognitive capacities...left her emotionally defenseless in the face of her own reason. (pp. 25–26)

Thus, counseling for the gifted and creative is a necessary response to a unique set of emotional needs; it is important both to support healthy emotional development and to prevent social and emotional problems.

THE GIFTED AS A SPECIAL NEEDS GROUP

There is a great deal of misunderstanding about giftedness. Anyone in a counseling capacity is likely to encounter numerous individuals who do not understand that the gifted have special needs. Therefore, to be an effective advocate, the counselor of the gifted must have an appropriate rationale for supporting identification, curricular modifications, and counseling interventions for this group of children.

The necessity of special provisions for the gifted can be understood most clearly when this population is perceived as a legitimate part of special education. Without the shield of special education, it is difficult to justify why gifted children should have differentiated programs. Exceptional children of all types are significantly different from the norm; therefore, they fail to thrive without modifications. The purpose of special provisions for exceptional children, whether educational or counseling, is to *respond to their unique needs*. Although it is relatively clear that children in every other branch of special education have unique needs, this assumption has not been widely endorsed for the gifted and has to be made explicit.

Under the rubric of special education, one can see that the distance from the norm of those who are developmentally advanced parallels the distance of those who are developmentally delayed, and that the unique needs attendant to that difference increase in direct proportion to the degree of exceptionality. The gifted are traditionally defined as students whose IQ scores are 2 standard deviations above the mean [approximately 130 IQ], comprising the top 2 percent of the population. Although this stringent definition has been replaced by newer ones that include a broader spectrum of capabilities and different types of talents, the most extraordinarily gifted still are neglected. The following analogy helps to bring this point home.

As can be seen in Figure 1.1, the top 2 percent correspond to the group whose IQ scores fall 2 standard deviations below the norm [below 70 IQ], a population whose needs are so clearly differentiated that they are protected by both federal and state mandates. Individual intelligence tests, comprehensive psychological assessment, staffings, individualized educational plans, certified teachers, modified curriculum, and due process are all required by law for students more than 2 standard deviations below the mean. At 3 standard deviations below the mean [approximately 55 IQ] even greater intervention is needed, such as partial or full-day self-contained placements. At 4 standard deviations below the mean [approximately 40 IQ], children need continuous supervision. (In some experimental settings, certain developmentally disabled children may be "mainstreamed," with a full-time aide to assist each of them, but they would be unable to handle the regular curriculum.) Yet, students who score 2, 3, 4, or more standard deviations above the mean are often placed in regular classrooms with no modifications of any kind, and frequently their parents are derided for attempting to secure "special treatment" for their children (e.g., see George, 1988). A continuum of services should be made available to the gifted, similar to that which is available for the disabled. (See Figure 1.2.)

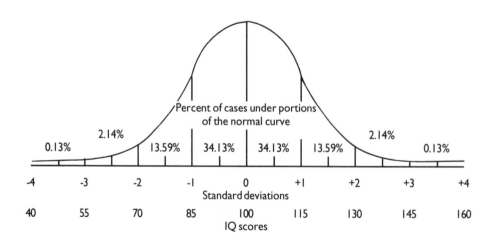

Figure 1.1
THE THEORETICAL CURVE OF DISTRIBUTION OF INTELLIGENCE

The situation is further complicated by unconscious hostility in society toward children who are thought of as "intellectually advantaged." Resentment toward gifted children on the part of administrators, psychologists, counselors, and teachers has been well documented (J. Gallagher, 1991; Marland, 1972; Singal, 1991). Whereas other exceptional children receive sympathy, often the gifted are targets of antagonism, which increases their emotional vulnerability (Kline & Meckstroth, 1985). (e.g., "If you're so gifted, why are you running down the hall?")

Advocates of the gifted must be prepared to deal with the perennial charge of "elitism." It is ironic that football heroes and Olympic medal winners are exempt from this charge. Athletically advanced youth are the pride of the nation; no one would dream of holding them to the level of their less talented peers as part of a misguided program of egalitarianism. The accusation of "elitism" has been misdirected at the gifted—elitism is actually a function of socioeconomic class rather than of intellectual differences. There is no evidence that grouping gifted children fosters snobbery (Newland, 1976). On the contrary, a false sense of one's importance is more likely to result from being "top banana" in one's class all the way through school with no equally able peers and no need to study because the work is too easy. Grouping gifted children together usually cures any illusions of superiority. Hollingworth (1930) observed:

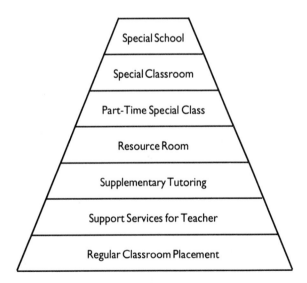

The continuum of services available for meeting the needs of disabled children. Most are served in the regular classroom with increasing amounts of support depending upon the severity of the problem.

Figure 1.2
CONTINUUM OF SERVICES

> Many of our pupils had their first experience of being equaled or surpassed at school work when they entered the special class. Several interesting episodes arose to suggest that conceit was corrected, rather than fostered, by the experience of daily contact with a large number of equals. (p. 445)

As advocates, we need to clarify the distinction between giftedness and socioeconomic advantage. Giftedness cuts through all social strata, and all racial, ethnic, and economic groups. Gifted education is most needed for children from less economically advantaged families who depend on public education for the development of their children's talents. Children from families with greater resources have other alternatives such as private schools, tutoring, and homeschooling. It is the talented poor who suffer the most when programs for the gifted are cut.

In attempts to cope with the charged political climate around the concept of giftedness, gifted education has become more and more broadly defined, so that more children can be considered "gifted," "talented," "creative," and "potentially gifted." Now it is common for gifted programs to involve 5, 7, 10, 15, 25, and as much as 33 percent of the population. The irony is that the broader the net, the less differentiated the needs of the students, and the less justifiable the gifted program. The small amount of available funds is spread so thin that a differentiated program is hardly feasible. An enrichment program that serves the top 10 percent 45 minutes a week is likely to be attacked as an unnecessary frill because "all students" could benefit from such enrichment.

The result is that the educational needs of the gifted and highly gifted are usually neglected, which in turn affects their morale, motivation, social relationships, aspirations, sense of self-worth, and emotional development. Counseling for the gifted is needed to help these students cope with society's attitudes toward them, as well as to help them find their way through an educational system that is not designed to optimize their progress. Counselors can provide emotional support to individual students and their parents, institute preventive counseling groups, work with individual teachers to obtain curricular modifications for gifted students, or work at the building level to establish appropriate programs.

In addition to helping gifted students deal with the impact of the external conditions listed above, the counselor must be sensitive to the unique internal conditions of this group. These internal variables—for example, intensity, sensitivity, and perfectionism—are illumined through the lens of Dabrowski's "Theory of Emotional Development" (Dabrowski, 1972; Dabrowski & Piechowski, 1977; Piechowski, 1991a), the only psychological theory specific to the development of giftedness and creativity (Piechowski, 1979). Dabrowski studied the mental health of intellectually and creatively gifted children and adults. His insights provide a foundation for understanding the complex inner life of the gifted throughout the life span, as well as their differentiated counseling needs.

DABROWSKI'S THEORY

Kazimierz Dabrowski (1902–1980), a Polish psychiatrist and psychologist, survived both world wars. During World War II, at the risk of his life, he gave asylum to Jews escaping from the Nazis. He was imprisoned by both the Nazis and the Communists, tortured, and forbidden to continue his professional practice (Nelson, 1989, 1991). His theory grew out of his own confrontation with death, suffering, and injustice and his desire to understand the meaning of human existence. During the wars, he witnessed acts of complete self-sacrifice in the midst of incomprehensible inhumanity and puzzled that both could exist in the same world.

As a youth, Dabrowski was repelled by the cruelty, duplicity, superficiality, and absence of reflection he saw in those around him. He searched for individuals who were "authentically ideal, saturated with immutable values, those who represented 'what ought to be' against 'what is'" (Dabrowski, in Piechowski, 1975, p. 234). In the biographies of eminent individuals and saints, he found the immutable values he sought and agonies that matched his own. After digesting an untold number of biographies of gifted, creative, and eminent people, Dabrowski continued his search in the laboratory and the clinic. He studied artists, actors, dancers, and intellectually gifted children and youth.

Dabrowski's private practice attracted creative adolescents and adults. In their struggle to attain something nobler in themselves, his clients displayed an emotional richness similar to that which he had seen in his biographical studies of the eminent. They could not reconcile themselves to concrete reality; instead, they clung to their creative visions of what ought to be. They searched for "a reality of higher level. And often they were able to find it unaided" (Dabrowski, in Piechowski, 1975, p. 236). These clients experienced intense inner conflict, self-criticism, anxiety, and feelings of inferiority toward their own ideals. The medical community labeled these conflicts as "psychoneurotic" and attempted to "cure" the clients by eliminating their symptoms. Dabrowski saw these same symptoms as an inseparable part of the quest for higher-level development. He fervently desired to convince the profession that inner conflict is a *developmental* rather than a degenerative sign.

From these observations, Dabrowski developed his "Theory of Positive Disintegration," in which he proposed that advanced development requires a breakdown of existing psychological structures in order to form higher, more evolved structures. The emotional makeup and intellectual capacity of the individual determine the extent of development possible. Inner conflict generates the tension that impels the individual toward higher levels of functioning. Positive disintegration is a disillusion of current ways of thinking and being in the world in the service of greater compassion, integrity, and altruism; it is marked by heightened creativity (Dabrowski, 1964). Negative disintegration, in contrast, is a breakdown that has no moral or ethical component; it is self-centered, containing none of the seeds that would enable the person to reintegrate on a higher level. The counselor's job is to distinguish between these two different experiences.

Dabrowski's theory emphasizes the role of emotions in human development, so since his death it has come to be known as "Dabrowski's Theory of Emotional Development." Independent support for some of Dabrowski's tenets comes from the research of Shula Sommers (1981). As described earlier, Sommers found strong correlations between cognitive complexity, emotional responsiveness, and structured value systems in college students. Cognitive complexity enables the person to take other viewpoints and to recognize injustice, creating a strong value system from which to evaluate life events. These evaluations activate rich emotional responses: individuals with well-developed value systems tend to be more emotionally reactive when they see behavior that violates their values. Sommers's findings echo Dabrowski's (1972) observations of the interplay of intellectual and emotional overexcitabilities in the gifted person's pursuit of higher values.

The relationship between cognition and emotion, the development of value structures, and the heightened intensity of the gifted and creative are all addressed in Dabrowski's theory. Intensity, so characteristic of the gifted, is explained in terms of *overexcitabilities*—greater capacities to respond to various stimuli. Others also have theorized that the gifted come equipped with supersensitive nervous systems which enable them to assimilate extraordinary amounts of sensory stimuli (Blackburn & Erickson, 1986; Cruickshank, 1963; Whitmore, 1980). "By its very intensity, a high kind of creativity may cause nervous strain and tension, and a supersensitivity of the nervous system may be conducive to both inner conflict and creative expression" (Cruickshank, 1963, p. 494). Whitmore (1980) adds that supersensitivity makes the gifted acutely perceptive and sensitive, more discriminating of the details of stimuli, and more analytical and critical of themselves and others.

> This physiological characteristic of the gifted child accounts for the tendency of young gifted children to be described frequently as "hyperactive" and highly "distractible." The supersensitive nervous system requires much activity, and the child needs help to learn how to screen out some stimuli and to focus on a selected few in order to increase concentration and effective assimilation of input without undue fatigue. (p. 147)

The expanded awareness of the individual, deriving primarily from inborn emotional, intellectual, and imaginational overexcitabilities, eventually leads to the development of value structures which guide development in adolescence and adulthood. Both the overexcitabilities and the developing value system create a unique inner life which marks the gifted as different from their peers. These differences, often misunderstood, underscore the need for counseling. Counseling via a Dabrowskian perspective goes beyond the sphere of social adjustment and career planning; it focuses instead on the powerful force of inner conflict in the development of value structures.

Dabrowski's theory is composed of two parts: the overexcitabilities and levels of development. The strength of these overexcitabilities, along with special talents and abilities, constitutes the individual's "developmental potential"—that is, potential for self-actualization and higher level development (Piechowski, 1979, 1991b). The overexcitabilities are discussed first because they appear in childhood.

The Overexcitabilities

The overexcitabilities described by Dabrowski (1938) are observable in infancy and thought to be innate. They represent expanded awareness and a heightened capacity to respond to stimuli of various types. Dabrowski postulated five overexcitabilities (OEs): *psychomotor, sensual, imaginational, intellectual,* and *emotional.* The term *overexcitability,* translated from Polish, means "superstimulatability," and carries with it positive connotations: an unusual capacity to care, an insatiable love of learning, vivid imagination, endless energy, and so forth. The OEs are an abundance of physical, sensual, creative, intellectual, and emotional energy. The strength of these overexcitabilities—particularly imaginational, intellectual, and emotional OEs—is positively related to advanced emotional development in adulthood. In studying a group of gifted children and youth in Warsaw in 1962, Dabrowski (1972) found that every one of them showed considerable manifestations of the overexcitabilities. Table 1.1 indicates the forms and expressions of the OEs used in the assessment and coding process.

Individuals with the gift of extra physical energy are "doers"—highly active and constantly on the go. Surplus energy is shown in rapid speech and gestures, marked enthusiasm, love of fast games and sports, nervous habits, and impulsiveness (Piechowski, 1991a). Schetky (1981) notes that gifted children have "high energy drive both physical and psychological" and that they can be "physically and mentally exhausting to live with" (p. 2). One of the earliest signs of *Psychomotor OE* is less need for sleep in infancy (Munger, 1990; Schetky, 1981). A parent of a highly gifted child remarked, "When other babies were getting 12 hours of sleep, I was lucky if he slept 6 hours. I figured he was smarter than other children his age because he had been awake twice as long" (Silverman & Kearney, 1989, p. 52). Children with high Psychomotor OE occasionally are misdiagnosed as hyperactive (Schetky, 1981; Whitmore, 1980). Hyperactive children tend to lack voluntary control of attention and behavior, such as interrupting and then losing the thread of the conversation. Gifted children who are high in psychomotor energy are simply very active, with few other symptoms of hyperactivity. They are capable of focused attention and intense concentration when they are interested; aimless activity seems to occur most often when there is insufficient mental stimulation.

By itself, Psychomotor OE does not differentiate gifted from average

Table 1.1
FORMS AND EXPRESSIONS OF PSYCHIC OVEREXCITABILITY

PSYCHOMOTOR

Surplus of energy

Rapid speech, marked enthusiasm, fast games and sports, pressure for action, acting out

Psychomotor expression of emotional tension

Compulsive talking and chattering, impulsive actions, nervous habits (tics, nailbiting), workaholism, acting out, compulsive organizing, competitiveness

SENSUAL

Sensory pleasure

Seeing, smelling, tasting, touching, hearing

Sensual expression of emotional tension

Overeating, sexual overindulgence, buying sprees, wanting to be in the limelight

Aesthetic Pleasures

Appreciation of beautiful objects (gems, jewelry, etc.), writing styles, words

INTELLECTUAL

Probing questions; problem solving; learning

Curiosity, concentration, capacity of sustained intellectual effort, avid reading, detailed planning

Theoretical thinking

Thinking about thinking, analytical thinking, introspection, love of theory and analysis, moral thinking and development of a hierarchy of values, conceptual and intuitive integration

IMAGINATIONAL

Free play of the imagination

Frequent use of image and metaphor, facility for invention and fantasy, facility for detailed visualization, poetic and dramatic perception, animistic and magical thinking

Spontaneous imagery as an expression of emotional tension

Animistic imagery, mixing truth and fiction, elaborate dreams, illusions, detailed visual recall, fears of the unknown, tendency to dramatize

EMOTIONAL

Intensity of feeling

Positive feelings, negative feelings, extremes of emotion, complex emotions and feelings, identification with others' feelings, laughing and crying together

Somatic expressions

Tense stomach, sinking heart, blushing, flushing

Inhibition (timidity, shyness)

Strong affective memory

Fears and anxieties, feelings of guilt

Concern with death, depressive and suicidal moods

Relationship feelings

Emotional ties and attachments, concern for others (empathy), sensitivity in relationships, attachment to animals, difficulty adjusting to new environments, loneliness, conflicts with others over depth of relationship

Feelings toward self

Self-evaluation and self-judgment, feelings of inadequacy and inferiority

Source: Adapted from "Developmental Potential" by M. M. Piechowski, in *New Voices in Counseling the Gifted* (p. 31), edited by N. Colangelo and T. Zaffrann, 1979, Dubuque, IA: Kendall/Hunt. Copyright 1979 by Kendall/Hunt Publishing Co. Used with permission.

development in children, adolescent, or adult populations. It must be integrated with other OEs before it becomes developmentally significant (Manzanero, 1985; Piechowski & Cunningham, 1985). But many actualized individuals (e.g., Albert Schweitzer and Mother Teresa) have been known for their unusual physical energy and capacity for working excessively long hours.

Sensual OE may be the most elusive of the overexcitabilities to measure and understand. It is marked by heightened experience of the senses, sensualism, sexuality, aesthetic appreciation, and desire for physical admiration. Individuals who love to touch different textures, who delight in particular smells such as paint and tar, or who cherish the memory of certain foods are showing signs of Sensual OE. In infants, this OE may be expressed in throwing off blankets and in extreme reactions to certain clothing (Meckstroth, 1991). Other signs include intense reaction to noise and immediate crying when diapers get wet. Colic and food allergies, both common among the gifted, may be manifestations of this OE; the child has enhanced sensitivities to foods and pollutants. Mothers report having to cut labels from children's clothes and having to be particularly careful about the placement of sock seams on toes because their children react so strongly (Meckstroth, 1991). Some children hate the textures of certain foods and are remarkably sensitive to small differences in their chemical content—for example, they can taste the difference in Coca Cola processed in different factories (D. Lovecky, personal communication, April 8, 1992). Freed (1990) observes:

> In addition to their perfectionism, I have noted that children with IQs above 140 seem to have heightened sensory awareness. They taste more acutely, smell everything, observe more in their environment. They get so much information that they have trouble filtering it out. They are constantly bombarded by stimuli. (p. 11)

Reactions such as these may continue into adult life. One respondent wrote, "My mornings were difficult, for my clothes had to exert the same pressure on both sides of my body. One stocking had to be exactly as tight as the other or I couldn't function" (Piechowski, 1979, p. 33).

An adult gifted population was found to be higher than an unselected group in Sensual OE (Silverman & Ellsworth, 1980); however, in studies conducted to date no differences in Sensual OE have been revealed between gifted and average children (Rogers, 1986), or between gifted and average adolescents (S. Gallagher, 1985; Schiever, 1985). Since observation seems to refute these results, it may be that Sensual OE is less conscious or less amenable to study by means of the essay format used to assess the overexcitabilities. Piechowski and Colangelo (1984) found levels of Sensual OE to be depressed in gifted adolescents, compared with two adult samples, which may indicate that Sensual OE increases with age. It is also plausible that adolescents are reluctant to reveal in a questionnaire information that is of an intensely personal nature (e.g., concerning their sexual feelings).

The other three overexcitabilities bear a more direct relationship to giftedness. *Imaginational OE*—unusual visualization abilities, vivid visual recall, dreaming in color, inventiveness, love of poetry and drama, active fantasy life—is closely allied with creativity. Artists and creative children are particularly high in Imaginational OE (Piechowski, Silverman, & Falk, 1985; Schiever, 1985), and gifted adolescents have been found to be consistently higher than their average peers in this domain (S. Gallagher, 1985; Piechowski & Colangelo, 1984; Schiever, 1985).

Early signs of Imaginational OE include imaginary companions and mixing of truth and fiction. Gifted children who have imaginary companions have more of them than do average children (Rogers, 1986), sometimes creating entire families or communities. One child traveled with a family of imaginary mice! Older children are attracted to science fiction and science fantasy. They frequently express themselves in metaphor, or in such great detail that adults *beg* them to get to the point. Sometimes it is difficult for them to express their thoughts in words because they think in images. Children high in Imaginational OE may be given to nightmares. They also have a great sense of humor which sometimes borders on the bizarre.

Intellectual OE is particularly correlated with intellectual giftedness: curiosity, concentration, theoretical thinking, introspection, extensive reading, capacity for sustained intellectual effort, love of learning and problem solving, and moral concern. One of the earliest and most enduring signs of Intellectual OE is intellectual curiosity. Gifted children are given to probing questions from the time they first learn to talk. The following examples are from a study conducted by Rogers (1986) of gifted and average children:

> Almost all of the gifted children were perceived by their parents as asking "probing" rather than simple questions. At the age of 18 months, one child wondered, "What is air? How high does it go? Why doesn't it all float away?" A three-year-old boy wanted to know how airplanes work and how people breathe. Another three year old asked, "Will I still be me when I grow up?" Global and abstract issues occupied the minds of several of these youngsters. One child asked detailed, probing questions about politics, nuclear war, world peace, starvation, pollution, energy and so forth. (Rogers & Silverman, 1988, p. 16)

All gifted samples studied scored high in Intellectual OE, and artistically gifted adults were found to be as high as the intellectually gifted in this domain (Piechowski & Cunningham, 1985). But Piechowski (1979) warns that Intellectual OE is not the same as intelligence. Not all intelligent individuals are intellectuals or have high levels of Intellectual OE. For example, there are those with high IQs who excel in practical intelligence but have little interest in cultural events, literary pursuits, or learning new theories.

The last, and perhaps most important of the overexcitabilities, is *Emotional OE*—the capacity for emotional depth, attachment to people and animals, intensity, sensitivity, empathy, self-criticism, inhibition, fears, guilt, and anxiety. Gifted children, adolescents, and adults exhibit high levels of

Emotional OE (S. Gallagher, 1985; Piechowski & Colangelo, 1984; Schiever, 1985; Silverman, 1983; Silverman & Ellsworth, 1980). Again and again we see signs of Emotional OE in gifted children beginning early in life. The following are examples from case files at the Gifted Child Development Center:

> B is a very sensitive child. Although not overly physically affectionate to many, his feelings for others are very deep—he feels hurt and pain when he feels he has displeased someone and also feels great pride, especially toward the achievements of his younger sibling. (Age 4)

> R had early awareness and empathy with others' feelings.... She has amazing tolerance and emotionally is beyond her age. She wears her heart on her sleeve and is honest in her feelings with adults as well as with other children. (Age 4)

> M is a very loving and compassionate child. Cannot stand to hear a baby crying. Puts his hands over his ears if he hears anything too loud or too violent. His feelings are hurt in an instant. Concerned about the welfare of others. (Age 3¾)

> I first observed R's great sensitivity at the age of 5½ months.

> K is very hard on herself. She doesn't forgive herself easily if she has hurt someone's feelings or makes a mistake.... She has a special sensitivity rarely seen in other children her age. (Age 4) (Silverman, 1986, p. 16)

These extraordinary levels of sensitivity do not disappear with age. Gifted adults retain their emotionality; often they are perceived as being "too sensitive." Emotional OE can be seen clearly in the following passage written by a gifted adolescent:

> We are not "normal" and we know it; it can be fun sometimes but not funny always. We tend to be much more sensitive than other people. Multiple meanings, innuendos, and self-consciousness plague us. Intensive self-analysis, self-criticism, and the inability to recognize that we have limits make us despondent. In fact, most times our self-searching leaves us more discombobbled than we were at the outset. (American Association for Gifted Children, 1978, p. 9)

One of the greatest gifts a counselor can give gifted young people is an appreciation of their sensitivities, intensities, and passions. Feeling everything more deeply than others do is both painful and frightening. The quote above illustrates how often adolescents with a high degree of emotional OE feel abnormal. In addition, there is often the secret fear, "There must be something wrong with me.... Maybe I'm crazy—nobody else seems to be bothered by this but me." It doesn't help when people say "You're too sensitive" or "Lighten up!" What does help is a supportive adult who takes time to listen to these children's feelings and who explains that such feelings are *normal* for gifted persons—that they come with the territory. A reassuring adult can dispel children's fears and help them find ways of coping with their strong emotions. But the first step is honoring those emotions, in boys as well as girls.

The Levels of Development

The second part of Dabrowski's theory involves five levels of adult development: self-interest, group values, transformative growth, self-actualization, and attainment of the personality ideal. The first and last levels can be thought of as relatively stable states, with well-integrated structures, whereas the three transition states are flexible enough to allow for growth and development. The levels are summarized in Table 1.2.

Table 1.2
DABROWSKI'S THEORY OF POSITIVE DISINTEGRATION

DABROWSKI'S THEORY OF POSITIVE DISINTEGRATION

Level I: Primary Integration
At Level I, Primary Integration, egocentrism prevails. A person at this level lacks the capacity for empathy and self-examination. When things go wrong, someone else is always to blame; self-responsibility is not a Level I characteristic. With nothing within to inhibit personal ambition, individuals at Level I often attain power in society by ruthless means.

Level II: Unilevel Disintegration
At Level II, individuals are influenced primarily by their social group and by mainstream values, or they are moral relativists for whom "anything goes," morally speaking. They often exhibit ambivalent feelings and indecisive behavior because they have no clear cut set of self-determined internal values. At Level II, inner conflict is horizontal, a competition between equal, competing values.

Level III: Spontaneous Multilevel Disintegration
At Level III, multilevelness arises. The person develops a hierarchical sense of values. Inner conflict is vertical, a struggle to bring one's behavior up to higher standards. There is a dissatisfaction with what one is, because of a competing sense of what one could and ought to be (personality ideal). This internal struggle between higher and lower can be accompanied by existential despair, anxiety, depression, and feelings of dissatisfaction with the self (inferiority, disquietude, astonishment).

Level IV: Organized Multilevel Disintegration
In comparison to those at Level III (the level of emotional tumult), individuals at Level IV are well on the road to self-actualization. They have found a way to reach their own ideals, and they are effective leaders in society. They show high levels of responsibility, authenticity, reflective judgment, empathy for others, autonomy of thought and action, self-awareness, and other attributes associated with self-actualization.

Level V: Secondary Integration
At Level V the struggle for self-mastery has been won. Inner conflicts regarding the self have been resolved through actualization of the personality ideal. Disintegration has been transcended by the integration of one's values and ideals into one's living and being. The life is lived in service to humanity. It is lived according to the highest, most universal principles of loving, compassionate regard for the worth of the human individual.

Source: Reprinted from "Dabrowski's Theory of Positive Disintegration" by K. C. Nelson, *Advanced Development, 1,* 1989, pp. 5–9. Adapted and reprinted in "Self as Phoenix: A Comparison of Assagioli's and Dabrowski's Developmental Theories" by E. Maxwell, *Advanced Development, 4,* 1992, p. 35.

At the lowest level, individuals have little concern for others, no intro-spection, and an absence of inner conflict. Instead, they externalize all conflict and blame others. They have a "What's in it for me?" orientation. Goals are limited to financial success, power, glory, and conquest. They embrace the ideal of competitiveness; they are fierce competitors and usually win. With no guilt or shame to give them second thoughts, it is easy for them to attain positions of leadership in a competitive society. Our society respects and rewards this type of self-serving consciousness.

At Level II, individuals are motivated by desire for approval, fear of punishment, and ambivalences and ambitendencies. Ambivalences are con-flicting desires such as approach/avoidance conflicts; ambitendencies are changeable and conflicting courses of action and self-defeating behaviors (Dabrowski & Piechowski, 1977). As there is no inner core of values from which to make solid judgments, these individuals are easily swayed. "What will people think of me if I...?" dominates their thought processes and becomes the basis for their decisions. Their indecisiveness makes them good candidates for manipulation by self-assured leaders, who are actually less evolved on Dabrowski's scale than themselves. At Level II, the psychological structure of self-centeredness has begun to break down. There is much more awareness of and concern for others. But their insecurity makes relationships frail because these individuals need others to validate their self-worth.

Dabrowski was most interested in the third, fourth, and fifth levels of development, which he called "multilevel development." Level III marks the transition into advanced development; it is the point at which the personality truly acquires depth, three-dimensionality. Individuals begin to develop a hierarchical set of values and to experience their own inadequacies intensely. An impassioned search for self-perfection originates at this level. "Positive maladjustment" (Dabrowski, 1972), a key manifestation of Level III, means being out of sync with one's peer group whose norms are incompatible with one's own, higher-level values. Their sense of honesty, for example, often gets the gifted into trouble. It takes them a very long time to learn that people often say things they don't mean and that this is socially expected (as shown in the movie, *Little Man Tate*). The issue of honesty is discussed further in chapter 2.

Inner conflict, central to Level III, has been noted in gifted adolescents (Silverman & Ellsworth, 1980). The exceptional awareness of highly gifted adolescents predisposes them to moral conflicts between "what is" and "what ought to be," both in themselves and in society. It is enlightening for the adolescent who may have begun this process of self-examination to learn that feelings of guilt, shame, dissatisfaction with self, and idealism accom-pany the Level III experience. It is also helpful to know that there is light at the end of the tunnel, that this intense level of questioning oneself actually leads somewhere positive (Nelson, 1989). It appears to be a necessary step in the process of self-actualization (Maslow, 1971).

Many who make the transition to multilevel development do not do so consciously. The path is tortuous, and there is no guarantee that the destination will be reached. Instead, these individuals are "thrown into their destinies" by circumstances that seem beyond their control. The disintegrative process happens to them spontaneously, either through external events such as the loss of a loved one, a brush with death, a mystical experience, or unconscious awareness that they are ready to take the next step in their development. Whether the choice is conscious or unconscious, individuals at Level III are most in need of counsel. The transformation is disorienting and frightening, and it helps to have a light to guide the way. At higher levels, the choice to evolve is made consciously and the pain of disintegration is not feared because the individual understands its purpose and necessity.

At Level IV, the gap between the ideal and the real narrows as individuals learn how to live in accordance with their ideals. "What ought to be *will* be" becomes the metaphor for the self-actualizing life. Individuals who attain this level of development are committed to responsibility and service to others. They have an unshakable set of values and a strong sense of integrity. They are no longer at the mercy of lower drives; they have overcome aggressiveness in themselves. Self-deprecation and disapproval of others gives way to self-acceptance, acceptance of others, and the ability to look at oneself and others objectively and compassionately. This is the level from which moral exemplars emerge, people whom gifted students can study as role models. Level IV is similar to Maslow's level of self-actualization (Maslow, 1971), and the methods devised to study individuals according to Dabrowski's theory are equally applicable to the study of Maslow's self-actualizers (Brennan & Piechowski, 1991).

Level V is the attainment of the personality ideal; it is marked by universal values, resolution of inner conflict, authenticity, harmony, altruism, and empathy for all living creatures. Mother Teresa and Dag Hammarskjöld are considered to have reached this highest level of development (Dabrowski & Piechowski, 1977). A recent study (Piechowski, 1991b) has uncovered yet another remarkable moral exemplar. Peace Pilgrim gave up all of her possessions except those she could carry in her pockets and walked penniless throughout the United States for twenty-eight years, covering well over 25,000 miles on foot, helping individuals to find inner peace and become activists for peace. Her philosophy, her total dedication to service, her living "to give instead of living to get" (Peace Pilgrim, 1982, p. 7) indicate that she attained the highest level in Dabrowski's schema (Piechowski, 1991b). In Peace Pilgrim we see the complete integration of all the overexcitabilities.

Although Dabrowski's levels of development do not apply to children, adolescents find exposure to this part of his theory reassuring and inspiring. It gives meaning to their own struggle to define themselves in a world that is often bereft of values.

The Relationship Between the Overexcitabilities and the Levels

The overexcitabilities of gifted children are the seeds of their self-development, the sands in the oysters that create the pearls through irritation. Because gifted children are bombarded with so much internal stimulation they must continuously exert conscious control over their internal worlds. Different patterns of OEs connote different types of giftedness (Piechowski & Colangelo, 1984), but all of these patterns bring excessive information into the system and involve powerful drives which need to be channeled. The rich, turbulent, intense inner worlds of the gifted cause a heightened awareness of the pain and suffering of others, higher levels of moral concern, higher expectations of themselves, and greater commitment to serve. Advanced development in adulthood is the result of the interaction in childhood between these internal forces and external events.

Children who experience intense physiological reactions to a variety of stimuli must continuously make choices in order to function. A gifted child high in all the OEs may simultaneously have a strong desire to continue a book she has begun (Intellectual OE); experience a physical need to play baseball with her friends (Psychomotor OE; also Emotional OE); feel intensely hurt by one of her friends and want to avoid her (Emotional OE); have an almost uncontrollable urge to go out for a sundae (Sensual OE); and imagine in great detail what would happen if she chose to do anything but her homework (Imaginational OE; Emotional OE). Which of these urges will she respond to? In selecting one, she must suppress the others and exercise control over impulses that are exceedingly potent. This provides daily practice in setting priorities and gaining inner directedness, the same skills needed later in life to construct a set of values for oneself. In one of the few glimpses of her childhood that Peace Pilgrim provided, she illustrates how important the ability to set priorities was to her later development:

> [As a child] I was preparing for the pilgrimage when I chose my rule of "first things first" and began to set priorities in my life. It led to a very orderly life and it taught me self discipline—a very valuable lesson, without which I could never have walked a pilgrimage. I carried it right into my adult life. (Peace Pilgrim, 1982, p. 1)

Dabrowski (1972) maintained that when Emotional, Imaginational, and Intellectual OEs surpass Sensual and Psychomotor OEs in strength, there is greater developmental potential to attain high levels of personality development. This is exactly the pattern found in a study of gifted adults (Silverman & Ellsworth, 1980): Emotional and Intellectual OEs were the most powerful overexcitabilities represented, with Imaginational OE significantly higher than in nonselected groups, but of less strength than the other two. The same pattern emerged in studies of gifted adolescents (S. Gallagher, 1985; Piechowski & Colangelo, 1984; Schiever, 1985). Dabrowski's observations of the developmental significance of these OEs have been at least partially confirmed by Lysy and Piechowski (1983), who determined that the combination of Intellectual and Emotional OE accounted for 48 percent of the variance in levels of development.

Although most studies of gifted populations have focused on overexcitabilities rather than levels, case studies indicate that individuals who have attained advanced development were clearly gifted (Brennan, 1987; Brennan & Piechowski, 1991; Grant, 1990; Piechowski, 1978, 1990, 1991b). Intelligence, however, is an insufficient predictor of multilevel development; emotional overexcitability of significant strength must also be present.

As suggested earlier, the strength of the OEs, combined with talents and special abilities, theoretically predicts "developmental potential" to attain higher levels of development in Dabrowski's framework. Developmental potential adds an important dimension to our understanding of the traits of giftedness and provides a new direction for understanding the development of gifted individuals throughout the life span. Piechowski (1986) writes:

> The concept of developmental potential...broadens the conception of giftedness by addressing the personality correlates of high ability. This model also suggests a method of identifying individuals with high potential beyond the traditional IQ tests, and binds the goals of their education to self-actualization and advanced moral development, rather than merely to productivity in adult life. (p. 190)

ADVANCED DEVELOPMENT IN ADULTHOOD

The natural trajectory of giftedness in childhood is not a six-figure salary, perfect happiness, and a guaranteed place in *Who's Who*. It is the deepening of the personality, the strengthening of one's value system, the creation of greater and greater challenges for oneself, and the development of broader avenues for expressing compassion. Advanced development in adulthood is the commitment to becoming a better person and helping to make this a better world. Sometimes that results in fame which was not particularly sought as a goal. And sometimes one's contribution is of a quieter nature. Piechowski (1989) describes one of the less obvious pathways to enhancing society:

> The great achievers and the eminent as a rule have a parent or mentor especially devoted to them.... No doubt it takes considerable dedication and integrity to live for the child but not through the child, to cherish and guide rather than to want to own. Thus, the nurturing generations appear to be necessary to the achieving ones. The idea behind this view is simply to acknowledge the great importance of those who nurture the talents of their children. (p. 25)

In the achievement orientation to giftedness, there is no place for a "gifted mommy." Yet, when White (1990) asked three of Leta Hollingworth's above-180-IQ subjects, one man and two women, what they considered to be their greatest achievements, the man referred to his mathematical theories and the two women replied, "my children." All three devoted some part of their lives to improving education. Harris (1992) reported similar findings with a larger sample of students who were enrolled in Hollingworth's experimental classes:

> Most of the subjects in the Hollingworth group, about 85%, also speak of achievement in terms of their children and personal satisfaction, along with feelings of peace, happiness, and creativity with relation both to the arts and to family life. (p. 102)

There has to be room in our conceptions of giftedness for the attainment of moral, emotional, spiritual, and nurturant goals—so that parents, counselors, and teachers are not perceived as "less gifted" than those who attain eminence.

EMOTIONAL EDUCATION

Healthy emotional development is clearly as important as academic achievement, but it has not been valued enough to date to create the kinds of environments in which that emotional development can be nurtured. The work of Leta Stetter Hollingworth stands out as one notable exception: "Leta Hollingworth... was the first to contribute evidence indicating that gifted children do have social/emotional needs meriting attention" (Colangelo, 1991, p. 273). Kerr (1990) describes Hollingworth as "the first and greatest counselor to the gifted and talented" (p. 178). Hollingworth not only studied gifted children in clinical settings, she created educational environments for the primary purpose of nurturing their emotional development. She was well aware of the adjustment difficulties of the gifted and endeavored throughout her lifetime to help others see the need for special educational and counseling provisions for them.

> The psychologist who is professionally acquainted with children who test above 130 IQ will be able to formulate clearly certain special problems of adjustment, observed in the case study of these children, which arise primarily from the very fact that they are gifted.... The more intelligent the child, the more likely he is to become involved in these puzzling situations. (Hollingworth, 1931, p. 3)

Lewis Terman also observed the precariousness of the gifted young person in society, and concurred with Hollingworth that the difficulties increase with higher intelligence.

> Precocity unavoidably complicates the problem of social adjustment. The child of eight years with a mentality of twelve or fourteen is faced with a situation almost inconceivably difficult. In order to adjust normally such a child has to have an exceptionally well-balanced personality and be well nigh a social genius. The higher the IQ, the more acute the problem. (Terman, 1931, p. 579)

Leta Hollingworth designed special classes for the gifted which offered what she termed "emotional education" (1939, p. 585). Components of her program included placement with like-minded peers to prevent social isolation; fast-paced instruction, cutting in half the amount of instructional time devoted to the basics (now known as "telescoping" or "compacting"); appropriate academic curriculum, sufficiently challenging so that the children enjoyed

learning and were motivated to work hard; thematic education, "The Evolution of Common Things," in which the children designed the curriculum
according to their own interests and curiosity; independent study and small-
group projects; extensive classroom discussion; teaching the children how to
handle the apparent foolishness of others with patience and love; helping them
learn to balance candor with tact; biographical study to expose the children to
role models of others like themselves who had sustained effort against odds
and contributed to society; and training in the fine art of argumentation,
including "argument with oneself," "argument with others in private, involving etiquette and the art of polite disagreement," and "argument in public"
(p. 585). Infused throughout this program was a beautiful set of human values:
basic respect for humanity, awareness of our global interdependence, and
commitment to service.

Thus, Hollingworth provided the first model for the integration of affective and cognitive development within the regular curriculum. Follow-up
studies indicate that Hollingworth's program had a profound, lifelong impact
on the students (Harris, 1992; White 1990). Harris (1992, p. 102) asked these
individuals, some almost seventy years later, "From your point of view, what
constitutes success in life?... The replies in the Hollingworth group quite
evidently mirrored the curriculum. Their answers were strongly focused on
societal connection, awareness and sensitivity to others as elements inseparable from self-actualization, and definitions of success."

CONCLUSION

In traditional educational perspectives, we inadvertently foster a type of self-
centered competitiveness in life in which the gifted are perceived as having an
edge. This framework does little to attract empathy for the unique needs of the
gifted. The school reform movement is moving education away from competitive structures toward more cooperative plans. However, there is even less
empathy for the gifted within this movement. In the name of cooperation,
often the gifted are held back to the rate of less advanced students. A truly
humanitarian framework honors the unique learning styles and learning rates
of all students. Natural collaborations are formed of students with similar
interests and abilities. The school becomes a community of learners, each
pursuing his or her own passions as well as absorbing a specific body of
knowledge. Emotional development is given equal importance with cognitive
development; therefore, groups are formed for the purpose of dealing with
affective and social issues. Community service is an integral part of the
program (see chapters 10 and 14). The works of Hollingworth (1926, 1939,
1940) and Roeper (1990) stand as guides for the design of such programs.
Until emotional education of gifted students becomes widespread, counselors
will have a great responsibility for preserving these children's emotional
health.

REFERENCES

Altman, R. (1983). Social-emotional development of gifted children and adolescents: A research model. *Roeper Review, 6,* 65–68.

American Association for Gifted Children. (1978). *On being gifted.* New York: Walker.

Blackburn, A. C., & Erickson, D. B. (1986). Predictable crises of the gifted student. *Journal of Counseling and Development, 9,* 552–555.

Brennan, T. P. (1987). *Case studies of multilevel development.* Unpublished doctoral dissertation, Northwestern University, Evanston, IL.

Brennan, T. P., & Piechowski, M. M. (1991). The developmental framework for self-actualization: Evidence from case studies. *Journal of Humanistic Psychology, 31*(3), 43–64.

Clark, B. (1992). *Growing up gifted: Developing the potential of children at home and at school* (4th ed.). New York: Macmillan.

Colangelo, N. (1991). Counseling gifted students. In N. Colangelo & G. A. Davis (Eds.), *Handbook of gifted education* (pp. 271–284). Needham Heights, MA: Allyn & Bacon.

Columbus Group. (1991, July). Unpublished transcript of the meeting of the Columbus Group, Columbus, OH.

Cruickshank, W. M. (1963). *Psychology of exceptional children and youth* (2nd ed.). Englewood Cliffs, NJ: Prentice-Hall.

Dabrowski, K. (1938). Typy wzmozonej pobudliwosci: psychicnej (Types of increased psychic excitability). *Biul. Inst. Hig. Psychicznej, 1*(3–4), 3–26.

Dabrowski, K. (1964). *Positive disintegration.* Boston: Little, Brown.

Dabrowski, K. (1972). *Psychoneurosis is not an illness.* London: Gryf.

Dabrowski, K., & Piechowski, M. M. (1977). *Theory of levels of emotional development* (Vols. 1 & 2). Oceanside, NY: Dabor Science.

Delisle, J. R. (1990). The gifted adolescent at risk: Strategies and resources for suicide prevention among gifted youth. *Journal for the Education of the Gifted, 13,* 212–228.

Freed, J. N. (1990). Tutoring techniques for the gifted. *Understanding Our Gifted, 2*(6), 1, 11–13.

Gallagher, J. J. (1991). Educational reform, values, and gifted students. *Gifted Child Quarterly, 35,* 12–18.

Gallagher, S. A. (1985). A comparison of the concept of overexcitabilities with measures of creativity and school achievement in sixth grade students. *Roeper Review, 8,* 115–119.

Genshaft, J., & Broyles, J. (1991). Stress management and the gifted adolescent. In M. Bireley & J. Genshaft (Eds.), *Understanding the gifted adolescent* (pp. 76–87). New York: Teachers College Press.

George, P. (1988). Tracking and ability grouping. *Middle School Journal, 20*(1), 21–28.

Gowan, J. C. (1974). *Development of the psychedelic individual.* Northridge, CA: John Curtis Gowan.

Grant, B. (1990). Moral development: Theories and lives. *Advanced Development, 2,* 85–91.

Harris, C. R. (1992). The fruits of early intervention: The Hollingworth group today. *Advanced Development, 4,* 91–104.

Hollingworth, L. S. (1926). *Gifted children: Their nature and nurture.* New York: Macmillan.

Hollingworth, L. S. (1930). Personality development of special class children. *University of Pennsylvania Bulletin. Seventeenth Annual Schoolmen's Week Proceedings, 30,* 442–446.

Hollingworth, L. S. (1931). The child of very superior intelligence as a special problem in social adjustment. *Mental Hygiene, 15*(1), 1–16.

Hollingworth, L. S. (1939). What we know about the early selection and training of leaders. *Teachers College Record, 40,* 575–592.

Hollingworth, L. S. (1940). Old heads on young shoulders. *Public Addresses* (pp. 104–110). Lancaster, PA: Science Press Printing.

Hollingworth, L. S. (1942). *Children above 180 IQ Stanford-Binet: Origin and development.* Yonkers-on-Hudson, NY: World Book.

Horowitz, F. D. (1987). A developmental view of giftedness. *Gifted Child Quarterly, 31,* 165–168.

Jacobs, J. C. (1971). Rorschach studies reveal possible misinterpretations of personality traits of the gifted. *Gifted Child Quarterly, 16,* 195–200.

Kerr, B. (1990). Leta Hollingworth's legacy to counseling and guidance. *Roeper Review, 12,* 178–181.

Kerr, B. A. (1991). *A handbook for counseling the gifted and talented.* Alexandria, VA: American Counseling Association.

Kline, B. E., & Meckstroth, E. A. (1985). Understanding and encouraging the exceptionally gifted. *Roeper Review, 8,* 24–30.

Lombroso, C. (1905). *The man of genius* (2nd ed.). New York: Robert Scott.

Lysy, K. Z., & Piechowski, M. M. (1983). Personal growth: An empirical study using Jungian and Dabrowskian measures. *Genetic Psychology Monographs, 108,* 267–320.

Manaster, G. J., & Powell, P. M. (1983). A framework for understanding gifted adolescents' psychological maladjustment. *Roeper Review, 6,* 70–73.

Manzanero, J. (1985). *A cross-cultural comparison of overexcitability profiles and levels of emotional development between American and Venezuelan artists.* Unpublished master's thesis, University of Denver.

Marland, S., Jr. (1972, March). *Education of the gifted and talented.* Report to the Congress of the United States by the U. S. Commissioner of Education. Washington, DC: U.S. Government Printing Office.

Maslow, A. H. (1971). *The farther reaches of human nature.* New York: Viking.

Maxwell, E. (1992). Self as Phoenix: A comparison of Assagioli's and Dabrowski's developmental theories. *Advanced Development, 4,* 31–48.

Meckstroth, E. (1991, December). *Coping with sensitivities of gifted children.* Paper presented at the Illinois Gifted Education Conference, Chicago.

Morelock, M. J. (1992a, February). *The child of extraordinarily high IQ from a Vygotskian perspective.* Paper presented at the Esther Katz Rosen Symposium on the Psychological Development of Gifted Children, University of Kansas, Lawrence.

Morelock, M. J. (1992b). Giftedness: The view from within. *Understanding Our Gifted, 4*(3), 1, 11–15.

Munger, A. (1990). The parent's role in counseling the gifted: The balance between home and school. In J. VanTassel-Baska (Ed.), *A practical guide to counseling the gifted in a school setting* (2nd ed., pp. 57–65). Reston, VA: The Council for Exceptional Children.

Nelson, K. C. (1989). Dabrowski's theory of positive disintegration. *Advanced Development, 1,* 1–14.

Nelson, K. C. (1991, November). *Meet Kazimierz Dabrowski: Theorist as role model.* Paper presented at the National Association for Gifted Children 38th Annual Convention, Kansas City, MO.

Newland, T. E. (1976). *The gifted in socio-educational perspective.* Englewood Cliffs, NJ: Prentice-Hall.

Peace Pilgrim. (1982). *Peace Pilgrim: Her life in her own words.* Santa Fe, NM: Ocean Tree.

Piechowski, M. M. (1975). A theoretical and empirical approach to the study of development. *Genetic Psychology Monographs, 92,* 231–297.

Piechowski, M. M. (1978). Self-actualization as a developmental structure: A profile of Antoine de Saint-Exupery. *Genetic Psychology Monographs, 97,* 181–242.

Piechowski, M. M. (1979). Developmental potential. In N. Colangelo & R. T. Zaffrann (Eds.), *New voices in counseling the gifted* (pp. 25–57). Dubuque, IA: Kendall/Hunt.

Piechowski, M. M. (1986). The concept of developmental potential. *Roeper Review, 8,* 190–197.

Piechowski, M. M. (1989). Developmental potential and the growth of self. In J. VanTassel-Baska & P. Olszewski-Kubilius (Eds.), *Patterns of influence on gifted learners: The home, the self, and the school* (pp. 87–101). New York: Teachers College Press. (Quotation from unabridged version, available from author, Northland College, Ashland, WI).

Piechowski, M. M. (1990). Inner growth and transformation in the life of Eleanor Roosevelt. *Advanced Development, 2,* 35–53.

Piechowski, M. M. (1991a). Emotional development and emotional giftedness. In N. Colangelo & G. Davis (Eds.), *Handbook of gifted education* (pp. 285–306). Needham Heights, MA: Allyn & Bacon.

Piechowski, M. M. (1991b, May). *Giftedness for all seasons: Inner peace in a time of war.* Presented at the Henry B. and Jocelyn Wallace National Research Symposium on Talent Development, University of Iowa.

Piechowski, M. M., & Colangelo, N. (1984). Developmental potential of the gifted. *Gifted Child Quarterly, 28,* 80–88.

Piechowski, M. M., & Cunningham, K. (1985). Patterns of overexcitability in a group of artists. *Journal of Creative Behavior, 19*(3), 153–174.

Piechowski, M. M., Silverman, L. K., & Falk, R. F. (1985). Comparison of intellectually and artistically gifted on five dimensions of mental functioning. *Perceptual and Motor Skills, 60,* 539–549.

Robinson, N. M., & Noble, K. D. (1991). Social-emotional development and adjustment of gifted children. In M. C. Wang, M. C. Reynolds, & H. J. Walberg (Eds.), *Handbook of special education. Research and practice: Vol. 4. Emerging programs* (pp. 57–76). New York: Pergamon Press.

Roedell, W. C. (1984). Vulnerabilities of highly gifted children. *Roeper Review, 6,* 127–130.

Roedell, W. C. (1989). Early development of gifted children. In J. VanTassel-Baska & P. Olszewski-Kubilius (Eds.), *Patterns of influence on gifted learners: The home, the self, and the school* (pp. 13–28). New York: Teachers College Press.

Roeper, A. (1982). How the gifted cope with their emotions. *Roeper Review, 5*(2), 21–24.

Roeper, A. (1990). *Educating children for life: The modern learning community*. Monroe, NY: Trillium.

Rogers, M. T. (1986). *A comparative study of developmental traits of gifted and average children*. Unpublished doctoral dissertation, University of Denver.

Rogers, M. T., & Silverman, L. K. (1988). Recognizing giftedness in young children. *Understanding Our Gifted, 1*(2), 5, 16, 17, 20.

Schetky, D. H. (1981). A psychiatrist looks at giftedness: The emotional and social development of the gifted child. *G/C/T*, Issue No. 18, 2–4.

Schiever, S. W. (1985). Creative personality characteristics and dimensions of mental functioning in gifted adolescents. *Roeper Review, 7,* 223–226.

Sebring, A. D. (1983). Parental factors in the social and emotional adjustment of the gifted. *Roeper Review, 6*(2), 97–99.

Silverman, L. K. (1983). Personality development: The pursuit of excellence. *Journal for the Education of the Gifted, 6*(1), 5–19.

Silverman, L. K. (1986). Personality development and the gifted. *Mensa Bulletin*, No. 299, 14–16.

Silverman, L. K., & Ellsworth, B. (1980). The theory of positive disintegration and its implications for giftedness. In N. Duda (Ed.), *Theory of positive disintegration: Proceedings of the third international conference* (pp. 179–194). Miami, FL: University of Miami School of Medicine.

Silverman, L. K., & Kearney, K. (1989). Parents of the extraordinarily gifted. *Advanced Development, 1,* 41–56.

Singal, D. J. (1991). The other crisis in American education. *The Atlantic Monthly, 268*(5), 59–74.

Sommers, S. (1981). Emotionality reconsidered: The role of cognition in emotional responsiveness. *Journal of Personality and Social Psychology, 41,* 553–561.

Terman, L. M. (1931). The gifted child. In C. Murchison (Ed.), *A handbook of child psychology* (pp. 568–584). Worcester, MA: Clark University Press.

Terrassier, J. C. (1985). Dyssynchrony-uneven development. In J. Freeman (Ed.), *The psychology of gifted children* (pp. 265–274). New York: Wiley.

Tolan, S. (1989). Special problems of young highly gifted children. *Understanding Our Gifted, 1*(5), 1, 7–10.

Webb, J. T., Meckstroth, E. A., & Tolan, S. S. (1982). *Guiding the gifted child: A practical source for parents and teachers*. Columbus: Ohio Psychology.

White, W. L. (1990). Interviews with Child I, Child J, and Child L. *Roeper Review, 12,* 222–227.

Whitmore, J. R. (1980). *Giftedness, conflict, and underachievement*. Needham Heights, MA: Allyn & Bacon.

The Quest for Meaning: Counseling Issues with Gifted Children and Adolescents

2

Deirdre V. Lovecky

In counseling gifted children and adolescents, one becomes part of their quest for meaning, a guide, or companion as it were, on the journey into the unknown self. Like the Knights of the Round Table searching for the Holy Grail, gifted students explore the self within and the world without in hopes of reaching understanding. This search for meaning has been described by a number of writers (Ogburn Colangelo, 1979; Piechowski, 1986; Roedell, 1984; Silverman, 1983a; Willings, 1985) and suggests that gifted young people have particular issues in psychosocial development. Unfortunately for many gifted children, social and emotional concerns and problems associated with psychosocial development are often misunderstood by the adults in their lives.

It is still assumed by most mental health practitioners, including school counselors and school psychologists, that gifted people have no special needs. No one would think of saying that developmentally disabled children had no special issues; yet, just that is done with the gifted even though they are as different from average students as are the developmentally disabled. (See chapter 1.) For example, no one these days would expect to be able to meet all the educational and developmental needs of a child with an IQ of 50 in a regular classroom, but they do expect to do just that with children with IQs of 150, though both IQs are equally different from the norm (3.33 standard deviations from the mean).

In fact, most counselors are quite unlikely to discover the literature on the effects of giftedness on social and emotional functioning because much of it is published in specialized journals. Only a few voices have found their way into the mainstream mental health literature (Freeman, 1983; Post, 1988; Wendorf & Frey, 1985). Consequently, most practitioners dealing with gifted children in counseling or psychotherapy may ignore the fact of their giftedness. Children treated by such practitioners may experience that even their counselor does not really understand what is wrong.

The literature on social and emotional adjustment of gifted children suggests that, as a group, they show good emotional adjustment (Franks & Dolan, 1982; Janos, Fung, & Robinson, 1985; Terman, 1925; Tidwell, 1980) and good peer relations (Austin & Draper, 1981; Janus, Marwood, & Robinson, 1985). Nevertheless, some literature suggests that there may be certain emotional and behavioral issues associated with being gifted which become increasingly problematic the more highly gifted a person is (Hollingworth, 1942; Janos & Robinson, 1985; Roedell, 1984). Other authors suggest specific areas of vulnerability that might predispose gifted children to risk. These include heightened sensitivity, emotional intensity and reactivity, perfectionism, feeling different, and experiencing dyssynchronous development of intellectual, social, and emotional areas (Betts & Neihart, 1988; Ehrlich, 1982; Freeman, 1983; Gross, 1989; Janos, Fung, & Robinson, 1985; Kitano, 1990; Kline & Meckstroth, 1985; Lovecky, 1990a, 1990b, 1991; Morelock, 1992; Piechowski, 1986, 1991; Roedell, 1988; Roeper, 1982, 1989; Roth, 1986; Silverman, 1983b; Silverman & Ellsworth, 1980; Tolan, 1989; Webb, Meckstroth, & Tolan, 1982; Whitmore, 1980).

A recognition of the specific counseling needs of gifted children in a more preventive framework is suggested by a number of authors (Betts, 1986; Culross & Jenkins-Friedman, 1988; Davis & Rimm, 1979; Hollinger & Fleming, 1988; Miller & Silverman, 1987; Ogburn Colangelo, 1979; Perry, 1986; Piechowski, 1986; Sanborn, 1979; Silverman, 1983b; Willings, 1980; Zaffrann & Colangelo, 1979). (See chapter 4.)

CHARACTERISTICS OF GIFTEDNESS

There appear to be five traits that may produce potential inter- and intrapersonal conflict in gifted children: divergent thinking ability, excitability, sensitivity, perceptiveness, and entelechy. The first three are derived in part from Torrance's (1961, 1962, 1965) descriptions of gifted children. The last two were developed from discussions with gifted adults (Lovecky, 1986) and from talking with gifted children and their parents. Although these traits appear to be an integral part of giftedness, their behavioral manifestations can vary, depending on such psychological and physiological factors as age, sex, tolerance for ambiguity, degree of introversion/extraversion, preference for certain types of sensory stimulation, and locus of control.

Several of these traits may coexist in the individual, though which ones predominate and whether the manifestations are seen as more positive or more negative vary across individuals. The gifted people whose experiences were the basis for this chapter all exhibited several of the traits. The traits themselves are neutral, but their behavioral manifestations give them social and emotional significance. It is others' perceptions of these traits that are regarded as particular strengths or weaknesses in the gifted person.

Gifted people in counseling may experience difficulties with one or more of the traits. It is both the degree of intensity of the behavior and its specific manifestations, particularly those that relate to self-esteem and a sense of connectedness to others, that need to be considered. Traits are described as if only one predominates in order to clarify which issues may result from each trait; nevertheless, the traits do overlap to some degree.

The original study was based on observations of sixteen gifted adults who were colleagues, friends, acquaintances, and psychotherapy clients (Lovecky, 1986). The current expansion includes information obtained from observations of a much larger sample of both gifted adults (80) and gifted children (75), ranging in age from four to eighty-three years. About half were female and half were male. Females predominated among the adults, and males among the children. About 85 percent of the children were psychotherapy clients. Identification of giftedness in the children was based on a variety of criteria including obtained IQ scores over 130, achievement scores above the 95th percentile, or independent evidence of high creativity (achievement in a field of creative endeavor that was original and above the child's age expectations).

Anecdotal and observational data, which were the basis for this chapter, were gathered in the form of journal notes and correspondence with a number of parents of gifted children. These data were used to delineate the five traits. Further exploration focused on biographies of well-known gifted people, particularly those who exemplify certain aspects of the five traits. Application of more refined research methodology, as opposed to this more intuitive approach based on observations, will provide a more elaborate elucidation of the impact of giftedness on the lives of those concerned.

TRAIT DESCRIPTIONS

Divergent Thinking Ability

Tom is a highly creative boy.[1] His drawings leap off the page, having a three-dimensional quality unusual for his age. He also manages to incorporate a sense of adventure and action. Tom spends much of his time preoccu-

---

[1] In order to preserve confidentiality, all anecdotes used in this chapter are fictionalized composites of several children. All identifying information has been removed and no example is exactly like any real child seen in counseling by the author.

pied with his fantasy life which he incorporates in the drawings. The margins of school papers are well figured, but often schoolwork is incomplete. Tom asks a great many questions about things that interest him, especially the weather. He is surprisingly knowledgeable about Chaos theory but fails easy tests on the four basic food groups. Parents and teachers wonder what is going to become of Tom.

A preference for unusual, original, and creative responses is characteristic of divergent thinkers. There appear to be two types: those whose divergent thinking is circumscribed to certain times and subjects, and those who fantasize much of the time (Lovecky, 1990b; 1991). Lynn and Rhue (1988) identified 2.6 percent of their 6,000 subjects as extreme fantasizers. Creativity was a special strength of this latter group.

Divergent thinkers are often high achievers in adulthood, innovative in a number of fields, task committed, self-starters, highly independent individuals who use their capacity for innovation and imagination to enhance their emotional well-being. Many theoretical scientists, writers, artists, composers, and philosophers are divergent thinkers. Darwin, Einstein, Freud, Mozart, Georgia O'Keefe, Thoreau, and the French Impressionists are all examples of gifted adults who have successfully used their divergent thinking abilities.

As children, divergent thinkers are often negatively reinforced for their curious questions, unusual responses and digressions, dislike of working in groups, and rather morbid imaginations. There is less acceptance of the divergent thinking of girls because people expect less conformity of boys and more of girls. Girls who ask impertinent questions and do not accept the status quo are not conforming in the expected way.

Children who are divergent thinkers find it hard to organize thoughts, feelings, and materials, both at home and at school. Although it is somewhat acceptable for adults to be absentminded, it is not acceptable for schoolchildren. For highly divergent thinkers, however, many adult organizational schemata seem alien. The standards adults use to organize schoolwork are frequently based on a linear format that gives divergent thinkers difficulty. They see problems as wholes, and dividing them up into what appear to be arbitrary parts does not seem reasonable to them; in fact, they cannot think this way at all. In addition, decision making and setting priorities are difficult because all the thoughts and feelings of the divergent thinker are interconnected; thoughts and feelings all seem to be equally interesting and important. Finding a starting place is impossible for the child.

Many have a unique style of learning. They are immersion learners, who want to find out everything about a subject at once, and then go on to something else. The artificial boundaries around subjects in school chafe at them. Also, they like to follow the novelty of an idea, see where something leads, and show a lack of interest in the usual rewards offered in school. The ability to make something happen or the novelty of an idea is often more rewarding than an adult-initiated reward system. Because of this, divergently thinking children may appear to adults to be bossy, stubborn, rebellious, unmotivated, inattentive, attention seeking, and tactless. Adults admire the creative story, poem, drawing, musical composition, or mathematical derivation, but they are apt to have trouble with the concept that the essence of creative thinking is rejection of, and rebellion against, some accepted standard. For the majority of divergent thinkers, there is little tolerance for deviations from the status quo.

Divergent thinkers also have to deal with being different. Although they do not accept the status quo, conform well, or fit in with peers and are often subjected to teasing, they do not know why they are different, or why they upset other people. Often they feel entirely alone, with no one to understand them, even their own families. A number of such youngsters become severely depressed in adolescence because both self-esteem and a sense of connection to others is affected.

Counseling Issues

Gifted children and adolescents who are divergent thinkers come to counseling with a number of specific issues. Receiving so little validation for the self fosters a corresponding internal negative self-image. They have difficulty understanding both how other people behave and what motivates other people's behavior, especially toward them. Because their thoughts and feelings are so interconnected, it is hard for them to assign feelings to an event, or to think about it in a problem-solving fashion; they are distrustful of efforts to get them to pin themselves down to one feeling or one thought. Accurate empathy can be difficult for counselors to achieve because divergent thinkers are difficult to understand; consequently, there are more failures of empathy with divergent thinkers than with other sorts of people. Counselors who work with divergent thinkers need to be honest about the complexity of issues and about the difficulty in understanding. They need to emphasize their sincere desire to understand. Helping the child build a stronger internal sense of self and forging a connection to at least one other person are the major goals.

The counselor working with divergent thinkers needs to help them develop and consolidate a sense of being their real selves. Because of the degree of social censure for originality and difference, many such gifted children and teens are at risk for developing false selves that they show the world; often these are conforming, ungifted selves. This is, for some, an effective disguise; it preserves a sense of self-integrity because the student is really wearing a mask and knows he or she is "in hiding." Others experience more of a conflict, however, because they come to see the false self as the valued self, and the divergent, creative self as unacceptable and not valued. For these children, finding people who will validate their creative selves is essential because it allows them to be their divergent selves in a positive way. This, then, develops self-worth and self-esteem.

In addition to the validation counselors give such children directly through the counseling relationship, bibliotherapy is useful in helping divergently thinking children to understand that they are not alone. Others feel the same way they do. (See chapter 4 and the reading list in the Appendix.)

It is also important for the counselor to pay attention to the tendency of the divergent thinker to be an immersion learner because this affects what the child is able to utilize in counseling. For example, the child who immerses the self in material and makes interconnections to what else is known will be busy thinking about this as the counselor tries to go on with another aspect of the problem or issue at hand. Paying attention to the content of other people's words and feelings is often an issue for these gifted children, and they frequently lose the focus of the conversation in their own puzzlement about things. This affects them also in school where they have trouble seeing the point the teacher is making, deciding what is the important piece to remember for the test, and how to organize main ideas into a sequence.

The job of the counselor is to help the child learn how to listen in a more focused fashion both to social conversations and to classroom material. Since schools are difficult places to be different and original, some students may need the counselor to advocate for them for a different educational arrangement (alternative school, accelerated program, individual studies). Helping to find a mentor who can work with strengths and interests often helps such children grow in their talents while surviving less-than-accommodating school situations. Some need to know that it is good to follow their own vision as long as they realize the cost of doing so. Others need help in deciding when to follow their own vision and when to borrow someone else's notes and memorize them for the test.

Gifted adolescents are particularly at risk for social ostracism. Many are more interested in following their own inner vision than in conforming in ways that will bring acceptance from peers. However, they are not always happy about the results. These students need help from the counselor in learning to process decisions about such things as not going to the prom or participating in peer group activities, so that the adolescent feels support for the decision while understanding the consequences for not participating in peer life.

Excitability

Cindy cried too much according to her teachers and parents. She cried when she was angry, afraid, worried about displeasing others, or feeling overwhelmed by sadness for other people. Cindy did not go to the movies or watch much television because she could not stand conflict. She even avoided arguments with friends. Her worst problem, though, was her fears, which were legion. In fact, Cindy anguished over all the evil she felt in the world to the extent that she could not sleep at night.

A high energy level, emotional intensity and reactivity, and high arousal of the central nervous system characterize the trait of excitability. All three aspects are not necessarily exhibited in one person (Lovecky, 1990b).

Gifted adults with this trait are able to focus their concentration and attention for long periods of time, have a wide variety of interests, and do many things well. They enjoy the excitement of taking risks and meeting challenges. Their high energy level allows them to produce prodigiously whatever most captures their interest, and they often pave the way for others to follow with refinements of their innovative ideas. This is what happened when Thomas Edison's refinements in telegraphy were kept and used by Western Union and Bell Telephone (Cousins, 1965). Many well-known inventors, explorers, and entrepreneurs are high in this trait, including Nellie Bly, Christopher Columbus, Leonardo da Vinci, Amelia Earhart, and Thomas Edison.

Gifted children, high in the trait of excitability, are often difficult to live with. Some have such high energy levels they at times appear to be hyperactive; nevertheless, when stimulated by challenging material, they are able to concentrate and organize themselves quite well. These gifted children have a high need to explore the environment and eagerly seek new experiences. If not provided with interesting material, and space to explore, they become bored and overactive. Many are stimulus-seekers, requiring greater levels of stimulation to moderate their behavior. If this is not provided, they seek to provide it for themselves. Thomas Edison was often in trouble as a child. Only when allowed to work and to experiment on his own was he able to flourish. This he did through managing a newspaper and candy concession on the railroad trains while using the baggage car as a mobile laboratory. He was thirteen years old (Cousins, 1965).

To many high-energy children, the pace of the world seems too slow. They may have a decreased need for sleep. Coupled with a high energy level and increased need for stimulation and parental attention, this can be exhausting for parents. Nevertheless, when properly channeled, their energy and excitement can be useful in organizing and stimulating others. And when these are combined with imagination and a creative drive, these children can generate impressive responses to challenge. For example, one child, a chess prodigy described by Feldman (1986), began his own snow-shoveling business at age twelve, soon earning enough money to buy a snowblower. Later teen ventures included a landscaping business, part interest in a gas station, ownership of several trucks, a large inventory of equipment, and several employees. The year after high school this man sold all his businesses for a huge profit. In the lives of many of this nation's successful entrepreneurs are other examples of such childhood ventures.

Because of the need for stimulation, many high-energy children become conditioned to a need for novelty. They are eager to start new projects and are enthusiastic about the initial stages, but once the novelty wears off and the details of completion need to be addressed they lose interest. Sometimes a cycle of high interest and great enthusiasm, followed by a loss of interest and failure to finish, occurs on every project the child attempts. This can lead to problems with self-esteem because the child does not obtain the personal reward of satisfaction for completion of something, nor recognition of task mastery. Over time the child can come to doubt his or her own abilities.

Other children with the trait of excitability are stimulus-avoiders. They find stressful the amounts of stimulation that most people find comfortable. In situations in which there is a high degree of sensory stimulation, they feel irritable, overwhelmed, and often frightened. They may also be more emotionally reactive, have greater difficulty turning off thoughts and feelings than most people, feel things more intensely, and exhibit prolonged emotional responses such as laughing or crying. They seem to have difficulty with the ordinary stresses of life such as schoolwork and social demands. Peers are experienced as too active, too noisy. High anxiety levels, fears, and phobias may develop.

The child who avoids situations and people because of difficulty with the stress engendered by sensory overload may not find it easy to gain the support of adults or peers. Such children are often regarded as troublesome by adults because they are seen as extreme and unpredictable in their responses. Peers may give them a wide berth. To them, the child is special but in a highly negative way. Such children are often the butt of peer teasing and bullying.

Counseling Issues

For children high in the trait of excitability, one counseling issue is the difficulty they have with self-regulation and self-control. Others include maintaining a level of arousal that feels comfortable both to the child and to others and finding satisfaction in creative endeavors and intellectual pursuits rather than in novelty or gratuitous stimulation.

Counselors need to be aware that whereas many of the strategies used with Attention Deficit Disordered children may be helpful to these gifted children (including positive reward systems, cognitive and self-control measures, imagery, problem solving, and relaxation techniques), an approach that depends on a high degree of structure and adult-set rewards will not work. This sort of child needs some structure, but also needs a high degree of both flexibility and challenge. Often, given proper support and instruction in self-regulation techniques, the child finds a suitable structure. Unique needs for certain levels of stimulation and intellectual challenge, and the drive to seek novelty, will result in some children rebelling against the behavioral programs as practiced in many school systems and as taught to parents. The highly active child can benefit from learning to use time to structure activities; for example, finishing a set task in a certain time and then doing a task of the child's own choosing. He or she will also require activities that base rewards in accomplishment and the subsequent satisfaction, as well as in novelty. It is crucial that these children learn to finish at least some tasks. Specific self-control measures such as working individually without demanding attention, use of relaxation strategies and self-talk to reduce stress, humor to defuse conflictual situations, and learning to judge more accurately the quality as well as the completeness of tasks may be of help in learning to manage the tendency to run from one novel task to the next.

Many of these gifted children have poor self-esteem related to the discomfort others experience in being around them and to the subtle emotional withdrawal and avoidance that can subsequently occur. Both the stimulus-seeker and the stimulus-avoider have difficulty. For some, the only effective strategy is to try to regulate the amount of stimulation received by changing the environment. This requires choosing activities that help maintain a moderate level of arousal. Most schools require concentrated attention on rote task material. Trying to balance these requirements with their own high needs for stimulation can be overwhelming. The ideal school situation would be one in which periods of activities requiring intellectual and creative stimulation alternate with more routine practice tasks.

Gifted children who are stimulus-avoiders require therapeutic help in managing their high degree of arousal. They may need to learn to manage the environment to eliminate extraneous stimulation and to avoid experiencing some types of stimulation. For example, they can learn to exercise choices about what they watch on television, what movies they see, what they read, and what they listen to. Other adaptive strategies such as pacing themselves so that they finish things in their own time, and using self-monitoring techniques and desensitization, can be helpful.

Gifted children with self-regulation issues often have trouble in their relationships with others. Counselors need to understand both the feelings of the child caught in an uncomfortable physical state and the unsympathetic responses of others to the seeming negativity of the child's behavior. If these children can learn to recognize cues of impending loss of control (tantrums, tears, feelings of dread or despair, need to move or run) and use some strategies to help alleviate the feelings (relaxation, moving to another environment or task, isolation to calm down, shift of attention to a more pleasant thought, self-talk), the conflictual situation can be defused by changing how the child approaches the problem. Adults are more likely to be sympathetic to a child who appears to be trying to cope. These children can also be taught how others might feel when confronted with their behavior, and what they can do to reestablish a connection to the other person (calm down, ask for a change of place or task, ask for appropriate attention, use of self-praise and self-correction, empathy for the other person's feelings, apologizing). Finally, direct interpersonal support often reduces anxiety and helps the child feel secure enough to try again.

Sensitivity

Mark felt a great compassion for suffering animals. He took every fallen baby bird into his heart, and he also knew how best to care for them. He regularly found homes for stray dogs and cats. In addition to giving his personal attention to animals, Mark was an effective fund-raiser for the local Animal Rescue League. He also promulgated the needs of third world countries for veterinary services and sound, ecologically based land management to preserve wildlife. Mark's passion was his involvement in preserving almost-extinct species. When he grew up, Mark wanted to work on conservation projects which would teach people in many countries that their lives are inexorably enmeshed with that of the wildlife around them.

A depth of feeling that results in a sense of identification with others (people, animals, nature, the universe) characterizes the trait of sensitivity. Passion and compassion are two different aspects (Lovecky, 1990b). Passion refers to the depth of feeling that colors all life experiences and brings an intensity and complexity to the emotional life of the gifted individual. Passion is also part of creative endeavors. Passionate people can form deep attachments and react to the feeling tone of situations; they may think with their feelings. Dorothea Lange (Meltzer, 1985), the well known documentary photographer during the Depression and in the 1940s, used her feelings about her subjects to express herself in her art. The feeling evoked by her photographic subjects was what was important, not the photograph per se.

Another aspect of sensitivity has to do with compassion. Not all gifted people exhibit compassion, but those who do find they make commitments to other people and to social causes that involve caring for others and wanting to decrease the pain they feel in others. This commitment to decrease suffering may be direct, as in the example of Mother Teresa of India, or at more of a distance, through the witnessing and recording of atrocities so that all the world may know. Nellie Bly (Carter, 1987) recorded the abuses toward the mentally ill by pretending to be insane and being admitted to an asylum. Her reporting of what she experienced led to reforms in mental health by the City of New York in 1887.

Poets, some investigative reporters, Peace Corps workers, people who volunteer to work to combat poverty, those who fight to save wildlife, many peace activists, and some political and religious leaders may be gifted and high in sensitivity. Examples include John James Audubon, Louisa May Alcott, St. Francis of Assisi, Elizabeth Blackwell, Dorothy Dix, Gandhi, Martin Luther King, Jr., and Albert Schweitzer.

In childhood, the passion side of sensitivity can lead to an intense commitment to people and ideas. This sort of child may be dedicated to friendship, not seeing the faults of others but focusing instead on the potential within. Even if hurt over and over, the child will not give up the alliance. He or she feels that if, somehow, the key to understanding the other could be found, then of course they would be friends. For example, as a teenager, Martin Luther King, Jr.'s forgiveness of a college student who threatened to kill him led to real change in the assailant (Milton, 1987).

Sensitive gifted children can bring their passion to bear on causes ranging from national issues to personal ones. The child simply has faith that success will occur. This dedication and commitment to a goal will bring the child into conflict with adults, but it will also result in a sense of alliance with the universe. This is a powerful reward, and far outweighs all the pain of the conflict that occurred before the goal was attained.

Sensitive and compassionate gifted children are highly empathic. They seem not only to know what others feel, but to actually feel the feelings within themselves. This is particularly true of intense and negative feelings. Whereas most children know when a parent is angry, sensitive gifted children feel the anger inside themselves. However, while experiencing the feeling of anger, they are unable to find the antecedent event that triggered the feeling. If they learn to set some interpersonal boundaries between self and others and can distinguish whose feelings are whose, empathy and compassion can lead to making personal choices that are mutually beneficial in relationships.

Children who feel the feelings of others and are unable to set interpersonal boundaries may feel too much pain coming from other people. Feeling so overwhelmed, they are likely to try to cope by either withdrawing or trying to make others happy. Those who withdraw still feel other people's pain, but actively avoid people and situations that tend to produce negative feelings. The result may be isolation and disconnection from others. Those who try to cope by making and keeping others happy may take on too much responsibility for the emotional tone of interactions. They come to feel they are responsible for how others feel; if others feel bad, it must be the gifted child's fault. Some children develop a sort of perfectionism as a style of dealing with the stress of feeling others' feelings, that is, they attempt to avoid negative confrontations by trying to be exceptionally good (perfect) at all times.

Counseling Issues

Gifted children who are very sensitive bring the sensitivity with them to counseling. They are able to unconsciously read the counselor's feelings; consequently, they may try to please the counselor, or stay isolated and remote. Often they work to avoid confrontations because anger and conflict are so painful and confusing. Counselors need to be aware of the underlying assumption of personal responsibility which the child makes in dealing with all kinds of feelings in order to help the child to learn that he or she is not responsible for the outcome of all interpersonal interactions.

Many sensitive, compassionate gifted children can be called "gifted givers." These are children who give without expecting a return, without measuring the cost to themselves or others. Giving seems to them a natural thing to do when confronted by someone else's needs. In fact, they often have a lot to offer, and giving is rewarding to them. Thus, they may try to give to the counselor, sometimes to meet what they perceive to be a need of the counselor (and they can be quite correct) and sometimes for the sheer joy of sharing themselves through giving. The counselor must consider the needs of gifted givers carefully and allow them the joy of such sharing of self with an accepting other. To entirely discourage giving from this sort of child might mean rejecting an important part of the self. On the other hand, the counselor needs to help these gifted children understand why they give in each instance, and under what circumstances giving can be unacceptable. Some need to understand the interpersonal consequences of giving too much. Also, some gifted givers feel such a need to give it never occurs to them to think about receiving. Counselors may need to suggest that receiving can also be a type of gift that one allows of another person. Some give so much their families take them for granted. These children need to learn the essential difference between selfishness and having a self.

In working with sensitive gifted children who feel others' feelings but have not yet learned to establish appropriate boundaries, counselors need to offer concrete suggestions. For example, to develop boundaries means to build appropriate interpersonal distance between the self and others' emotional states. Actual physical distancing techniques may be helpful; for example, the child leaves the room and assesses what he or she is feeling, and was feeling prior to the problem. The child then returns and tries to problem solve. It is also helpful to discuss the difference between empathy (accurate understanding of another's viewpoint) and compassion (caring) as the child struggles to see things from a different perspective without feeling responsible for causing the feelings. Sometimes mental imagery helps, for example, taking a deep breath and relaxing, and then building a transparent wall between the self and others. It lets the gifted child see and hear the other but not feel invaded by the other's feelings. Some of the children may have intense family needs and be in the role of co-dependents. In addition to needing some of the same sorts of help that children of alcoholics need, they also have to learn to recognize that the core of the problem can be that they actually feel what others feel.

Empathic, compassionate children often form deep bonds with others, including animals. The child who is compassionate with animals often seems to recognize what animals feel, and is someone animals seem to like and trust. Children who form deep bonds with other people may choose a younger or disabled child or an elderly person; sometimes they choose the counselor. These children, who are gifted at loving, need to recognize the specialness of this bond, and to learn that such bonds are rare and that expectations for forming such deep bonds may need to be realistic. Sometimes adults in the child's life, as well as the child, need to understand the underlying, but often subtle, reciprocity of such bonds because on the surface, they may seem to be one-sided.

Perceptiveness

Helen was twelve when she was asked to join a cheating co-op at her junior high school. She was surprised at the extent to which cheating took place at

her school, and the ignorance of teachers about it. She declined to partici-
pate, and after much soul-searching decided to inform the principal. To her
astonishment, he appeared angry at her, refused to take action saying she
had no proof, and told her she was a troublemaker. Later, her parents, who
supported her action, told her about the problems whistle-blowers face
when administrators turn a blind eye to dishonesty, giving tacit permission
for such behavior.

Seeing several points of view simultaneously, understanding several layers of self within another, and getting quickly to the core of an issue are characteristic of gifted adults with the trait of perceptiveness. This intuition helps them to understand the meaning of personal symbols and to see beyond the superficiality of a situation to the person beneath (Lovecky, 1990b). Margaret Mead, for example, was able to use her unique insight and intuition to understand symbols embedded in culture. Her ideas revolutionized both anthropology and the way society has come to view sexual development. This same capacity for insight earlier in her life suggested to her that she neither hide her intelligence nor force herself to compete intellectually with others at too early an age (Mead, 1972).

Insight, intuition, and the ability to read several layers of feeling simultaneously allow perceptive gifted people to rapidly assess people and situations. In fact, they are often skilled at sensing the dyscongruency between exhibited social facades and real thoughts and feelings.

The recognition of and need for truth is important to perceptive gifted people. Justice and fairness are also issues. Recognizing that life is often unfair, they nevertheless try, within their own lives, to be fair and just to others.

Some religious and political leaders, scientists, philosophers, therapists, artists, writers, and poets may be especially gifted with perception. Examples include Emily Dickinson, Langston Hughes, Anne Hutchinson, Abraham Lincoln, Margaret Mead, and Shakespeare.

In childhood, perceptiveness manifests itself as intuition, insight, and a high regard for truth and fairness. Martin Luther King, Jr., at age fourteen, saw the irony inherent in winning first prize in an oratory contest for his speech on "The Negro and the Constitution," only to be forced to move to the back of the bus on the way home (Milton, 1987).

Perceptive gifted children are able to grasp patterns in material otherwise seen as disparate, find the hidden meanings in what they read and hear, and understand the reality beneath the surface in the statements of others. Because they value truth and fairness so much, they see clearly the implicit unfairness in how many adults treat children. The idea of social facade and different faces shown in different roles can be puzzling to them. Why someone would be nice to your face and mean behind your back makes no sense. To these children, the truth is an absolute; they both seek and tell the truth, frequently with little regard for feelings. Often they find themselves in the role of the boy in The Emperor's New Clothes, albeit with very different results.

Children with the trait of perceptiveness appear to ask themselves two different questions: "Why am I so different from others?" ("What is wrong with me?"); or "Why don't others see what I see so clearly?" ("Why are they so stupid?"). Some children seem to polarize to one or the other position; others seem to change from one point of view to the other (Lovecky, 1990a).

Children who feel the self is different (and therefore wrong) really try to understand how others think. They believe the best of others, and often respond positively to negative comments and criticisms from others. Because they do not realize that others are not as perceptive as they are, these gifted children feel that whatever negative comments are made about them must be true. They think the other person must see a defect within them that they are blind to but that is obvious to others. That the other person might be less idealistic, mistaken, petty, jealous, or acting from limited perceptions will not occur to them. Over time, perceptive children can develop a negative self-image based on taking to heart the conflicting negative comments made by others, feeling defective in some mysterious way, and coming to distrust the validity of their own thoughts and feelings.

The second type of child does not understand why others are so lacking in perceptiveness. It is perfectly obvious what is right, and the rest of the world seems out of step. These children expect adults to practice what they preach, to be paragons of virtue, truth, fairness, and justice. Some gifted children have trouble with differences of opinion because to them there is only one truth. This rigid concept of right and wrong is a developmental issue for all children, but it is a particular problem for very insightful children who are, nevertheless, developmentally in an either/or stage. They are apt to have trouble with adults they regard as misinformed or foolish. To them it makes no sense that a person would not want to know the truth, wish to have a mistake corrected, or learn a better way to do something. The foolishness of adults in authority over them can be difficult to tolerate, and may lead to continual conflict for these children.

To the perceptive child, searching for truth, having to know the right answer, or being absolutely fair can supersede an awareness of others' needs. The risk of such a strong internal drive is severe disappointment in adults and in the adult world. Gifted children may come to feel betrayed by adults and disillusioned by the mores that adults hold up as desirable but do not really practice themselves. This leads to difficulty in knowing how to trust, with subsequent lack of development of internal security. As these children grow older they may become cynical and arrogant. The negativity toward adult authority that can develop brings more negativity from adults. Over time, fewer and fewer supportive adults appear in their lives.

If perceptive gifted children are to become successful gifted adults, they need to learn to trust their own perceptions while understanding the limitations of others, to build a positive self-image despite negative and often inaccurate feedback from adults, and to find a basis of connectedness to the adult world. This can occur only if gifted children receive adult support, acknowledgment of the accuracy of their insights, and some understanding of how others think and feel.

Counseling Issues

The most important counseling issue for highly perceptive gifted children is learning when and how to trust their own perceptions, and how to assess what they are told about themselves by others. In fact, the existential question faced by such children, as they grow up, is how to learn to be trusting (but not naive) in an untrustworthy and untruthful world. In counseling, it is the development of the trusting relationship, based on mutual respect, that teaches these children to examine carefully what others say about them, and to judge the validity of particular comments in light of what they know to be true about themselves. Differences of opinion and interest are another area to be explored in an effort to understand what truth is, and how it is derived by many people.

In helping gifted children to learn to trust their own perceptions, the counselor needs to take care to really understand these perceptions. Because these children are also perceptive about the counselor's weaknesses and vulnerabilities, the accuracy of their perceptions can be immediately judged. This may be uncomfortable for the counselor at times, but the acknowledgment of the truth of the child's perceptions, and the means the counselor uses to deal with faults and vulnerabilities, can be helpful to the child in coming to terms with the problem of feeling defective. Once the child is able to judge the accuracy of perceptions, the counselor can help the child decide what to do with the knowledge. This means teaching the child that other opinions also count, feelings are as important as truth in many situations, and there is room for negotiation and compromise without dishonesty becoming an issue. The encouragement of more awareness of others' feelings allows the child to hold perceptions in mind while evaluating the best course of action.

Perceptive children may need help in understanding that others are less perceptive than they; in fact, such perceptiveness is a rare gift. These children may need to learn about the different layers within people. They also need to realize that they see more consequences, ramifications, and parts to situations than do most other people. Thus will these gifted children learn to suffer the foolishness of others a bit better. If they can understand how others think and feel and the basis from which most decisions are made, gifted children can come to understand why most people do not like to have mistakes pointed out to them, or why they will continue to pursue a course of behavior that seems wrong to the child. Some children also need to learn the interpersonal hazards of needing to be absolutely correct at all costs.

It can be helpful to these children to learn when feelings will be a more important focus than the truth. Many have trouble making that judgment, so counselors can be helpful in taking the role of the other person and thinking aloud about what happens between the child and the other. Learning to watch others and wait to use information rather than immediately responding to a cue can be helpful in discovering the motivations of other people. Some children also profit from an approach that requires them to watch others the way an anthropologist might in order to gain information about the underlying dynamics of people in different situations. This can help the children learn why someone is two-faced, or repeats troublesome behavior. This "Margaret Mead" approach helps them to learn how the truth might look to someone else, as well as what dishonesty really is. From such understanding can come the sense of trust about others in relation to the self that so many perceptive children lack.

Some highly intuitive and sensitive children can read below the surface so well that their perceptions scare them. They (and others) may believe they have psychic abilities or can read minds. Some make intuitive predictions about what might happen. These children need unconditional positive support from the counselor who tries to understand how they feel. Many such children feel responsible for what happens. What they need is help in learning that the overwhelming feelings they have come without their consent, and that they are only responsible for their own actions, not for events that occur that are beyond anyone's control. Developing a positive sense of using perceptiveness can help these gifted children become adults able to use their abilities wisely while feeling intimately connected to the deepest core of other people.

Entelechy

When Angel's older brother was diagnosed with AIDS, their father threw him out. Luis went to live with a friend. Angel, who was nine at the time, was forbidden to see him. Angel thought their father was wrong in his attitudes about homosexuality and AIDS, and began a campaign to remind him of his love for Luis, who, as eldest son, he had held closest to his heart. Angel induced their father to accept Luis's being gay, and to understand that he was probably going to lose Luis from AIDS without saying good-bye unless he let Luis into their lives again. Eventually the father went to see his son, and reconciled. He had been shamed into going by his young child who truly loved both Luis and him without reservation.

Derived from the Greek word for having a goal, entelechy is a particular type of motivation, need for self-determination, and an inner strength and vital force directing life and growth to become all one is capable of being (Lovecky, 1990b). Gifted people with this trait are often attractive to others who feel drawn to their openness and their dreams or visions. Being near someone with this trait gives others hope and determination to achieve their own self-actualization.

These gifted people are deeply involved in making their own destiny.

This "will to be" enables them to continue on despite what are sometimes tremendous obstacles. They believe in themselves, even when no one else does. Because of their tremendous strength of will and personal courage, they may inspire, and sometimes shame, others. Great teachers, therapists, social reformers, statesmen, and some types of artists can be so gifted. Examples include Bronson Alcott, Helen Keller, Abraham Lincoln, Camille Pissarro, Carl Rogers, and Eleanor Roosevelt.

Gifted children with the trait of entelechy are highly motivated, exceptionally single-minded in the pursuit of their own goals, and incredibly strong of will. For example, Abraham Lincoln was so determined to get an education that he read even while doing physical labor, walked miles to borrow books, and never neglected a chance to hear a lecture, or talk with an author. In a frontier community that prized hunting prowess, he gave up hunting at an early age (North, 1956). Children high in entelechy find the same independence, strength of will, and inner spirit to surmount tremendous difficulties. These difficulties might be environmental, as Lincoln experienced, or personal, as in the case of Eleanor Roosevelt, who overcame her shyness, insecurity, and eagerness to please in order to become an effective campaigner for human rights (Faber, 1985).

Children high in entelechy appear to elicit positive responses from adults who admire their spirit and see something special within. For example, Mary McLeod Bethune, the African-American educator, as a child, was considered special by her entire community. When asked to pick one child to receive a higher education, she was the one selected (Meltzer, 1987). Some gifted children survive childhood because of this ability to elicit caring and help from others. For many, their specialness is the source of a mentor relationship which can continue into adulthood.

Children high in entelechy may have unlikely friendships. Because they are drawn to the specialness of others, they may see the inner spirit of those different from themselves. Some appear to have a type of charisma that allows them to successfully lead peers in group activities. They are the ones to whom others turn for support and encouragement, and they may provide the motivation that allows various factions to work together on a project. Often they can help others rise above the usual petty jealousies and rivalries because they inspire others to be better than they ordinarily would be.

The specialness of the gifted child may become a liability. Though these children do not see themselves as special, many adults treat them as if they do. Some try to break the child's strong spirit; they see the specialness as threatening. Lincoln's father may have felt this as he sent young Abe out for hire as a slaughterer of livestock after the boy would no longer hunt or kill (North, 1956). To insecure adults, the child with so much inner spirit can seem a reprimand of their own shortcomings, and they may then give the child a difficult time. Thus, the child experiences adults as people who treat them in extreme ways: either exceptionally willing to help, or always finding fault, making life difficult, and trying to humiliate them in the guise of teaching humility.

These gifted children may find that others' needs always seem to come first, and the harder they try to meet all the needs, the more frustrated, disappointed, and disillusioned they feel. Often too much is expected. Despite their charisma, these children are not necessarily popular. Instead, they are the ones everyone else relies on. By the end of high school many feel burned out, have little idea who they are apart from others' expectations of them, and feel burdened with all the essential, but unglorified, work of any group venture. For the gifted child with entelechy, developmental tasks involve finding inner resources that are not dependent on meeting the needs of others, and evolving a sense of self that does not alternate between feeling extremely positive and special or extremely negative and alienated.

Counseling Issues

Because these are often children who are inspiring to be with, they may become special to the counselor, who serves in the role of trusted adult friend and who helps them learn to understand others. Issues involve developing internal security and avoiding vulnerable self-esteem created from the confusion they feel in the responses obtained from others. The extreme contrast between the positive responses of those seeing them as special for certain traits and the negative responses of those threatened by those same traits means that the child has trouble seeing the self clearly. The counselor needs to help the child learn to focus on a more balanced view of self as a person with strengths and weaknesses, rather than someone special or bad as defined by someone else.

Because many of these children are so strong-willed, it is helpful if the counselor deals directly with the self-defeating aspects of this behavior. A strong-willed child often becomes a foil in eliciting negative interactions with others and needs help in learning to use the strength of will more positively. A strong-willed person is someone whose vision of how things should be is very strong, and who has an extremely powerful pull toward self-determination.

Labels given the child are often negative: rebellious or stubborn, for example. Recognition that the negative side is only part of the picture is important, because being strong in will also means one makes commitments, is assertive, and has a sense of what is right for the self. Counselors need to experience, through their own use of empathy, what the world of such children is like in order to understand why they feel so strongly about an issue, that is, what it represents to them. Only in this way can these gifted children learn to compromise and listen to the reasoning of others. The counselor can also help them see what is positive about a stance and how to effect a positive influence in an interaction. Finally, recognizing that some adults are beyond change might be helpful. Strategies for dealing with situations when one is in a weaker position are also useful.

Counselors will need to recognize the extreme loneliness of some gifted children. Children high in the trait of entelechy need particular help in learning how to recognize and find true friends. Those whose self-image is bound up in meeting others' needs must learn that others will always want too much, and it is never the gifted child's turn to receive unless he or she sets such parameters from the beginning. The tasks of learning to set limits on what one will do and saying "no" are important, as is learning the pleasures to be obtained from one's own company and one's own self-affirmation.

The pursuit of a special dream is often a need of gifted children who are high in entelechy. A goal upon which to focus, through the medium of the dream, can help such children to manage their strong wills, determination, and personal power in more positive ways. Counselors may have to advocate for children by helping them find resources and people who will help focus their energies on exciting and challenging pursuits. These special mentor relationships provide an interpersonal connection in which the specialness of the child is valued, and the strengths of the child enhanced.

CONCLUSION

Gifted young people often have an intense need to find meaning: the meaning of life, the meaning of who they are inside themselves, the meaning of interpersonal relationships to them. This search for self is the basis of development of both identity and good self-esteem if the gifted student is able to discover and learn to treasure his or her own uniqueness, and to find some means of connection to others. Counselors working with gifted young people need to recognize their special problems and issues and guide them in learning about their divergent thinking ability, excitability, sensitivity, perceptiveness, and entelechy in positive and growth-enhancing ways.

REFERENCES

Austin, A. B., & Draper, D. C. (1981). Peer relationships of the academically gifted. *Gifted Child Quarterly, 25,* 129–134.

Betts, G. T. (1986). Development of the emotional and social needs of gifted individuals. *Journal of Counseling and Development, 64,* 587–589.

Betts, G. T., & Neihart, M. (1988). Profiles of the gifted and talented. *Gifted Child Quarterly, 32,* 248–253.

Carter, M. (1987). Nellie Bly. *Cricket, 15*(1), 55–60.

Cousins, M. (1965). *The story of Thomas Alva Edison.* New York: Random House.

Culross, R. R., & Jenkins-Friedman, R. (1988). On coping and defending: Applying Bruner's personal growth principles working with gifted/talented students. *Gifted Child Quarterly, 32,* 261–266.

Davis, G. A., & Rimm, S. (1979). Identification and counseling of the creatively gifted. In N. Colangelo & R. Zaffrann (Eds.), *New voices in counseling the gifted* (pp. 225–236). Dubuque, IA: Kendall/Hunt.

Ehrlich, V. Z. (1982). *Gifted children.* Englewood Cliffs, NJ: Prentice-Hall.

Faber, D. (1985). *Eleanor Roosevelt. First lady of the world.* New York: Viking Kestrel.

Feldman, D. H., with Goldsmith, L. (1986). *Nature's gambit.* New York: Basic Books.

Franks, B., & Dolan, L. (1982). Affective characteristics of gifted children: Educational implications. *Gifted Child Quarterly, 26,* 172–178.

Freeman, J. (1983). Annotation. Emotional problems of the gifted child. *Journal of Child Psychology and Psychiatry, 24,* 481–485.

Gross, M. (1989). The pursuit of excellence or the search for intimacy? The forced-choice dilemma of gifted youth. *Roeper Review, 11,* 189–194.

Hollinger, C. L., & Fleming, E. S. (1988). Gifted and talented young women: Antecedents and correlates of life satisfaction. *Gifted Child Quarterly, 32,* 254–261.

Hollingworth, L. (1942). *Children above 180 IQ Stanford-Binet: Origin and Development.* Yonkers-on-Hudson, NY: World Book.

Janos, P. M., Fung, H., & Robinson, N. M. (1985). Perceptions of deviance and self concept within an intellectually gifted sample. *Gifted Child Quarterly, 29,* 78–82.

Janos, P. M., Marwood, K. A., & Robinson, N. M. (1985). Friendship patterns in highly gifted children. *Roeper Review, 8,* 46–49.

Janos, P. M., & Robinson, N. M. (1985). Psychosocial development in intellectually gifted children. In F.D. Horowitz & M. O'Brien (Eds.), *The gifted and talented: Developmental perspectives* (pp. 149–195). Washington, DC: American Psychological Association.

Kitano, M. K. (1990). Intellectual abilities and psychological intensities in young gifted children: Implications for the gifted. *Roeper Review, 13,* 5–10.

Kline, B. E., & Meckstroth, E. A. (1985). Understanding and encouraging the exceptionally gifted. *Roeper Review, 8,* 24–30.

Lovecky, D. V. (1986). Can you hear the flowers singing? Issues for gifted adults. *Journal of Counseling and Development, 64,* 590–592.

Lovecky, D. V. (1990a). Psychotherapy with gifted children. In P. A. Keller & S. R. Heyman (Eds.), *Innovations in clinical practice: A source book* (Vol. 9, pp. 119–130). Sarasota, FL: Professional Resource Exchange.

Lovecky, D. V. (1990b). Warts and rainbows: Issues in the psychotherapy of the gifted. *Advanced Development, 2,* 65–83.

Lovecky, D. V. (1991). The divergently thinking child. *Understanding Our Gifted, 3*(3), 1, 7–9.

Lynn, S. J., & Rhue, J. W. (1988). Fantasy proneness: Hypnosis, developmental antecedents, and psychopathology. *American Psychologist, 43,* 35–44.

Mead, M. (1972). *Blackberry winter.* New York: William Morrow.

Meltzer, M. (1985). *Dorothea Lange. Life through the camera.* New York: Viking-Penguin.

Meltzer, M. (1987). *Mary McLeod Bethune. Voice of Black hope.* New York: Viking-Penguin.

Miller, N. B., & Silverman, L. K. (1987). Levels of personality development. *Roeper Review, 9,* 221–225.

Milton, J. (1987). *Marching to freedom. The story of Martin Luther King, Jr.* New York: Dell.

Morelock, M. J. (1992). Giftedness: The view from within. *Understanding Our Gifted, 4*(3), 1, 11–15.

North, S. (1956). *Abe Lincoln. Log cabin to White House*. New York: Random House.

Ogburn Colangelo, M. K. (1979). Giftedness as multilevel potential: A clinical example. In N. Colangelo & R. Zaffrann (Eds.), *New voices in counseling the gifted* (pp. 165–187). Dubuque, IA: Kendall/Hunt.

Perry, S. (1986). I'm gifted, but I'm not supposed to know it. *G/C/T, 9*(3), 55–57.

Piechowski, M. M. (1986). The concept of developmental potential. *Roeper Review, 8,* 190–197.

Piechowski, M. M. (1991). Emotional development and emotional giftedness. In N. Colangelo & G. Davis (Eds.), *Handbook of gifted education* (pp. 285–306). Needham Heights, MA: Allyn & Bacon.

Post, R. D. (1988). Self-sabotage among successful women. *Psychotherapy in Private Practice, 6,* 127–130.

Roedell, W. (1984). Vulnerabilities of highly gifted children. *Roeper Review, 6,* 127–130.

Roedell, W. (1988). "I just want my child to be happy": Social development and young gifted children. *Understanding Our Gifted, 1*(1), 1, 7, 9–11.

Roeper, A. (1982). How the gifted cope with their emotions. *Roeper Review, 5*(2), 21–24.

Roeper, A. (1989). Empathy, ethics, and global education. *Understanding Our Gifted, 1*(6), 1, 7–10.

Roth, H. (1986). Personality patterns and counseling styles. *G/C/T, 9*(3), 58.

Sanborn, M. P. (1979). Differential counseling needs of the gifted and talented. In N. Colangelo & R. Zaffrann (Eds.), *New voices in counseling the gifted* (pp. 154–164). Dubuque, IA: Kendall/Hunt.

Silverman, L. K. (1983a). Personality development: The pursuit of excellence. *Journal for the Education of the Gifted, 6*(1), 5–19.

Silverman, L. K. (1983b). Issues in affective development of the gifted. In J. VanTassel-Baska (Ed.), *A practical guide to counseling the gifted in a school setting* (pp. 6–21). Reston, VA: Council for Exceptional Children.

Silverman, L. K., & Ellsworth, B. (1980). The theory of positive disintegration and its implications for giftedness. In N. Duda (Ed.), *Theory of positive disintegration: Proceedings of the third international conference* (pp. 179–194). Miami, FL: University of Miami School of Medicine.

Terman, L. M. (1925). Mental and physical traits of a thousand gifted children. *Genetic studies of genius* (Vol. 1). Stanford, CA: Stanford University Press.

Tidwell, R. A. (1980). Psychoeducational profiles of 1593 gifted high school students. *Gifted Child Quarterly, 24,* 63–68.

Tolan, S. (1989). Special problems of young gifted children. *Understanding Our Gifted, 1*(5), 1, 7–10.

Torrance, E. P. (1961). Problems of highly gifted children. *Gifted Child Quarterly, 5*(2), 31–34.

Torrance, E. P. (1962). *Guiding creative talent*. Englewood Cliffs, NJ: Prentice-Hall.

Torrance, E. P. (1965). *Gifted children in the classroom*. New York: Macmillan.

Webb, J. T., Meckstroth, E. A., & Tolan, S. S. (1982). *Guiding the gifted child*. Columbus: Ohio Psychology.

Wendorf, D. J., & Frey, J. (1985). Family therapy with the intellectually gifted. *The American Journal of Family Therapy, 13*(1), 31–38.

Whitmore, J. R. (1980). *Giftedness, conflict, and underachievement.* Needham Heights, MA: Allyn & Bacon.

Willings, D. (1980). *The creatively gifted.* Cambridge, England: Woodhead-Faulkner, Ltd.

Willings, D. (1985). The specific needs of adults who are gifted. *Roeper Review, 8,* 35–38.

Zaffrann, R. T., & Colangelo, N. (1979). Counseling with gifted and talented students. In N. Colangelo & R. T. Zaffrann (Eds.), *New voices in counseling the gifted* (pp. 142–153). Dubuque, IA: Kendall/Hunt.

3   A Developmental Model for Counseling the Gifted

Linda Kreger Silverman

In the first two chapters we discussed various attributes of the gifted personality. In this chapter a model for counseling the gifted, which has been derived from the unique characteristics of this population, is presented. Regardless of the talent domain in which giftedness expresses itself, gifted and talented individuals share certain intellectual and personality traits, which appear early in life and tend to remain throughout the life span. Both the intellectual and the personality differences of this group must be taken into account in designing appropriate counseling programs to meet their needs.

The intellectual and personality characteristics provide the windows through which these children view the world. All of their experiences are filtered through these lenses. They can be clear, bright, undistorted reflections, they can be colored to shade the child from too much stimulation, or, if the child feels vulnerable, they can be like one-way mirrors in which the child sees out but others cannot see in. The counseling interventions are life preservers for these children, preventing alienation, depression, underachievement, and damage to their self-esteem. These interventions foster a sense of self-efficacy and facilitate the process of self-actualization. Emotional development takes place through interaction with four external contexts—the home, the school, the community, and peer relations—as well as the internal context of the inner psychic milieu. These contexts are all potential support systems in the process of personal growth and development. Even when one of these contexts appears damaging, it is possible to restructure that part of the system so that it can lend its support. The various chapters in this book provide guidance for how these support systems can be mobilized to assist the development of the child.

The goals of developmental counseling appear varied, but they are simply different facets of a fully developed Self that can express its uniqueness for the greater good. The outcomes are represented by a clear, deep pool of wisdom and self-knowledge. Our desire is for these individuals to live lives deeply imbued with immutable values, to have the wisdom to choose the path of integrity, the compassion to choose the path of service, and the moral courage to become their best selves in the face of a world that often settles for less. It is with these goals in mind that we offer a developmental model for counseling the gifted. (See Figure 3.1.) The model can be perceived in a lighthearted way—taking one's life preserver and shades into the pool of knowledge. It can also be understood at a deeper level, as the struggle of an individual with a unique world view to attain wisdom and self-actualization in an unsupportive world. The support systems that can be mobilized on the child's behalf, and the interventions that can be put in place, do more than save the child from drowning; they act as a catalyst in the development of higher-order values. This means that, with support, the individual becomes morally committed to using his or her gifts to help all of society—the pool of humanity in which we are all interdependent.

CHARACTERISTICS OF THE GIFTED AND COUNSELING RESPONSES

The following list of characteristics is fairly typical of a large spectrum of the gifted population. The intellectual characteristics are evident in intellectually gifted children and tend to increase in strength in accordance with IQ; most would obtain across all talent domains as well. In addition, these characteristics have personality correlates. The pairs listed below are but a sampling of myriad possibilities. *All* of the intellectual traits are dynamically interrelated with *all* of the personality traits, and certain clusters of traits are more salient in some personalities and less so in others. These characteristics interact with degree of intellectual difference, overexcitabilities, and talents. Counselors need to understand these essential facets of the gifted person and to employ them constructively in the therapeutic process. In this section each of these pairs will be discussed as well as their counseling implications.

Intellectual Characteristics	Personality Characteristics
Exceptional reasoning ability	Insightfulness
Intellectual curiosity	Need to understand
Rapid learning rate	Need for mental stimulation
Facility with abstraction	Perfectionism
Complex thought processes	Need for precision/logic
Vivid imagination	Excellent sense of humor
Early moral concern	Sensitivity/empathy
Passion for learning	Intensity

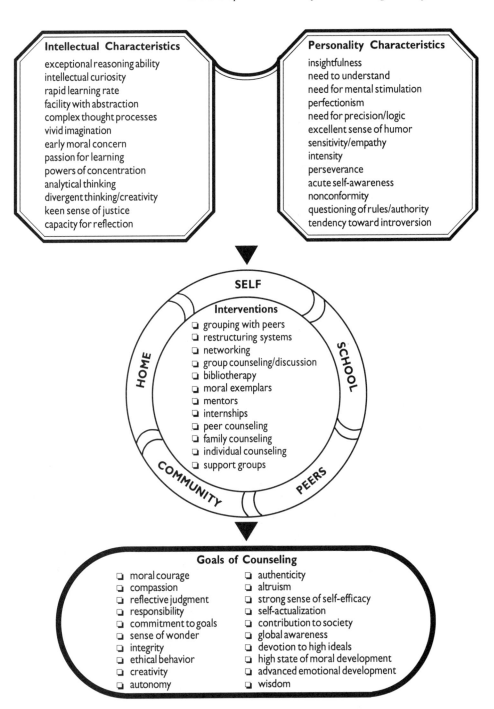

Intellectual Characteristics

exceptional reasoning ability
intellectual curiosity
rapid learning rate
facility with abstraction
complex thought processes
vivid imagination
early moral concern
passion for learning
powers of concentration
analytical thinking
divergent thinking/creativity
keen sense of justice
capacity for reflection

Personality Characteristics

insightfulness
need to understand
need for mental stimulation
perfectionism
need for precision/logic
excellent sense of humor
sensitivity/empathy
intensity
perseverance
acute self-awareness
nonconformity
questioning of rules/authority
tendency toward introversion

SELF

HOME

SCHOOL

Interventions

❏ grouping with peers
❏ restructuring systems
❏ networking
❏ group counseling/discussion
❏ bibliotherapy
❏ moral exemplars
❏ mentors
❏ internships
❏ peer counseling
❏ family counseling
❏ individual counseling
❏ support groups

COMMUNITY

PEERS

Goals of Counseling

❏ moral courage
❏ compassion
❏ reflective judgment
❏ responsibility
❏ commitment to goals
❏ sense of wonder
❏ integrity
❏ ethical behavior
❏ creativity
❏ autonomy

❏ authenticity
❏ altruism
❏ strong sense of self-efficacy
❏ self-actualization
❏ contribution to society
❏ global awareness
❏ devotion to high ideals
❏ high state of moral development
❏ advanced emotional development
❏ wisdom

Figure 3.1
A DEVELOPMENTAL MODEL FOR COUNSELING THE GIFTED

Powers of concentration	Perseverance
Analytical thinking	Acute self-awareness
Divergent thinking/creativity	Nonconformity
Keen sense of justice	Questioning of rules/authority
Capacity for reflection	Tendency toward introversion

Insightfulness

Exceptional reasoning ability enables an individual to be more *perceptive and insightful,* grasping the essential elements of situations (Lovecky, 1992). When Cornell and Grossberg (1989) asked parents to write their own definitions of giftedness, perceptiveness emerged as the most frequently mentioned characteristic by 40 percent of the respondents. This quality also leads to problem finding and problem solving. In Parkinson's (1990) study in Australia, 68 percent of the parents of gifted children said that their children had unusual approaches to problem solving and unusual solutions, and 70 percent felt that their children possessed "superior powers of reasoning,...of understanding meanings, and of seeing relationships" (p. 11).

The student's advanced reasoning skills become immediately apparent at the outset of individual counseling sessions through his or her vocabulary level and the sophisticated manner in which thoughts are expressed. An effective counselor understands the asynchrony—recognizes that the student is mentally much older than he or she is physically—and communicates directly with that "older self." The older part of the student is assumed to have more wisdom to offer to the current situation. At the same time, the counselor maintains awareness that the student is an amalgam of many developmental ages (Tolan, 1989), and that his or her needs and life experiences are age-appropriate (Morelock, 1992). The student's reasoning skills and capacity for insight are continuously called into play in the therapeutic process. The counselor acts as a facilitator to help the student draw upon inner resources to resolve problems effectively. Brainstorming techniques can be carried over from the classroom to the counseling session and brought to bear on personal difficulties.

It is exciting for a counselor to work with a student who is insightful. But there are drawbacks as well, many of which are elucidated in chapter 2 in Lovecky's description of the perceptive child. Gifted students are so fascinated with ideas that they can turn counseling sessions into intellectual exercises. Insight becomes an end in itself rather than a means to a greater end. It is important for the counselor not to be swept away by the great idea chase. Two caveats to keep in mind: (1) insights are not a substitute for feelings; the insightful student may need to be continuously refocused on his or her feelings; (2) insights are not a substitute for actions; change requires not just understanding but commitment to *use* that understanding. Insights need to be translated into action plans.

The Need to Understand

Intellectual curiosity is in itself both an intellectual and a personality aspect because the *need to understand* drives the individual to seek knowledge. Curiosity is one of the earliest traits observed by parents of gifted children (Louis & Lewis, 1992; Munger, 1990; Parkinson, 1990). Eighty-one percent of the parents in Parkinson's (1990) study indicated that their children were curious, investigative, and asked penetrating questions; 66 percent described their children as persistent in examining and exploring stimuli to know more about them. Roeper (1991) suggests that this drive is maintained throughout the life span.

> *Gifted adults are often driven by their giftedness.* Gifted individuals do not know what creates the drive, the energy, the absolute necessity to act. They may have no choice but to explore, compose, write, paint, develop theories, educate children, conduct research or whatever else it is that has become uppermost in their minds. They need to know; they need to learn; they must climb the mountain because it is there. This "driven-ness," this one-track-mindedness, may keep them from sleeping or eating...for the duration of their specific involvement.
>
> Where does this drive in the gifted originate? It is in part a psychological need. It grows from the need to make sense of the world, to understand the world, to create one's own world. It is a need for mastery—intellectually, creatively, physically. (pp. 90–91)

Almost all gifted students are curious about their own psychological makeup and are fascinated with the subject of what makes them tick. Psychology courses can be offered, or psychology can be infused in seminars, discussion groups, and other special provisions. Gifted students usually enjoy taking personality inventories and learning more about intrapsychic and family dynamics. *Psychology for Kids* (Kincher, 1990) provides forty personal-style inventories for students aged ten and above.

Their natural curiosity can be integrated into the counseling process by having gifted students perceive themselves as experimental subjects in a research design of their own construction. They learn to observe themselves under various conditions. They can take notes, keep diaries, make charts, or numerically rate affective states. "What would happen if...?" questions can be raised to help them see different potential actions and consequences. The student-as-researcher can also monitor his or her own progress with different self-chosen interventions.

The Need for Mental Stimulation

Gifted children crave a great deal of mental stimulation even from infancy. Infant studies show that precocious infants quickly lose interest in familiar stimuli (habituation) and prefer novelty (Fisher, 1990; Storfer, 1990). Their remarkable memories, advanced rate of development, and *rapid learning rate* are observable in early childhood (Louis & Lewis, 1992; Parkinson, 1990). The foremost characteristic of giftedness mentioned by all of the parents in

Parkinson's (1990) study was unusual memory; 88 percent indicated that their children learned easily and readily.

A major problem for gifted students in school is the mismatch between their rapid learning rate and the pace of most of their classes (Feldhusen, 1992; Robinson & Noble, 1992). Lovecky (1992) and Tolan (1985) maintain that highly gifted children cannot concentrate on schoolwork that is unstimulating. Their minds take off on journeys that are beyond their control.

> Jim very much wanted to please the teacher. Yet, every time he started a page of problems, he would find himself in trouble for not working. Jim's brain could not work with the material offered, and his mind would not focus on the task. Given material at his level, Jim had no trouble with concentration or completing tasks. (Lovecky, 1992, p. 4)

According to Lovecky, an intense *need for mental stimulation* differentiates the exceptionally gifted from their more moderately gifted peers. "Exceptionally gifted children have minds that never turn off. Isaac Asimov...author of over 400 books, has described his need for stimulation as so pressing that he counts the holes in acoustic ceiling tiles" (1992, p. 3). Apparently, Sir Francis Galton also had a penchant for counting things. He counted anything and everything imaginable—yawns and fidgets of an audience at a concert as a measure of boredom to the 20,000 brush strokes used by the artist who painted his portrait! (Schultz, 1981).

The child's excellent retention, rapid learning rate, and need for mental stimulation should be able to be dealt with effectively in the school setting. As an advocate, the counselor can facilitate programmatic, curricular, and instructional modifications. Teachers can be encouraged to use a diagnostic/prescriptive approach with the student (Nelson, 1992), assessing what he or she knows before teaching to make sure the student isn't covering the same ground twice. Ability grouping allows the pace of instruction to be accelerated. Independent projects, grade acceleration, advanced coursework, enrichment opportunities, testing out of courses, curriculum compacting, and magnet schools can all be explored as means of keeping the child intellectually stimulated and challenged. The counselor needs to be aware of private school options, community resources for enrichment, and even resources for homeschooling, should the school prove inadequate to the task of providing sufficient stimulation for the child.

Excellent memory has its down side, for it means that the individual has intense affective memory as well (Piechowski, 1991). Gifted students vividly recollect each failure and every humiliation, reliving these experiences years after they have occurred. It is a challenge for counselors to break the self-defeating cycle that perpetuates feelings of helplessness and bitter resentment. Role playing can be useful, allowing the student to reexperience the situation from a place of empowerment rather than victimization. The reenactment may replace the old memory and help the student realize that new skills are available in case a similar situation should occur in the future.

The student's need for mental stimulation must also be addressed in the counseling sessions. The pace of the session may need to be quickened. Some students enjoy reading about the psychological theories being employed by the counselor, and can participate more fully when they feel better informed about the process.

Perfectionism

Facility with abstraction and *perfectionism* are probably the most striking facets of giftedness, but their relationship may seem somewhat obscure. As they are key elements to understanding the gifted, a more elaborate explanation follows. Snyderman and Rothman (1988) polled 661 psychologists to determine if there is any professional agreement about the nature of intelligence. Contrary to the media's message that there is no shared view in the field, 99.3 percent considered abstract reasoning an essential component of intelligence.

> It can be reasonably concluded that when different psychologists and educators use the term "intelligence" they are basically referring to the same concept, having to do with capacity to learn and with more complex cognitive tasks like abstract reasoning and problem solving.... In many ways, Terman's 1921 definition of intelligence as abstract thinking remains at the heart of current thought about intelligence. (pp. 56–57)

Capacity for abstract thought is the *sine qua non* of giftedness. It is evident early in life, differentiating gifted preschoolers from less able peers (Lewis & Louis, 1991; Louis & Lewis, 1992).

Whereas abstract reasoning is the most accepted aspect of giftedness, perfectionism is the least understood and most maligned, even though the latter is a direct result of the former. Perfection is an abstract concept. It is an awareness of what is possible—an abstract ideal, beyond that which currently exists in concrete reality. Dabrowski's Level III conflict between "what is" and "what ought to be" (Dabrowski, 1970, p. 106) is the search for ideals of a higher order. From a Dabrowskian perspective, perfectionism is a positive quality in the personality—the striving for self-perfection that propels the individual toward higher level development (Silverman, 1990).

Perfectionism is also a function of the asynchronous development of the gifted child. When the mind develops faster than the body, the reasoning and values of the child are more like those of his or her mental peers than like those of age-mates. The child sets standards for him- or herself based upon this advanced awareness. Sometimes the child's body will not be sufficiently developed to keep the promises the mind has made, as in the example in chapter 1 of the child who cannot shape clay with five-year-old fingers to match the vision of her eight-year-old mind. Frustration ensues. It appears to others that the child is being "too perfectionistic" by setting such impossible standards. But when it becomes clear that the part of the child setting the standards is quite advanced, then those standards appear more reasonable. It becomes the job of anyone acting in a counseling capacity to help that advanced part of the child understand the physical limitations of other parts of the system.

Numerous educators and clinicians have recognized the perfectionistic tendencies of gifted children (e.g., Adderholdt-Elliott, 1987; J. Gallagher, 1990; Hollingworth, 1926; Karnes & Oehler-Stinnet, 1986; Kerr, 1991; Manaster & Powell, 1983; Robinson & Noble, 1991; Roedell, 1984; Whitmore, 1980), but even within gifted education, this trait is usually seen in a negative light, and often blamed on the child's parents.

> Perfectionism here is defined as a complex of characteristics and behaviors including compulsiveness with regard to work habits, overconcern for details, unrealistically high standards for self and others, indiscriminate acquiescence to external evaluation, and rigid routines.... Although the commonsense notion of the causes of perfectionism tends to lay the blame for the perfectionistic child squarely on "pushy," exacting parents, clinical experience shows this conclusion to be unwarranted. Many perfectionistic gifted children are the products of relaxed, easy-going parents with realistic expectations.... It seems possible that certain children are simply *born* with the combination of temperaments that create a need for an orderly environment, or conversely, an aversion to chaos. (Kerr, 1991, p. 141)

Roedell (1984) and Robinson and Noble (1991), however, discuss the positive as well as negative aspects of this quality. "In a positive form, perfectionism can provide the driving energy which leads to great achievement" (Roedell, 1984, p. 128).

> Holding and attaining high standards leads to achievement, efficacy, and energy,... optimism and self-confirmation,...high self-esteem...and of course the positive effects of attaining the goal, be it a creative product, a new skill, or whatever. Much more attention has been given to negative concomitants of perfectionism, such as depression, shame and guilt, shyness and procrastination,...as well as overemphasis on the future without appreciation for one's own progress, all-or-none thinking, and rigidity...
>
> ...There are several reasons to expect that gifted children would develop high standards. They are not only more capable than other children of meeting expected goals, but they are also used to doing so and therefore optimistic about future attainment. They are able to envision goals which are more complex, detailed, mature, complete, and perhaps more "creative" than those of their age peers, and are more likely to have older friends with a more mature and competent frame of reference. (Robinson & Noble, 1991, p. 65)

Curiosity and perfectionism are relentless drives in the gifted personality. Neither can be turned off or "cured," nor should they be. The gifted mind will always question, even when it is dangerous to do so. And the gifted will continuously set unrealistic standards for themselves, will fight windmills and city hall, will persist when others have given up, will maintain their visions of what is possible even in the face of disaster. They will push themselves beyond all reasonable limits to achieve goals that they feel are important. Without perfectionism, there would be no Olympic champions, no great artistic endeavors, no scientific breakthroughs, no exquisite craftsmanship, no moral leaders. It is a basic drive to achieve excellence.

It is a sad commentary on contemporary values that we have come to view this powerful force as a disease of the mind and spirit. Bookstores are filled with self-help books on how to rid oneself of perfectionism. A therapist or counselor who does not understand this important facet of the gifted personality, who perceives perfectionism as an undesirable, neurotic tendency to be rooted out of the client's makeup, can be damaging to the individual. Counselors who understand giftedness respect this quality and help the individual learn how to use it productively in their lives.

As part of the equipment of the personality, perfectionism can be used in a positive way to achieve excellence, or it can be used in a negative way—to beat oneself over the head for past mistakes. To use perfectionism productively, the student must learn how to set priorities. The student who tries to be perfectionistic in too many areas at once is likely to get intensely frustrated. If writing the finest treatise the teacher has ever seen on the plight of whales is that important, then an A on the math test may have to be sacrificed. Can the student live with a B in math for the sake of a good cause? Another positive approach to take with perfectionism is reframing the notion of "mistakes" as "learning experiences" and stepping stones to future accomplishments (Blackburn & Erickson, 1986; Webb, Meckstroth, & Tolan, 1982). A scientist searching for a cure for cancer is going to face thousands of "failures" before success is reached. Walker (1991) provides this apt anecdote as a case in point:

> Thomas Edison tried 1,500 different filaments for the light bulb before finding the right one. After the last experiment, an assistant asked, "Well, Mr. Edison, how do you feel about having 1,500 failures to your credit?" Edison replied, "No, they weren't failures. We now know 1,500 light bulb filaments that don't work!" (p. 68)

These attempts can be viewed as errors or as simply roads in the maze of life; each blind alley narrows down the possibilities and brings the seeker that much closer to the goal.

Perfectionists need counselors to have faith in their vision, faith in their ability to reach their goals. When someone believes in them, these individuals find the courage to surmount obstacles and reach for the stars. Idealism should be fostered rather than stifled. We need idealists; we need those who set high standards for themselves and are willing to sweat and sacrifice in order to further their own evolution and the evolution of society.

The Need for Precision

Gifted children have logical imperatives, much like moral imperatives, which ensue from their *complex thought processes*. They expect the world to make sense and they react very strongly when it doesn't. Parkinson (1990) found that 70 percent of the children in her study preferred complex ideas and became irritated or bored by routine. A related trait is their *need for precision* and exactness. This is particularly noticeable in the highly gifted (Kline & Meckstroth, 1985).

> *Exactness* in all mental performances is characteristic, and keen love of precise facts. Allied to this is the perception of things in their multitudinous relationships, with frequent use of the phrase, "Well, that depends." A young child who spontaneously utters the phrase, "That depends," is sure to catch the attention of one who thoroughly knows gifted children. (Hollingworth, 1927, p. 4)

The ability to perceive the "multitudinous relationships" of things can make decision making difficult. Nothing is as simple as it seems. True-false questions are a nightmare, and multiple-choice are almost as confusing. These students see many more possibilities than are offered in a paper/pencil objective test. "That depends..." doesn't count on a forced-choice measure. For these reasons, highly gifted students may do poorly on group tests designed for age peers. Discrepancies between group IQ measures and individual intelligence measures are greatest for the highly gifted (Pegnato & Birch, 1959).

The need for the world and the people in it to be logical often results in argumentativeness. The student feels a compelling need to correct errors, to set the record straight, to call attention to cases that disprove a particular statement. This demand for accuracy, exactness, precision of thought and expression does not enhance social relations. Teachers dislike being corrected, especially in front of their students, and other students will shun a know-it-all. The counselor can assist the student in recognizing how critical he or she appears to others. Social skills can be taught, and alternative ways of relating can be practiced in individual or group counseling sessions.

Another facet of the complexity of the young person's thought processes is the ability to see many layers of meaning in each situation. "Multiple meanings, innuendos, and self-consciousness plague us" (American Association for Gifted Children, 1978, p. 9). Mixed messages are quickly absorbed by gifted minds, leaving them in a state of confusion and embarrassment in social situations. To which of these messages are they supposed to respond? What if they choose incorrectly? While their classmates are viewing things simply in black/white terms, gifted students are coping with endless shades of gray.

In counseling sessions, much of the time can be spent listening to the students' internal arguments or their need to refine their thoughts so that they are communicating *exactly* what they are trying to say. Sometimes this need for exactitude interferes with communication, keeping the counselor in the role of observer of the student's thought processes, rather than as a participant in a two-way dialogue. The counselor can gradually help the student learn listening skills and how to participate in the natural flow of conversation. Sessions are often spent listening to all of the intricate details of an event because there are so many interrelated variables that need to be explained. After gathering the essential information, the counselor may need to interrupt the internal argument or the detailed explanation in order to focus the student's attention on one aspect of the problem that can be addressed. Part of the counselor's responsibility is to help students sort through the massive amounts of information generated by their complex thought processes, and help them distinguish the relevant from the irrelevant, so that they can make decisions and take action.

Excellent Sense of Humor

Perhaps the most delightful aspect of giftedness is that it comes with a keen *sense of humor*. This trait has been included in numerous checklists of the characteristics of giftedness, but only recently has this observation been empirically tested. Shade (1991) found that gifted students respond to and comprehend various forms of verbal humor to a significantly greater degree than students from the general population. Hollingworth (1940) called this quality in the gifted their "saving sense" (p. 274) because it enables them to cope with the foolishness they see all around them. The relationship between humor and *vivid imagination* may not be immediately apparent. Those who possess a good sense of humor often "see" absurdities and incongruities in situations. Their imaginations exaggerate the comical aspects of events. Dabrowski originally perceived humor as a function of heightened imagination [imaginational overexcitability] (Dabrowski & Piechowski, 1977), but it also appears to have an intellectual component [intellectual overexcitability]. "Understanding incongruity involves a mental process having many similarities to problem solving.... In humor, as in problem solving, there are elements which have to be perceived and understood in their interrelationships" (Ziv & Gadish, 1990). The type of humor in which individuals engage reflects their level of development as well (Dabrowski & Piechowski, 1977). Maslow (1970) noted that self-actualizers have a philosophical, unhostile sense of humor.

Humor definitely has a place in the repertoire of the counselor. It has been found to be therapeutic by a number of counseling theorists. Berg and DeMartini (1979) outline the uses of humor in counseling the gifted, including social facilitation, anxiety release, self-expression, diagnosis of psychological functioning, motivation, facilitating the development of insight, and self-development toward self-actualization. The skillful counselor can help gifted students use their sense of humor to cope with situations that appear maddening. For example, Kramer (1986) used humor in career awareness seminars to help gifted adolescent girls grapple with the inequities of women in the work world. She recommends the use of humor "as a coping device to promote relaxation and a relief of tension" (p. 130). However, humor must be used cautiously, and timing is essential. At no time is sarcasm appropriate. Humor appears to be most effective after the counselor and the student have developed a solid ground of trust, when it is relevant to the topic discussed, and when "attitudes and conflicts...are near to the student's awareness" (Berg & DeMartini, 1979, p. 203).

Sensitivity/Empathy

Dabrowski's theory is particularly valuable in understanding the *sensitivity* and intensity of the gifted individual. Sensitivity and *empathy* are expressions of emotional overexcitability, whereas *moral concern* appears to be a function of intellectual overexcitability, related to the development of a hierarchy of values (Piechowski, 1979). When moral concern fuses with empathy, it transforms into moral commitment. Early concern with moral issues has been observed frequently in the gifted (Hollingworth, 1942; Munger, 1990; Passow, 1988; Silverman & Ellsworth, 1980; Ward, 1985):

> The highly gifted also deal with complex moral issues at a very tender age. A 5 year old said to her mother, "Mommy, did you kill that chicken? If you did, I'm not going to eat it." One 9 year old refused to eat any living thing that had to die for him, which left him very little to eat. More than one highly gifted child has become a vegetarian in a meat-eating family. They tend to ask difficult questions: "What is evil?" "Why is there violence?" "Is there a God?" "What happens when you die?" "How do we know we aren't part of someone else's dream?" (Silverman, 1989, p. 76)

A mother who brought her seven-and-a-half-year-old daughter for an assessment echoes many parents who believe their children's moral awareness is inherent: "B. has a strong sense of right and wrong. It almost seems that she came this way. We have been guides and examples of strong principles, but B. almost knows what is good and what is not by instinct." In response to items on a sentence completion test, an underachieving ten-and-a-half-year-old gifted boy said, "I dream of...*a better world—loving and caring*"; "If I could only...*draw the world more peaceful*"; "What makes me sad...*is people who don't seem to care about people*"; "I want to know...*why the world can't get along, because I think they could*"; "I worry most about...*what'll happen if the world keeps fighting.*"

Examples of sensitivity in gifted children and the associated research were presented in chapters 1 and 2. Sensitivity and empathy are related, but they do not always occur together. Some children are extremely sensitive to criticism, and get their feelings hurt easily, whereas they are not as aware of the feelings of others. Many gifted children are protective of younger children, disabled children, and the elderly, but some of these same children show lack of concern for the feelings of siblings or children their own age.

There are, however, some gifted children who are genuinely empathic in all situations. These children might be considered "emotionally gifted" (Piechowski, 1991; Roeper, 1982). "[Emotionally] gifted children show enormous empathy with others, surpassing at times the compassion of adults who are more limited by society's expectations" (Roeper, 1982, p. 24). For example, a four-year-old boy was described on a parent questionnaire as "incredibly mature in his relationship skills.... He has never hit, kicked or pushed a sibling, friend or anyone else." His father continued:

[A] is an incredible peace maker as well as leader. Is able to keep harmony in groups of one to ten of all different age groups. Is accommodating by suggesting methods of problem resolution acceptable to the group and insuring everyone is happy....

A is an exceptionally gentle and kind boy. I have never seen him hit or push and, in fact, have had to teach him that it is not good to let his little brother hit him.... He is extremely loving (e.g., he sings, "I'm so glad when Daddy comes home" every day to me). He daily praises my wife and I for taking care of his baby brother. He has an intense love of games and frequently seeks out adults to play with him. When he plays with his friends, he will help them find the best move in a game and deliberately lose—all the while telling his friend how good they are at the game.... He is easily upset if he believes someone else has been treated unfairly (e.g., was sobbing because someone had taken his friend's toy—the friend was not crying).

Another parent said that her child had "awareness and concern for others' feelings—to a degree that almost defied belief. Near-total lack of sibling rivalry...[she] has excellent refusal skills and can rarely be convinced by others to do anything she perceives as wrong, unsafe, or boring."

K [age nine] is both a sensitive and a sensible child. From an early age she has exhibited an unusually keen awareness of the world around her, particularly as it relates to the feelings and needs of others. Until recently she has seemed often to be burdened by the weight of knowledge she has not had the emotional maturity to deal with....

Over the past six months or so we have noticed big changes in K. She is noticeably happier, less moody, more comfortable with who she is, less put out by others' failings. She seems to have come to some sort of personal decision to be who she is instead of who her teachers or peers think she ought to be.

In this vignette, we see the unusual sensitivity and empathy of the emotionally gifted child, and we are also given some clues as to the type of counseling response needed. Sensitive children need to be given permission to be who they are. The expression "too sensitive" should be stricken from our vocabularies. In a world that lacks sensitivity, those who are perceived as "overly" sensitive may have exactly the degree of sensitivity that would be required to find a solution to homelessness or to save the planet from self-destruction. (See chapter 2 for the counseling implications of sensitivity.)

Intensity

Passion for learning may seem a strange item to include in a list of intellectual characteristics. Passion is so clearly an emotional term. Yet, the love affair that gifted children have with learning does not lend itself to cold, impersonal terminology. They are fascinated with ideas, new words, patterns and relationships. Students enrolled in an International Baccalaureate program have shared that the most exciting part of the program is the opportunity to learn with other students who "love learning." They don't have to hide their love of knowledge the way they had to in heterogeneous classes. "Having a group of students all interested and knowledgeable in a subject area and teaching each other has been *wonderful*" (S. Jones, personal communication, February 5, 1990).

Intensity is actually connected with all of the characteristics since the overexcitabilities can be thought of as intensities. One aspect of this trait is the intense manner in which gifted children pursue their interests. They often go through periods in which they are only interested in dinosaurs, or astronomy, or circuits, or computers, or Greek mythology, and they want to know everything there is to know about that one area. They become totally preoccupied, asking endless questions, learning vast amounts of material, unable to think of anything else—eating, sleeping, breathing dinosaurs, for example, until their energies are spent. When they have satisfied their curiosity, they go on to another area of absorption.

> *[At the age of two, B's] first major area of interest was Outer Space, which he pursued by collecting numerous books on the subject, building models of spaceships with me, visiting the Kennedy Space Center, collecting NASA videos, etc. His second passion was Greek Mythology, starting in his third year, pursued by having us read every book we could find on the subject to him.... By the time he was four, he had memorized most of the gods in both the Greek and Roman.... Probably his next love was/is baseball. He has about 1,000 cards...many of which he has memorized. Last summer, for example, he spent hours to most of a given day memorizing and sorting the cards. This has blossomed into him studying pitching techniques of various pitchers and imitating them when he plays baseball....*

Public schools are rarely set up to accommodate the intense fascination with learning that gifted children bring with them (Ward, 1985). If these students were allowed to pursue their passions, school would remain exciting and alive for the entirety of their education. Instead, education is usually chopped up into subject areas presented in 20- to 40-minute time blocks, in keeping with typical attention spans of age-mates. The gifted are subjected to a steady diet of review, and new material is presented at such a slow pace that these students have difficulty paying attention. Independent projects should be a regular part of the curriculum for gifted children.

Gifted young people pursue self-development with the same zeal they have for other areas of knowledge. But those children who have lost their passion for learning during school hours will sometimes have their motivation rekindled by a sensitive counselor who understands how to use their interests to make school relevant (Emerick, 1992). The counselor as advocate can also attempt to make the school environment more responsive to the student. One highly gifted teen has a regular column in a large city newspaper, but he is getting Ds in language arts because he cannot bring himself to do the busy-work that has been assigned to him. He has asked his counselor to negotiate with his English teacher to give him more independent study projects instead of the regular homework. In chapter 2, Lovecky describes additional counseling interventions in her discussion of students high in "excitability."

Perseverance

Gifted children often have greater *powers of concentration* than their peers if they are truly interested in what they are doing. Long attention span is apparent in early childhood (Rogers, 1986):

> One parent commented, "He would play games longer than playmates and get upset when they stopped playing and would leave." A second reported, "She would work on a puzzle or a book for over a half-hour when she was only two." (Rogers & Silverman, 1988, p. 5)

However, "concentration can be a problem for exceptionally gifted children when material does not offer sufficient intellectual stimulation" (Lovecky, 1992, p. 4). Focusing energy is also difficult for gifted children with attentional deficits. *Perseverance* is related to attention span and the ability to concentrate. It is also tied to the will—the tenacity of the child. Some gifted children are, by nature, very purposive (Ward, 1985), whereas others are more engaged in the process itself, and when they lose interest in the process the goal becomes meaningless. Most gifted children are more process-oriented than goal-oriented; perseverance usually increases with maturity.

In the counseling process, perseverance is needed to help the student change patterns he or she desires to change. Perfectionism without the recognition that "practice makes perfect," or the willingness to put in the effort, often leads to underachievement. Counselors can support students in attaining their goals by encouraging them when they get frustrated or reach an impasse in their progress. The counselor can acknowledge each step toward success, as well as the hard work involved. (See chapter 4.)

Acute Self-Awareness

Highly gifted children are often *analytical thinkers* (Altman, 1983). They have discriminating tastes, often rating experiences, people, food, music, and so forth. They excel at critical examination: they can take things apart in their minds and see all the intricate ways in which they could be improved—including themselves. *Acute self-awareness* ensues when that incisive intellect is focused inward. A parent of a seven-year-old writes:

> *This leads me to his love of analytical problem solving. When he was three, he started to show us his ability to work through problems. If puzzled he would verbalize at length about the problem and "theorize" solutions. It seemed rather funny to us to watch him pace the kitchen floor espousing his*

thoughts! Much of these early sessions were about human relations such as love, marriage, who hit whom on the playground and why, etc. When he asked questions about religion, specifically about God, His power, death, etc., we were rather surprised. These were in-depth questions, not just "Can He see me if I'm bad?"...Psychologically, B. can be a handful. He can go through periods of intense self-criticism which are quite difficult for all of us.

Unless students learn to temper this trait with self-acceptance they can brutalize themselves. Through positive reflection, counselors can help students appreciate themselves and realize that the choices they made were the best ones available to them at the time.

Analyzers worry a great deal, trying to prepare themselves for the worst by imagining all the things that could go wrong and then guarding against these consequences as well as they can. Life is lived as an insurance policy against disaster, and when something unpredicted occurs, they engage in self-flagellation with self-statements such as, "I should have known that..." Visualization can be a powerful tool in redirecting the student's energies from negative to positive outcomes. For example, an effective gestalt technique is to have the student visualize the worst possible outcome of a situation that is causing anxiety (the "catastrophic fantasy"), then visualize the best possible outcome (the "anastrophic fantasy"), and then collapse the two images into one to get a more realistic picture of what is likely to happen. Reality is usually not as bad as we fear nor as good as we would wish.

Nonconformity

It is common today to hear the gifted and creative described as if they were two discrete groups. Yet, the gifted have traditionally been acclaimed for their *creativity*. Goethe, Leibnitz, John Stuart Mill, and Sir Francis Galton were among "the most intelligent persons who have been tested or whose biographies have been examined" (Boring, 1950, p. 461), and they were certainly more than just good lesson learners. All were predicted to have IQs in the 200 range, and their creative contributions are staggering. Gifted adults tend to be creative (Albert, 1980; Rocamora, 1992; Roeper, 1991) and the creative tend to be gifted (Gowan, 1979). According to Rocamora (1992), self-actualizing gifted adults "have a relentless curiosity and divergent thinking ability" (p. 76).

The gifted derive enormous satisfaction from the creative process.... I believe the whole process is accompanied by a feeling of aliveness, of power, of capability...and of transcendence of the limits of our own body and soul. The "unique self" flows into the world outside. It is like giving birth. Creative expression derives directly from the unique Self of the creator, and its activation brings inherent feelings of happiness and aliveness, even though they may be accompanied by less positive emotions, such as sadness, fear and pain. Underneath all is the enormous joy of discovery and personal expression....

> *Just as the creative process creates a feeling of happiness, the greatest unhappiness can occur if it is interfered with or not allowed to happen.* In that case the inner pressure cannot be released. (Roeper, 1991, p. 91)

Albert (1980) found high levels of creativity in his study of exceptionally gifted boys and even higher levels in their parents. Louis and Lewis (1992) found that creativity and imagination distinguished gifted children from others at three years of age or younger. Like adults, gifted children need opportunities for creative expression. When these avenues are blocked, the drive can be diverted into destructive channels. Some gifted children are extremely divergent thinkers (Altman, 1983). Lovecky (1991) defines divergent thinkers as "those who prefer unusual, uncommon, original and creative responses...though they might not produce concrete products" (p. 7). In chapter 2, Lovecky presents guidelines for counseling divergent thinkers.

Nonconformity is often a concomitant of creativity which can cause problems with peers and teachers. The counselor's role is to honor the uniqueness of creative students, while helping them to effectively bridge the gap between themselves and others. A counselor can help students differentiate between "positive maladjustment" (Dabrowski, 1972) and rebellion. If the student refuses to acquiesce to the norms of the group because of higher moral standards, then nonconformity is to be lauded. On the other hand, if the nonconformity draws its strength from insecurity and a desire to prove something to the group, then there are issues to be worked out in therapy.

Questioning of Authority

It seems as if gifted children's first words are "it's not fair." They are quick to respond to perceived injustices to themselves and others from the time they are very young. *A keen sense of justice* invariably leads to *questioning of rules and authority figures* (Munger, 1990; Schetky, 1981). When the gifted child perceives those in authority as illogical, irrational, erroneous, or unjust, negativism toward authority is likely to develop (Hollingworth, 1940).

Questioning is natural for an inquisitive mind. For many highly gifted children, questioning and arguing are forms of mental exercise, engaged in for pure pleasure and as a method of learning, as well as to win a point. An exercise was done in a freshman college class in an engineering program to teach the students about different learning styles. The class was divided into four groups based upon results of the Myers-Briggs Type Inventory (Myers, 1962): Intuitive Feelers (NF), Intuitive Thinkers (NT), Sensing Feelers (SF), and Sensing Thinkers (ST). The groups were asked to discuss the question, "How do you learn best?" The first answer that appeared on their sheet of butcher paper for the Intuitive Thinking group was *"ARGUE"*—in large block letters! Many highly gifted boys are NTs, with an unbeatable combination of incisive logic and highly developed intuition. They are born to argue and usually win. They have a potential future in the courtroom.

In some families, argumentation is a basic form of communication.

Everyone understands the rules of the game, and the most persuasive member not only wins the mental battle of wits, but is appreciated for his or her cleverness. The Intuitive Thinker is excellent at forensics, can easily argue opposing points of view, and will often play devil's advocate in conversations, simply to hear the other person's rationale—which will be advocated later in another discussion. However, the world is not composed entirely of Intuitive Thinkers, so these individuals are very intimidating to every other personality type. Some NTs, who have underdeveloped emotional sensitivity, may be highly competitive and hooked on winning. Their sharp intellectual fencing skills need to be tempered with understanding of other people's feelings and reactions to their argumentativeness.

Counseling helps the young person understand others' needs and discomfort with constantly being challenged. Other types of social interaction can be introduced and rehearsed. The student can learn effective conflict resolution and negotiation skills that come from a win–win orientation. These can be practiced with teachers, parents, siblings, and peers, while the student monitors others' reactions to these new skills. The counselor can engage the student in abstract discussions of the value of mercy and justice. Books, films, plays, and real-life situations dealing with this theme can be shared. The student can be asked, "When is mercy more appropriate than justice?"

With younger children, the concept of fairness can be expanded to reciprocity. The child who cries "It's not fair" can be asked, "Is what you want 'fair' for just yourself or is it fair for everyone involved?" It helps to appeal to the child's advanced reasoning abilities and capacity to take other points of view. It is also helpful to have discussions about global interdependence and the need for cooperative models to replace competitive ones in order for the planet to survive. Students who must win every argument and who are very threatened unless they are right all the time have low self-esteem. Individual and family counseling may be needed to get to the root of the problem. More on questioning authority can be found in chapter 7.

Introversion

The *capacity for reflection* is an admired trait—at least philosophically; yet, our society rewards impulsivity. The studies of wait-time in classrooms bear this out. In analyzing taped classroom discussions, Rowe (1974) discovered that *teachers tend to wait less than one second for students to reply to their questions*. Intelligence tests give bonus points for speed, penalizing reflective thinkers. Newer instruments, like the Wechsler Preschool and Primary Scale of Intelligence-Revised (WPPSI-R) and the Wechsler Intelligence Scale for Children-III (WISC-III) put even greater emphasis on speed of responding than older IQ tests.

> The biggest negatives for gifted assessment are the new emphasis on problem-solving speed on the WPPSI-R [and] the substantially increased stress on performance time in the WISC-III compared to the WISC-R.... The speed factor will

penalize gifted children who are as reflective as they are bright, or who tend to go slow for other non-cognitive reasons such as a mild coordination problem. (Kaufman, 1992, p. 158)

So much for valuing reflection! There are counseling courses to teach verbal assertiveness; verbal domination is supported in courtrooms, legislative meetings, and academic discussions. Our society is great at talking and poor at listening—a reflection of the general competitiveness that roams unfettered in our culture.

The capacity for reflection is greatest among *introverts*. Introverts are a minority group in our gregarious society, comprising about 25 percent of the American population (Bradway, 1964; Myers, 1962). It is important for those who counsel gifted children to understand this personality type, since at least half of the gifted population are introverts (S. Gallagher, 1990; Hoehn & Bireley, 1988; Myers, 1962). Shelagh Gallagher (1990) studied 1,725 adolescents enrolled in three programs for talented students and found that 50 percent were introverted. In our studies of the highly gifted at the Gifted Child Development Center, it appears that introversion increases with IQ (Silverman, 1986; see also, Dauber & Benbow, 1990); more than 75 percent of the children with IQs above 160 are introverted—three times the national average.

The main difference between introverts and extraverts is the source of their energy. Extraverts get energy from people and objects outside of themselves, whereas introverts gain energy from within themselves. A second major difference is that the extravert has a single-layered personality, whereas the introvert has a private self and a public self (the "persona"). Behaviorally, this means that introverts try to be perfect in school, store up all their negative feelings inside, and then dump them at home on the person they trust the most and feel the safest with—usually Mom.

Jung (1938) created this terminology; he was an introvert, and he did not consider introversion of lesser value than extraversion. Individuals have degrees of introversion and extraversion in their personalities, and the degree to which one pole dominates the personality can be measured with the Myers-Briggs Type Indicator (Myers, 1962), the basis of all personality and learning inventories today. Unfortunately, the short forms all shortchange introversion, without recognition of the important role it plays in personality development. Essential differences between extraverts and introverts are listed below:

Extraverts	**Introverts**
Get energy from interaction	Get energy from inside themselves
Feel energized by people	Feel drained by people
Have a single-layered personality (same in public and private)	Have a persona and an inner self (show best self in public)
Are open and trusting	Need privacy
Think out loud	Mentally rehearse before speaking
Like being the center of attention	Hate being the center of attention

Learn by doing	Learn by observing
Are comfortable in new situations	Are uncomfortable with changes
Make lots of friends easily	Are loyal to a few close friends
Are distractible	Are capable of intense concentration
Are impulsive	Are reflective
Are risk-takers in groups	Fear humiliation; quiet in large groups

The following are examples of introverted children: "[J] doesn't like to be singled out at school." "[M] is very shy in large groups of people, more open in one-on-one encounters. M. is cautious and reserved when he's encountering new situations—he will observe, rather than participate." "[J] is quick to tire when around people too much, and insists that weekends be kept as free of planned activities as possible. She seems very refreshed if she can spend a couple of uninterrupted hours in her room drawing or reading."

[L] is a very polite child away from home. She is angry and disagreeable in her home environment. She is unable to express her feelings.... [L] has had one good friend.... [L] plays by herself at school and does not enter into a group unless she is invited and is interested in what they are doing.... She resists change and does not react well to changes in plans. She needs plenty of advanced warnings of new events, changes to methods or changes to her "expectations."

Family dynamics can be vastly improved through an understanding of introversion. An extraverted parent who demands that an emotional situation be discussed "*right now*" is inviting a tantrum. Extraverted spouses who want to discuss a deeply moving play immediately afterward are in for stony silences from introverted mates. Introverts need time to reflect, time to let emotions settle down before they can verbalize them, time to ponder possible solutions to problems. Discussions should be postponed for at least twenty-four hours to let the introvert have time to "think about it."

More than anything, introverts need respect for their introversion. Parents and teachers are not working overtime to turn extraverts into introverts, but they do try to remake introverts into extraverts. One rarely hears a parent complain, "My child plays outdoors too much. I wish she'd spend more time by herself reading." Introverts read more than extraverts, partly because it is a societally accepted means of gaining some needed alone time. Counselors can help parents and teachers accept that introversion is perfectly normal, and not in need of curing. Counselors are trained to protect confidentiality, and they can teach parents and teachers the importance of maintaining the confidentiality of an introverted child. These children have a deep, inherent need for privacy, they get embarrassed easily by either public censure or praise, and they need time to reflect. A good book to share with families and teachers that discusses introversion in children is *Please Understand Me* (Keirsey & Bates, 1978).

Differences in introverts' and extraverts' approaches to counseling are amusing. The extravert comes to the counseling session, talks nonstop for fifty minutes, providing every internal and external detail imaginable, leaving the counselor no room to get a word in edgewise, and then leaves feeling much better, thanking the counselor for all of the "help" on the way out. If the counselor dares to offer solutions prematurely, the client may feel misunderstood, and that his or her problem has been trivialized. All the extravert needs is a sounding board, someone to listen while he or she thinks aloud. Extraverts solve their problems by talking about them to other people. This is part of the externalization of their thought processes. They sort their thoughts through verbalization.

Introverts, on the other hand, rarely talk to others about their problems. They stew over them, going over and over the situation in their minds like a broken record until they are about to explode. If they finally are driven to seek advice from a counselor, that's exactly what they want: advice. They don't want to talk about it or think about it anymore; they just want solutions. It is like pulling teeth to get them to elaborate, to give the counselor enough detailed information to be helpful. Interactions between counselors and clients of different personality types can be comical. Introverted counselors think extraverted clients spend too much time "reporting" and never get to the point, while extraverted counselors think introverted clients are noncommunicative and withholding! It helps to understand one's own personality type as well as the client's.

Taken all together, these various characteristics and their interactions indicate why gifted children need specialized counseling services. A counselor without training in the unique qualities of the gifted is likely to misunderstand any number of these traits and be counterproductive to the student's development.

SUPPORT SYSTEMS

There are five contexts that can be influenced to support the development of the child:

1. Home environment
2. School environment
3. Peer relations
4. Community resources
5. The Self (intrapsychic milieu)

Within each milieu, several factors need to be taken into account. For example, in the *home environment*, the constitution of the family, their socioeconomic status, their value system, the child's placement within the family, their attitudes toward the child and toward giftedness, all affect the manner in which the family will be able to nurture the child's abilities. Parents need information about the personality characteristics associated with giftedness so that they can understand their children more fully and respond to their needs appropriately. Family counseling is discussed in chapter 7.

The *school environment* is the central context of this book. It is assumed that the school has major responsibilities for promoting the gifted child's intellectual and emotional development. Although there are numerous constraints—budgetary, time, attitudes, lack of trained personnel—there are also many facilitative factors within the educational environment. It only takes one advocate within the system to enhance the quality of the child's school experience. That person can be a regular classroom teacher, a specialist on giftedness, a counselor, a school psychologist, a principal, a social worker, a superintendent. The critical role each of these individuals can play is discussed in chapter 8. Schools can be restructured to meet the affective needs of gifted students in many ways: ability grouping in the classroom, arranging mentorships and internships, forming after-school support groups, emphasizing affective development within the curriculum, providing opportunities for group counseling with a trained facilitator, and freeing the counselor's time for preventive counseling with gifted groups, individuals, and families.

When gifted children are asked what they most desire, the answer is often, "a friend." The child's experience of school is completely colored by the presence or absence of *relationships with peers*. One of the most damaging assumptions of school systems is that gifted children need to relate socially with children their own age, regardless of ability. Forced interaction on the basis of age is as ludicrous for children as it would be for adults. Gifted children develop true friendships with others who have similar interests, in much the same manner as adults develop friendships. When the school acts as a clearinghouse for bringing like minds together, it becomes a powerful force in the positive social development of gifted children. This has been shown by the longitudinal studies of the children enrolled in Leta Hollingworth's experimental classes (Harris, 1992). However, when the school purposely separates gifted children from each other in order to enforce a social/political agenda, the results are often counterproductive to healthy social attitudes. Children who cannot connect with others like themselves are at risk for social alienation, scapegoating, damaged self-esteem, antisocial reactions, withdrawal from social interaction, and depression. It is ironic that we think of the regular classroom as good for "socializing" the gifted; often it has exactly the opposite effect.

The *community* is a valuable source of adult role models, mentors, and moral exemplars, individuals who pursue their lives and work with passion, and who can guide the young gifted person to the development of his or her own passions. Parent advocacy groups can serve a networking function to bring gifted children together for social purposes and intellectual stimulation. Universities and colleges often offer Saturday programs, summer enrichment programs, and after-school activities for gifted students. These institutions sponsor national talent searches, which enable gifted junior high school students to be identified inexpensively, recognized for their achievements at award ceremonies, and served through high-powered, accelerated coursework on campus. Science centers, planetariums, museums, zoos, community schools, and departments of parks and recreation are additional community resources that can bring together gifted children who have common interests.

All of these environmental support systems can be mobilized to enable the gifted child to develop optimally. But there is still the *internal world of the individual* to be considered. The unique intellectual and personality characteristics listed above lead to inner experiences that are markedly different from other children's. These experiences need interpretation by understanding adults in order for them to be integrated in a healthy manner. Parents are their children's first counselors and best advocates; therefore, they need to be sensitized to the special qualities of their children's inner life and to their unique needs. Without that knowledge, it is easy to be swayed by current educationisms which could be harmful to the child (e.g., "Boys with summer birthdays should always be held back"; "These children need to learn how to get along in the *real* world"; "Children who are pushed ahead never make good social adjustments"; "By third grade, all the other children will catch up"). Parents need protection from bad advice.

INTERVENTIONS

Types of Interventions

- ❏ Grouping with peers
- ❏ Restructuring systems
- ❏ Networking
- ❏ Group counseling/discussion
- ❏ Bibliotherapy
- ❏ Moral exemplars
- ❏ Mentors
- ❏ Internships
- ❏ Peer counseling
- ❏ Family counseling
- ❏ Individual counseling
- ❏ Support groups

Counseling interventions can take many forms. The most in-depth type of counseling occurs in an individual setting with a trained psychotherapist (psychiatrist, psychologist, social worker, or licensed/certified counselor). Individual counseling should not be reserved for those who are in psychological trouble; on the contrary, a trained counselor can *prevent* psychological disturbances from occurring. All gifted individuals can profit from individual therapy at some point in their lives, as long as the practitioner is aware of the unique intrapsychic milieu of the gifted. Within this context, deep feelings, past experiences, and unresolved conflicts can be explored. The therapist can: (1) help the client come to terms with his or her differences; (2) help the person realize the potent developmental forces fueling the struggle to become; (3) engage the client in a dialogue to refine his or her personal philosophy; (4) focus the client's energies on reaching aspirations; (5) support attempts to change attitudes and behaviors; and (6) monitor progress and applaud successes. Counseling needs to be seen as a positive support system for healthy self-development. (See chapter 4.)

Individual counseling is expensive, so alternative forms of counseling should be made available within the schools. Preventive counseling groups can be set up by the school counselor or the gifted education specialist. (See chapters 5 and 6.) Peer counseling has been shown to be an effective avenue of support, particularly when the peers are matched by ability and personality type. Support groups can be organized during or after school hours. Bibliotherapy can occur in the regular classroom, if the teacher is aware of resources that can direct the child to books in which characters are dealing with issues similar to those of the child. (See chapter 4 and the reading list in the Appendix.)

GOALS OF DEVELOPMENTAL COUNSELING

In a developmental model of counseling, the ultimate goal is the self-actualization of the individual. There is recognition of the developmental potential of the child, and the individual is seen as an evolving system. The focus of counseling is on growth toward high ideals. These ideals include the following:

❏ Moral courage	❏ Authenticity
❏ Compassion	❏ Altruism
❏ Reflective judgment	❏ Strong sense of self-efficacy
❏ Responsibility	❏ Self-actualization
❏ Commitment to goals	❏ Contribution to society
❏ Sense of wonder	❏ Global awareness
❏ Integrity	❏ Devotion to high ideals
❏ Ethical behavior	❏ High state of moral development
❏ Creativity	❏ Advanced emotional development
❏ Autonomy	❏ Wisdom

CONCLUSION

When we truly respect the developing Self of the gifted child (Roeper, 1992), we recognize that our role is to facilitate that development. These children are our future leaders, and we have a moral responsibility to do more than just fill their minds with knowledge. Knowledge without wisdom and ethics is dangerous. We cannot inculcate the values we desire, but we can inspire their development through our own attitudes and actions. We are these children's role models, and if we embody these ideals in our own lives, we teach them more from who we are than from anything we say or do. And we will learn from them as well.

REFERENCES

Adderholdt-Elliott, M. (1987). *Perfectionism: What's bad about being too good?* Minneapolis, MN: Free Spirit.

Albert, R. (1980). Exceptionally gifted boys and their parents. *Gifted Child Quarterly, 24,* 174–179.

Altman, R. (1983). Social-emotional development of gifted children and adolescents: A research model. *Roeper Review, 6,* 65–68.

American Association for Gifted Children. (1978). *On being gifted.* New York: Walker.

Berg, D. H., & DeMartini, W. D. (1979). Uses of humor in counseling the gifted. In N. Colangelo & R. T. Zaffrann (Eds.), *New voices in counseling the gifted* (pp. 194–206). Dubuque, IA: Kendall/Hunt.

Blackburn, A. C., & Erickson, D. B. (1986). Predictable crises of the gifted student. *Journal of Counseling and Development, 9,* 552–555.

Boring, E. G. (1950). *A history of experimental psychology* (2nd ed.). Englewood Cliffs, NJ: Prentice-Hall.

Bradway, K. (1964). Jung's psychological types. *Journal of Analytical Psychology, 9,* 129–135.

Cornell, D. G., & Grossberg, I. N. (1989). Parent use of the term "gifted": Correlates with family environment and child adjustment. *Journal for the Education of the Gifted, 12,* 218–230.

Dabrowski, K., with Kawczak, A., & Piechowski, M. M. (1970). *Mental growth through positive disintegration.* London: Gryf.

Dabrowski, K. (1972). *Psychoneurosis is not an illness.* London: Gryf.

Dabrowski, K., & Piechowski, M. M. (1977). *Theory of levels of emotional development* (Vols. 1 & 2). Oceanside, NY: Dabor Science.

Dauber, S. L., & Benbow, C. P. (1990). Aspects of personality and peer relations of extremely talented adolescents. *Gifted Child Quarterly, 34,* 10–15.

Emerick, L. J. (1992). Academic underachievement among the gifted: Students' perceptions of factors that reverse the pattern. *Gifted Child Quarterly, 36,* 140–146.

Feldhusen, J. F. (1992). Early admission and grade advancement for young gifted learners. *The Gifted Child Today, 15*(2), 45–49.

Fisher, K. (1990, April). Interaction with infants is linked to later abilities. *The APA Monitor* (American Psychological Association), p. 10.

Gallagher, J. J. (1990). Editorial: The public and professional perception of the emotional status of gifted children. *Journal for the Education of the Gifted, 13,* 202–211.

Gallagher, S. A. (1990). Personality patterns of the gifted. *Understanding Our Gifted, 3*(1), 1, 11–13.

Gowan, J. C. (1979). Creativity and the gifted child movement. In J. C. Gowan, J. Khatena, & E. P. Torrance (Eds.), *Educating the ablest: A book of readings on the education of gifted children* (2nd ed., pp. 4–17). Itasca, IL: F. E. Peacock.

Harris, C. R. (1992). The fruits of early intervention: The Hollingworth group today. *Advanced Development, 4,* 91–104.

Hoehn, L., & Bireley, M. K. (1988). Mental processing preferences of gifted children. *Illinois Council for the Gifted Journal, 7,* 28–31.

Hollingworth, L. S. (1926). *Gifted children: Their nature and nurture.* New York: Macmillan.

Hollingworth, L. S. (1927). Who are gifted children? *Child Study, 5*(2), 3–5.

Hollingworth, L. S. (1940). Intelligence as an element in personality. In G. M. Whipple (Ed.), *Intelligence: Its nature and nurture: Part I. Comparative and critical exposition.* 39th yearbook of National Society for the Study of Education (pp. 271–274). Bloomington, IL: Public School Publishing.

Hollingworth, L. S. (1942). *Children above 180 IQ Stanford-Binet: Origin and development.* Yonkers-on-Hudson, NY: World Book.

Jung, C. G. (1938). *Psychological types or the psychology of individuation.* (H. G. Baynes, Trans.). London: Kegan Paul, Trench, Trubner & Co., Ltd.

Karnes, F., & Oehler-Stinnet, J. (1986). Life events as stressors with gifted adolescents. *Psychology in the Schools, 23,* 406–414.

Kaufman, A. S. (1992). Evaluation of the WISC-III and WPPSI-R for gifted children. *Roeper Review, 14,* 154–158.

Keirsey, D., & Bates, M. (1978). *Please understand me: Character and temperament types.* Del Mar, CA: Prometheus Nemesis Books.

Kerr, B. A. (1991). *A handbook for counseling the gifted and talented.* Alexandria, VA: American Counseling Association.

Kincher, J. (1990). *Psychology for kids: 40 fun tests that help you learn about yourself.* Minneapolis: Free Spirit.

Kline, B. E., & Meckstroth, E. A. (1985). Understanding and encouraging the exceptionally gifted. *Roeper Review, 8,* 24–30.

Kramer, L. (1986). Career awareness and personal development: A naturalistic study of gifted adolescent girls' concerns. *Adolescence, 21,* 123–131.

Lewis, M., & Louis, B. (1991). Young gifted children. In N. Colangelo & G. A. Davis (Eds.), *Handbook of gifted education* (pp. 365–381). Needham Heights, MA: Allyn & Bacon.

Louis, B., & Lewis, M. (1992). Parental beliefs about giftedness in young children and their relation to actual ability level. *Gifted Child Quarterly, 36,* 27–31.

Lovecky, D. V. (1991). The divergently thinking child. *Understanding Our Gifted, 3*(3), 1, 7–9.

Lovecky, D. V. (1992). The exceptionally gifted child. *Understanding Our Gifted, 4*(4), 3–4.

Manaster, G. J., & Powell, P. M. (1983). A framework for understanding gifted adolescents' psychological maladjustment. *Roeper Review, 6,* 70–73.

Maslow, A. H. (1970). *Motivation and personality* (2nd ed.). New York: Harper & Row.

Morelock, M. J. (1992, February). *The child of extraordinarily high IQ from a Vygotskian perspective.* Paper presented at the Esther Katz Rosen Symposium on the Psychological Development of Gifted Children, University of Kansas, Lawrence.

Munger, A. (1990). The parent's role in counseling the gifted: The balance between home and school. In J. VanTassel-Baska (Ed.), *A practical guide to counseling the gifted in a school setting* (2nd ed., pp. 57–65). Reston, VA: The Council for Exceptional Children.

Myers, I. B. (1962). *Manual: The Myers-Briggs type indicator*. Palo Alto, CA: Consulting Psychologists Press.

Nelson, K. C. (1992). Curriculum compacting: A model for teacher/specialist/parent collaboration. *Understanding Our Gifted, 4*(5), 5–6.

Parkinson, M. L. (1990). Finding and serving gifted preschoolers. *Understanding Our Gifted, 2*(5), 1, 10–13.

Passow, A. H. (1988). Educating gifted persons who are caring and concerned. *Roeper Review, 11,* 13–15.

Pegnato, C. W., & Birch, J. W. (1959). Locating gifted children in junior high schools: A comparison of methods. *Exceptional Children, 25,* 300–304.

Piechowski, M. M. (1979). Developmental potential. In N. Colangelo & R. T. Zaffrann (Eds.), *New voices in counseling the gifted* (pp. 25–57). Dubuque, IA: Kendall/Hunt.

Piechowski, M. M. (1991). Emotional development and emotional giftedness. In N. Colangelo & G. Davis (Eds.), *A handbook of gifted education* (pp. 285–306). Needham Heights, MA: Allyn & Bacon.

Robinson, N. M., & Noble, K. D. (1991). Social-emotional development and adjustment of gifted children. In M. C. Wang, M. C. Reynolds, & H. J. Walberg (Eds.), *Handbook of special education: Research and practice: Vol. 4. Emerging programs* (pp. 57–76). New York: Pergamon Press.

Robinson, N. M., & Noble, K. D. (1992). Acceleration: Valuable high school to college options. *The Gifted Child Today, 15*(2), 20–23.

Rocamora, M. (1992). Counseling issues with recognized and unrecognized creatively gifted adults, with six case studies. *Advanced Development, 4,* 75–89.

Roedell, W. C. (1984). Vulnerabilities of highly gifted children. *Roeper Review, 6,* 127–130.

Roeper, A. (1982). How the gifted cope with their emotions. *Roeper Review, 5*(2), 21–24.

Roeper, A. (1991). Gifted adults: Their characteristics and emotions. *Advanced Development, 3,* 85–98.

Roeper, A. (1992). The reality of the self. *Advanced Development, 4,* 59–60.

Rogers, M. T. (1986). *A comparative study of developmental traits of gifted and average children.* Unpublished doctoral dissertation, University of Denver.

Rogers, M. T., & Silverman, L. K. (1988). Recognizing giftedness in young children. *Understanding Our Gifted, 1*(2), 5, 16, 17, 20.

Rowe, M. B. (1974). Relation of wait-time and rewards to the development of language, logic, fate control: Part II. Rewards. *Journal of Research in Science Teaching, 11,* 291–308.

Schetky, D. H. (1981). A psychiatrist looks at giftedness: The emotional and social development of the gifted child. *G/C/T,* Issue No. 18, 2–4.

Schultz, D. (1981). *A history of modern psychology* (3rd ed.). New York: Academic Press.

Shade, R. (1991). Verbal humor in gifted students and students in the general population: A comparison of spontaneous mirth and comprehension. *Journal for the Education of the Gifted, 14,* 134–150.

Silverman, L. K. (1986). Parenting young gifted children. *Journal of Children in Contemporary Society, 18,* 73–87.

Silverman, L. K. (1989). The highly gifted. In J. F. Feldhusen, J. VanTassel-Baska, & K. Seeley (Eds.), *Excellence in educating the gifted* (pp. 71–83). Denver: Love.

Silverman, L. K. (1990). The crucible of perfectionism. In B. Holyst (Ed.), *Mental health in a changing world* (pp. 39–49). Warsaw: The Polish Society for Mental Health.

Silverman, L. K., & Ellsworth, B. (1980). The theory of positive disintegration and its implications for giftedness. In N. Duda (Ed.), *Theory of positive disintegration: Proceedings of the third international conference.* Miami, FL: University of Miami School of Medicine.

Snyderman, M., & Rothman, S. (1988). *The IQ controversy, the media and public policy.* New Brunswick, NJ: Transaction Books.

Storfer, M. (1990). *Intelligence and giftedness.* San Francisco, CA: Jossey-Bass.

Tolan, S. S. (1985). Stuck in another dimension: The exceptionally gifted child at school. *G/C/T,* Issue No. 41, 22–26.

Tolan, S. (1989). Special problems of young highly gifted children. *Understanding Our Gifted, 1*(5), 1, 7–10.

Walker, S. Y. (1991). *The survival guide for parents of gifted kids: How to understand, live with, and stick up for your gifted child.* Minneapolis: Free Spirit.

Ward, V. S. (1985). Giftedness and personal development: Theoretical considerations. *Roeper Review, 8,* 6–10.

Webb, J. T., Meckstroth, E. A., & Tolan, S. S. (1982). *Guiding the gifted child: A practical source for parents and teachers.* Columbus: Ohio Psychology.

Whitmore, J. R. (1980). *Giftedness, conflict, and underachievement.* Needham Heights, MA: Allyn & Bacon.

Ziv, A., & Gadish, O. (1990). Humor and giftedness. *Journal for the Education of the Gifted, 13,* 332–345.

PART II

The Counseling Process

Techniques for Preventive Counseling

4

Linda Kreger Silverman

Intricate thought processes and complex emotions are held in delicate balance in the gifted individual. Idealism, self-doubt, perceptiveness, excruciating sensitivity, moral imperatives, desperate needs for understanding, acceptance, love—all impinge simultaneously. Their vast emotional range can make gifted students appear contradictory: mature and immature, arrogant and compassionate, aggressive and timid. "These youngsters have strong needs to stand out, and yet they yearn to be unnoticed" (Ford, 1989, p. 134). Semblances of self-assurance often mask deep feelings of insecurity. The journey to discovering that which is finest in oneself is precarious, and those who embark upon this journey sometimes falter and lose their way.

WHY IS PREVENTION NEEDED?

Greater awareness of the world situation, of injustice, of the way things ought to be, coupled with the feeling of powerlessness, can throw gifted young people into despair (Delisle, 1986; Hollingworth, 1942; Strip, Swassing, & Kidder, 1991). Even students who appear well adjusted and achieve high grades in school often suffer from feelings of inadequacy because their successes fall far short of their goals (Yadusky-Holahan & Holahan, 1983). And beyond all these internal variables, gifted children face the task of living in a culture that rejects their differences, that tells them in a thousand subtle and not-so-subtle ways it's not okay to be gifted. "Our children are taught to don masks before they recognize their own faces. They are made to put their tender, pliable forms into prefabricated shells" (Drews, 1972, p. 3). They may respond to societal pressures by hiding their abilities, withdrawing from painful social interaction, rebelling and acting out in the classroom, or experiencing quiet desperation.

All of these factors clearly indicate the importance of counseling services for gifted students. However, elementary counselors are rare, and the enormous caseloads of middle and high school counselors (usually over 300 students) force them to focus on students who seem to have the most pressing concerns. This crisis orientation leads to neglect of the gifted, whose needs are not as obvious. Our society adheres to the philosophy, "If it ain't broke, don't fix it." But a broken child, a broken spirit, is hard to mend, and the alarming number of suicides among high-achieving adolescents should alert us to the fact that for some of our youth, intervention may come too late.

Suicide is the second leading cause of death in adolescents and young adults; it is estimated that 5,000 to 7,000 young people take their own lives every year, and 400,000 attempt to do the same (Strip, Swassing, & Kidder, 1991). These statistics are staggering. We are not certain if gifted students are at higher risk than their peers for suicide, but we do know that students who took their lives in high school and college were often high achievers (Delisle, 1986, 1990; Farrell, 1989; Hayes & Sloat, 1990; Kerr, 1991b; Lajoie & Shore, 1981; Leroux, 1986).

One study conducted at 129 high schools revealed 42 cases of suicide attempts, 8 of whom (19 percent) were identified as gifted students. Five of the 8 were gifted underachievers (Hayes & Sloat, 1990). Harkavy and Asnis (1985) found that almost 9 percent of the students at a high school for the gifted reported at least one suicide attempt. In a preliminary study conducted with coordinators of gifted programs in the state of Colorado, I found that seasoned professionals (more than three years in their position) perceived gifted students to be at greater risk for suicide than their classmates. No suicide completions were reported, but there were several suicide attempts, and suicidal ideation was quite common.

> A major difficulty confronting counselors, educators, and researchers is why some youth experience these life stressors with seemingly little negative impact on their self-worth, while other teens—who may appear to be quite similar to their more mentally healthy peers—experience such pain that suicide is seen as a viable alternative. (Delisle, 1990, pp. 214, 216)

It is speculated that gifted youth are high risks for suicide because of their unusual sensitivity and perfectionism (Delisle, 1986). These students may be visited by despair at failing to reach their ideals, humiliation at having their imperfections revealed, or depression from struggling in vain to grasp the meaning of their existence. In addition, extreme cases of introversion may lead to isolation (Kaiser & Berndt, 1985). Those in greatest peril are those who are alienated from their families. Most attempt or commit suicide because of the severity of their problems, not because of their giftedness (Kerr, 1991b).

However, alienation, humiliation, isolation, or depression, when experienced with the characteristic intensity of the gifted, can be fatal.

The pain borne of experiencing life at a deep level can be constructive as well as destructive. According to some theorists, inner conflict is potentially transformative and can be used to further development (Assagioli, 1965; Dabrowski, 1972; Jung, 1954). Such constructive use of psychic pain requires guidance. The gifted need significant adults in whom to confide, whose judgment is trustworthy and whose support can be relied upon. Some children are fortunate enough to receive this kind of guidance from parents or mentors, but most young people who experience intense inner conflict have no one to turn to who understands what they are going through. Therapists are seldom engaged for a variety of reasons: expense, parental attitudes toward therapy, and most of all, lack of recognition of the existence of the problems. There is also a conspicuous absence of awareness of the unique emotional needs of the gifted in the field of psychology. Counselors, school psychologists, and clinical psychologists receive no training about giftedness.

Counselors trained to deal with the psychological needs of gifted young people are not an extravagance—they can save young people's lives. Whereas the number of suicides is increasing at a frightening rate (Delisle, 1986), the number of counselors in the public schools is decreasing due to budget cuts. Ideally, each school district should employ a counselor whose sole function is preventive counseling of gifted students. In large school districts, several such counselors are needed. The emotional needs of gifted children must not be neglected—the costs are too great. Let us hope that it does not require a series of tragedies to call attention to the severity of this neglect.

PREVENTIVE COUNSELING FOR THE GIFTED

A developmental approach to guidance and counseling is one that is concerned with the ongoing growth of the child and not with *putting out fires* as they occur in the child's life.... As long as the counselor simply intervenes instead of preventing, the mental health needs of gifted children will remain unmet.

No one teaches reading by providing instruction only after children develop reading problems. (Culross, 1982, p. 24)

The importance of preventive counseling has not been recognized even within the field of gifted education (Blackburn & Erickson, 1986; Culross, 1982). "Counseling is described as a remedial activity for students who have already exhibited problems.... rather than...[as a means of] preventing the evolution of these problems" (Blackburn & Erickson, 1986, p. 552). With prevention rather than remediation as the goal, counselors would not only intervene when problems have reached the point of crisis, they would be able to plan developmental counseling programs to facilitate the emotional well-being of gifted children.

Counselors play an essential role in guiding the development of gifted students. They can help students understand their abilities; design programs of challenging, accelerated coursework; acquaint them with the options and opportunities available both in and after school; help them explore career goals, colleges, and scholarship opportunities; and remain available to these students throughout their years at a particular school for emotional support and consultation around personal issues. In addition to these responsibilities, the counselor can be an advocate, intervening with parents, teachers, and others when necessary, to explain students' needs, enable them to progress at their own rate, and prevent scapegoating. They can also serve as guides to parents, providing information about educational alternatives and assisting with problems encountered at home (Colangelo, 1991). (See chapter 7.) In school districts using individualized education plans (IEPs) for gifted students, the counselor may be in charge of designing the plan, monitoring its implementation, and possibly implementing parts of it.

In most school districts, however, these counseling needs are not addressed. Counselors may not even know which students are gifted or have the time to meet with them. I have observed schools in which even the most obvious needs of the gifted are not met, on the assumption that these children can take care of themselves. The student develops coursework plans based on what his or her friends are taking. The counselor rubber-stamps the student's selections, without discussing available options or attempting to match coursework with the student's abilities or aspirations. The student receives no guidance in career planning, selecting a college, applying for admission, or winning a scholarship. If the student's educational needs are of only perfunctory concern to the counselor, it is clear that his or her emotional needs will be ignored.

Counseling is only considered necessary when a gifted student is underachieving or appears to have behavioral or emotional problems (Blackburn & Erickson, 1986; Culross, 1982). But counselors can actually *prevent* the development of behavioral disorders and help students develop coping skills to circumvent emotional problems. We need a new, proactive conception of counseling that recognizes the needs of the child *before* crises arise. The predictable developmental crises of gifted students suggested by Blackburn and Erickson (1986) include: (a) uneven development in the primary grades, particularly for boys with motoric lags; (b) underachievement in upper elementary grades due to lack of a challenging curriculum; (c) conflict for gifted girls between achievement and popularity in early adolescence; (d) difficulty in selecting a career in late adolescence due to multipotentiality; and (e) the inability to cope with less than complete success in college or adult life. "If these students are to survive the crises of growing up gifted, they must have the support and skills needed to convert each predictable obstacle into a challenge" (Blackburn & Erickson, 1986, p. 554).

Goals for a developmental counseling program based on the needs of the gifted would include:

❑ Understanding of their strengths and weaknesses (Kerr, 1991a)
❑ Self-acceptance and recognition of their limitations (Culross, 1982)
❑ Commitment to nurturing their abilities (VanTassel-Baska, 1991)
❑ Development of internal locus of control (Perrone, 1986)
❑ Acceptance of mistakes as learning experiences (Webb, Meckstroth, & Tolan, 1982)
❑ Conflict resolution skills (Betts, 1986)
❑ Problem-solving skills (Culross, 1982)
❑ Awareness, understanding, and acceptance of others (Betts, 1986)
❑ Communication skills (Betts, 1986)
❑ Ability to be assertive rather than aggressive (Blackburn & Erickson, 1986)
❑ Interpersonal skills (Betts, 1986; VanTassel-Baska, 1991)
❑ Leadership and decision-making skills (Perrone, 1986)
❑ Knowledge of stress reduction techniques (Genshaft & Broyles, 1991)
❑ Ability to view themselves and events with humor (Blackburn & Erickson, 1986)

A preventive counseling program might involve weekly meetings in which students discuss issues of mutual concern. (See chapter 5.) In addition, preventive counseling could teach students techniques of peer counseling: how to be aware of the signs of severe crises in their friends, effective methods of gaining assistance, some crisis intervention techniques, questioning and active listening skills, conflict resolution and negotiation skills, and methods of reducing stress in their peers. Peer counseling techniques for crisis intervention are offered by Strip, Swassing, and Kidder (1991).

Given today's educational climate, most school districts seem light-years away from employing counselors specifically for the gifted; nevertheless, it is essential that *someone* in each school be available to meet the counseling needs of these students. Gifted coordinators and resource teachers should receive training in counseling so that they can take on this function. A school social worker who has received training in the emotional needs of the gifted might be given special responsibilities with this group.

When a practitioner's understanding of the affective needs of the gifted is wedded to knowledge of counseling skills, the result is a teacher-counselor prepared to deal with the emotional development of the gifted. This book discusses the counseling needs of the gifted, and suggests some approaches for meeting those needs, but it cannot provide all of the skills necessary to be a successful teacher-counselor. Coursework in counseling techniques is highly recommended for all concerned professionals. It is unfortunate that there are so few specific courses available in counseling the gifted. Hultgren (1981) found that out of a list of twenty-four competencies in gifted education, counseling was ranked 14th in importance by both practitioners and university personnel. Given the critical needs of the students, special training in counseling the gifted should be a mandatory part of every training program in gifted education.

COUNSELING ISSUES OF THE GIFTED

Polling over 400 gifted students, Galbraith (1985) identified "eight great gripes" (p. 15) of gifted children: not being told what giftedness is all about; feeling different and not accepted; parents, teachers, and friends expecting them to be perfect; being bored at school; being teased by other students; having few friends who really understand them; feeling overwhelmed by too many career choices; and worrying about world problems they feel helpless to do anything about. In addition, some gifted students feel isolated, hide their talents to fit in with peers, are intolerant of others, refuse to do repetitive assignments, resist authority, have high levels of anxiety, have difficulty accepting criticism, lack motivation, or are depressed.

Some of these issues are external in origin, caused by lack of acceptance and understanding of the gifted in our society. Others stem from the inborn characteristics discussed in chapters 2 and 3, personality and learning styles, asynchronous development, and a highly sensitive nervous system. External and internal factors interact to create a unique set of concerns for gifted students, the most salient of which appear to be:

❑ Feeling different
❑ Confusion about the meaning of giftedness
❑ Lack of understanding from others
❑ Fear of failure
❑ Perfectionism
❑ Existential depression

A child who *feels different* from other children is likely to interpret this difference to mean, "Something must be wrong with *me*" (Janos, Fung, & Robinson, 1985, p. 78). Some of the resulting anxiety can be allayed through appropriate counseling at the time of identification (Colangelo, 1991; Ross, 1964). For the student who is never recognized as gifted, or who is recognized but never told that he or she is gifted, feelings of being unacceptable and inferior to other people can remain a haunting reality—sometimes for an entire lifetime.

Identified gifted children also pay a heavy toll for society's *confusion about the nature of giftedness*. They are often genuinely perplexed about the meaning of giftedness (Ford, 1989). Definitions are so varied that children come to believe their abilities are situational. "I used to be gifted in elementary school, but I'm not gifted anymore." From the time children are identified as gifted, a series of questions plague them: "What is my 'gift'?" "Where did it come from?" "Will it go away?" "What will be expected of me now?" "What if I fail to live up to their expectations?" "Why me?"

An excellent resource to use with elementary school gifted students is *Giftedness: Living with It and Liking It* (Perry, 1985). The book is an entire unit on understanding giftedness, with the following sections:

"What is it and who's got it?"
"How do you get it?"
"Identifying it."
"It and other people."
"It and you."
"Misuses and abuses of it."
"Doing something with it."
"Living with it and liking it."

Every gifted program should include a counseling component, and the first counseling task should be helping students understand giftedness as it is defined by that program. For example, if high scholastic achievement is the main criterion for selection in the program, students should be made aware that they have academic talent that will serve as a foundation for success in college. This information is particularly important for girls (Kerr, 1991a), who often doubt their abilities and think their grades are simply the result of their teachers being nice to them.

Students can be informed that their giftedness means that they need different learning experiences from some of their classmates. They can learn about their learning styles and patterns of strengths and weaknesses. They can be helped to understand that they will excel in some areas and be surpassed in others—which does not mean that they have failed. Being the best in everything is an unrealistic goal; if achieved, it simply implies the lack of sufficiently challenging companions. The sooner a gifted student meets equally capable classmates, the easier it is for him or her to give up the expectation to be the best in all subjects.

Children need to be prepared to deal with *misunderstanding and the potential hostility of others* toward their abilities. Parents and teachers may unrealistically expect gifted children to be good at everything (Clinkenbeard, 1991; Galbraith, 1985). "If you're so gifted, how come you can't spell?" They may be teased by other children, and called names such as "bookworm," "egghead," "brain," "nerd," and "computer." A counseling program can help children discuss ways to respond to these taunts. More important, it can give children emotional support to help them resist internalizing these messages.

Fear of failure haunts most gifted children, particularly introverts. Introverts are not comfortable revealing weaknesses to others. They want the world to see only their finished products, not the false starts and blind alleys traversed to get there (Keirsey & Bates, 1978). We can assist introverted gifted children by respecting their privacy needs and allowing them to learn new skills in a safe atmosphere, with as few onlookers as possible.

Children who exhibit a visual-spatial learning style also appear to have difficulties with risk taking and accepting failure (Silverman, 1989). They learn by visualizing relationships and perceiving the gestalt—the whole. Many parents remark that their children "just know" things; when the children are asked how they arrived at their conclusions, they can't explain. Before they reach school age, some of these children do highly complex puzzles and mazes, take apart mechanical objects and reassemble them, and remember vividly the layout of a place they visited once when they were toddlers. They master complex skills by observing rather than by trial and error. One six-year-old girl refused to touch her new two-wheeler for months. Then one day she got on the bicycle and rode it perfectly. She explained to her puzzled parents that she had pictured herself on the bike and taught herself how to maintain her balance.

If spatial learners don't know the answer to a question, they often become panic-stricken because they do not have a route they can take to reach the solution. For most people, learning is a sequential, step-by-step process. Instead, spatial learners visualize all of the elements of a problem coming together into a pattern; this happens all at once, not in a step-by-step fashion. When asked a question, at first they may not know the answer, and then, quite suddenly, they do know. For them, there are only beginning and end points, and no secure strategies for getting from one point to another. This makes new situations particularly anxiety provoking. For such children to arrive at a correct answer requires a leap of faith that the muse will come and the pattern will announce itself in their minds.

The computer is an invaluable asset for introverts and visual-spatial learners. It allows the children to make their mistakes in private. It casts no aspersions on the child's character when he or she makes an error. It never raises an eyebrow and exclaims, "I'm surprised you didn't know that!" It uses a visual mode of learning, capitalizing on the strengths of the visual-spatial learner. The computer does not seem to care how long it takes the child to succeed. It is very "forgiving"—always providing another opportunity for success. The computer allows for continuous progress, challenging the child at his or her own level. The computer is a perfectionist, like the child: close is never good enough! Perhaps we can take some lessons from the computer in dealing with gifted children's perfectionism.

Here are some examples of *perfectionism* taken from case files at the Gifted Child Development Center:

J (age 4) seems to have qualities of a perfectionist. Things are to be done correctly and he doesn't easily accept alternate ways of doing them. At 18 months, he used to line cars, shoes, cards, etc. in perfect rows and from smallest to largest...

M (age 10) is extremely intense, self-critical, and tends to be impatient with other children. M is sensitive to criticism and is acutely aware of the fairness or justice of a given situation. She tends to be a perfectionist in matters that she considers important. Once involved in an activity, she demonstrates a great deal of determination to perfect her performance of that activity.

Students can be helped to cope with perfectionism by the counselor's accepting it as a basic part of giftedness, emphasizing its positive aspects, and acknowledging the anxiety and frustration it provokes. Attaining excellence usually takes more time and hard work than attaining mediocrity. Only those who believe it is possible to reach their goals will put forth the effort. The more difficult the goal, the more anxiety and frustration will be generated. When children experience these feelings, they should be led to understand that such feelings are to be expected whenever one takes on a difficult challenge, and that they have the inner strength to surmount those feelings.

It is important for perfectionists to learn to set priorities and avoid overcommitting themselves (Kerr, 1991b). It may be possible to attain a near-perfect report given enough time, but impossible to attain a measure of perfection in all subjects and several after-school activities simultaneously. When students become overextended and anxious over too many commitments, it is time to call a halt to the activity level, examine what is really important, and curb self-defeating behavior. (More about perfectionism can be found in chapter 3.)

Depression can result from too much pressure, overcommitment, loneliness, dependence on extrinsic motivation, extreme competitiveness, and other stressors (Kerr, 1991b). Gifted students may also suffer from a premature type of "'existential depression' [which] stems from their intense concerns about the basic problems of human existence" (Webb, Meckstroth, & Tolan, 1982, p. 193).

> Premature existential depression...occurs in gifted children and adolescents when their capacity for absorbing information about disturbing events is greater than their capacity to process and understand it.... Some gifted students seem to experience existential depression as a result of having wrestled with concepts with which even the wisest of adults have struggled. The meaning of life, the inevitability of death, and the beginning and end of the universe are all subjects that may lead to depression in the child or adolescent who is attempting to understand them. Perhaps the depression results from the incongruence between the child's developmental stage and intellectual abilities. (Kerr, 1991b, p. 138)

Kaiser and Berndt (1985) report that one-eighth of the 175 gifted junior and senior high school students they studied experienced pervasive feelings of depression, anger, and loneliness. Berndt, Kaiser, and van Aalst (1982) found that a substantial number of gifted students suffer from a type of "success depression" involving guilt, low self-esteem, and helplessness in the face of a high degree of stress. They provide evidence that students who have received guidance toward self-actualization and the development of a sense of meaning are less likely to be depressed.

GROUP AND INDIVIDUAL COUNSELING

Counseling can be helpful in teaching students a variety of interpersonal skills (Betts, 1986). Perrone (1986) suggests that "gifted students can...be helped to develop empathy, social skills, social assertiveness, leadership skills, decision-making skills, and self-evaluation skills through individual and group counseling" (pp. 564–565). Highly self-critical children may be unduly harsh in their criticisms of others. Children can be taught how to make friends and how to be a friend, to be sensitive in their interactions with others, to compliment as well as criticize, and to give constructive criticism in a caring manner. In an atmosphere that fosters respect and caring, students can unlearn dysfunctional attitudes about others, and replace them with healthy attitudes of mutual support and respect.

Counseling Groups

Traditionally, at the middle and high school levels, the strong emphasis on mastery of specific subject areas has left little room in the curriculum for emotional development. However, some innovative districts have instituted counseling seminars for middle and high school gifted students which have been very effective. For example, the Aurora Public Schools, in Colorado, developed a comprehensive affective curriculum for middle school gifted students. The curriculum concentrated on the following topics:

- ❏ Understanding Giftedness
- ❏ Self-Expectations
- ❏ Dealing with Expectations of Others
- ❏ Feeling Different
- ❏ Peer Pressure
- ❏ Sensitivity
- ❏ Tolerance
- ❏ Family Structure
- ❏ Responsibility for Others
- ❏ Career Exploration
- ❏ Leadership Training (Beville, 1983)

Topics such as these are generic concerns of gifted students and lead to lively discussions. Students share their experiences and give each other suggestions for coping with similar problems. The Aurora affective development program incorporates simulations and structured group activities, and is conducted by the teacher of the gifted. Chapter 5 contains guidelines for counseling ("discussion") groups conducted by teacher/counselors.

A counseling group can also be more open-ended rather than topical in nature. This format works best under the guidance of a trained counselor. Students take turns sharing issues of immediate concern in their lives and gaining assistance from group members. Sessions usually begin with a question such as, "Who has an issue you would like to share with the group today?" The counselor needs some training in group processes to draw in different members of the group, note levels of discomfort that might be expressed nonverbally, and move the group along at a productive pace. Role-playing can be used in a group setting to facilitate awareness of other points of view, resolve conflicts, and practice negotiation skills.

In some communities it has been suggested that if a counseling group is good for gifted students, it would be good for all students. Preventive counseling, however, is only effective when students feel safe. The problems experienced by the gifted are often related to their lack of emotional safety in a heterogeneous group. Gifted students have different issues from their age-mates, and they will not reveal their true concerns in a mixed-ability group. They have many devices for hiding their abilities so that they are not teased by the others. This is a serious issue which leads to inauthenticity and inner conflict. The issue would not come up or be resolved in a heterogeneous group. It is much more likely that a group of students who are all hiding to some degree will be able to encourage each other to find better ways of coping with their differences. (See chapter 5 for more on this issue.)

Individual and Family Counseling

The gifted student who makes statements such as "I wish I were dead" should be involved in individual counseling, whether or not it is supplied by the school. It is unwise to assume that these are just "attention-getting behaviors." All such cries for help must be taken seriously, and responded to promptly by parents, peers, teachers, and counselors to prevent escalation into suicide attempts. Gifted students are capable of making suicide attempts appear to be accidents, and they may skip many of the typical steps, such as dropping hints (e.g., "I probably won't be there next week"), giving away prized possessions, making sure pets will be cared for, losing interest in achievement, appearance, or their usual activities, isolating themselves, and so forth. They may be slippery in counseling sessions as well, assuring the counselor that everything is fine (Kerr, 1991b). Therefore, suicidal students need to be monitored carefully, and they should not be left alone. Counselors should be well acquainted with crisis intervention techniques and approaches to suicide prevention (Kerr, 1991b).

Some additional signs that individual counseling is needed include:

❏ Intense competitiveness
❏ Social isolation
❏ Alienation within the family
❏ Inability to express or control anger
❏ Excessive manipulativeness
❏ Chronic underachievement
❏ Depression or continual boredom

❑ Sexual acting out
❑ Evidence of any kind of abuse
❑ Recent traumatic experiences or loss of loved ones

Children under the age of ten often profit from play therapy, in which they have a chance to act out their frustrations and inner conflicts with puppets, dolls, and toys while they engage in conversation about their feelings and actions with the therapist. Older students prefer a more adultlike talking therapy. In any event, the counselor or therapist should be thoroughly experienced in working with gifted children and youth. Otherwise, some of the symptoms of giftedness might be misinterpreted, or the child may manipulate the therapist.

Individual counseling may also be sought by adolescents and adults as part of their plan for self-development. Counseling can assist youths in selecting careers, preparing for marriage, gaining greater self-awareness, learning conflict resolution skills, dealing with existential issues, developing independence, and actualizing their potential. Family counseling can increase harmony in the family system and enable each member to understand each other's personality types and roles. Counseling should be viewed in a positive light and actively sought for prevention rather than just remediation.

DABROWSKI'S THEORY AS A FRAMEWORK FOR COUNSELING

Young people often internalize messages from the society that are counterproductive to healthy emotional development. They are made to feel that they should not have problems or "negative" feelings such as anger, hurt, or unhappiness. They should not be "overly" sensitive or experience inner conflict. People who have these feelings are called "immature," "maladjusted," or, worse, "mentally unstable." When sensitive gifted students feel a great deal of pain in relation to an incident others see as "trivial," they may come to perceive themselves according to these negative labels. "There must be something wrong with me because I feel this way." Well-meaning adults may respond to the student by saying, "Don't BE that way." If the messages of "Don't be the way you are" are too strong, the young person may become severely depressed.

Dabrowski's theory (Dabrowski, 1972) is most beneficial in terms of the changes in attitude it promotes in both the counselor and the student. The counselor comes to view intense inner experiences as positive signs of development, rather than as negative indicators of emotional disturbance. Using the Dabrowskian model, the counselor *does not* attempt to help the student resolve his[1] problems. Support is given without taking sides on the issues involved, or

---

[1] Note: For the sake of clarity, the counselor will be referred to as "she" and the student as "he" throughout the next few sections.

all sides of an issue are validated. In this way, the young person feels that his issues are real and important, rather than trivial and easily resolved by an outsider. The student remains in conflict as long as necessary in order to come to some inner resolution on his own. The counselor is in no hurry to "cure" the student because she deeply believes in the value of inner conflict for personal growth, and in the student's ability to cope adequately, given sufficient time and encouragement.

Ogburn Colangelo (1989) describes an application of the theory with a gifted college freshman experiencing conflict between her need to develop her own special abilities and her attachment to family members who do not support the development of these talents. The strategies used by the counselor to foster personal growth in the student were *supporting* and *reframing*.

> To support is to validate existing behaviors, attitudes, and emotions. ...To reframe is to assign a new meaning to existing behaviors, attitudes, and emotions—to help the client understand aspects of herself differently, namely in terms of the process of development. The theory details which behaviors, attitudes, and emotions to reframe and provides both the rationale for the reframing and the framework into which the behavior is placed. (p. 88)

In this particular case, the counselor validated the student for the strength of her attachment—her ability to experience relationship. At the same time, she invited the young woman to look within herself to discover her own internal pressures toward self-actualization. The counselor helped the student recognize that these two needs might present conflict, and that the conflict was healthy, since both desires were healthy. She also helped the student to acknowledge her strengths: her sense of responsibility to her family, her awareness of her own talents, and her willingness to determine her own future. While encouraging the young woman to trust her own judgment, the counselor at no time dismissed the negative consequences the student might face by following her own path instead of the one designed by her parents.

The counselor was able to see the problem from the student's point of view, and the difficulty of the choices to be made. She listened, helped the student sort out the problem by herself, and gave her confidence in her strengths and her ability to cope with the situation.

> So, in counseling Sara we want to act as nourishers, not so much of the talent itself, but of the emotional structure from which the talent comes. We can accomplish this by supporting and reframing already existing strengths which might stimulate the client to continue that growth. (Ogburn Colangelo, 1979, p. 186)

From the perspective of Dabrowski's theory, the sensitive counselor can remove much of the anxious overlay, the misperceptions that prevent gifted students from achieving a degree of self-acceptance. The counselor validates the student's feelings, helping him see that his emotional responses are healthy. She respects the student's problems, both the nature of the conflicts and the fact that he has these inner growth experiences. The counselor serves as an interpreter of the student's inner world to parents, teachers, and others who might not understand. She helps the student reframe negative attitudes toward his conflicting feelings, which eliminates self-doubt and self-deprecation. Clients who have been exposed to Dabrowski's theory in my counseling practice experience an immense sense of relief and renewed hope. When inner conflicts are perceived as developmentally healthy, resistance melts, and new sources of energy are mobilized for coping with difficult periods.

INDIVIDUAL COUNSELING TECHNIQUES

Until trained professionals are available, the brunt of the responsibility for meeting the child's emotional needs will rest on classroom teachers and parents. All personnel who work with gifted students should be prepared to act in a counseling capacity (Parke, 1990). The next two sections contain counseling techniques for the counselor-in-training. Parents, teachers, coordinators, principals, and students themselves can master most of these techniques. Additional training and experience in courses, workshops, and personal counseling will enhance these skills.

Although counseling approaches may differ, their effectiveness rests on a single principle: respect for other human beings. A teacher who can truly respect a student is likely to become the child's confidant, friend, and counselor. There are three necessary components in a counseling relationship, all of which can be seen as facets of respect: genuineness, unconditional positive regard, and accurate empathy (Rogers, 1961). Genuineness is authenticity or honesty, which forms the basis of trust. Unconditional positive regard means overcoming one's natural tendency to judge others, and appreciating the person aside from his actions. Accurate empathy is the ability to enter another's world, to feel as he feels. When one has "walked a mile in another's shoes," she gains great respect for the person's inner conflicts. If one sees easy solutions to another's problems, this is usually an indication of insufficient empathy.

The essential elements of good counseling are similar, regardless of different philosophical orientations (Garfield, 1986). Good counselors ask pertinent questions, listen well, give honest feedback, sincerely respect the client and his problems, and, by providing a safe, confidential, nonjudgmental atmosphere, enable the client to share deep feelings.

One main way in which therapies differ is the amount of direction the counselor provides (Corey, 1991). In working with the gifted, it is better to give too little than too much direction. These children are capable of high-level problem solving, and may simply need these capabilities stimulated. They often resent someone else's answers to their problems and reject advice. They prefer a good listener who can guide them through the problem-solving process, and perhaps offer insights into the problem itself that would change their perspective. A teacher/counselor can use a nondirective approach, providing a safe haven for the student to explore his own problems; in this way, there is less risk of giving unwanted advice, angering parents, or eliciting censure for practicing therapy without a license.

The following suggestions may be useful to a novice counselor, a teacher/counselor, a peer counselor, or any other individual who takes on a counseling role without the benefit of extensive training.

Invite the student to share feelings. A counseling session usually begins with an open-ended question—that is, a question that requires more than a one-word, "yes–no" type of response. The question conveys caring and readiness to listen. The counselor may also offer an observation of the student's emotional state that will encourage the expression of feelings.

"What has been happening with you lately?" "You've been looking down in class. What's been going on?" "You look sad today. What are you feeling?" "What's happened since we talked last?"

Actively listen. Listening may seem too obvious to mention, but it is not as easy as it sounds. We are all easily distracted by our own thoughts, and it is difficult to give our full attention to another person. For some gifted students, the counseling session may be among the rare times they receive the undivided attention of an adult. Active listening is the key to effective counseling. The counselor indicates through body posture, facial expression, and eye contact that she is receptive to the student's feelings and experiences (Egan, 1990). She also conveys warmth, sincerity, and safety during the listening process. All of this is done through nonverbal communication.

Ask for more information. Active listening also involves responding to the information given with questions, statements, observations, nodding, and gestures. The communication process resembles a conversation between two close friends that is focused primarily on only one of them. The listener continuously probes for more information, never assuming she fully understands the situation described.

"Tell me more about..."
"What happened when you...?"
"I don't see the connection between..."
"Why do you suppose he...?"

In this way, the counselor draws out experiences, perceptions, and feelings, both for her own benefit and for the student's. As the student shares different facets of the situation out loud, he has more conscious awareness of the elements and motives at play. Simply talking in depth about a problem often gives birth to its resolution.

Paraphrase to obtain feedback on what you are hearing. Paraphrasing is another form of active listening. The listener restates the information that the student is sharing. There are various levels at which paraphrasing takes place

(Egan, 1990). At first, the restatement is quite literal. The counselor rechecks her understanding of the information given. She may mirror the student's words, intonation, even facial expressions: "I hear you saying... Is that correct?" At another level, the counselor summarizes the content conveyed, rephrasing the information in her own words. At a third level, the counselor infers the feelings from the content, and reflects them back to the student: "It sounds like you felt humiliated by that experience." "You're angry that..."

Encourage expression of emotions. Dealing with the student's feelings in a situation is more effective than discussing the events. The events cannot be changed, but one's feelings, attitudes, and perceptions can be altered, thus paving the way for changing one's behavior in future situations. The counselor encourages the student to share the full gamut of his emotions: "How did you feel when...?" "How do you feel now?"

Negative feelings are often unacceptable in the home environment, so the counselor may need to reassure the student that all of his feelings are acceptable: "I can understand how you would feel that way." If the student is having difficulty expressing an emotion, the counselor may reflect the emotional content back, checking to see if the reflection is accurate: "You were furious, weren't you?" "I would have been crushed."

Share personal experiences that are relevant. The counselor's personal experience may form the basis of rapport with the student (Egan, 1990). It is appropriate for the counselor to share these experiences as long as she does not get so wrapped up in her own story that she steals center stage from the student. A rule of thumb is to keep self-disclosure as brief as possible, emphasizing how the counselor's experience relates to the student's experience. Self-disclosure is a particularly effective technique for teacher/counselors to use with gifted students. These children often feel so alone that it helps to know someone else has had similar feelings.

Provide encouragement by validating the student's strengths. Many capable students are unaware of their strengths. Gifted children can often recite extensive accounts of their shortcomings, partly because of their high standards and partly because they are used to downplaying their abilities in the attempt to convince themselves and their classmates that they're "just regular guys" (Ford, 1989). Some of the traits that they perceive as liabilities (e.g., compulsiveness and stubbornness) can be reframed as assets (e.g., determination and organization) (Corey, 1991; Dinkmeyer & Losoncy, 1980). The student needs the counselor's encouragement to recognize and use all of his inner resources and to gain the courage to change beliefs and behaviors that are self-defeating.

Support feelings without taking sides on the issue. It is important to validate the student's feelings without supporting one side of the issue or the other. In most cases, the student will offer only part of the story, either because of his current emotional state, or because he is consciously aware of only some elements in the situation and not others. When the counselor gives support to the student's current perceptions and beliefs, she may inadvertently freeze them, preventing the student from seeing new perspectives. This often occurs subliminally, through excessive verbal agreement and head-nodding. In contrast, the effective counselor recognizes that she is dealing with only partial information. She supports the person's feelings, while reserving judgment on the situation itself, and attempting to gain more data. For example, "You are really disturbed by the way you feel she treats you. Why do you stay in the relationship?"

Explore positive aspects of the problem. In the example from Ogburn Colangelo (1989) cited earlier, the counselor acknowledged the positive aspects of the conflict itself. When a student seeks counseling he is likely to describe all of the negative components that make the situation problematic. It is important to draw out the positive components to gain a more balanced picture of the complexity of the problem. For example, "If you were to leave home, what would you miss about your family?"

In changing behavior patterns, it is useful to explore with the student the benefits of the pattern he is trying to change. For example, if a student wants to lose weight, the counselor can have him list all of the ways in which the weight helps him, and all of the needs that food fulfills for him (Bandler & Grinder, 1979). Without this information, a weight loss program may prove ineffective because it does not deal with all of the issues involved.

Help clarify the problem. Much of the art of counseling is in problem clarification. Most counselors know that the problem originally presented may not be the real issue. Whereas the layperson may jump immediately to potential solutions, the counselor spends a considerable amount of time looking at the problem itself. It may have many facets, each of which must be examined separately. Gifted students often need help sorting through myriad events and impressions in order to form a statement of the problem. They can be asked to draw a picture of the problem as well as talk about it.

Help the student analyze and prioritize issues. Next, the counselor can help the student analyze the problem and prioritize issues to be resolved. Sometimes this involves creating lists of parts of the problem, such as those parts that can be changed most easily.

Determine what can be changed. Some facets in a situation can be altered and others cannot. The counselor can help the student sort through the various aspects and determine which can be changed. This means separating those that are under his control from those that are not. Often students believe that no part of a problem is under their control and that they are simply victims of unfair circumstances. Before change can take place, this perception must be challenged. As long as the individual feels like a helpless victim, all that can be hoped for in the counseling effort is an exchange of "ain't it awfuls" (Berne, 1964)—not improvement.

In any situation, the one aspect that can be altered is oneself. For improvement to occur, the individual must be willing to accept part of the responsibility for the problem. Ownership of the problem provides a foundation for goal setting and behavior change (Meichenbaum, 1985). The student must come to see which aspects of himself he can change to improve the situation.

Provide new perspectives. One of the advantages of talking to someone about a problem is the possibility of gaining a new perspective on the situation. A person who is not directly involved may offer new insights. An observer can also be more objective, and can see the issue within a different time frame. When a student is in pain, he may believe that he will be in pain forever. The counselor can assure him that he has not always been where he is now and that he will move through the current crisis.

A perceptive counselor gives not only objectivity, but also a helpful kind of subjectivity—her own personal insights into the problem. Sometimes these insights are directly related to the information given, or to the counselor's knowledge of the student's personality. At other times, the insights are from the counselor's personal experiences or from associations with others who have faced similar situations. There are also times when these insights are not easily traced. The counselor offers these intuitive responses as "hunches," which she checks out with the student: for example, "I just got this idea. Tell me if this fits for you."

Help the student examine basic assumptions. When rapport has been firmly established with the student, the counselor can begin to be more confrontive, stimulating the student to examine his beliefs and conflicts at a deeper level. Confrontation needs to be handled delicately, conveying complete acceptance of the student and belief in his ability to handle anything (Ellis, 1989). Basic self-defeating assumptions can be challenged gently: "What is the worst possible thing you can imagine that would happen if you got a C in the course?" "How likely is this to occur?"

Reflect discrepancies. As the student reveals more and more information, the threads of the conflict begin to surface. Often they appear as discrepant pieces of information, attitudes, or feelings. They may also become apparent through body language. For example, the student may be smiling while describing a sad event, or he may say he feels fine, while his foot swings rapidly back and forth. The counselor takes note of these discrepancies and calls them to the attention of the student at appropriate times during the session: "You're telling me that this didn't bother you at all, but what is your foot saying?" (Perls, 1973). The counselor might say, "I'm really confused by...," reflecting the inconsistencies presented. "Last week you indicated that your mother always is supportive of you, and this week you've brought up three incidents in which you felt that she hurt you." This type of reflection brings together elements of the inner conflict that the student might not have consciously connected.

Help the student set goals. Goal setting means making a commitment to change. Some students just want a shoulder to cry on; they are afraid of actually making changes. Through encouragement, the counselor helps the student perceive that a more harmonious way is possible and that it can be achieved. Only at this point is the student ready to explore options. It is important to first establish rapport through the previous processes before helping the student consider potential solutions.

Help the student explore options. Generating options is very much like brainstorming. Most gifted students have had some practice in brainstorming in their classes. The counselor acts as a guide, without offering suggestions until the student has exhausted his own ideas. Options can also be explored visually through diagrams. The options are not judged as adequate solutions until the end of the idea generation phase. The student selects the options with the most potential for success, and then prioritizes them, determining which he would like to attempt first.

Ask the student to observe before attempting change. The first step in changing a pattern is often the act of observation. As the student observes his own behavior, he begins to develop the "subject-object" in himself (Dabrowski, 1970, p. 178), a higher-order function that enables him to evaluate himself objectively. The counselor may ask the student to observe his own reactions for a week and notice under what conditions a particular pattern reoccurs. The observation can be very detailed, including thoughts, feelings, and the impact of one's behavior on others (Meichenbaum, 1986). The act of observation itself may prove ameliorative. Engaging the gifted student as an experimenter gives him a sense of control and reduces resistance to change.

Recognize and acknowledge progress. Implementing changes in one's life is a difficult, time consuming undertaking that requires patience; the counselor is there to provide support and feedback during the process. She warns the student that it might be two steps forward and one step backward. She prepares the student for plateaus encountered in the process. She acknowledges each step taken toward the student's goals, and reminds him of how far he has come from where he was at the beginning of the process. If he runs into a stumbling block, the counselor helps him to reevaluate the situation, and plan alternative courses of action where necessary. Even after the student has terminated the counseling sessions, the counselor maintains some contact, and is available to monitor the student's growth and development. She remains as a backup system to the student when future crises arise. Once the relationship between the counselor and the student is established, it remains intact, regardless of the extent of contact between them. This bond provides a healthy basis for establishing long-term relationships with others.

Know when to refer. At times, situations arise that are beyond the scope of the training, experience, and capabilities of even the most experienced counselor. A child might have a schizophrenic episode, need to be hospitalized, need medication, become alcoholic, overdose on drugs, be victimized by violence in the family, and so on. It is essential for the counselor to be familiar with agencies in the community that deal with specific types of problems, so that the student and his family can be referred for expert treatment. One individual cannot be expected to know how to deal effectively with every psychological problem with which she might be presented. It is as important to know when one is beyond one's level of competence as it is to know where to refer a child in need. This is particularly true for the novice counselor.

It is essential to maintain students' confidentiality and to explain the limits of that confidentiality. Protection of the student takes precedence over confidentiality. This is important for peer counselors to understand so that loyalty to friends does not overshadow the need to report self-destructive behavior to someone who can assist (Strip, Swassing, & Kidder, 1991). Additional counseling strategies that can be used effectively by noncounselors are stress reduction techniques and bibliotherapy.

STRESS REDUCTION TECHNIQUES

Stress management is an important facet of preventive counseling. Stress is the body's response when an individual feels unable to cope with circumstances—the signal system that he or she is in danger (Genshaft & Broyles, 1991). When stress is ignored, physical illness can result, as can depression and suicidal ideation. Therefore, reducing stress can prevent illness, emotional disturbance, and suicide.

Because of their asynchronous development and unique personality traits, gifted students are more susceptible to stress (Genshaft & Broyles, 1991; Kaiser & Berndt, 1985; Kerr, 1991b; Kline & Meckstroth, 1985). Some common stressors of gifted students include loneliness (Kaiser & Berndt, 1985), their feeling the need to hide their abilities in order to be accepted (Cross, Coleman, & Terhaar-Yonkers, 1991), excessively high standards (Buescher, 1991; Ford, 1989; Karnes & Oehler-Stinnet, 1986) academic pressures (Yadusky-Holahan & Holahan, 1983), high expectations from the community (Kerr, 1991b), and antagonism from classmates if they attempt to meet those expectations (Clinkenbeard, 1991; Ford, 1989). Perfectionism intensifies in adolescence (Buescher, 1991; Kline & Short, 1991) to the point where gifted students are often dissatisfied with their performance. Adolescent girls of high ability appear to be particularly vulnerable to depression and fear (Gilligan, 1991; Kline & Short, 1991; Petersen, 1988).

Some gifted children are extremely intense and easily overstimulated from birth (Turecki & Tonner, 1985). Life itself is stressful for these children. Parents can help easily stimulated children to relax at bedtime by singing to them and developing a calming routine at night, which might include back rubs, soothing music, and deep relaxation exercises. Older gifted students sometimes feel they are under extreme pressure by teachers, administrators, and parents to live up to others' expectations (Ford, 1989; Kerr, 1991b). These students can be helped to examine these expectations and gradually move from dependence on others' evaluations toward self-evaluation.

Gifted students can be taught how to deal with negative feelings when they arise so as not to be overpowered by them. The following set of steps has been found to be useful in helping students cope with stressful situations.

1. Become aware of the physical sensations of stress
2. Stop the interactions
3. Remove self from the situation
4. Find some place to be alone
5. Become aware of feelings
6. Express emotions
7. Do relaxation exercises
8. Try to understand reasons for the reactions
9. Take a different perspective on the situation
10. Develop a plan for resolving the conflict
11. Implement plan

There are physiological symptoms of stress which act as danger signals (Genshaft & Broyles, 1991). Some individuals even have a sophisticated code of body language—they feel different emotions in different parts of their bodies. Humiliation may cause a facial flush; stage fright may lead to a racing heartbeat or butterflies in the stomach; anger may be experienced as intense lower back pain; frustration may be felt as a tight neck and shoulders; hurt may manifest in teary eyes or headaches. A useful exercise with groups and individuals is to help them *become aware of the signals of tension*—their body's unique communication system.

What are you feeling?" "Where are you feeling this?" "Where in your body do you react when someone has just insulted you?" "Do you put a big hurt in the same place as a little hurt?"

Genshaft and Broyles (1991) recommend that gifted students develop a "warning signs checklist" (p. 83) of their own reactions, such as sleepiness, stomach-aches, mood changes, and so forth, to help them become aware of their body's messages.

Once the student is aware of his body's signal system, he can learn to pay attention to the signals and *stop whatever is causing the distress*. In most cases, it is possible to stop an interaction that is causing negative feelings, and to *remove oneself from the situation* until one can regain composure and control. Break time is permissible—even advisable—in the midst of an argument. Rather than storming out of the house and slamming the door, the young person can announce his need to discontinue the fight, and his intention to resume discussion or negotiations under less heated circumstances. He can then determine the time, place, and circumstances of the next encounter so that he will feel more in control of the situation.

Some possible interventions in the middle of a heated discussion are:

> *"I am uncomfortable with this discussion. Let's talk about it tomorrow when we've both had a chance to calm down." "I need some time to think about all this. I'm going to go for a walk and I'll be back in an hour." "I don't want to talk about this anymore right now; I'll call you as soon as I've had a chance to think it through."*

If all else fails, one can almost always buy a *few minutes of privacy* for personal refreshment: "Excuse me for a moment. Where is the rest room?"

Once the person has succeeded in extricating himself, he can allow himself to *become aware of his feelings*: pain, hurt, fear, frustration, anger... Venting the feelings is extremely helpful. There are numerous ways to *express emotions*: jogging... screaming... cleaning... attacking a punching bag in the gym... writing hate letters and then ripping them up... drawing... crying... pounding a pillow... conjuring up imaginary conversations. Release of tension through physical exercise restores energy to the system and helps the individual feel calmer and more able to cope (Genshaft & Broyles, 1991). Journal writing is also useful for highly verbal gifted students to express their emotions, sort feelings, and record information which can later be analyzed for possible solutions. Preference for either a verbal or a nonverbal way to release tension is often related to the individual's temperament.

The expression of emotion can be delayed until the student is in a safe environment. In planning for such occasions, the student can brainstorm all the ways of releasing pent-up emotions that might work for him. When there is strong rapport between the counselor and the student, some of these methods can be attempted with the counselor's guidance.

After the emotion is expressed, the next step is *relaxation*. Gifted children with high overexcitability levels need relaxation techniques to assist them in coping. Deep breathing is usually helpful, as is tightening and relaxing every part of the body separately from head to toes. Creative visualization (e.g., the ocean or a favorite place) can also have a calming effect, as can soft music with a slow tempo. Biofeedback equipment is becoming increasingly popular and accessible as a means of stress reduction. It would be valuable to have biofeedback equipment in every school, along with instruction as to its proper use. Gifted students can quickly master the principles and learn to control their autonomic nervous systems.

When he has succeeded in calming himself down, the gifted student can bring his analytical strengths to the situation, and *try to understand the reasons for his reactions*. Is it the person's tone of voice? Are there discrepancies between the person's words and body language? Does the event trigger the memory of an upsetting experience in childhood? He can attempt to *look at the problem objectively from many different perspectives*. He can begin to examine reasons for the other person's behavior.

The next step is *conflict resolution*. Experience in creative problem solving is particularly valuable in this phase of the process. The gifted student constructs as many alternatives as possible for dealing with the situation more effectively. If time permits, this can be done with the help of a friend or counselor. An important skill in conflict resolution is *negotiation*. Many students do not know how to ask for what they want, how to hear what another person needs, and how to negotiate to the point at which everyone is satisfied and a win-win result is achieved. These skills can be taught by the counselor or teacher/counselor.

The last step is *implementation of the plan*, following through with the negotiations at a time and place of the individual's choosing. If the plan is unsuccessful, alternative strategies can be constructed. If this process is done with the aid of a counselor, the student can rehearse conversations or negotiations in a safe environment before attempting them. He can imagine the consequences and plan strategies for coping with the negative ones. He can also visualize positive outcomes. The counselor can teach him how to approach situations cooperatively and create allies out of his "opponents."

> Approaches to managing stress include teaching the individual to be aware of bodily responses to stress, identifying faulty beliefs that may exacerbate stress, developing positive coping strategies, and practicing relaxation techniques. Individuals working with gifted adolescents experiencing stress also may find it helpful to teach positive problem-solving strategies or increase certain daily activities such as physical exercise or writing. Perhaps the most important assistance may be in the form of emotional support from a close adult. (Genshaft & Broyles, 1991, p. 86)

BIBLIOTHERAPY

> I was alone. I'd always been alone.... If I was alone, OK, it was better to accept it, not pretend. I was a kind of person that just does not fit into this kind of society. To expect anybody to like me was stupid. What should they like me for? My big brain?... Nobody likes brains. Brains are very ugly things. Some people like them fried in butter, but hardly any Americans do. (*Very Far Away from Anywhere Else*, LeGuin, 1976, p. 61)

One of the most effective counseling tools available to parents, teachers, counselors, and the gifted child is bibliotherapy. Bibliotherapy is the use of children's books to help understand and solve personal problems (Frasier & McCannon, 1981). It is particularly effective with the gifted, since these students usually have advanced reading skills and are often avid readers. They are capable of seeing the metaphoric implications of the material, not only for the characters in the plot, but also for themselves. Intellectual, imaginational, and emotional overexcitabilities are all highly stimulated by good literature. Gifted children often become so "lost" in their reading that they may not even hear their names being shouted from a distance of three feet! Children who are lonely often find their friends in books.

As part of a developmental counseling program, therapeutic reading enables the child to try various approaches vicariously without real-life consequences (Frasier & McCannon, 1981). Students may find this method less threatening than direct counseling, and often teachers are more comfortable with this technique than with other counseling strategies. Bibliotherapy increases a student's self-knowledge and knowledge of others. Identification with the characters can lead to release of emotions and insights about problems (Halsted, 1988). In a therapeutic reading program, the counselor or teacher/counselor draws the student into discussing the personal meaning of the story, through such questions as, "Have you ever been in a position similar to...'s?" "What did you do?" "What do you think ... would have done in your place?"

A children's librarian should be consulted for assistance in locating appropriate books that deal with the presenting issues. There are several reference books available at public libraries that catalog children's literature according to the issue or problem area addressed. The most popular of these is *The Bookfinder 4: When Kids Need Books* (Spredemann-Dreyer, 1989). The guides are annotated and indicate appropriate reading level. *Counseling Children* (Thompson & Rudolph, 1983) contains a mini-guide of suggested reading for children on the following topics: abandonment, adoption/foster homes, child abuse, death, divorce, family, friendship—sense of belonging, and single parents. It also includes a short reading list of books about gifted children.

Some authors specialize in writing about and for the gifted, such as E. L. Konigsburg (e.g, *(George)*, 1970); Madeleine L'Engle (e.g., *A Wrinkle in Time*, 1962); Stephanie Tolan (e.g., *Pride of the Peacock,* 1986); Katherine Paterson (*Bridge to Teribithia*, 1977); and Ursula LeGuin (e.g., *Very Far Away from Anywhere Else*, 1976). Sisk (1982) describes two bibliotherapy units, using Danziger's *The Cat Ate My Gymsuit* (1974), and Blume's *Otherwise Known as Sheila the Great* (1972). (See the Appendix for additional books.) The works of these authors are thoroughly enjoyed by gifted children and adults alike. They can be read and discussed by an entire class, or they can be read aloud by the teacher; they are also favorites for bedtime and family reading. Frasier and McCannon (1981) present a framework for using bibliotherapy with gifted children, and list books about the gifted, organized around three topics: personal problems, social problems, and educational/vocational problems. Biographical study can be therapeutic as well, since it presents role models to the student (Hollingworth, 1942).

Bibliotherapy appears to be particularly useful in helping gifted students cope with existential depression (Kerr, 1991b). An annotated list of books appropriate for counseling gifted students has been developed by Schroeder-Davis (1990) and is included as an Appendix in Kerr's (1991b) book, *A Handbook for Counseling the Gifted and Talented*. These children's books adhere to the following criteria:

1. They are good literature. That is, independent of their relevance to the gifted, the books are well written and fun to read. Many are by award winning authors or have won awards themselves.

2. Giftedness is important, but not necessarily central to the story. The book must be *concerned* with the gifted, but not "about" giftedness.
3. Readers should be able to identify with the characters, themes, and conflicts. Therefore, portrayals that are rich, varied, and realistic rather than stereotyped or derogatory should be chosen. (Kerr, 1991b, p. 139)

The books listed in our Appendix also fit Schroeder-Davis's criteria. They are excellent children's literature, written by well-known authors; each features a gifted child as the protagonist. To determine the types of issues addressed in these books for therapeutic reading purposes, please consult *The Bookfinder 4* (Spredemann-Dreyer, 1989). Also, in-depth reviews of several of the books appear in "The Reading Room," a regular feature in the journal *Understanding Our Gifted* by the novelist Stephanie Tolan.

No age levels have been indicated in our book list, as gifted children's reading ability usually far exceeds their chronological age. The designation "Young Adult" indicates that material contained in the book is more appropriate for adolescents. It appears that children who read well beyond their age level often come across sexually explicit material, and there is no evidence that this is harmful. An extremely cautious children's librarian assures me that children gloss over material they do not fully understand. However, exposure to violence and gross injustice can have devastating effects on gifted students, bringing to their awareness information they cannot bear. We do little to protect children from violence in the media, and parents need to be guided in helping their children cope with the amount and intensity of violence to which they are exposed.

A therapeutic reading program involves more than just reading; it provides the opportunity for discussion and sharing of insights. This can be done on a group or individual basis. The facilitator needs to be thoroughly familiar with the books in order to lead an effective discussion. The Great Books Foundation (1974) provides a wonderful program to train parents and teachers to lead insightful discussions of literature. *Exploring Books with Gifted Children* (Polette & Hamlin, 1980) is a good resource for appropriate reading materials and discussion questions. The types of questions suggested help children to extricate the deeper significance of their reading. A newer book by Polette (1984), *Books and Real Life: A Guide for Gifted Students and Teachers*, contains perceptive questions for teachers to ask to guide students' reading. Another excellent resource is Halsted's (1988) *Guiding Gifted Readers from Pre-School to High School*. This book is particularly valuable for helping gifted students deal with unanswerable questions. Flack and Lamb (1984) present activities for students to engage in after reading some of the most recommended books about gifted children. Two additional resources are *Books for the Gifted Child* (Hauser & Nelson, 1988) and *Reading Ladders for Human Relations* (6th ed.) (Tway, 1981).

CONCLUSION

The counseling needs of the gifted are unique and varied. They can profit from preventive group counseling, individual counseling, career counseling, peer counseling, and bibliotherapy. Because of the intensity with which they experience life, gifted students may be at risk for depression and self-destructive behavior. Increased counseling services for some gifted students could mean the difference between achievement and underachievement, between peace and despair, between friendship and loneliness, between life and death. Counselors need to be trained in the emotional characteristics of the gifted. Teachers need to be trained in counseling techniques to function as teacher/counselors. Special training in counseling the gifted should be available in all graduate programs in gifted education. The whole milieu of school can be constructive or destructive, depending upon the extent of our understanding of and responsiveness to gifted students' emotional needs.

We have only begun to explore the emotional development of the gifted. We know that gifted children are highly sensitive, and that this sensitivity must be nurtured in order to develop the child's emotional health. We also know that the levels of sensitivity, perfectionism, and overexcitabilities shown by gifted students are not highly valued in society. If ever there was a good reason for gifted programs, it would be to provide a safe haven for the emotional development of these children. If we fail to provide the kind of understanding they so desperately need, we transform emotional sensitivity into emotional disturbance, and we risk losing these individuals permanently. This is a risk none of us can afford to take.

REFERENCES

Assagioli, R. (1965). *Psychosynthesis: A manual of principles and techniques*. New York: Hobbs, Dorman.

Bandler, R., & Grinder, J. (1979). *Frogs into princes: Neurolinguistic programming*. Moab, UT: Real People Press.

Berndt, D. J., Kaiser, C. F., & van Aalst, F. (1982). Depression and self-actualization in gifted adolescents. *Journal of Clinical Psychology, 38,* 142–150.

Berne, E. (1964). *Games people play: The psychology of human relationships*. New York: Grove Press.

Betts, G. T. (1986). Development of the emotional and social needs of gifted individuals. *Journal of Counseling and Development, 64,* 587–589.

Beville, K. (1983). The affective development curriculum. In S. M. Perry, *The Aurora gifted and talented handbook for middle school*. Aurora, CO: Aurora Public Schools.

Blackburn, A. C., & Erickson, D. B. (1986). Predictable crises of the gifted student. *Journal of Counseling and Development, 9,* 552–555.

Blume, J. (1972). *Otherwise known as Sheila the great*. New York: Dell.

Buescher, T. M. (1991). Gifted adolescents. In N. Colangelo & G. A. Davis (Eds.), *Handbook of gifted education* (pp. 382–401). Needham Heights, MA: Allyn & Bacon.

Clinkenbeard, P. R. (1991). Unfair expectations: A pilot study of middle school students' comparisons of gifted and regular classes. *Journal for the Education of the Gifted, 15,* 56–63.

Colangelo, N. (1991). Counseling gifted students. In N. Colangelo & G. A. Davis (Eds.), *Handbook of gifted education* (pp. 273–284). Needham Heights, MA: Allyn & Bacon.

Corey. G. (1991). *Theory and practice of counseling and psychotherapy* (4th ed.). Pacific Grove, CA: Brooks/Cole.

Cross, T. L., Coleman, L. J., & Terhaar-Yonkers, M. (1991). The social cognition of gifted adolescents in schools: Managing the stigma of giftedness. *Journal for the Education of the Gifted, 15,* 44–55.

Culross, R. R. (1982). Developing the whole child: A developmental approach to guidance with the gifted. *Roeper Review, 5*(2), 24–26.

Dabrowski, K., with Kawczak, A., & Piechowski, M. M. (1970). *Mental growth through positive disintegration.* London: Gryf.

Dabrowski, K. (1972). *Psychoneurosis is not an illness.* London: Gryf.

Danziger, P. (1974). *The cat ate my gymsuit.* New York: Dell.

Delisle, J. R. (1986). Death with honors: Suicide and the gifted adolescent. *Journal of Counseling and Development, 64,* 558–560.

Delisle, J. R. (1990). The gifted adolescent at risk: Strategies and resources for suicide prevention among gifted youth. *Journal for the Education of the Gifted, 13,* 212–228.

Dinkmeyer, D. C., & Losoncy, L. E. (1980). *The encouragement book: Becoming a positive person.* Englewood Cliffs, NJ: Prentice-Hall.

Drews, E. (1972). *Learning together: How to foster creativity, self-fulfillment, social awareness in today's students and teachers.* Englewood Cliffs, NJ: Prentice-Hall.

Egan, G. (1990). *The skilled helper* (4th ed.). Pacific Grove, CA: Brooks/Cole.

Ellis, A. (1989). Rational-emotive therapy. In R. J. Corsini & D. Wedding (Eds.), *Current psychotherapies* (4th ed., pp. 197–238). Itasca, IL: F. E. Peacock.

Farrell, D. M. (1989). Suicide among gifted students. *Roeper Review, 11,* 134–139.

Flack, J. D., & Lamb, P. (1984). Making use of gifted characters in literature. *G/C/T,* Issue No. 34, 3–11.

Ford, M. A. (1989). Students' perceptions of affective issues impacting the social emotional development and school performance of gifted/talented youngsters. *Roeper Review, 11,* 131–134.

Frasier, M. M., & McCannon, C. (1981). Using bibliotherapy with gifted children. *Gifted Child Quarterly, 25,* 81–85.

Galbraith, J. (1985). The eight great gripes of gifted kids: Responding to special needs. *Roeper Review, 8,* 15–18.

Garfield, S. L. (1986). An eclectic psychotherapy. In J. C. Norcross (Ed.), *Handbook of eclectic psychotherapy* (pp. 132–162). New York: Brunner/Mazel.

Genshaft, J., & Broyles, J. (1991). Stress management and the gifted adolescent. In M. Bireley & J. Genshaft (Eds.), *Understanding the gifted adolescent* (pp. 76–87). New York: Teachers College Press.

Gilligan, C. (1991). Women's psychological development: Implications for psychotherapy. In C. Gilligan, A. G. Rogers, & D. L. Tolman (Eds.), *Women, girls & psychotherapy: Reframing resistance* (pp. 5–31). New York: Haworth Press.

Great Books Foundation. (1974). *Getting into books.* San Mateo, CA: Author.

Halsted, J. (1988). *Guiding gifted readers from pre-school to high school: A handbook for parents, teachers, counselors and librarians.* Columbus: Ohio Psychology.

Harkavy, J., & Asnis, G. (1985). Suicide attempts in adolescence. Prevalence and implications. *New England Journal of Medicine, 313,* 1290–1291.

Hauser, P., & Nelson, G. A. (1988). *Books for the gifted child.* New York: R. R. Bowker.

Hayes, M. L., & Sloat, R. S. (1990). Suicide and the gifted adolescent. *Journal for the Education of the Gifted, 13,* 229–244.

Hollingworth, L. S. (1942). *Children above 180 IQ Stanford-Binet: Origin and development.* Yonkers-on-Hudson, NY: World Book.

Hultgren, H. M. (1981). *Competencies for teachers of the gifted.* Unpublished doctoral dissertation, University of Denver.

Janos, P. M., Fung, H. C., & Robinson, N. M. (1985). Self-concept, self-esteem, and peer relations among gifted children who feel "different." *Gifted Child Quarterly, 29,* 78–82.

Jung, C. G. (1954). *The development of personality.* (R. F. C. Hull, Trans.) Bollingen Series 20. Princeton, NJ: Princeton University Press.

Kaiser, C. F., & Berndt, D. J. (1985). Predictors of loneliness in the gifted adolescent. *Gifted Child Quarterly, 29,* 74–77.

Karnes, F., & Oehler-Stinnet, J. (1986). Life events as stressors with gifted adolescents. *Psychology in the Schools, 23,* 406–414.

Keirsey, D., & Bates, M. (1978). *Please understand me: Character and temperament types.* Del Mar, CA: Prometheus Nemesis Books.

Kerr, B. A. (1991a). Educating gifted girls. In N. Colangelo & G. A. Davis (Eds.), *Handbook of gifted education* (pp. 402–415). Needham Heights, MA: Allyn & Bacon.

Kerr, B. A. (1991b). *A handbook for counseling the gifted and talented.* Alexandria, VA: American Counseling Association.

Kline, B. E., & Meckstroth, E. A. (1985). Understanding and encouraging the exceptionally gifted. *Roeper Review, 8,* 24–30.

Kline, B. E., & Short, E. B. (1991). Changes in emotional resilience: Gifted adolescent females. *Roeper Review, 13,* 118–121.

Konigsburg, E. L. (1970). *(George).* New York: Atheneum.

Lajoie, S., & Shore, B. (1981). Three myths? The overrepresentation of the gifted among dropouts, delinquents, and suicides. *Gifted Child Quarterly, 25,* 138–143.

LeGuin, U. (1976). *Very far away from anywhere else.* New York: Bantam.

L'Engle, M. (1962). *A wrinkle in time.* New York: Farrar, Straus & Giroux.

Leroux, J. (1986). Suicidal behavior and gifted adolescents. *Roeper Review, 9,* 77–79.

Meichenbaum, D. (1985). *Stress inoculation training.* New York: Pergamon Press.

Meichenbaum, D. (1986). Cognitive behavior modification. In F. H. Kanfer & A. P. Goldstein (Eds.), *Helping people change: A textbook of methods* (3rd ed., pp. 346–380). New York: Pergamon Press.

Ogburn Colangelo, M. K. (1989). Giftedness as multilevel potential: A clinical example. *Advanced Development, 1,* 87–100. [Originally appeared in its entirety in N. Colangelo & R. T. Zaffrann (Eds.), *New voices in counseling the gifted* (pp. 165–187). Dubuque, IA: Kendall/Hunt]

Parke, B. N. (1990). Who should counsel the gifted: The role of educational personnel. In J. VanTassel-Baska (Ed.), *A practical guide to counseling the gifted in a school setting* (2nd ed., pp. 31–39). Reston, VA: The Council for Exceptional Children.

Paterson, K. (1977). *Bridge to Teribithia.* New York: Thomas Y. Crowell.

Perls, F. (1973). *The Gestalt approach and eye witness to therapy.* New York: Bantam Books.

Perrone, P. A. (1986). Guidance needs of gifted children, adolescents, and adults. *Journal of Counseling and Development, 64,* 564–566.

Perry, S. M. (1985). *Giftedness: Living with it and liking it.* Greeley, CO: Autonomous Learner Publications (ALPS).

Petersen, A. (1988). Adolescent development. *Annual Review of Psychology, 39,* 583–607.

Polette, N. (1984). *Books and real life: A guide for gifted students and teachers.* Jefferson, NC: McFarland.

Polette, N., & Hamlin, M. (1980). *Exploring books with gifted children.* Littleton, CO: Libraries Unlimited.

Rogers, C. R. (1961). *On becoming a person: A therapist's view of psychotherapy.* Boston: Houghton Mifflin.

Ross, A. O. (1964). *The exceptional child in the family.* New York: Grune & Stratton.

Schroeder-Davis, S. (1990). *Affirming giftedness through fiction.* Unpublished doctoral dissertation, College of St. Thomas, St. Paul, MN.

Silverman, L. K. (1989). The visual-spatial learner. *Preventing School Failure, 34*(1), 15–20.

Sisk, D. A. (1982). Caring and sharing: Moral development of gifted students. *The Elementary School Journal, 82,* 221–229.

Spredemann-Dreyer, S. S. (1989). *The Bookfinder 4: When kids need books.* Circle Pines, MN: American Guidance Service.

Strip, C., Swassing, R., & Kidder, R. (1991). Female adolescents counseling female adolescents: A first step in emotional crisis intervention. *Roeper Review, 13,* 124–128.

Thompson, C. L., & Rudolph, L. B. (1983). *Counseling children.* Pacific Grove, CA: Brooks/Cole.

Tolan, S. S. (1986). *Pride of the peacock.* New York: Scribner's.

Turecki, S., & Tonner, L. (1985). *The difficult child.* New York: Bantam.

Tway, E. (1981). *Reading ladders for human relations* (6th ed.). Washington, DC: American Council on Education.

VanTassel-Baska, J. (1991). Teachers as counselors for gifted students. In R. M. Milgram (Ed.), *Counseling gifted and talented children: A guide for teachers, counselors, and parents* (pp. 37–52). Norwood, NJ: Ablex.

Webb, J. T., Meckstroth, E. A., & Tolan, S. S. (1982). *Guiding the gifted child: A practical source for parents and teachers.* Columbus: Ohio Psychology.

Yadusky-Holahan, M., & Holahan, W. (1983). The effect of academic stress upon the anxiety and depression levels of gifted high school students. *Gifted Child Quarterly, 27,* 42–46.

5

Group Counseling with Gifted Students

Nicholas Colangelo and Jean Sunde Peterson

One of the idiosyncrasies of schooling is the overt and covert effort to keep gifted students isolated. There is worry that identifying students as gifted and then grouping them together in any way might lead to elitism, track systems, and negative feelings in students not so identified. The debates on these issues abound, with many opinions based on single-case experiences, emotional reactions, and little systematic evidence.

Grouping gifted students appears to be most palatable when oriented toward academic areas such as mathematics or reading, though even then it is sometimes suspect. When gifted students are grouped for a math class, they interact about mathematics and motivate and stimulate each other. We consider these to be positive outcomes that justify grouping by academic content.

However, interactions focusing on academic content are not enough for maximal development of gifted students. These students also need opportunities to interact with their peers for self-discovery and communication of interpersonal and intrapersonal issues. In the school setting, gifted students have considerably more opportunity to learn about science than to learn about the "self"—at least more opportunity to *discuss* science. It is our observation that many gifted students are smarter about coursework than about themselves. They often lack the human relations and leadership skills necessary to using their talents (Blackburn & Erickson, 1986). They sometimes lack the wisdom needed for wise academic planning (Colangelo & Kerr, 1990; Kerr, 1981, 1991; Kerr & Colangelo, 1988; Perrone, 1986, 1991). Hypersensitivity often contributes to difficulties during developmental transitions, makes the gifted vulnerable when there is family dysfunction, and contributes to high levels of self-criticism and perfectionism and problems in relationships. In fact, they might be handicapped by their giftedness in interpersonal relationships. In addition, their high capability and sometimes unique learning styles often make them fit poorly into the system.

However, they also *share* many concerns with their age peers. Certainly they are not exempt from the problems associated with adolescence, including mood swings and depression. Just like others, their families move, friends move away, parents divorce and remarry, close relatives die, and relationships break up. They might live recklessly for a time, experimenting with alcohol, other drugs, and sex, or flirting with crime. They might develop eating disorders. They might have relatively weak areas academically. They might lack motivation and eventually might even drop out of school. They might not get along with their parents or siblings and might even suffer from abuse. Like others their age, they are trying to navigate successfully the transition to adulthood.

Much of counseling in schools is problem-oriented. Counselors spend considerable time handling problem situations for students in trouble. This is legitimate and necessary. However, we advocate for more developmental approaches to counseling (see Colangelo, 1991), whereby the focus is on establishing an atmosphere that is conducive to exploration of self and to counseling functions that provide opportunities for social and emotional growth, rather than simply corrective measures.

We can offer no more powerful tool for the social and emotional growth of gifted students than group counseling. Group counseling is a rich arena where students can share with one another their struggles and questions about growing up and about what it means to be "gifted." They seldom, if ever, have such an opportunity.

However, we do not believe that simply "sitting around" talking about feelings and values is enough. Group counseling is a structured situation with a trained leader, for example, a counselor or trained group facilitator who has knowledge of both gifted children and group dynamics.

WHAT CAN COUNSELING GROUPS DO FOR GIFTED STUDENTS?

Students grow by having opportunities to discuss feelings and perceptions in an atmosphere of trust and understanding. They also need to share with peers— and "peers" for gifted students are those who have had similar experiences and who can respond at the same level. To think of peers as only age-mates is a trivialization of the concept. A peer is more a soul-mate or mind-mate than an age-mate. Gifted students might not have the opportunity to talk to one another about what it means to be gifted or how it feels to understand what many age-mates cannot seem to grasp. Even when they experience many of the same problems as less capable students, they are hesitant to discuss them with those they feel cannot understand them. That hesitancy is significant in considering whether gifted students should be in mixed-ability counseling groups. Differences in verbal ability or differences in ability to think complexly might have something to do with their reluctance to self-disclose in such situations. They are much more willing to discuss problem situations openly with those of similar intellect, whether adult or age-peer. A homogeneous counseling group, according to ability, is often the only avenue to such communication.

Gifted students sometimes "hide" who they are, including their intellect. They also often hide distress and fears behind a facade of self-assurance. In group counseling they are encouraged to share their vulnerabilities and doubts, their strengths and solidity, and their perhaps unique passions with others who understand and accept them. When gifted students are given a chance to meet regularly as a small group for the purpose of self-discovery, for most of them it is their first opportunity to share with "peers." If a rationale is needed for group counseling with gifted students, it is that in the course of school life, such a situation usually does not happen naturally.

Counseling groups can take gifted students momentarily out of the competitive academic realm, where personal issues are not dealt with, and give them an experience in the less judgmental affective realm, where no one dominates and where no grades are given. In these groups, problems common to the gifted, including insomnia, dealing with their own and others' expectations, and perhaps not "fitting in," can be discussed openly. Groups, when they are effectively led, can help competitive and perfectionistic gifted students to move out of "one-up," academic-issues-oriented, performance-based interactions to an affirmation of humanness and commonality. That kind of affirmation is important for success in present and future relationships.

Likewise, gifted students who have not embraced the inherently competitive academic environment can find, in nurturant groups, affirmation for intelligence that may or may not be affirmed elsewhere. Nonschool achievement can be communicated and celebrated, and various *kinds* of intelligence can be recognized (see Gardner, 1983; Ramos-Ford & Gardner, 1991). Personal worth can be defined in terms other than academic results. An atmosphere of a new kind of risk taking, which is difficult for many perfectionistic gifted children, can be created together and enjoyed.

Achievers and underachievers can break down stereotypes of each other in counseling groups. When underachievers share fears and disillusionment, they are seen as more than just stereotypical bravado, insolence, laziness, or rebellion, if, in fact, one of these is their "label." Achievers become more than a gradepoint.

Groups can also allow those who are perpetually "nice"—not necessarily ungenuinely—to relax and express anger or frustration. Groups can allow those who are usually negative, rebellious, or hostile to express those *and* positive feelings in an atmosphere of acceptance. Those with tense anger under a tight "lid" can be encouraged to "put words on it."

Peterson (1990) speaks of what groups of gifted high school students typically communicate:

> I have learned that articulating both strengths and weaknesses is difficult for most, and that many have a hard time "selling themselves" for fear of appearing arrogant. Certain "weaknesses" are common: many procrastinate, are hypersensitive and highly self-critical, lack self-confidence, worry a lot, and are pessimistic, messy, argumentative, shy, impatient, and stressed. These qualities are sometimes a matter of shame to them. The chance to hear that others share these traits is helpful. Most are astounded that everyone feels shy in certain circumstances, for example. Most assume that everyone else has it more "together" than they themselves do.
>
> ...Many receive mixed signals from parents: "be social, but get the grades." Most prefer to sit in the rear of the classroom, and many never volunteer in classroom discussions. There is a great fear of being misunderstood. Most want "baking time" for their thoughts and feel teachers want short, quick, superficial answers in class. It is also difficult for them to ask for help, and they perceive that teachers feel "you should know this if you're so bright." There is a strong need to "be known" by teachers. They perceive that teachers "like" them when they talk to them about other things or call them by name in the halls, or call on them in class. Most, however, feel that teachers are reluctant to give them "strokes." They recommend that teachers "look twice" at the students who are argumentative, creative in doodling, resistant to homework, and daydreaming in class, and yet doing well on tests.
>
> There is a strong need for them to learn how to relax, since their antennae work overtime. Most of these students say they appreciate teachers who engage their minds in the classroom: they don't enjoy being bored. They are very concerned about finding their special niche in the adult world. Their multi-talentedness makes choices extremely difficult, and, perfectionists that they are, they assume that they must find the "perfect" college, profession, and mate. (pp. 21–22)

The most common feedback at the end of a year of growing intimacy and comfort in discussion groups is "I never knew anyone else felt like that—thought like that." The distressing self-centeredness of adolescents, who self-consciously imagine criticism in an "imaginary audience" (Elkind, 1981), is dangerous, in that lonely self-criticism and the perceived negative judgment of others can contribute to despair. Group discussions, when they are carefully, sensitively, and equitably led, can normalize the "weird thoughts" of adolescents and let tense shoulders relax.

SHOULD THEY BE CALLED "COUNSELING GROUPS"?

Gifted students are often reluctant to go to counselors. It is not that they have less need. One bright senior girl commented, "We just hide it better." If "gifted" refers to all with high potential, and not just those who are motivated enough to achieve well, then a great number of gifted students are as much in need of support and guidance as anyone in the school system. Certainly it is not just underachievers who have counseling needs; achievers, too, have both unique and common social and emotional concerns. Both groups must deal with the expectations of others and expectations within themselves. Faculty and administrators should not assume that either group is exempt from family dysfunction, conflict with parents or siblings, devastating events involving loss, transitions related to divorce and remarriage, relationship problems, depression, and general self-doubt. Both groups have a heightened sensitivity that sometimes makes developmental and environmental transitions more difficult than they are for others.

However, these students are aware of the stigma of psychological help, and many believe counseling is only for "others." Too many feel they should solve their problems themselves, given their high capability. Furthermore, whether they are valued highly for their minds and achievement or are hassled for *not* "meeting their potential," most do not seek out adults to express their fears and discouragements, stresses and sadness. Achievers often doubt that anyone understands that they might have self-doubt, and underachievers often assume that either everyone is too concerned or not enough concerned about their well-being.

Even when they know they should ask advice, they are sometimes hesitant, as expressed by one senior boy just before graduation: "Counselors have to devote so much time to problem kids. I was really worried about college, but I felt I had no adult that I had a right to seek advice from. Discussion group seemed almost like therapy for me. The divorce discussion was especially helpful." His family situation had left him with no ready assistance outside of school, and teachers and counselors assumed he was "taken care of."

These issues underscore the fact that there is a problem in how to advertise the groups. Calling them "counseling" groups may get no response at all. In our experience, the use of any descriptor associated with counseling or counselors seems to *turn away* gifted students. Having the gifted education teacher co-facilitate groups with a respected counselor is one alternative that helps to remove stigma. Obviously, if groups are used in a nonschool context, or if there is mutual agreement about their therapeutic purpose, less hesitancy about the term *counseling* is warranted.

In a school setting, calling them "discussion" groups and bringing students together individually or in small or large groups for a detailed explanation of the group activity seem to yield better results. Achievers can be told that groups deal with the "stress of expectations" and guidance about friends and academic choices. Underachievers may respond best when approached as "interesting," "complex" people, who can add immensely to a group of students with high capability, who will come together to discuss common concerns with "intellectual nimbleness." They can be told that it will be a nongraded, noncompetitive, relaxed activity, where they can learn from each other, and where each person will be valued.

Achieving high school students can even be enticed by "If I can get to know you better, I can write more than just a generic recommendation for you." This thought has also been helpful: "I've never respected students less from getting to know them better." It has been our experience that students have a desire to be acknowledged on a personal level by some adult in the system. The group situation provides a valuable opportunity for this to happen.

For our purposes here, we will continue to refer to the groups as "counseling groups," since, in fact, they serve that purpose. In practice, however, we recommend using "discussion groups" to identify or promote them.

GETTING STARTED

At the secondary level, it is best to make the groups voluntary. They can be scheduled during a lunch period or study hall or before or after school hours, beginning perhaps the third or fourth week of the school year, after initial communication to prospective participants, registration, and "sorting" according to class schedules have been completed. In gifted programs where students already meet regularly for various classes or activities, teachers might include weekly counseling groups. Students should be informed about the purpose and possible areas of discussion before the groups begin, however.

Students may not know each other at the outset, being brought together only because they share an available time slot and giftedness. Because dialogue is therefore sometimes difficult to establish without some prompt or catalytic information, especially when some feel both skeptical and vulnerable, it is a good idea to have a focus for each session. It is important that initial sessions deal with topics that are both nonthreatening and stimulating. Usually, dealing with "giftedness" is a good way to begin, "getting it out in the open" for both achievers and underachievers, and forcing all to acknowledge it and hopefully to affirm it as a given. They enjoy discussing the multidimensional facets of giftedness, including their decisions about how they will and will not demonstrate their giftedness. Initial questioning might include the following:

- ❑ What does it mean to be gifted?
- ❑ What do your parents think about your being gifted? Your teachers? Your peers? Your siblings?
- ❑ How is being gifted an advantage for you? A disadvantage?
- ❑ Have you ever deliberately hidden your giftedness? If so, how? Why?
- ❑ Would you rather be a gifted girl or a gifted boy? Why?
- ❑ How would it be (or how is it) to be gifted and African American? Latin American? Asian American? Native American?
- ❑ What are common stereotypes of gifted students? Do any fit you? Which ones definitely do not?
- ❑ When did you first realize you were more intelligent than most others your age? Did knowing that change anything in your life?
- ❑ Is there a time in school (elementary, middle school, high school) when it is especially difficult to be gifted? Easier? Why?

These questions are by no means exhaustive, and they invariably lead to other related questions and concerns.

Pertinent to these questions, it might be noted that a study of attitudes of gifted students about their own giftedness (Kerr, Colangelo, & Gaeth, 1988) found that they saw giftedness as an academic advantage, but a social disadvantage. Colangelo (1991) reported that groups of gifted students talked about "deliberate underachievement," i.e., purposely getting lower grades so that peers would be more accepting of them. Studies concerning gender and ethnicity (Colangelo & Kerr, 1990; Kerr & Colangelo, 1988) show that both aspects are important as related to giftedness. Students find it easy and stimulating to discuss such issues, and they gain insight into these areas through discussion.

Most respond well to this kind of beginning. The fact that the facilitator appears to see giftedness as worthy of discussion—and worthy of serious concern—sends a powerful message of affirmation to both achieving and underachieving gifted students. Most will return for the second session.

Faculty may worry that the groups are simply vehicles for "teacher-bashing," and parents sometimes wonder if they are used to air family linen. Therefore, it is important to inform both groups, in newsletters or through conversation, about general and specific topics that are discussed. Furthermore, some gifted students themselves do not appreciate "just rapping." Many are reluctant to give up even one hour per week for unfocused repartee. These, who are perhaps quite "structured" in lifestyle and in personality, like to experience something specific.

"Counseling" is basically "talking together" in an atmosphere of honesty and respect. Gifted students need to know that. No counselor or teacher should approach group counseling with the objective that students should be "fixed" or "repaired." Whether the leader is a trained counselor or a gifted education teacher with good instincts and sensitivity, good discussion groups can serve an important counseling function—and can also communicate that counseling can be a valid, meaningful, edifying, and inspiring activity for people of high capability. It should not be assumed that all students will be eager to participate. However, careful and sensitive promotion of the groups and able, responsive leadership, session by session, can establish group interaction that can be an especially meaningful experience in a gifted program.

INSTRUCTIONAL OBJECTIVES

The following are some instructional objectives of counseling groups for gifted children:

1. To help gifted students understand what being "gifted" means.
2. To help gifted achievers and underachievers discover commonalities and break down stereotypes of each other.
3. To help gifted students gain comfort with their capabilities and

develop coping strategies for dealing with the burdens of capability.
4. To help them understand and deal with their own and others' expectations.
5. To help them deal with their multipotentiality regarding career goals and make good decisions (e.g., college and career).
6. To help them deal with procrastination and perfectionism.
7. To help them learn to enjoy the present, instead of being preoccupied with, and anxious about, the future.
8. To help them learn to seek help when it is needed and to see counseling in a less stigmatized way.
9. To help gifted boys and girls deal with issues related to gender.
10. To help them explore ethnic issues related to giftedness.
11. To help those who are overly concerned with pleasing others to pay attention to "self."
12. To help them understand teachers and the realities of dealing with the broad population in the classroom.
13. To help them solve problems involving conflicts with teachers and other students and deal successfully with "the system."
14. To help them understand their own learning and thinking styles and how these have an impact on their interacton with others in the school setting.

The following are instructional objectives that apply to all students, but which are also important for the gifted:

1. To help them learn to articulate feelings.
2. To help them gain insights about their interaction with family, peers, and teachers.
3. To help them with developmental issues, such as physical changes, gaining an identity, and separation from family.
4. To help them deal with stress.
5. To help them deal with family issues, including conflict with parents and siblings.
6. To help them develop social skills, including being able to read interpersonal nuances accurately and give and receive compliments.
7. To help them develop both self-awareness and self-esteem.

SETTING THE AGENDA FOR THE GROUPS

A facilitator must be wise and sensitive both when setting a group agenda and when leading sessions. When the purpose of the groups is to provide experience in articulating feelings and personal concerns, the students can establish both content and pace to a great extent. Ideally, that should be the case. However, the leader will need to be alert to potential problems in this regard.

Content should, of course, be appropriate and helpful to all participants. Therefore, a few dominant personalities must not be allowed to set the agenda for everyone. There is also a need to be equitable in discussion, and the facilitator can help dominant personalities give shy or quiet students adequate opportunity to express themselves and to be assisted in problem solving. At all levels, but especially with younger children, the facilitator needs to guide the discovery process carefully. Particularly in the school setting, care must be taken not to frighten away those who are unsure about the experience.

The facilitator must monitor nonverbals in the group in order to detect discomfort or desire to speak, encourage contributions from everyone, protect/ prevent them from being indiscreet in revelations, remind them periodically about confidentiality, and steer the conversation gently and unobtrusively toward appropriate closure. All of these tasks require a great deal of concentration and sensitivity in a leader.

We recommend that the groups be somewhat focused in content, but flexible. Being able to describe various content areas helps "recruitment" at the secondary level in a school setting. It helps to be able to list them for doubting faculty members, administrators, or parents. Focus also makes it easier to remember strands from previous sessions that need to be brought up again. In addition, focus helps to satisfy those students who like to "cover something specific" or feel that they "got something out of" each session.

Sample topics that can be adapted for use at any age level are these·

1. Giftedness—what it is; what the concerns are; what the stereotypes are; how others feel about it; how we feel about it.
2. Where gifted children can find unconditional support.
3. Dealing with our own and others' expectations.
4. Stress—what it is; coping strategies; sorting out stress points; deciding what can and cannot be changed; looking at "stress rhythms" at home and at school.
5. Anger—learning to recognize it, express it, talk about it.
6. Sadness and depression—learning to articulate feelings during "low times"; dealing with others who are sad.
7. Relationships with others—what a friend is; how one "makes friends"; how we can "read" what others do not put into words.
8. When we worry that we are "too much"—or too shy, too lazy, too strange, too perfectionistic, too nice, too talkative, too assertive, etc.
9. Perfectionism—what it is; what is "sacrificed"; what it affects.
10. "Passion areas"—dinosaurs, robots, music, history, space....
11. Change—dealing with it; learning to express feelings about it.
12. Giving support to others—learning how to give compliments and other verbal and nonverbal support to classmates, family, teachers; learning how to build bridges for mutual support.
13. Where we feel comfortable and where we do not; where we feel

"smart" and where we feel "stupid"; where we feel confident and where we do not.

14. Where we need courage in life.
15. Dealing with family transitions (divorce, remarriage, moving, death, unemployment, illness, etc.).
16. Heroes—who are they?
17. Optimism vs. pessimism—ways of looking at life.
18. "Intensity cycles" in gifted children regarding strong interests.
19. Having friends of different ages.
20. What can and cannot be changed in our lives.
21. Being afraid.
22. Tact—what it is; who has modeled it for us; why it is important in social interaction; how to ask, and not demand.
23. Appropriate assertiveness for having needs met.
24. Leaning on others for support—developing relationships with peers, teachers, counselors, mentors.
25. Learning and thinking styles; classroom behavior.
26. Learning to deal effectively with "the system."

High school students can add topics related to college and career concerns, sexuality and adolescent relationships, goals and expectations for adulthood, moral decision making, sex role expectations, and debatable issues, such as whether the gifted have a greater responsibility to society than others do.

Middle school students, with their concerns about finding personal identity, might explore topics related to image, self-perception versus others' perception, mood range, rumors and gossip, popularity, maturity, and "being difficult to raise."

Expectations regarding insight and abstraction should differ according to age and grade level. Some topics challenge them to explore areas they are not used to contemplating, and these might require "wait time" for thoughtful response. However, these students generally do not find it difficult to generate animated discussion, especially when topics are introduced effectively. The challenge is usually *ending* the discussions, rather than starting them.

Most gifted students seem to feel that focus is good. Many have said that they would probably never discuss many of the areas on their own, and they become informed through the insistence on focus, yet in a flexible, conversational atmosphere. The focus also demands that difficult areas be pursued and not avoided. However, focus does not mean that new strands cannot be followed. One senior recommended, as he concluded three years in groups, "One thing you absolutely cannot change is the form of the discussions. If you start talking about one thing and end up talking about something else, go with the flow. That is the way to get the most insight."

We have found that it is helpful not to announce in advance the "focus for the day." Many topics do not appeal to students at first glance, but can become quite engrossing during a group session. Eventually, students begin to trust the judgment of the facilitator regarding topics. Students can also be asked for input regarding possible topics, some of which might require research on the part of the facilitator and might necessitate a week's delay. There should also be the option that a critical, current, personal student issue within the group can become the focus of that day. If there is a trauma in the school, groups are an ideal setting for letting students vent feelings related to it. Most important is the need for the facilitator to maintain a nonthreatening, responsive, attentive, courteous, respectful atmosphere in the group, one that can nevertheless accommodate intense emotion when it arises.

One graduating senior, a veteran group member, put it well: "We were never told to 'pipe down' or 'stay on track.' If we happened to go off the subject, we just went with it. And many of our better discussions happened like that." A facilitator can deftly guide discussions to accommodate a multitude of strands, leading the group to closure and unobtrusively helping them to stay somewhat focused. The students might not even notice that guidance.

WHAT MAKES THE IDEAL GROUP?

The best groups in our experience with the gifted have included both achievers and underachievers. Those achievers with high perfectionism and competitiveness might be articulate about political issues, academic matters, and possibly other people, but often are not experienced in, and are not secure about, expressing their own social and emotional concerns. Underachievers, like achievers, come in many varieties, of course, but often they are particularly sensitive and expressive about emotions, and that can enhance group interaction. Perhaps they have had more overt personal conflict with parents and teachers over academic matters. Perhaps others have assumed feelings in them more so than with high achievers. Mixed groups give underachievers a chance to be known by achievers, and achievers have an opportunity to learn to know those with priorities different from theirs. They can compare stress levels, values, and coping styles. Both seem to benefit from contact with each other.

Even though gifted children may have intellect and interests similar to others across several age levels, for interaction about social and emotional matters it is best to strive for homogeneity regarding age. In high school, sophomores do not respond to specific college and career topics as seniors do. Juniors often are more concerned about managing the new stress of advanced courses and pressures for performance than about the crunch of college applications and college selection. In the middle school, seventh graders can have social and emotional concerns that are quite different from eighth-graders'. Small schools, however, often have the problem of not having enough gifted students to create groups that are homogeneous in age. In this case, identification can be broadened to include others of *nearly* the same age level.

It is also best, according to our experience, to mix genders for most purposes. Same-sex groups miss the opportunity to learn about the opposite sex through forthright discussion. Particularly with males, same-sex groups tend to be more protective of image and therefore less able to remove protective facades than mixed groups. At all ages, mixing genders offers a chance for both to establish honest, open exchange and for female students to practice appropriate assertiveness in a group situation including male students. It also offers an opportunity to practice social skills. The particular concerns of gifted boys and gifted girls can be dealt with beneficially in both same-sex and mixed-sex groups. Certainly, some situations and some issues make single-sex discussions more appropriate.

Optimal group size seems to vary according to age level and composition of the group. At the high school level, twelve seems to be maximum, and eight minimum. Sometimes when the number is below eight, familiarity and lack of seriousness can become a problem. When there are more than twelve, it is difficult to hear from everyone adequately in a given session.

At the junior high or middle school level, groups should be kept at approximately eight, since class periods are usually shorter, and students often need time to articulate complex thoughts and attain depth. At the elementary level, six to eight seems to be a good range for similar reasons. For groups with a distractible and "kinetic" majority, it sometimes is best to keep the numbers around six. For groups where such students are not the majority, the presence of a large number of less distractible students is beneficial.

We have found that forty to sixty minutes is an appropriate length for meeting time and a length that is possible in most settings. Shorter segments usually do not provide adequate time to develop depth in discussion, and longer meetings go beyond the attention spans and physical comfort levels of many.

STRUCTURING THE GROUP SESSION

In order to communicate "safety" for comfortable dialogue, we have found that having something that requires brief written responses helps students to sort, assess, and objectify feelings prior to beginning the discussion. That is, of course, not always necessary or even helpful, particularly when *expressing* emotions is beneficial. However, asking students to answer questions about when they were last sad for more than a day, for example, among perhaps a dozen questions about physical and behavioral manifestations of stress, gives them time to ponder the topic for the day while "settling in." Students can also be asked about their usual classroom behaviors, seating preferences, interaction with teachers, parental expectations, stress points, perfectionism, strengths and weaknesses, sources of frustration and anger, self-perception, heroes, mixed messages, loss, loneliness, fears, and anxieties in this manner. Filling out a brief questionnaire seems to give students a chance to look inside quietly and focus on the topic for the session, while nevertheless paying attention to incidental conversation and repartee. Invariably, when the discussion begins, they are ready to share, and they are eager to hear what others have written. They can then interact spontaneously—beyond the questionnaire. Questionnaires seem to promote seriousness and genuineness. We recommend that the facilitator also fill out whatever form is being used, in order to serve as a role model and to communicate that there are commonalities across age categories as well as within them.

Going around the group for comments based on questionnaire responses also ensures that *everyone* has a chance to develop skills in articulating complex feelings orally. The facilitator needs to make sure that all are heard from. It should be pointed out, however, that no one is *required* to speak. Anyone can "pass" on any item or in any discussion. Sometimes it takes several weeks before a particular student shares a thought spontaneously. Usually, however, all will share something written in response to a carefully written questionnaire item. Apparently that seems less threatening than informal dialogue to reticent group members—especially at the outset. Telling them they can "edit" questionnaire responses, if they choose, works well at older age levels for encouraging reluctant students. Most groups, and most students, share willingly. However, the shy, the threatened, and the skeptical, particularly, often respond best initially when they can "report" what they have written. Obviously, if using questionnaires seems altogether unnecessary for certain groups or if students become resistant to using them, they should not be used.

For some topics, perhaps five or ten minutes of information by the facilitator is needed to lay the groundwork for discussion—for example, in regard to depression, eating disorders, nonverbal messages, perfectionism, stress, or date rape, all of which are topics particularly pertinent for gifted adolescents. Compliance and lack of assertiveness make many gifted girls vulnerable to date rape. Perfectionism has more dimensions than most have thought about. Some gifted individuals are not adept at reading nonverbal messages and need information about both what nonverbals are and what importance they have. Students also probably could use more information about eating disorders, which can occur among the gifted. Informational prompts of many kinds can be effective catalysts for discussion.

BRINGING IN SPEAKERS

Especially for older students, guest speakers from the community can provide insights regarding career satisfaction, career paths, being "square pegs in round holes," struggles with moral and ethical issues in the adult world, meeting a "nemesis," or dealing with multipotentiality. College students home for school breaks might shed light on college adjustment, changing majors, finding friends, developing identity in a new setting, academic challenges, and separating from parents healthily. Mental health professions might speak about family issues related to adolescence. Students can ask questions in interview fashion, or questions can be submitted to the speakers in advance, and the facilitator can guide the discussion. Subsequent group meetings can involve discussion of insights gained from the speakers.

In addition, speakers from various ethnic backgrounds might discuss how various cultures view giftedness and what gifts are particularly valued in these cultures. Counseling groups that are multicultural can use group members as resources. Groups are an ideal setting for both consciousness-raising in regard to understanding and tolerance and for exploration of various cultural attitudes.

GROUP DYNAMICS AND GROUP COUNSELING TECHNIQUES

Many counselors have been trained to use their skills for individual counseling in a group setting and call it "group counseling." Group counseling is quite distinct from individual counseling, although they are not mutually exclusive. While many of the skills gained in doing one-on-one counseling are useful and applicable to group work, such skills are not the essence of group counseling. To rely on individual skills in a group setting is not to make full use of group dynamics. By analogy, it would be like driving a four-cylinder engine with only two cylinders functioning.

The essence of group counseling is to *transform* students from *spectators* into *participants*. While there is evidence of the positive effects of being a spectator in a group, it pales compared to the evidence of being a participant (Yalom, 1985). To be a spectator in a group means to observe and listen, but to be only tangentially associated with the topic of discussion. A group is not effective when the primary role of its members is as spectators.

A counselor can transform spectators into participants by taking opportunities to connect any topic of discussion to individual members. A specific example, using the concepts of *vertical* and *horizontal* self-disclosure, may be helpful here.

A student may be talking about her feelings about being labeled "gifted." The counselor can ask her questions to help her elaborate on these feelings: "How long have you felt this way?" "Is it changing at all for you?" "Who knows that you feel this way?" These questions help the student talk more about her feelings and lead to *vertical* self-disclosure because they help to "build" more information on how the student feels about labeling. As this "mound" of information is built, the rest of the students in the group are listening, perhaps nodding in agreement, and being empathic. Theirs is primarily a spectator role, albeit a sympathetic and interested one, in that they are observing this interaction between the one student and counselor.

In this same situation, the counselor can transform the group members from spectators to participants by moving from vertical self-disclosure to *horizontal*. Instead of asking for more information on the feelings about labeling, the counselor can ask the student, "Who in this group do you think feels the same way you do?" "Who in this group do you think feels most different from you about labeling?" These questions are horizontal in that they connect students to one another. The students in the group are no longer simply listening to the girl talk about labeling (spectators); now they are actively involved (participants) in their own feelings about labeling and perceptions.

In every group there are countless opportunities to take what a student says and make horizontal connections. Every horizontal connection makes better use of group dynamics and generates more energy and participation.

Another technique for transforming spectators into participants is to focus on the group as an *entity* rather than as individuals. Counselors are trained to attend to individual comments and nonverbals. However, in addition to such individual attending, group counselors need to attend to the group as a whole. The counselor needs to pay attention to the "atmosphere" of a group. Is the group excited? Is it enjoying itself? Is it trusting? For a counselor to address the group as an entity enhances each member's feeling of being part of the group. For example, a comment by the counselor such as "I think we really enjoy each other during group time" addresses the collective, rather than a particular student. Such statements help everyone feel a greater participation and ownership in the group. If the group is going well, all feel they have contributed. If the group is struggling or stuck, then all are part of the process. Group entity statements help members feel they are constantly contributing to the life of the group. There are countless occasions in the course of group counseling for a counselor to address the "group as an entity." Each time, the emphasis is on the *participatory* aspect of the group, rather than on the *spectator* aspect.

One last technique focuses not so much on transforming spectators into participants as on helping students to pay better attention to the processes in their group. In perhaps the last three to five minutes of every session, the counselor can ask one student to "*process* for the group"—i.e., articulate to everyone what he or she thought happened in the group as it went about its task for that session. This is "group process time."

This simple technique accomplishes several important tasks. First, in time, it gives each student a chance to share what he or she has observed in the group. It also offers other students a chance to hear the perspective of one member on what happened during a session. To paraphrase T. S. Eliot, one can have the experience, but miss the meaning. This technique minimizes the possibility of missing the meaning. Second, ending every session with group process time is a good way to summarize and "tie up" the session. It also prevents some last-minute concerns from coming up that cannot be discussed for lack of time. Third, the group process time can be an excellent stem for the start of the next group session. For instance, it is not uncommon in groups to have a student start a session with "When Bob did group process last week, he said some things that I saw very differently. I want to talk about how I saw them." With that, the group session is off to a good start.

TIPS FOR PROSPECTIVE FACILITATORS

Group work about affective concerns can teach gifted education teachers or counselors about gifted children in ways that textbooks cannot. It can be "mutuality in learning" in the best sense. In fact, it has been our experience that presenting the groups as a means for "teaching me about kids like you" is effective for encouraging students to participate. That approach also encourages the facilitator to be quiet and listen to the students, something that is often difficult for adults to do.

There is perhaps a need to include one cautionary note at this point. Gifted education teachers who do not have counselor training should be instructed about counseling ethics, particularly in regard to confidentiality, since that might become an issue for students, facilitator, faculty, parents, or administration as a group develops. Students must be able to trust the facilitator absolutely in order for groups to function optimally. However, they should be advised early that the leader is a mandatory reporter for child abuse or neglect and for anyone who is deemed to be a danger to self or others. It is advisable for the leader to obtain parental permission in writing for participation, and such a signed document might include references to confidentiality. Care in that regard usually alleviates future problems, especially if there are parental questions about what might have been said in a group. If the facilitator is a trusted individual, parents are usually glad that their children have such an opportunity for increasing self-awareness and support.

Counselor training, or at least some degree of academic work in counseling, is encouraged for leaders of groups. However, a teacher who is sensitive to the needs of the gifted, who is neither intimidated by them nor in awe of them, who does not have personal "agendas" with them, and who is willing to "learn by doing" can manage discussion groups for gifted students quite adequately. It is advisable then, as mentioned earlier, that they are not called "counseling" groups officially, that the noncounselor leader does not declare that he or she is a counselor, and that students are not led to believe that the leader is a trained counselor. Because gifted education teachers are probably trusted as understanding the special needs of the gifted, gifted students are usually willing to participate openly. One student put it this way: "It is nothing more than having a person there to talk with who has dealt exclusively with people who are similar to you—not with the whole student body." That seems to be the key to having enough trust to let down the guard and "be real."

We recommend highly that noncounselor leaders seek advice from counselors on the staff, if they do not co-facilitate groups with a trained counselor from the outset. Attending skills, basic listening skills, monitoring of nonverbals, and strategies and techniques for eliciting discussion and gaining closure can be discussed and modeled by the trained counselor. These can then be practiced.

It is good to *process* the group experience now and then, asking the students for feedback about how they felt during particular segments of the session and assessing group dynamics in general. However, it is our experience that students resist whatever makes the experience "self-conscious," and a facilitator must therefore be sensitive about when and how often such processing should take place. Processing is particularly important when there are times of tension within the group, when someone is suggesting dropping the activity, when someone's mannerisms or responses become an issue for the group, when the group has a difficult time generating discussion, or when the leader needs suggestions about how to facilitate interaction more effectively. Some groups need to process more often than others.

It is probably inevitable that there will be individual spin-off from the groups. When there is trust established between the facilitator and a particular student, there is likelihood that the student will seek out the leader individually if there is a crisis or special need. At these times, too, the noncounselor facilitator ought to be in touch with the student's counselor for advice and direction. If a student approaches the facilitator outside of the group with "I need to talk to you," the response should be "Of course." However, it might be prudent to remind the student, "Remember, I'm not a trained counselor, but I'll certainly listen, and we can always check with your counselor if we think it necessary." It is imperative to recognize one's limits of expertise and to make a referral when appropriate. Staff counselors or administrators can provide guidelines for referral. Since one can never anticipate what might occur in or outside of a group, it is best to be informed about options in regard to certain situations that might arise.

It is helpful for group leaders to bring together the school counselors to explain the plan for group work with gifted students. It is appropriate to remind them that gifted children are often reluctant to see counselors or therapists, and that the group experience is important, both for helping children learn to articulate personal concerns and for lessening the stigma associated with asking for help.

The presence of counseling groups for gifted students in a school setting sends many messages to others in that environment. It communicates something about needs of the gifted. It models primary prevention in counseling. It is also good public relations for a gifted program (Peterson, in press).

Most facilitators find that leading a group is both easier and more difficult than anticipated. Experience is a good teacher, and the satisfaction in gaining expertise and comfort as a leader can be immense. Gifted children are complex. A group facilitator must be able, or must learn, to accommodate their strengths as well as their fragility and their critical and self-critical natures. Gifted students are eager to make sense of themselves and their world, and they need more guidance than even teachers who work with them every day are likely to guess. The group experience can be invaluable for them, and it can also provide an invaluable opportunity for the facilitator to gain insights about them both collectively and as individuals.

CONCLUSION

Group counseling can effectively help gifted students develop socially and emotionally. Yet, it is rare that gifted students have opportunities to engage in group activities when the primary purpose is personal growth, not academic development. Group counseling is a unique counseling situation that requires specific knowledge and skills to make optimal use of group dynamics, which is the essence of group counseling. Group dynamics are most viable when group members are transformed from spectators into participants. Fundamental techniques for such transformation can be integrated by a counselor or trained facilitator. Stimulating topics can provide information, lead students to important insights, and generate energetic interaction. Clarity of purpose and specific focus can also communicate unrecognized needs to others in the school setting. Effective group counseling of gifted students needs both sensitivity to the social and emotional needs of the gifted and specific expertise in group processes. We hope that school counselors and others with special awareness of gifted concerns will recognize the potential for personal growth when gifted children can share their feelings and perceptions in a group counseling setting.

RECOMMENDED READINGS

This chapter by no means addresses all the intricacies of group counseling. It is part of school counselors' training to receive some fundamentals in group counseling. For noncounselors who want to do some focused reading on group counseling, we recommend the following readings. None of these focus on gifted students, but we have found them useful regarding principles of group dynamics.

Corey, G. (1990). *Theory and practice of group counseling* (3rd ed.). Pacific Grove, CA: Brooks/Cole.
Gazda, G. M. (1989). *Group counseling: A developmental approach* (3rd ed.). Needham Heights, MA: Allyn & Bacon.
Johnson, D. W., & Johnson, F. P. (1987). *Joining together: Group theory and group skills* (3rd ed.). Englewood Cliffs, NJ: Prentice-Hall.
Kerr, B. (1991). *A handbook for counseling the gifted and talented*. Alexandria, VA: American Counseling Association.

Yalom, I. D. (1985). *The theory and practice of group psychotherapy* (3rd ed.). New York: Basic Books.

REFERENCES

Blackburn, A. C., & Erickson, D. B. (1986). Predictable crises of the gifted student. *Journal of Counseling and Development, 64,* 552–555.

Colangelo, N. (1991). Counseling gifted students. In N. Colangelo & G.A. Davis (Eds.), *Handbook of gifted education* (pp. 273–284). Needham Heights, MA: Allyn & Bacon.

Colangelo, N., & Kerr, B. (1990). Extreme academic talent: Profiles of perfect scorers. *Journal of Educational Psychology, 82,* 404–409.

Corey, G. (1990). *Theory and practice of group counseling* (3rd ed.). Pacific Grove, CA: Brooks/Cole.

Elkind, D. (1981). *Children and adolescents: Interpretive essays on Jean Piaget* (3rd ed.). New York: Oxford.

Gardner, H. (1983). *Frames of mind.* New York: Basic Books.

Gazda, G. M. (1989). *Group counseling: A developmental approach* (3rd ed.). Needham Heights, MA: Allyn & Bacon.

Johnson, D. W., & Johnson, F. P. (1987). *Joining together: Group theory and group skills* (3rd ed.). Englewood Cliffs, NJ: Prentice-Hall.

Kerr, B. (1981). *Career education for the gifted and talented.* Columbus, OH: ERIC Clearinghouse for Adult, Career, and Vocational Education.

Kerr, B. (1991). *A handbook for counseling the gifted and talented.* Alexandria, VA: American Counseling Association.

Kerr, B., & Colangelo, N. (1988). The college plans of academically talented students. *Journal of Counseling and Development, 67*(1), 42–48.

Kerr, B., Colangelo, N., & Gaeth, J. (1988). Gifted adolescents' attitudes toward their giftedness. *Gifted Child Quarterly, 32*(2), 245–247.

Perrone, P. A. (1986). Guidance needs of gifted children, adolescents, and adults. *Journal of Counseling and Development, 64,* 564–566.

Perrone, P. A. (1991). Career development. In N. Colangelo & G. A. Davis (Eds.), *Handbook of gifted education* (pp. 321–327). Needham Heights, MA: Allyn & Bacon.

Peterson, J. S. (1990, July/August). Noon hour discussion: Dealing with the burdens of capability. *The Gifted Child Today, 13*(4), 17–22.

Peterson, J. S. (in press). Peeling off the elitist label: Smart politics. *The Gifted Child Today.*

Ramos-Ford, V., & Gardner, H. (1991). Giftedness from a multiple intelligences perspective. In N. Colangelo & G. A. Davis (Eds.), *Handbook of gifted education* (pp. 55–64). Needham Heights, MA: Allyn & Bacon.

Yalom, I. D. (1985). *The theory and practice of group psychotherapy* (3rd ed.). New York: Basic Books.

Counseling Gifted Learning Disabled: Individual and Group Counseling Techniques

6

Sal Mendaglio

Gifted students who underachieve academically are a perennial concern. Recently it has come to light that many underachievers are gifted children with hidden learning disabilities. This chapter is based on the writer's clinical experience in working with these students, their families, and their teachers. Work with students has included both individual and group counseling. Selected interviewing techniques are described and illustrated using excerpts from counseling sessions. A multidimensional approach is recommended when counseling gifted learning disabled students. For counseling effectiveness, it is important to involve both parents and teachers in the helping process. The techniques described below are also useful in interviewing these significant adults.

Gifted Learning Disabled Students

In the last decade, a new label has been born—the gifted learning disabled. Like other labels in special education, the definition is imprecise. Essentially, it refers to those children who meet the criteria for definitions of both "gifted" and "learning disabled." A perusal of various conceptualizations of learning disabled (LD) suggests that writers in the field agree on the presence of three main criteria for inclusion. First, the student must possess an average or above average level of intelligence. Second, the individual is to be characterized by significant underachievement. For some, this means that the individual is to be at least one grade level below his or her peers in areas such as language arts or mathematics. For others, this is expressed in more statistical terms, such as performance at least one standard deviation below the mean on an achievement test. Third, the student must have difficulties with skills such as encoding and decoding of language.

After reviewing twenty-eight recent editions of textbooks dealing with LD, Hammill (1990) reports that eleven definitions of LD are currently prominent. Hammill prefers the National Joint Committee on Learning Disabilities definition (NJCLD):

> Learning disabilities is a general term that refers to a heterogeneous group of disorders manifested by significant difficulties in the acquisition and use of listening, speaking, reading, writing, reasoning, or mathematical abilities. These disorders are intrinsic to the individual, presumed to be due to central nervous system dysfunction, and may occur across the life span. Problems in self-regulatory behaviors, social perception, and social interaction may exist with learning disabilities but do not by themselves constitute a learning disability. Although learning disabilities may occur concomitantly with other handicapping conditions (for example, sensory impairment, mental retardation, serious emotional disturbance) or with extrinsic influences (such as cultural differences, insufficient or inappropriate instruction), they are not the result of those conditions or influences. (NJCLD, 1988, cited in Hammill, 1990, p. 77)

Mercer (1986) states that the various definitions of LD may be categorized into three groups: brain injury, minimal brain dysfunction, and learning disabilities. He suggests that terms such as *brain injury* and *minimal brain dysfunction* have been discarded because of negative reactions from parents and professionals. Parents disliked the term *brain injury* because of the permanence it implied. Professionals found both *brain injury* and *minimal brain dysfunction* of little value in categorizing or teaching these students. As to the question of incidence of LD, Mercer reports that estimates vary from 1.5 to 4.63 percent of the population, depending on how stringently the criteria are applied.

Gifted Learning Disabled and Underachieving Gifted

For purposes of counseling, students who possess the dual exceptionalities may be viewed as a subcategory of underachieving gifted students. Support for this perspective stems from recent literature on LD as well as literature on the gifted learning disabled (Silverman, 1989). Hammill (1990) believes that there is a growing consensus regarding the definition of LD; others, however, view with concern the problems resulting from the confusing number of definitions and identification processes used. Samuel Kirk (1987), who coined the term *learning disability*, stated recently: "Surveys of children placed in public school classes for LD have demonstrated that approximately half of the children assigned to these classes are underachievers, but are not necessarily learning disabled" (p. 174). After a thorough review of the history and various definitions of LD, Berk (1983) concluded that LD has become a category of underachievement.

Silverman (1989) contrasted Whitmore's (1980) characteristics of gifted underachievers with a list of characteristics of gifted learning disabled. She concluded:

> The lists of key characteristics of learning-disabled gifted children and gifted underachievers derived from various studies are virtually identical. This may seem less surprising when one realizes that both populations have been identified through discrepancies between performance on measures of aptitude and achievement and thus the groups overlap. (p. 37)

SELF-PERCEPTION: AN ACCURATE REFLECTION OF SIGNIFICANT OTHERS' CONFUSION?

It seems that school professionals, including teachers, counselors, psychologists, and administrators, are still perplexed by dual exceptionality. Even some academics in special education speak of gifted *or* learning disabled, and it is difficult to convey to them the notion of gifted *and* learning disabled. This is particularly true when programs for gifted students are, in fact, programs for high achieving students only. And so, some bewilderment and resistance from these professionals is to be anticipated initially, even though the notion of gifted learning disabled has been discussed in the literature since the early 1980s (Fox, Brody, & Tobin, 1983).

Parents may also have some difficulty understanding the label; though, given their vested interest, they are usually more receptive. Like other parents of exceptional children, they tend to be highly motivated to read and learn as much as they can about the label.

Confusion over gifted learning disabled is also evident in the self-referent statements made by these children. This is best illustrated by the words some of the students use to describe themselves. During one-on-one interviews, ten gifted learning disabled adolescents were asked about their reactions to the label. The responses were summed up by Chris, who responded, "How can I be dumb and smart at the same time?" Poor self-esteem is said to characterize children who experience difficulties with school achievement. In addition, it seems that gifted children with learning disabilities have an added dimension of uncertainty with respect to their self-perception.

Outside of school, these children may have a different perception of self, with an accompanying higher level of self-esteem. Some speak with great enthusiasm about their abilities in other areas, such as computer games, athletics, and hobbies. For example, young adolescent students have described their escapades as a "skater" (one who skateboards), or their involvement in role-playing games (of the Dungeons and Dragons variety). Still others described their sophisticated electronics projects using lasers, and hobbies such as clock-making. It is difficult to tell whether their enthusiasm is merely bravado—a defensive facade to protect themselves against the anxiety associated with poor school performance—or a genuine sense of well-being derived from their achievements in nonschool areas. There is some indication that gifted learning disabled students are more creative and have more productive extracurricular interests than other gifted students (Baum, 1988).

EMOTIONAL AND INTERPERSONAL ASPECTS

Possessing both superior potential and learning disability results in the experiencing of a variety of negative reactions toward school achievement. These include frustration, anger, and resentment. Lewis and Michaelson (1983) note that emotions are evaluative responses of relatively short duration. The emotional experiences that are discussed here are better represented as "chronic" emotions. Kemper (1978) suggests the term *affects* for such recurring emotions.

School and academic achievement represent a recursive reality in young people's lives: each day gifted learning disabled students are confronted with a series of stimuli that activate their negative emotions. At home, they may also experience this activation through regular reminders of their weak school performance, such as questioning about school by well-intentioned parents. The scenario tends to result in negative affective experiences. Often these affective reactions go unexpressed, contributing to poor family and social interactions. When the affects are manifested they may take the form of aggressive, acting-out behavior. Frustration may be displaced onto classmates or siblings.

Emotions and affects that go unexpressed for long periods of time eventually have their day. These children may overreact to objectively trivial demands or comments from parents. These infrequent explosions may give the child a "Jekyl and Hyde" quality. It is disturbing to see a usually easygoing child transformed into a furious one. Parents, teachers, siblings, and classmates tend to develop reduced tolerance for such a child. If the behaviors persist, adults soon become discouraged and may even begin to avoid the young person. At school, the child's behavior may become a source of stress for the teacher. At home, it may negatively affect the quality of the marital relationship. Observations of this type lead to the conclusion that counseling with gifted learning disabled children needs also to focus on parents, family members, and teachers. A primary objective here is to assist these significant others in understanding the emotional experience of the child. When parents and teachers begin to identify their overreactions, they can, with assistance, be of greater therapeutic value, since such a process forestalls the adult's emotional reaction to the child.

ISSUES RELATING TO INTERVENTION

There are several issues in counseling these students that need to be addressed: the necessity of focusing on the affective domain, the importance of a multidimensional approach, and the relationship between the counselor's attitude and technique.

Necessity of Focusing on the Affective Domain

A perusal of the literature in LD (e.g., Wong, 1987) and gifted learning disabled (Baum, 1984, 1988) suggests that insufficient attention has been paid to the affective domain. The perspective adopted in this chapter is that the affective domain, and by implication the interpersonal sphere of functioning, takes priority over other foci of intervention. Whereas direct teaching is an integral part of certain approaches to counseling, here the "curricula" consist of topics such as *communication skills, concepts relating to behavioral change, self-esteem, self-awareness and acceptance of self and others*. By the time a gifted child with learning disabilities is referred for counseling, the emotional reactions and patterns of interaction among the child, parents, and teachers are well established. These entrenched patterns become serious obstacles to all forms of intervention. The barriers need to be removed before change in academic achievement can be expected. School-related matters such as study skills may be treated, but the professional counselor should not be expected to deal with academic concerns directly. These are the teacher's, or tutor's, responsibility. In a very real sense, the counselor plays an important support-ive role to the teacher's efforts to instruct the gifted learning disabled student.

A primary task of counselors is the education of parents and teachers vis a vis the goals of the counseling process. Counselors need sufficient self-awareness and security to acknowledge what they can and cannot deliver. Furthermore, they must direct the counseling process toward an in-depth exploration of the affective domain, facilitating appropriate expression of emotion and the reduction of tensions among the student, parents, and teach-ers, and eventually engage them in problem-solving activities.

Multidimensional Approach

The counselor should implement a multidimensional approach with these students. Giftedness and learning disabilities are conditions residing within the child, but they have multiple implications for the child and his family and teachers. Given the central importance of the school experience for a child, these exceptionalities affect not only the child's learning, but the quality of his family and peer relations. The context of giftedness and learning disabilities is social in nature.

The view implicit in this discussion is that this dual exceptionality exerts an interactive influence on all of the parties involved. The parents are nega-tively affected by the child's difficulties. After some time they may feel discouraged and helpless. Given the characteristics of giftedness, the child feels frustrated when the attention is focused on her deficits and not on her abilities. Also, she may be affected by perceived criticism or impatience from parents and teachers whose own feelings of frustration are inappropriately expressed toward her.

In this analysis, it is more appropriate to use the term *student system*, rather than student. The problem may be resident within the child, but the intervention requires the designation of parents and teachers as clients of the counselor as well. This does not mean that parents and teachers are the cause of the problem. It is difficult to ascertain its etiology. However, parents and teachers may unwittingly exacerbate the problem. One of the preliminary functions of the counselor is to enhance the significant adults' awareness of their style of interaction with the child to determine its level of effectiveness. Specifically, it is essential to investigate the extent to which parents and teachers encourage appropriate emotional expression in the child. In addition, it is important to assess the degree to which communication with the child is pressuresome and negatively toned.

It must be emphasized that in this writer's approach, direct work with the child is not necessarily the main function of the counseling process. A general rule of thumb is: The younger the child, the more work is done through the adults. Of course, the child is certainly a focus of the counselor's attention. Interviews with the child are necessary to provide the counselor with a direct observational base for generating hypotheses regarding the child's attitudes, values, and self-perceptions. Furthermore, the child requires an opportunity to present his perspective.

Attitudinal Context

Prior to presenting selected interviewing techniques, it is necessary to note the central role attitudes play in their administration. The counselor's attitudes toward the student system, the presenting problem, giftedness, and learning disabilities are all vital considerations in the success or failure of techniques. We know some of this from our own day-to-day experience—the impact of interpersonal communication is not in what people say to us but in how they say it. For example, when one spouse asks another "What's wrong?" the verbal response "Nothing" may be strongly contradicted, depending on how it is said. The counselor's attitudes contribute to how a technique is used. Both clinical experience with clients and supervisory experience with counseling students have shown that a well-established technique or strategy may prove useless if a counselor administers it in an atmosphere of impatience with, intolerance for, or misunderstanding of the client.

INDIVIDUAL OR GROUP PLACEMENT?

A primary consideration is the selection of either group or individual counseling. This depends on a number of factors, such as the status of the individual student, the availability of sufficient students to form a group, and the feasibility of scheduling in a school setting. Both counseling modalities require regular parental involvement in the interventions used.

Proponents of specific counseling approaches will advocate the use of their particular choice of one-on-one, family, and group modalities for all counseling situations and presenting problems. By adopting an eclectic approach to counseling we are not bound by the constraints of one position. Although some counselors believe that a "case" must be made for the use of group counseling, human beings are essentially social animals whose daily transactions involve small groups. This is particularly true of children and adolescents.

A major reason for using group work is the therapeutic value in students learning that others share similar problems. This is supported by the success of many self-help groups that have developed over the years. When one finds that he or she is "not the only one" there is an immediate sense of relief, particularly for gifted children with learning disabilities, a group with relatively low incidence within a school jurisdiction. These students often have deficits in social skills, or, at times, display antisocial behavior. The small group is an ideal vehicle for learning and practicing social competencies such as communication skills. It may also prove useful in developing fundamental attitudes such as empathy for others.

Counseling groups can also be applied effectively to gifted children who have experienced chronic ostracism from their classmates. Here they can engage in social interaction with intellectual peers, which often results in the development of friendships and provides a break from the child's usual sense of isolation. Daily school experience for gifted learning disabled students is likely to be frustrating because of their inability to shine in academic pursuits, and painful if they are rejected by their peers. Even when attempting to make social contact with classmates these children may be greeted with obvious disdain.

In observing young people in the group setting, it can be seen that students are more receptive to each other than to adults. Feedback from a peer may be more potent, or may be accepted sooner in the process than it would be from an adult professional. Similarly, a parent attempting to change a teenager's behavior may face verbal resistance, whereas the same request made by another teenager results in compliance. This is particularly true in early adolescence—thirteen to fifteen years of age—when the effects of the peer group are said to be most powerful. However, peers do not necessarily provide curative feedback to each other. The counselor needs to guide the process so that constructive rather than destructive comments are made.

With some students, one-on-one counseling is preferred. It may then be followed up with group sessions. The gifted learning disabled child who has a need to experience catharsis because of emotional trauma should be seen individually. Here the counselor has an opportunity to focus exclusively on the needs of that child. Also, students who display aggressive behavior in classrooms are probably best served in one-on-one sessions. The shy, withdrawn child should receive individual treatment because the demands of the group situation may be particularly stressful. It must be emphasized that the "extreme" types of students described here may eventually benefit from group sessions. Initially, however, these students seem to require more attention

from the counselor, especially when they have experienced rejection from significant adults. Counselors who wish to use group methods with such students should use individual counseling sessions as a form of pre-training for their participation in a group.

Sometimes the initial demeanor of the participants in a group is such that, regardless of the skill of the counselor, very little work can be accomplished. Conducting group sessions with ten children seeking attention and displaying a variety of disruptive behaviors may prove challenging and somewhat frustrating for the counselor. Experience in small-group counseling with adolescents suggests that, for gifted learning disabled students who are deficient in social skills or who engage in inappropriate behaviors, the group process benefits greatly from the involvement of peers who possess better attitudes and skills and can thereby serve as role models.

CONFIDENTIALITY

Whether one uses an individual or group modality, confidentiality is an important consideration. This is a complex matter, especially when one is working with young people. The counselor is ethically bound to protect information that a client reveals, whether that client is a child or an adult. On the other hand, parents as well as teachers and other school personnel need information gleaned in the counseling process. In order to foster a trusting relationship, the child or adolescent must be convinced that the counselor will not divulge information to others without his or her permission. By protecting the student's privacy, the counselor displays respect for the young person.

Here is a straightforward way of handling the demands of codes of ethics regarding confidentiality and the significant adults' need to know. The counselor can make the following type of statement to the child during their initial encounter:

Counselor: The way I help people is by having them talk to me about things they usually don't tell others. They need to talk about their thoughts and feelings. I would like you to understand that what people tell me is confidential. That means that what you tell me will not be told to anybody else without your permission.

When I work with kids your age I have found that it is helpful if their parents and their teachers know some of the things they tell me. It's best when the kids can tell their parents themselves. Sometimes they find it easier if I tell them.

When I feel it is important that your mom and dad know something, I will ask you: "Would you mind if I told your parents, [child's name]?" If you say no, I promise that I will not tell them. Do you understand this?

Student: Yes.

Counselor: Do you have any questions about this?

When the counselor encounters some significant information that is unknown to parents, she may approach the student in the following manner:

Counselor: You know, K..., we've been talking about your relationship with your father. I wonder, do you think he knows how hurt you feel because he doesn't do things with you?

K: No, I don't think he knows that. It's not the kind of thing we talk about.

Counselor: I think it would be very helpful if he did know. I would like it if you told him how you felt.

K: I'm not sure I can do that.

Counselor: I can help you do that or I can tell him for you.

It is also important to explain to the young person the limits of confidentiality: that it is necessary to report if individuals are planning to harm themselves or others. The counselor has an ethical responsibility to protect students from harm.

GROUP CHARACTERISTICS

There are several key characteristics of groups: composition, size, cohesion, and level of structure.

Composition and Size

Anyone who has experience using groups with children and adolescents knows that composition of the group is an important element in determining its evolution and ultimate success. A group composed of only highly aggressive or uncommunicative members will prove extremely challenging to the group leader. As mentioned, counselors are urged to ensure that the group include some individuals who can act as role models, or at least who are more adept socially than others. This is not always easy to arrange. In a school setting, particularly one with programming for gifted students, this can be done, especially if the school also has an established peer-helping program.

With respect to the size of the group, it seems that an optimal range is eight to twelve members. Experience suggests that an ideal size is ten.

Cohesion

Cohesion refers to the feeling of togetherness that should develop in a group. Cohesion is the "psychological glue" (Blocher, 1987) that holds a group of individuals together. This has been associated with a variety of positive group counseling aspects, from enhancing self-disclosure among members (Yalom, 1985) to successful outcomes (Kapp, Glasser, & Brissenden, 1964). The mutual bonding that occurs motivates members to become active participants in the group process.

Some factors that may facilitate the development of cohesion are student-dependent while others are related to the counseling process. The cluster of characteristics shared among the students may foster a sense of togetherness. Perceived similarity serves to engender a feeling of solidarity.

The counselor's initial approach to the group can be critical. The group members need to learn about each other quickly and feel mutually accepted. The counselor needs to facilitate group members' appropriate self-disclosure. Group discussion must be guided from an initial superficial level—factual information—to more meaningful self-disclosure as the group process develops. In addition, mutual acceptance among members will be encouraged as the counselor models a nonevaluative attitude in the course of interacting with each member.

Level of Structure

One of the methods of categorizing various approaches to group counseling is through the amount of structure that group members experience. At the highly structured extreme are guidance groups whose purpose is to dispense information, usually dealing with educational or vocational planning. At the other extreme are encounter groups, where group members grapple with ambiguity and the focus is the process itself toward some general therapeutic goal. Neither of these extremes is considered appropriate for use with the type of student and problems under discussion in this chapter. As indicated below, the type of group described here reflects a flexible structured approach.

INTERVIEWING TECHNIQUES

In this section we discuss techniques used in individual and group counseling. Some of these arise out of general counseling practices; others have been developed as a result of counseling experience with gifted children—gifted children with learning disabilities. Techniques used in group counseling are a combination of those used in individual counseling and some others that are appropriate when counselors need to contend with more people. This is not surprising since theoretical approaches to group counseling essentially reflect theories of counseling. And so we have, for example, psychoanalytic, person-centered, gestalt, and transactional analysis approaches to group counseling. The selected techniques discussed below are based on an eclectic view of group counseling.

Pre-Group Session

The purpose of the pre-group session is to prepare the student for participation in the group and to indicate the general goal of the group. The counselor uses this meeting to initiate the establishment of rapport with each student and to assess the student's suitability and motivation for becoming a member of the group.

Counselor: I believe your teacher and parents have told you about the group I am forming to try to help some kids.

K: Yeah, they both told me something about that.

Counselor: What did they tell you?

K: Not much except that you're trying to help some kids with problems.

Counselor: Did they tell you that I am interested in working with gifted kids who have learning difficulties?

K: Actually they said gifted learning disabled.

Counselor: Yes, that's right.

K: I guess that means me. What are we going to do in this group? Are you going to help us with our spelling? Stuff like that?

Counselor: No, my purpose is different. I'm more into helping people understand themselves and express their feelings. I'm a counseling psychologist working with gifted individuals and I am interested in helping kids like you talk about things like their reactions to being gifted and learning disabled...

K: Yeah, have I got reactions!

Counselor: Well, that's the kind of thing I'm interested in. You know, expressing your reactions and opinions about that. I arranged to meet with you to give you an idea of the kinds of things I would ask you to talk about and to see whether you would be interested in joining us. Shall we give it a shot for a few minutes right now?

K: Okay.

Counselor: Each session will begin with a topic that I will present and we'll talk about various things that the members might bring up as well. Let's start right now with reactions to the two labels. What do you think about being labeled "gifted" and "learning disabled"?

K: Well, it's really confusing to me. (pause)

Counselor: (allows pause to continue, then) Please tell me more about that.

K: (pause) It's just really confusing, that's all. I'm supposed to be gifted, yet I can't get good marks. I have a lot of trouble with writing and I can't do math.

Counselor: It sounds to me like you're confused and frustrated.

K: Yeah, I'm really frustrated, especially when my teachers and parents expect so much from me. Why can't they just leave me alone.

Counselor: (after pursuing the conversation a little longer) Well, K..., that's the kind of talking that would happen in the group. I'll try my best to help you talk about your feelings and how your school performance is affecting you. In my experience, talking about these things, and doing that in a group, can be very helpful to kids.

K..., you seemed to talk very freely just now. Do you think you would be able to talk like that with other kids?

K: I think so as long as I kind of knew them. Who would be in the group?

Counselor: Well, there would be other kids from your school. You probably know some already. There would be about ten or maybe twelve. And I think you are absolutely right—you have to get to know somebody first before expressing your feelings to them. I really appreciate how you have been able to talk so freely with me today.

There are a couple of other things that I want you to know. I plan to videotape the group sessions. And, we would meet once a week for about an hour for the next few months...

K: What will you do with the tapes?

Counselor: Well, I was coming to that. I will do two things. The tapes will be useful in helping me to understand how well we are all working. No one else will see them. The other thing is probably more interesting. I plan to use segments of our sessions to show in some of our group meetings.

K: We get to see ourselves? That's going to be different!

Counselor: Yes, I will use some segments to help you see yourself as others in the group may see you. I would expect you and the others to do things like take turns speaking, trying your best to listen, and make helpful comments during our meetings. Do you have any other questions?

K: No.

Counselor: Well, I have one for you: Would you like to participate in our group?

K: O.K.—especially if this is in class time.

Techniques for Either Individual or Group Counseling

This excerpt illustrates several techniques that are applied in a one-on-one interview, but that are equally applicable in group counseling, particularly in the early stages of the process.

Structuring

This refers to the counselors' outlining of the various pragmatic aspects of the process—purpose of the sessions; number in group; duration of meetings; expectations of the group leader. In addition, special matters are mentioned. In this case, videotaping is noted since permission is needed from the members. K's question allows the counselor to ensure that permission is given with informed consent. An important part of the structuring is providing the student with a sense of the type of talking that he will be engaged in, as a basis for informed consent when he is asked if he wishes to participate.

   The pre-session interview with each student is an excellent opportunity for the counselor to engage in structuring. It is a half-hour worth spending. It also affords students the occasion to have specific questions answered and the opportunity to decline participation. Regardless of age, this approach communicates directly to the student that his or her opinions are valued, and it reinforces freedom of choice, which is essential to the group process.

   A final point on structuring—it is not to be confused with the counselor's approach to counseling. Whether one is, relatively speaking, directive or nondirective in one's approach, the notion of structuring is still important. Structuring does not mean that the counselor necessarily directs the content of future sessions—she may or may not. Alternatively, she may adopt, as is done here, a "semi-directive" approach. In this chapter, structuring refers to the provision of information useful to students in deciding whether to become involved, and then guidance about the process they will experience.

Perception Checking

It is important for the counselor to know what the student understands about the group. Often, parents and teachers who have decided that some intervention will be beneficial for a child neglect to pass on to the child the information provided by the counselor. In the course of many initial interviews, it becomes clear that young students have been told nothing, or very little, about the process or the reason for being brought to the counselor. By first establishing how the child or adolescent perceives the program, the counselor can clarify misperceptions.

Open and Closed Questions

Counselors should use open questions to encourage elaboration on a topic and closed when a yes or a no is sufficient. "What are your reactions to being gifted and learning disabled?" is an example of an open question. This invites the student to elaborate on that issue. "Would you like to join our group?" is a closed question. It is acceptable because the counselor merely needs to hear a yes or a no from the student.

   Some professionals place a great deal of emphasis on the issue of questioning in counseling. This may be a confusing matter for novice counselors. Questioning, like so many other techniques in counseling, is inexorably bound to the notion of timing. The counselor needs to be mindful of distinctions such as closed and open questions—and the entire matter of the use of questions—in the initial phases of the process. Early on, especially in the first few sessions, or even in the first few minutes of a single interview contact, the counselor must acknowledge his ignorance of the student before him. It is important to use open questions and reflective-type comments to encourage the child's communication. Closed questions as a rule should be used as little as possible at this point because they may serve to reinforce a passive, minimally responsive stance. Once the counseling relationship is established and the student is communicating freely and spontaneously, counselors need not concern themselves with this matter. At that stage, closed questions will elicit as much material as open.

Exploration Phase

Elaboration on other issues will be presented under two broad phases of the counseling process: exploration and action. Of course, the content and purpose of sessions will vary from one phase to another. In the first sessions of the exploratory phase, such topics as the introduction of members and establishing the purpose of the group are discussed.

One of the difficulties in dealing with young people, especially in a group situation, is learning the jargon or latest adolescent argot. For example, when introducing himself, Kevin, fourteen, said, ". . . and I'm a D and D freak." Nick, fifteen, said, "My name is Nick and I'm a skater." For many adults these expressions are unfamiliar. The counselor should seek clarification rather than fake understanding.

Technique 1. Counseling in a Group

In the approach taken to the group situation, the initial phase, especially the first group session, is more "counseling in a group" than group counseling. That is, the counselor, in essence, uses individual interviewing techniques to assist participants in elaborating their opinions, rather than attempting to facilitate interaction between and among group members. This "counseling in a group" also allows the counselor to model effective communication, particularly effective listening, and to demonstrate pragmatic matters such as communication protocol within the group (e.g., others listen while one person speaks; everyone is given the opportunity to speak). With gifted children and adolescents who may have developed a low tolerance for rules, this approach is preferred to one in which the group members are presented with a list of do's and don'ts in the first session.

Technique 2. Flexible Structure and Counselor-Initiated Topics

This "interviewing with an audience" technique is done in a flexibly structured atmosphere that should permeate the entire group process. Sessions need some structure, and this is the counselor's responsibility—much like preparing a lesson plan—but the counselor, like any effective teacher, needs to take into account new information and adjust accordingly within the parameters of the process. Specifically, the counselor prepares topics for group discussion that are salient to the group and that are used to focus group participation, especially in the beginning phase of the group. The intent is to encourage group members to take responsibility and to initiate self-disclosure. The work of the group is to create a climate in which concerns can be shared, emotions associated with giftedness and learning disabilities expressed, and self-disclosure facilitated. The creation of such an atmosphere is a responsibility shared by all participants, with the counselor guiding the process toward that end.

Counselor-Initiated Topic: Dealing with Dual Exceptionalities

Counselor: You have been described using two labels: "gifted" and "learning disabled." What do these mean to you? Let's begin with "gifted."

T: You're better at things, better than the average person.

J: I think it's very complicated to go into every detail but...I think basically you have talents but it doesn't mean you'll do better than other kids. Like C... has a good vocabulary and he has put it to good use BUT he doesn't have to if he doesn't want to. He has to decide to do the work. It basically is a capacity.

Counselor: A potential to...

J: Yeah.

Counselor: It doesn't mean you will automatically do well.

J: Right.

Another member continues:

N: Nothing! I think it's a crock.

Counselor: It's a crock.

N: It's just a bunch of crap.

Counselor: It has no meaning for you.

N: It has meaning for me but I don't think it means much.

Counselor: It seems to me that you're saying that it means something pretty bad to you.

N: No, I'd rather be gifted than stupid or learning disabled completely.

The counselor should expect to hear the repetition of textbook definitions but elicit the students' own views:

K: Talented in a particular area.

Counselor: I'm getting confused. Some of you say gifted means being above average, K..., you're saying that gifted means talented...

K: Well, O.K., Mrs. T says that. Like talented is like you're talented in a few things. Gifted means that you're a bit better in everything.

Counselor: Yes, but what does it mean to *you*, K...?

K: I don't know, I've been gifted since grade three. I don't know anymore.

The above is one example of a counselor-initiated topic. A counselor working with a group should create her own list of topics for the sessions. These can be selected from lists of characteristics of gifted learning disabled students, from problems associated with either of these labels, and from recent research. The works of Whitmore (1980), Silverman (1989), and Baum (1984) are excellent sources for this purpose. (Also, see suggested topics in chapters 4 and 5.) The approach would be the same for each session: present topic, encourage expression of thoughts and feelings surrounding it; foster student-to-student interaction; *and* allow for the introduction of other meaningful topics by group members. Much like a good teacher who prepares a lesson plan but displays flexibility when the students' needs are different, the counselor initiates a topic but relinquishes it when another emerges. The rationale for this is simply that the goals of the group session are the important consideration—a topic is a means to an end. Here, the goals are self-disclosure and effective communication among group members who are learning to express their feelings appropriately and discovering that other children have similar difficulties.

Technique 3. Inclusion of Silent Members

Counselor: Let's give some others a chance to express their views. I'd like to hear from those who have not yet had a chance to speak. (pause).

This usually results in silent members speaking and voicing their opinions. If there is no response from those members targeted, then no pressure is applied and the discussion is turned back to the topic in general.

Counselor: I guess some of you have nothing to say at this point. (pause to allow reaction) Well, let's get back to what you were saying. Do you have anything further to add to this topic?

End of Exploration Phase

The exploration phase ends after sound working relationships are well established and group members have become proficient at self-disclosure and capable of appropriate emotional expression in the sessions. By the end of this phase, pertinent issues for each participant will have been identified. Further, the students' concerns are understood by both counselor and group members. When counseling is effective, the counselors' direction of this phase results in the students' acknowledging their contribution to their problems. Students become more responsible. In the approach to group counseling used here, it is the counselor's responsibility to assess whether the group has completed the exploratory phase. Counselors need to be prepared for the occurrence of some errors in judgment on their part. When these occur, it is important for the counselor to acknowledge this to the group and to return to unresolved issues before proceeding further.

The exploration phase concerns itself, by and large, with behavior and goals relevant to the facilitation of group cohesion and mutual understanding among group members. The goals of the action phase shift attention to the students' behavior in the outside world. Students are encouraged to take major responsibility for this phase, with the counselor acting as facilitator.

Action Phase

Once affective expression regarding the topics considered salient by the counselor has occurred, group members are directed to create plans of action for their individual situations. Here the focus is on what each student can do to improve his or her situation. These include improving relationships with parents, siblings, and teachers; achieving appropriate emotional expression outside of counseling; improving study habits; completing assignments and handing them in; and the like. It is important to urge participants to propose their own agendas, rather than the counselor preparing or suggesting plans of action. When students propose some course of action there is greater likelihood of their implementing it.

This request for student-initiated plans of action serves an important assessment function for the counselor. The students' response to this request indicates the level of responsibility that each participant is willing to adopt, the degree of intrinsic motivation within each student, and whether it is, indeed, time to progress to the action phase of counseling. One of the challenges in conducting effective counseling relates to the matter of timing. Throughout the process, counselors are constantly faced with the question: "Is this the right time for me to do or say this?" which essentially can be translated, "Is the student ready for this?"

The participants' responses to such requests alert the counselor to whether they are ready for this phase. If they demonstrate resistance, then the issues raised need to take precedence in the sessions. If no resistance is encountered, counselors proceed *as if* the students are ready. The term *as if* is used because only future student behavior will ensure that they are, in fact, ready for creating plans and refining them, and subsequent implementation and evaluation. The counselor needs to approach this entire matter with the knowledge that effective counseling often involves false starts. When participants experience these, the counselor needs to respond supportively and engage in an exploration of the obstacles impeding progress.

From a different vantage point, this issue relates to a discrepancy between the counselor's perception and the student's reality. When a counselor chooses to initiate an action phase, such a decision has been arrived at based on her perception of the student. Whether implicitly or explicitly, the counselor has made observations of the student that indicate a readiness for action. This matter is raised here because of a potential problem—the counselor might try to convince the student that he is ready—through logical analyses and the reporting of earlier student statements. In an extreme situation, the discrepancy between the student's reality—expressed as not being prepared for action—and the counselor's judgment may lead to a power struggle between the counselor and the student. Obviously, this must be avoided, since it would wreak havoc on the relationship between counselor and student.

Refinement and Support of Action Plans

Both the transitions from stage to stage and the early part of each stage clearly evidence that counseling is an art as well as a science. Once the counselor has ascertained that it is appropriate to engage participants in action, they need assistance in refining their plans. Students should be helped to ensure that plans are specific and attainable. Furthermore, the counselor seeks to support the students in their implementation of the plans. In general, the concept of "successive approximations of the goal" is useful here. Behaviorists take credit for this notion, but the writer prefers an earlier version, namely, the Taoist saying as paraphrased "A journey of a thousand miles begins with the first step." The first step in any action is of crucial importance.

In this case, the first step is the counselor's assisting students in the anticipation of the implementation of their plans. Once a realistic plan has been identified, the counselor asks the students to anticipate the outcome of their attempt to implement their first steps. In the course of this discussion, the counselor needs to focus attention on three possibilities: (1) success, (2) failure, and (3) lack of effort.

In general, the procedure involves asking the participants to imagine themselves implementing their plans. Their feelings associated with the imagery are explored. Then they are asked: "How would you feel if you succeed, fail, or if you decided not to try?" Each possibility is discussed in turn. It is very important in these discussions that the counselor communicate an understanding of the difficulty involved in overcoming the initial inertia or resistance to implementation. Furthermore, the young people need reassurance that any eventuality will be acceptable. Essentially, the counselor is required to provide a balance between encouraging students to implement their plans and simultaneously communicating that failure will not lead to criticism or disapproval. All of the counselor's behavior is geared to helping the students overcome the difficulties involved in the beginning stages of behavior change. The implementation is then assigned as homework.

In subsequent sessions, students are asked to report on their homework. They are asked for details of the events, and encouraged to disclose associated emotions. It is important to explore the rationales for successes as well as failures or no attempts. For successes to be sustained the participants need to know the reasons why they succeeded. Success needs to be the consequence of students' efforts and not simply chance or behavior changes in others. Failures need to be understood and encouragement to try again provided. When a student does not attempt the homework, one needs to investigate the issues of motivation, and possible social or environmental impediments to change. If genuine change is to occur and persist, it is important to instruct the students in the importance of conscious, deliberate effort on their part. Changes that occur by chance may not necessarily be maintained. The counselor assists the participants by this continuous interplay among being assigned homework, reporting on it, and articulation of the rationale for the performance and the emotions experienced during the performance.

CONCLUSION

Several issues related to intervention with gifted learning disabled students have been discussed in this chapter. First, counselor attitudes influence counselor communication patterns with the student system. A second issue is the primacy of the affective reactions of the child, parents, and teachers. Implicit in this is the need for a multifaceted approach when counseling with gifted learning disabled students. A number of strategies and interview techniques have been described. Many prove useful when applied appropriately and when parents and teachers are actively involved in the counseling process. Finally, the counselor must not forget the "gifted" aspect of these students, and efforts need to be made to help students use their gifts to help themselves.

REFERENCES

Baum, S. (1984). Meeting the needs of learning disabled students. *Roeper Review, 7,* 16–19.

Baum, S. (1988). An enrichment program for gifted learning disabled students. *Gifted Child Quarterly, 32,* 226–230.

Berk, R. A. (1983). Learning disabilities as a category of underachievement. In L. S. Fox, L. H. Brody, & D. Tobin (Eds.), *Learning-disabled/gifted children: Identification and programming* (pp. 51–76). Baltimore: University Park Press.

Blocher, D. H. (1987). *The professional counselor.* New York: Macmillan.

Fox, , L. H., Brody, L., & Tobin, D. (Eds.). (1983). *Learning-disabled gifted children: Identification and programming.* Baltimore, MD: University Park Press.

Hammill, D. D. (1990). On defining learning disabilities: An emerging consensus. *Journal of Learning Disabilities, 23,* 74–94.

Kapp, F. T., Glasser, G., & Brissenden, A. (1964). Group participation and self-perceived personality change. *Journal of Nervous and Mental Disorders, 139,* 255–265.

Kemper, T. D. (1978). *A social interactional theory of emotions.* New York: Wiley.

Kirk, S. A. (1987). Intervention research in learning disabilities. In S. Vaughn & C. S. Bos (Eds.), *Research in learning disabilities: Issues and future directions.* Boston: College-Hill.

Lewis, M., & Michaelson, L. (1983). *Children's emotions and moods: Developmental theory and measurement.* New York: Plenum Press.

Mercer, C. D. (1986). Learning disabilities. In N. G. Haring & L. McCormick (Eds.), *Exceptional children and youth* (4th ed., pp. 119–159). Columbus: Charles E. Merrill.

Silverman, L. K. (1989). Invisible gifts, invisible handicaps. *Roeper Review, 12,* 37–42.

Wong, B. Y. L. (1987). Conceptual and methodological issues in interventions with learning disabled children and adolescents. In S. Vaughn & C. S. Bos (Eds.), *Research in learning disabilities* (pp. 185–196). Boston: College-Hill.

Yalom, I. D. (1985). *Theory and practice of group psychotherapy (3rd ed.).* New York: Basic Books.

7

Counseling Families

Linda Kreger Silverman

A gifted child in the family is a mixed blessing. From birth on, these children present an unusual set of challenges. They tend to begin life as active babies, sleeping less than other infants, responding intensely to their environment, often colicky. They exhaust their primary caretakers with their constant need for stimulation. Two gifted children in a family may be highly competitive (Ballering & Koch, 1984). More than two and the parents are outnumbered. Despite rumors to the contrary, most parents do not pray to have gifted children. When they appear, parents are often puzzled as to how to meet their needs, and there is very little in the way of understanding or support in the community.

As discussed in chapter 1, gifted children have asynchronous development, which means that although their intellectual skills are advanced, their social and motor skills are usually age appropriate (Tannenbaum, 1992; Wright, 1990). The unevenness of their development leads to frustration—for themselves and for their parents. Decisions such as "Where should we send our child to school?" are quite simple for other families but agonizingly difficult for parents of advanced children. Grade placement is another problem. Peer relations can be a source of strain. Gifted children often enjoy playing with children older than themselves, mothering children younger than themselves, and talking to adults; however, their relations with children their own age usually leave something to be desired.

It is stressful raising a child with any type of exceptionality, but parents of gifted children have the added stress of being continuously discounted. There are great emotional risks in going to the principal and saying, "I believe my child is gifted and has special needs." Too often they hear the patronizing reply, "Yes, Mrs. Maxwell, *all* our parents think their children are gifted." Parents of disabled children do not receive this kind of treatment.

Being a parent of a gifted child is even harder than being a gifted child (Dirks, 1979); at least the child has some advocates. Parents need advocates, too. They need counselors who are knowledgeable about the gifted, who are not bent on looking for dysfunction, and who are equipped to give them guidance in dealing with the educational system and their complex home lives. This kind of guidance is usually not available within the school system and is difficult to locate outside of the system as well. However, in time, it is hoped that more counselors will become familiar with the unique issues of the gifted and their families and be able to serve this population effectively.

CONCERNS OF FAMILIES OF THE GIFTED

The unique concerns that motivate parents to seek psychological services can be divided roughly into six categories corresponding to the support systems in our model (see chapter 3): *The Child, Home, School, Peers, Community,* and *The Parent.* The "Self" has been split into two parts—child and parent—to distinguish issues in the child's development from issues in the parents' development. The first set of concerns involves the recognition and assessment of giftedness, coping with the characteristics of giftedness, and motivational issues. The second set involves the parents' perceptions of their competence in raising a gifted child, increased tension in families of the gifted, fostering self-discipline, and the question of early stimulation. School concerns include school and grade placement decisions and relations with school personnel. Peer relations are extremely important to most parents and children, and may require special attention. Parents need information about community resources. And, finally, the counselor is remiss if the focus is only on the needs of the child. When parents discover that their child is gifted, they have to deal with a profound set of implications that affect their self-perceptions and aspirations; they often need counseling to understand their own giftedness (Meckstroth, 1991).

THE CHILD

Recognition

Most parents begin to notice signs of giftedness in their children in the first five years. In Kaufmann and Sexton's (1983) study, 83 percent of the ninety-eight parents were aware of their children's abilities prior to school age. Gogel, McCumsey, & Hewett (1985) had similar findings two years later with 1,039 parents of identified gifted children: 87 percent recognized their children's abilities by the age of five. Seven percent suspected that their children were gifted before their infants were six months of age; 15 percent between six and twelve months; 23 percent between one and two years; and 25 percent between two and three years. Both studies consisted of samples drawn from parent groups throughout the country.

Parents are actually quite proficient at recognizing early signs of intellectual advancement in their children, with reported accuracy levels ranging from 47 to 90 percent (Hanson, 1984; Jacobs, 1971; Louis & Lewis, 1992; Robinson, 1987; Silverman, Chitwood, & Waters, 1986). Accuracy increases dramatically over four years of age—not because parents become more astute, but because children become infinitely easier to assess. Parents often fail to recognize their children's high abilities, especially if other family members and friends' children show similar advancement (Munger, 1990). Some are skeptical about the early identification of giftedness. A father once said to me, "But he's only five years old. What could he have *done* in five years to be gifted?" The assumption in his question is that giftedness equals extraordinary achievement. Early identification makes much more sense from a developmental vantage point.

What is it that parents perceive as giftedness in young children? First they notice the alertness and responsiveness of their infants (Gogel, McCumsey, & Hewett, 1985). Then they notice that their children progress through the developmental milestones at a faster pace than the baby books indicate (Hall & Skinner, 1980), particularly in the development of vocabulary, verbal abilities, memory and abstract reasoning ability (Lewis & Louis, 1991; Roedell, 1989). Then they realize that their children are quite advanced compared to their neighbors' children (Louis & Lewis, 1992). This is when mothers begin to worry that their child will be out of step with playmates or with the school curriculum. This is also the beginning of a continuous barrage of bad advice from well-meaning friends, relatives, educators, pediatricians, and writers of popular articles. The message is clear: *Don't encourage your child to be different.*

The methods of good childrearing behind this well-meaning advice are appropriate for average children (Ross, 1964; Schetky, 1981; Sebring, 1983) and are frequently no more applicable for children who are developmentally advanced than they would be for children who are developmentally delayed. However, because gifted children "look normal," it is more difficult for the adults in their lives to be aware of their unique needs. When parents are frequently accosted with "Now, don't push 'em" messages from relatives and friends, they are apt to distrust their own perceptions, leaving the child without any source of advocacy. Parents of young children are more likely to seek professional advice when they have matched their child's traits to a list of characteristics of giftedness (see Table 7.1) (Munger, 1990; Silverman, Chitwood, & Waters, 1986). Counselors with special training in the psychology of giftedness are needed to assist parents in understanding, nurturing, and maintaining some control of their gifted preschoolers.

Obtaining Assessments

Children who are developmentally atypical require thorough diagnostic evaluation; developmentally delayed children are guaranteed that right by law. (See chapter 1.) Early identification of disabled children is essential for their well-

Table 7.1
EARLY SIGNS OF GIFTEDNESS

❏ Unusual alertness in infancy
❏ Less need for sleep in infancy
❏ Long attention span
❏ High activity level
❏ Smiling or recognizing caretakers early
❏ Preference for novelty
❏ Intense reactions to noise, pain, frustration
❏ Advanced progression through the developmental milestones
❏ Extraordinary memory
❏ Enjoyment and speed of learning
❏ Early and extensive language development
❏ Fascination with books
❏ Curiosity; asks many questions
❏ Excellent sense of humor
❏ Keen powers of observation
❏ Abstract reasoning, problem-solving skills, ability to generalize
❏ Early interest in time

being because it enables *early intervention*. The same is true for the gifted. The earlier gifted children are identified, the more favorable their development (Hollingworth, 1942; Witty, 1958). As suggested in chapter 1, individual intelligence testing is the best means available for determining the degree of developmental asynchrony. Assessment provides valuable information about a child's relative strengths, weaknesses, learning style, and learning needs, and is the only way to detect learning disabilities in bright children. The ideal age for evaluation is during the preschool and primary years, before gifted girls go into hiding (Silverman, 1986).

Most families depend on schools to identify their children as gifted. This can be accomplished in states with mandated kindergarten through twelfth-grade programs, where individual testing is required by state guidelines—as long as there is some flexibility built into the system. However, numerous schools have abandoned their gifted programs (Benbow, 1992), and, because giftedness is usually defined as being selected for a gifted program, children in these schools are no longer being identified. In some schools, individual intelligence testing is available only for children with problems.

Typically, gifted programs begin in third grade (Roedell, 1989), and children are selected on the basis of gross screening devices: combinations of group achievement test scores, grades, and teacher recommendations (Gillespie, 1982). The criteria are achievement-oriented, and the number of children identified depends on budgetary considerations. When giftedness is equated with achievement, children who do not excel in their regular schoolwork will not be recognized, including gifted children with learning disabilities; the exceptionally gifted who are bored; culturally diverse students for whom the curriculum may be irrelevant; creative children who need different teaching styles; gifted girls, second-born children, and children with anti-intellectual peer groups who are hiding their abilities; introverts who don't speak up in class; and children for whom English is a second language. Only the scholastically gifted will be seen.

Even where group IQ tests are used as part of the selection process, the results are questionable because group and individual IQ tests are poorly correlated (Schecter, 1992). The inadequacy of this pervasive model is apparent when one looks at the methods used to identify children with developmental disabilities. No parent of a developmentally delayed child would allow his or her child to be labeled using group measures, grades, and teacher recommendations.

Parents who decide to obtain assessment of their children's abilities outside of school face another set of roadblocks. It is often difficult to find a psychologist or agency sufficiently experienced with gifted children. Introverted, perfectionistic children (and nine-year-old girls) will only answer questions they are absolutely certain they can answer accurately. An examiner who has no experience with the gifted may take each "I don't know" at face value, whereas a seasoned professional is able to draw more out of them (e.g., "Suppose you did know, what would the answer be?"). In addition, the accuracy of test interpretation and the value of specific recommendations vary dramatically with the experience of the test administrator (Baum, 1992; Meckstroth, 1989b). The best way for parents to find a knowledgeable, experienced examiner is through recommendations of other parents of gifted children.

Interpreting test scores for gifted children is complex because discrepancies in scores obtained on various instruments are much greater for the gifted than for any other population. The discrepancies are greatest in the highly gifted range, where 50 to 92 point differences have been found (Silverman & Kearney, 1989, 1992; Whitmore, 1980). The basic problems with group tests and the newer individual tests are *ceiling effects* (Hansen, 1992) and the emphasis on performance speed (Kaufman, 1992). Most tests have insufficient room at the top for children to demonstrate the full strength of their abilities. Therefore, if a student scores near the ceiling level of three subtests on a group or individual intelligence measure, it is recommended that he or she be given the Stanford-Binet (Form L-M) as a supplemental test (Silverman & Kearney, 1989, 1992). The old Binet has a higher range of items because it was designed to assess adults as well as children. Stanley (1990) considers it "the original examination suitable for extensive out-of-level testing" (p. 167). It would also be wise to use the old Binet for children younger than six (Vernon, 1987), or for children for whom response speed is a particular problem.

Another way to locate gifted students is through the national talent searches originated by Julian Stanley (1990), in which junior high school students take the Scholastic Aptitude Test (SAT) designed for high school seniors. The SAT as an above-level test taken in seventh grade is an excellent, inexpensive method of identifying gifted students. Some drawbacks are that gifted girls are less likely to be identified than gifted boys on this instrument (Silverman, 1986), the SAT may be biased against lower-income children (VanTassel-Baska, 1989), and seventh grade is late in the developmental sequence to identify giftedness. (See chapter 8 for more information about the SAT as an above-level test.)

After the child is identified, the counselor's job begins in earnest. Parents need guidance in understanding patterns of strengths and weaknesses, dealing with the implications of various ranges of ability, locating appropriate resources, sorting through the options, and coming to terms with the meaning of the child's giftedness for everyone in the family system. Ross (1964) maintains that the examiner who identifies the child as gifted has a responsibility to provide preventive guidance to the family. Although children seem to react favorably to the testing, it may take several months or even years for parents and siblings to adjust to the results of the assessment (Colangelo & Brower, 1987; Dirks, 1979).

Personality Characteristics

The personality characteristics of the gifted were discussed in detail in chapters 2 and 3. Certain of these traits cause more problems for parents than others. Children's argumentativeness and questioning of authority are frequently mentioned in the literature (Meckstroth, 1991; Munger, 1990; Schetky, 1981; Sebring, 1983; Whitmore, 1979). Parents seem to find children's persistent questions particularly annoying (Strom, Johnson, Strom, & Strom, 1992). These authors contend that questioning is natural for the gifted child; it reflects the child's growing independence and need to understand. "The nature and frequency of the gifted child's queries may not only vex the parents, but also lead them to construe such questioning as challenges to parental authority" (Sebring, 1983, p. 97). Sebring goes on to say that conflicts can be avoided if the parents understand that gifted children are independent thinkers and that when they argue they are really analyzing what is expected of them.

Another characteristic that causes a great deal of concern to parents is a child's introversion (see chapter 3). Introversion is not well understood in our society and needs to be explained to parents. They are quite relieved to learn that the naturally reticent behaviors of their child, their spouse, or themselves are healthy, rather than abnormal. In addition to the suggestions given in chapter 3, it is beneficial to administer the Myers-Briggs Type Indicator (MBTI) (Myers, 1962) to the entire family to help them understand the various personality types in the family and how they interact. The MBTI can be given to children with a sixth-grade reading level, although younger children will need to have some of the words explained. Children in second through fifth grade can take the Murphy-Meisgeier Type Indicator for Children (Meisgeier & Murphy, 1987). Through this process, family members come to appreciate each other's differences to a greater extent, and they stop trying to mold each other into their own likenesses.

Intensity, perfectionism, and heightened sensitivity are the three emotional tributaries that most often flow through the gifted personality. "There is among gifted individuals a greater intensity of feeling, greater awareness of feeling, and greater capacity to be concerned" (Piechowski, 1987, p. 22). Intensity is the hallmark of passion, an important variable in the achievement of excellence (Feldman, 1979), perfectionism is the driving force behind the pursuit of excellence, and heightened sensitivity is the basis of compassion. These three qualities combine to create a unique personality structure governed by the vision of the ideal. In adult life, they may create a powerful force for changing the world, but in childhood, these are very difficult traits to live with.

Guidance in dealing with intensity and emotional sensitivity in gifted children is provided by Piechowski (1991):

> The intensity of emotional reactions...in [gifted] children may sometimes be difficult to understand especially when...the child is strongly upset over "nothing." It requires considerable patience and knowledge of the child to see that this "overreaction" comes from the child's sensitivity and the need for his or her own order of things to be preserved.... To a sensitive and intense child who may be disequilibrated often by his or her own emotions, departure from something routinely expected, for example, the way a story is told, may be extremely upsetting simply because the need for support is all the greater. The strongest support, without doubt, is the parent's loving patience and acceptance. (pp. 287, 289)

It is confusing to raise a child who is at once many developmental ages. Parents need help in differentiating dysfunctional behavior from normal behavior for gifted children or typical behavior for children their child's age. For example, a five-year-old was being reprimanded by her mother for acting childish. "Act your age!" scolded her mother. "But, Mom, I'm acting like all the other kids in my class," the kindergartner retorted. When a child talks and reasons like a much older person, it is easy to forget what is age appropriate. Sometimes I tell parents to hold up their child's shoes to remind themselves of the age and maturity of the child. Whitmore (1979) points out that the child may not perceive a behavior (e.g., argumentativeness) as a problem, and that it may be more of a problem for the parents. In this case, the parents may need the counseling more than the child. Everyone in the family can profit from stress reduction techniques and communication and negotiation skills.

Motivation

Gifted children love to learn and they are continuously learning—even when they are not achieving in school. For example, when a group of underachieving teens who have formed a self-help group get together, they share with each other their interests, hobbies, and passions; they look at what is successful in their lives. One is wild about snakes and another is into computer programming. They are teaching each other how to take notes, how to remember homework assignments, how to make friends, how to feel differently about school and about themselves (Young & Johnson, 1991).

> "Some teachers are not so bad once you get to know them. My science teacher said he finally realized I knew the information better than anybody in the class and that my biggest problem was just reading the tests."

> "All I did was quit eating wheat and dairy, and my grades went right up to A's and B's." (p. 15)

Most of all, they are learning that they aren't alone.

> "We have found a way to feel better about ourselves. Through the peer group we are sharing our experiences and have actually begun to achieve some success at school. For the first time, we feel we can cope with school. We have a long way to go, but we are feeling an optimism we have never felt before." (p. 15)

One of the main reasons parents of gifted children seek counseling is their children's underachievement. Numerous factors that contribute to lack of motivation are discussed in chapter 12. In this section, I would like to share some insights gleaned through my clinical practice. Most of the underachieving students referred are boys, so I will use the generic "he." Girls also underachieve, but their patterns are usually different from boys, starting later and more related to socialization (Laffoon, Jenkins-Friedman, & Tollefson, 1989; Reis, 1987; Shaw & McCuen, 1960). (See chapter 14.)

Children who are underachieving should receive a thorough, comprehensive diagnosis as early as possible (Whitmore, 1980). It is important to ascertain whether the difficulty is short-term or long-term, school based or home based. I begin by asking the parents when they first noticed the problem. If they say that the child was an easy baby, wonderful for the first five years, and everything fell apart when he started school, it is likely that the problem is in part educational. On the other hand, if they say that their child has been difficult from birth, fights incessantly with siblings, and that life on the home front resembles a war zone, then it is apparent that family counseling is needed. A student who has been underachieving for less than a year can be turned around much more quickly than one who has developed a pattern of chronic underachievement for several years.

The next step is assessment, which includes an individual intelligence test, an achievement battery, a self-concept measure, a projective assessment (such as a sentence completion procedure), a Characteristics of Introversion in Children Scale (Silverman, 1985) completed separately by each parent and the child, an inventory of causes of underachievement completed by the child, a teacher checklist, the Myers-Briggs Type Inventory (Myers, 1962) for each family member, a detailed developmental questionnaire, and interviews. (Most of these measures are described in chapters 8 and 11.) Diagnostic assessment is indispensable in working with underachievers. Too many times a child is called "lazy" or parents are blamed when the problem may be physiological. Hidden learning disabilities have proved to be the primary cause of under-achievement in the population served by the Gifted Child Development Center (Silverman, 1989).

There is a remarkable consistency in the test profiles of underachieving gifted students: they tend to achieve high scores in vocabulary, abstract reasoning, spatial relations, and mathematical analysis, coupled with low scores in sequential tasks (e.g., repeating digits, repeating sentences, coding, computation, spelling). If the discrepancies are mild, the problem may be simply a mismatch between the student's spatial learning style and the teacher's teaching style. This can be ameliorated by providing the teacher with some different strategies for reaching the student (see Silverman, 1989) and by helping the student understand his own learning style.

However, if the discrepancies are severe (e.g., a Verbal/Performance split of 15 points or more, at least a 7-point spread between high and low subtest scores, or differences of 30 points between IQ and achievement scores), then the student may be learning disabled. It is extremely difficult to recognize learning disabilities in gifted students because the strengths and weaknesses often mask each other, making the children appear average. In addition, the newer tests (e.g., WISC-III, WPPSI-R) put so much emphasis on processing speed (Kaufman, 1992) that a gifted learning disabled child's IQ score is likely to be seriously depressed. The diagnostic checklist in Table 7.2 provides additional observational data to help determine if a learning disabil-ity is present. If many of these signs appear, the student needs a complete evaluation, followed by therapy. (See chapter 6 for group techniques.)

Different types of therapy are recommended depending on the profile that emerges from the assessment. Children with extremely low Performance scores on the Wechsler tests, in comparison with their Verbal scores, are routinely sent to a behavioral optometrist to see if they need glasses or vision training. If children have had a history of chronic *otitis media* (ear infections) and have low scores on the Digit Span test, the Central Auditory Processing Battery is recommended to diagnose auditory processing difficulties. Children with poor eye–hand coordination and speed often profit from sensorimotor integration therapy, using a computer for written assignments, and the elimi-nation of timed tests. (This should be noted in the students' records with the recommendation that they take SATs and ACTs under untimed conditions.) Children with cyclic mood swings or enuresis are referred to an allergist to rule out food allergies. If high levels of distractibility are evident during the testing, the parents are given a checklist of the symptoms of Attention Deficit Hyperactivity Disorder (ADHD), and further evaluation is recommended to see if medication is needed. If emotional difficulties surface, counseling or play therapy is recommended. Counseling is usually the last recommendation,

Table 7.2
DIAGNOSTIC CHECKLIST OF WRITING DISABILITY

1. Is his writing posture awkward?
2. Does he hold his pencil strangely?
3. Can you see the tension run through his hand, arm, face?
4. Does it take him much longer to write than anyone else his age?
5. Does he fatigue easily and want to quit?
6. Does he space his letters on the paper in an unusual way?
7. Does he form his letters oddly (e.g., starting letters at the top that others would start at the bottom)?
8. Does he mix upper and lower case letters?
9. Does he mix cursive and manuscript?
10. Are his cursive letters disconnected?
11. Does he prefer manuscript to cursive?
12. Does his lettering lack fluidity?
13. Does he still reverse letters after age seven?
14. Is his handwriting illegible?
15. Is his spelling poor?
16. Does he avoid writing words he can't spell?
17. Does he leave off the endings of words?
18. Does he confuse singulars and plurals?
19. Does he mix up small words, like "the" and "they"?
20. Does he leave out soft sounds, like the "d" in gardener?
21. Is his grasp of phonics weak? (Is it difficult to decipher what he was trying to spell?)

Source: From "Help for the Hidden Handicapped" by L. K. Silverman, 1991, *Highly Gifted Children, 1*(2), pp. 10–11.

after all of the physiological factors have been examined.

Educational options must also be evaluated before a student or family is placed in counseling. If the problem began when the child started school, then placement with another teacher or in another school may be the solution. We have to be careful not to assume that the problem always resides within the child (Roeper, 1992); inappropriate education diminishes a gifted student's motivation (Gross, 1992; Whitmore, 1989).

The Myers-Briggs Type Indicator (Myers, 1962) is helpful in assessing family dynamics. Clashes between parents and children often can be traced to differences in style. In most cases, gifted underachievers have very high Perceiving scores, whereas at least one of the parents has a very high Judging score. Perceivers are spontaneous, playful, interested in many things, and like to take in a great deal of information before they pull it all together. They are likely to go overboard on the research aspects of a project, wait until the night before the project is due to begin the writing, and then stay up all night. Perceivers who are chronic underachievers take in all the information but are unable to synthesize it and put it down on paper. They would probably perform well on an oral test because they do gain a considerable amount of knowledge. If a student is a high Perceiver and has a writing disability as described in Table 7.2, chances are that homework rarely gets turned in. Using a word processor for assignments often helps.

Judgers are organized, goal-oriented, and enjoy planning and completing tasks. They pay attention to deadlines and are punctual, if not early. Judgers are not exactly thrilled to have offspring who are Perceivers. Some of these Judgers may actually be "Reformed Perceivers" who learned a set of behaviors in order to survive and support a family. "Reformed Perceivers" are likely to be tougher on the child than natural Judgers because the child reminds them of their former selves.

The parent who was most like the child in learning style and behavior usually "gets on the child's case" the most. Very often these are father-son dyads. The father was an underachiever in school and the son mirrors those qualities that the father most disliked in himself. Discussions of learning style, personality style, and the combination of giftedness and learning disabilities help the father understand himself better, as well as understand his son. With the assistance of the counselor, the father begins to realize that he can become his son's greatest ally. He can teach his son how he compensated for his weaknesses or learned how to get organized. A deeper bonding ensues between the father and son through these discussions. Teachers who were among the "organizationally impaired" at some point in their lives are also effective in teaching underachievers organizational skills.

Additional strategies that have been employed with underachievers include tutoring (Freed, 1990); counseling groups for underachievers (see chapter 6); group counseling for families in which parents are matched with someone else's children (Shaw & McCuen, 1960); family counseling; role-playing (Olenchak, 1991); grade advancement (Rimm & Lovance, 1992); alternative schools; special class placement and interventions (Whitmore, 1980); individual plans with parent, teacher, and student (Fine & Pitts, 1980); adapting the curriculum to the student's learning style; teaching to the student's strengths; teaching the student compensation techniques; bibliotherapy; and using the student's interests to make school relevant (Emerick, 1992). The bottom line is that underachievement *can* be reversed.

THE HOME

Feeling Inadequate

Most parents are not joyously enthusiastic to learn that they have a gifted child. When I share test results with parents of exceptionally gifted children, the tissue box is always close by. For some, it is as big a shock as being told that their child is developmentally disabled. They mourn the loss of their fantasy of having a "normal" child (Meckstroth, 1991) whose needs will be easily taken care of within the regular classroom. Any exceptionality places a heavy burden of responsibility on the parent (Freeman, 1979; Ross, 1964); but parents of other exceptional children have societal support and sympathy, whereas parents of the gifted have neither (Schetky, 1981). They are called "elitist" and accused of seeking "to twist the structure of the schools to the benefit of their children" (George, 1988, p. 27) by zealots of the school reform movement.

Parents often feel inadequately prepared to meet the needs of a gifted child (Colangelo, 1991; Parker, Ross & Deutsch, 1980; Ross, 1964). These problems are compounded by many factors: myths and misinformation about the gifted (Dettman & Colangelo, 1980); blatant or covert hostility toward the intellectually advanced (Singal, 1991); lack of information about available resources (Dirks, 1979); and limited financial resources of parents (Bloom, 1985). Gifted children can be very expensive to raise, and there is no financial assistance available.

Increased Tension

There are reports in the literature of increased conflict in families when a child has been labeled gifted (Cornell, 1984; Dirks, 1979; Fine, 1977). Two frequent concerns are confusion about the child's role in the family and conflicting expectations of the child by the parents (Colangelo & Dettman, 1983; Fine, 1977). Delisle (1992) writes, "It is naive to believe that a characteristic as significant as giftedness would not have some unique impact on both the family and the child's role in the family, requiring some changes in parent-child interactions" (p. 189).

Several writers have indicated that there is jealousy and competitiveness in families in which there are gifted and "nongifted" siblings (Cornell, 1984; Grenier, 1985; Hackney, 1981; Pfouts, 1980; Sunderlin, 1981). However, Kaufmann and Sexton (1983) found that only 20 percent of the siblings of gifted children in their study had negative reactions, and Colangelo and Brower (1987) report that problems initially apparent disappeared within five years. In cases where there is increased friction, the gifted label usually catches the lion's share of the blame. Yet, one variable that has not been systematically investigated is the effect on children of being perceived as nongifted when they are equally as bright as an identified sibling.

When one child in the family is gifted, the rest usually are not far behind. A review of the IQ scores of 148 sets of siblings revealed that almost 36 percent were within 5 points of each other and 61.5 percent were within 10 points of each other (Silverman, 1988). Discrepancies greater than 10 points occurred when one of the siblings had a learning disability, one had a history of chronic ear infections, or there had been a substantial age difference between the siblings at the time of testing. The "nongifted" child, then, is most probably a gifted child who did not test as high as the identified sibling due to learning disabilities or other factors or who did not achieve well enough to gain acceptance in the gifted program. The factors that depressed the child's performance, coupled with the perception that the child is not as bright as his or her sibling, could account for a considerable amount of jealousy and competitiveness. Much of the jealousy is alleviated when the so-called nongifted child is properly identified.

Increased stress also occurs when the family is focused on the *achievements* of one child over other children or when children's achievements are compared (Delisle, 1992). Sloane (1985) reports that parents who have devoted their lives to the tennis champion, concert pianist, or Olympic swimmer in their families experienced occasional twinges at the neglect of other siblings. These problems may not be pervasive: VanTassel-Baska (1989) found that parents of disadvantaged children did not show preferential treatment to their high-achieving child. Tension is also created when parents hold different views of giftedness. In one study, parental relations were strained as a result of the child being identified as gifted in the school—mothers believed the designation whereas fathers were more skeptical (Cornell, 1983). Fathers tend to perceive giftedness as achievement, whereas mothers perceive giftedness in terms of developmental differences (Silverman, 1986). These discrepant points of view can be discussed in counseling, which usually leads to resolution of the conflict.

The counselor can dispel all the myths and misunderstandings about giftedness, and provide parents who need them with some basic parenting skills (such as remembering who's in charge, presenting a united front, and not comparing their children), but tensions are still likely to be present in the gifted family (Albert, 1978). The characteristics of gifted children—intensity, perfectionism, sensitivity, and argumentativeness—are not limited to one family member. Everyone shares in them to some degree. A perfect setting for high drama! Meckstroth (1989a) calls it "crisis cubed": "The effects of life situations, feelings, and ideas become magnified in the gifted family. It is as if there is a geometric progression of intensity with each family member involved" (p. 11).

The counselor can help the family understand that strong feelings are healthy. An introduction to Dabrowski's (1964) theory (see chapter 1) helps family members view their intense inner experiences as positive signs of development rather than as indicators of emotional disturbance. This frees energy consumed by self-denigrating beliefs, making it available for the development of successful coping mechanisms. As each member of the family gains self-understanding, there is more awareness of the emotional experience of others in the family. Compassion and problem solving grow out of this enhanced awareness.

Fostering Self-Discipline

Gifted youngsters have a keen sense of justice; they respond well to democratic approaches in which they have a voice in decision making and poorly to authoritarian parenting styles (Parker, Ross, & Deutsch, 1980). "'Do it because I said so!' is both ineffective and self-defeating" (Meckstroth, 1991, p. 105). Fortunately, most parents of gifted children reason with their children rather than resort to punishment and other forms of external power (Abelman, 1991). Nevertheless, many people in our culture take "ageism" for granted—the belief that adults have more power and therefore more rights and privileges than children. Gifted children do not share this assumption. "Respect your elders" is a hierarchical concept that leaves the young without respect. To bring this point home, I engage parents in the following exercise:

> *"Close your eyes and imagine that you are asking your mother-in-law to get off the phone. Observe everything you can about yourself. Now imagine that you are asking your child to get off the phone. What differences do you notice in your choice of words, tone of voice, facial expression, body posture, amount of wait time?"*

Parents usually laugh, but they gain an awareness of the difference in respect that they award individuals older and younger than themselves. The key to family harmony is respect for all members: a simple concept, but difficult to implement.

Montemayor (1987) has found that conflicts with adolescents are resolved by accepting children as peers and sharing power. This appears to be true with younger gifted children as well. Gifted children will behave manipulatively or disrespectfully in situations where they feel powerless or not respected. The antidote is to help parents create a family system with a balance of power, in which all members feel supported.

One method of balancing power in a family is by establishing a family council—usually a regularly scheduled meeting of the entire family. A family council provides direct experience in democratic decision making. Everyone is given an opportunity to air grievances, request changes in rules, learn negotiation skills, learn conflict resolution techniques, and practice effective communication skills on a routine basis. Family council meetings can also be a vehicle for building self-esteem and family solidarity. A time for compliments can be included as well as a time for complaints, and the meetings can end with shared activities such as reading aloud. Gifted children can participate competently in family council meetings at about seven years old, although even preschoolers respond well to this approach.

Home Stimulation

Researchers consistently have found parenting to be the most potent factor in the development of giftedness, creativity, and eminence (Albert, 1978; Bloom,

1985; Cox, Daniel, & Boston, 1985; Kulieke & Olszewski-Kubilius, 1989; Tannenbaum, 1992). Yet, many parents are confused as to how much and what type of home stimulation is appropriate (Colangelo & Dettman, 1983). Parents, particularly those who are also teachers, often apologize for their children's advancement (Roedell, 1989), saying anxiously, "Honestly, I didn't teach her to read. She just picked it up on her own." The fear that they will be seen as "pushy" prevents many parents from exercising their rightful role as educators.

A major study of individuals who achieved world class recognition by the age of thirty (Bloom, 1985) highlights the important role parents play and provides information about the most effective familial support for the development of talent.

> In summary, the parents of the athletes, musicians and artists believed in the importance of working hard and doing one's best. They organized their time, established priorities, and set standards for the completion of a task. (Sloane, 1985, p. 443)

> ...the parents' participation in the child's learning contributed significantly to his or her achievement in the field. ...these children could [not] have gotten good teachers, learned to practice regularly and thoroughly, and developed a value of and commitment to achievement in the talent field without a great deal of parental guidance and support. (p. 476)

Further insights about the role of the family in nurturing giftedness come from a study of the MacArthur Fellows, all of whom received substantial awards for their outstanding creativity (Cox, Daniel, & Boston, 1985).

> *Almost without exception the MacArthur Fellows pay tribute to their parents.* While the educational level of the parents varied, and the level of financial backing as well, virtually all the parents let their children know the value of learning by personal example. The parents supported without pushing. Their homes had books, journals, newspapers. They took the children to the library. The parents themselves read, and they read to their children. Most important, they respected their children's ideas. (p. 24)

Feldman (1986) describes the parents of prodigies quite similarly. He found them generally *responsive* rather than controlling: "The parents' role seems to be to respond, support and encourage" (p. 156). Families of early achievers usually are stable and cohesive; they establish patterns of achievement, independence, and perseverance in early childhood and focus attention and resources on their gifted children (Robinson & Noble, 1991). Perhaps the most striking impression from various studies is the high degree of parental involvement with their children (Gogel, McCumsey, & Hewett, 1985; Kulieke & Olszewski-Kubilius, 1989; Robinson & Noble, 1991; Silverman & Kearney, 1989). When parents of gifted children are asked to describe their interests, the first response of many mothers is "my children."

Gogel, McCumsey, and Hewett (1985) asked over a thousand families to list the most successful ways they work with their gifted children at home. The most cited activity was reading together. Second was consistent encouragement and praise for their children's achievements. Other methods listed included frequent conversations; participation in community activities; field trips to museums; vacations; discussions; listening; asking and answering questions. Additional research indicates that parents assist the development of their gifted young by providing strong family values, clear standards of conduct, and good role models (MacKinnon, 1962); mutual trust and approval (Piechowski, 1987); support of their children's interests (Bloom & Sosniak, 1981); emotional support from extended family members (VanTassel-Baska, 1989); encouraging curiosity and active exploration (Kulieke & Olszewski-Kubilius, 1989); holding high expectations for their children (Albert, 1978; Bloom & Sosniak, 1981); encouraging autonomy; valuing creative and intellectual endeavors; emotional and verbal expressiveness (Robinson & Noble, 1991); avid reading and reading frequently to children (Cox, Daniel, & Boston, 1985); quality time and communication (Delisle, 1992); and helping their children to believe in their dreams (M. Darnell, personal communication, November 15, 1988).

Parents should be encouraged to provide a stimulating home environment—including instruction—if the child is eager, interested, and enjoying the activities. If the experience is *fun* for both the parent and the child, it is not harmful. On the other hand, parents should be discouraged from pushing unwanted enrichment on their child. After reviewing all of the research on early development of giftedness, Tannenbaum (1992) presents this eloquent conclusion:

> All in all, giftedness develops through an array of uniquely exquisite efforts by a caretaker who cares for the child's special qualities and who takes wise steps to accelerate their ripening.... Children with superior inner resources can fulfill their promise only if the nurturance they receive is "tailor-made" to meet their special needs; but without the requisite inner resources in a child, no amount (or type) of nurturance can make the difference between mediocrity and excellence. (p. 128)

Ironically, the more skillful parents are at home stimulation, "the greater dissonance there will be when the child enters school" (Munger, 1990, p. 58).

THE SCHOOL

Determining Appropriate School Placement

Part of the guidance parents desire is information about options: public and private. The counselor needs to be aware of the availability of various special programs for the gifted and the supportiveness of administrative staff in different schools. This is particularly important in communities that have adopted a "schools of choice" philosophy, offer open enrollment, or use a voucher system. Within the public schools, several choices may be available (e.g., a pull-out program, a magnet school across town, cluster-grouping within the regular classroom). Parents may need to determine which of several alternatives is best for their child. A recurring question is the impact on social development of transporting children to a magnet or private school away from the neighborhood school. Parents are reassured to learn that gifted children often have different sets of peers for different types of activities (Roedell, 1985), and they usually develop two sets of friends: school friends and neighborhood friends.

If public school offerings are limited, private schools should be explored. Parents will want to know about current tuition rates, scholarship opportunities, and availability of before/after school care. The counselor can provide evaluation criteria for examining schools (e.g., Silverman & Leviton, 1991; see also criteria on p. 202 in chapter 9), or assist the parents in developing their own evaluation criteria, and even accompany the parents to observe one of the schools. Parents should visit several schools and determine which ones are responsive to giftedness, are within a reasonable distance, appear congruent with their own philosophy, and are affordable. After they have narrowed down the choice to two or three, they should take their child to spend a morning or afternoon in each environment and request input from the child. Even four-year-old gifted children are capable of selecting an appropriate school for themselves. They often notice factors that parents miss (e.g., how the children treat each other on the playground).

When public schools offer no gifted programs, private schools for the gifted are not available or affordable, or the child is highly gifted and bored (even in a gifted program), acceleration should be considered. This is often a loaded topic, but the familiar biases are not supported by research (Feldhusen, 1992; Feldhusen & Moon, 1992; Southern & Jones, 1991). Strong opposition to acceleration may be countered by sharing the studies, which are almost uniformly positive (Robinson & Noble, 1991). Although many children have benefited from acceleration, it remains unpopular with educators (Southern & Jones, 1991). "Indeed, school personnel frequently assume that cognitive maturity is altogether unrelated to psychosocial maturity and for that reason they take a strong stand against accelerative options" (Robinson & Noble, 1991, p. 60). Excellent criteria for determining whether early entrance or grade advancement is appropriate are provided by Feldhusen (1992).

Unfortunately, many parents are pressured to move in the opposite direction: to hold back instead of accelerate. Holding gifted boys back at the kindergarten level has become an accepted practice on the erroneous assumption that it will enhance their social relationships. Intellectually advanced boys are often branded "immature" because they refuse to play the "baby" games of their age-mates (see chapter 14). A more appropriate solution to social adjustment difficulties is finding the boy true peers—age-mates of similar ability with whom he can be socially comfortable.

When parents and teachers understand the implications of the differentness inherent in being gifted, they can create conditions that will support the child's positive social and emotional growth. The first step is to realize the inextricable link between social and cognitive development.... If the child also makes the discovery that communication with classmates is difficult, and that others do not share his/her vocabulary, skills or interests, peer interactions may prove limited and unsatisfactory. *We cannot ignore the gifted child's need for intellectual stimulation and expect social development to flourish.* (Roedell, 1988, pp. 10–11)

One additional option that should be mentioned is homeschooling. Home instruction is one of the fastest growing movements in American education, affecting anywhere from 100,000 to 1,000,000 children (Kearney, 1989). Families of highly gifted children frequently select this option for some period of time because it is difficult for them to find a suitable placement for their children. Robinson and Noble (1991) find it "disturbing to consider how high a proportion of eminent people in history were home tutored" (p. 60). Perhaps it is unrealistic to expect the schools to be able to handle adequately the full range of human abilities. The most frequently voiced drawback to home schooling is the lack of socialization opportunities. To meet social needs, homeschooling families get together for group instruction, participate in church groups, or enroll their children in a number of extracurricular activities such as those available through the Department of Parks and Recreation. In any event, parents often request information about state requirements for homeschooling, contacts with other homeschoolers, and resources and guidance for developing curriculum.

Assistance with School Personnel

A school counselor can help select the most effective teachers for the child and assist teachers in adapting their methods to meet the student's needs. At times, the counselor is also called upon to act as an advocate for the child. If a student is particularly unhappy, and the teacher is unresponsive to the parents' attempts to ameliorate the situation, the counselor may need to intervene. A typical situation is parents who feel their daughter would be better served in first grade and the kindergarten teacher who feels that the girl is not ready to leave kindergarten. The counselor can observe her in both kindergarten and first grade, request a staffing to discuss the placement, provide insights about the girl, and mediate between the teacher and the parent.

Another typical scenario is the case of the junior or senior high school student whose grades are D's and F's. At mid-term the boy's parents put him in counseling, but he does not see the point of trying to reverse the pattern. Even if he turned in all his assignments for the rest of the semester his final grade would reflect the months of noncompliance, so why bother? The counselor can intervene on the student's behalf, approach each teacher, explain that the youth is now in counseling, and ask that he be allowed a fresh start. This will enhance the potential effectiveness of the therapeutic intervention.

Parental persistence is apparently the key factor in success in working with schools (Gogel, McCumsey, & Hewett, 1985). Some of the techniques that parents reported were initiating contact with school personnel at all levels, volunteering parent services, and assuming leadership roles. If they encountered resistance, they usually asked a staff member to intercede on their behalf, sought outside testing, or changed schools.

A cooperative partnership between the home and the school is essential (Roedell, 1989). Colangelo (1991) describes a model for facilitating parent–school relationships involving four types of interactions: Type I, cooperative; Type II, conflict; Type III, interference; Type IV, natural development. The model provides counselors with a framework for understanding and improving communication between home and school.

PEER RELATIONS

Parents are often more concerned about their children's social adjustment than scholastic accomplishments (Anderson & Tollefson, 1991; Cornell, 1983; Roedell, 1988). Gogel, McCumsey, and Hewett (1985) found that parents' "most often mentioned personal wishes were for their children to be accepted by peers and that their children have good self-images" (p. 9). For gifted children also, the number one priority is often finding a friend. The most important factor in determining their friendship choices appears to be mental age (Gross, 1989).

Although there has been considerable controversy in the literature as to whether gifted children experience greater social adjustment difficulties than children of lesser capabilities, a recent, comprehensive review indicates that the majority of gifted students enjoy positive relations with peers (Robinson & Noble, 1991). According to the evidence presented, gifted children appear to be more mature than their age-mates in play interests, social understanding, choice of friends, fears, and world view. The picture is not as uniformly positive for the highly gifted, for adolescent girls, and for minority group members. (See chapter 14 for more information about social development and gender differences.)

Observation of the friendship patterns of the gifted reveals that they seek children with similar interests and abilities, and that age and sex are of lesser importance. Grouping gifted children together for instruction is one obvious way to enhance their social development. Programs for the gifted have a highly beneficial effect on social relationships (Feldhusen, Sayler, Nielsen, & Kolloff, 1990; Higham & Buescher, 1987; Kolloff & Moore, 1989; Olszewski-Kubilius, 1989).

> In an environment where all students are gifted and where intelligence and ability are highly valued, social relationships flourish. For many, this is the first time that they feel "average" or "normal," which for adolescents, can be a great relief. (Higham & Buescher, 1987, p. 88)

Contrary to superstitions that associations with other gifted students prevent these children from adjusting to the "real world," their ability to relate to heterogeneous groups increases by finding others like themselves.

Higham and Buescher (1987) report that there is a carryover effect from the positive social experiences of adolescents in summer enrichment programs to their regular school experiences: they feel more comfortable and socially adept. Once they find friends who truly appreciate them, laugh at their jokes, and enjoy their company, their self-confidence increases in other situations. They demand less from average peers because they know that somewhere someone likes them just the way they are.

When peer problems exist, the solution is usually to locate gifted peers (Roedell, 1985, 1988). Parents should be advised to enroll their children in self-contained classes for the gifted (public or private), pull-out programs, enrichment classes, or summer opportunities for the gifted in order to find friends for them. Support groups for parents of the gifted are another resource for locating children of similar abilities. In rural areas, pen pals or computer networking can reduce feelings of isolation.

Children learn to love others only when they have achieved self-love. The process usually involves the following stages: (1) self-awareness; (2) finding kindred spirits; (3) feeling understood and accepted by others; (4) self-acceptance; (5) recognition of the differences in others; and, eventually, (6) the development of understanding, acceptance, and appreciation of others. Counselors can help gifted children find true peers, help them gain self-acceptance, and guide them toward accepting others.

COMMUNITY RESOURCES

Counselors need to be acquainted with various resources in the community (Culross, 1982; Ross, 1964). They should be prepared to answer questions about after-school enrichment programs, early college entrance, simultaneous enrollment in high school and college, internships, mentorships, and scholarships. In addition, parents request information about local, regional, and national support groups and conferences; newsletters, magazines, and journals; books for parents of the gifted; and books and software for gifted children. (See Appendix for publications, bibliographies for both parents and students, and national resource centers for counseling and assessment.) If the family is unhappy with the neighborhood school, the counselor can investigate open enrollment policies within the district, enrollment in other districts, voucher systems, and private schools. If the student needs assistance in certain skill areas, the counselor should have on hand the names of competent tutors. As mentioned earlier in the chapter, referral sources of other professionals in the community should be provided for various difficulties revealed in the assessment: audiologists, optometrists, occupational therapists, speech therapists, play therapists, ADHD specialists and support groups, and allergists.

Extended family members cannot be overlooked as important sources of support for the gifted student, particularly those from disadvantaged backgrounds (VanTassel-Baska, 1989). Grandparents and other relatives should be included in family counseling efforts so that all those who have a direct impact on the child are thoroughly familiar with his or her strengths, weaknesses, and needs. If extended family is not available, mentors and role models can be sought from groups of retired persons or professional groups in the child's areas of interest. Local businesses can be contacted to provide computers and scholarship assistance to economically disadvantaged children with intellectual promise.

GIFTED CHILDREN, GIFTED PARENTS

Giftedness is a quality of the family, rather than a quality that differentiates the child from the rest of the family (Albert, 1978, 1980; Burks, Jensen, & Terman, 1930; Hollingworth, 1926; MacKinnon, 1962). When one parent's IQ is known, the child's IQ can often be predicted within 10 points. Therefore, when a child is identified as gifted, the parents are probably gifted, too (Kline & Meckstroth, 1985; Meckstroth, 1991; Tolan, 1992). It is painful for parents to acknowledge their own giftedness. However, "it is hard to help one's child resolve issues one has not yet resolved for oneself" (Tolan, 1992, p. 8). Tolan continues,

> Few gifted adults have come to terms with their own giftedness. As we set out to help our children come to terms with theirs, our blind spots, denials, cover-ups and strategies for self-preservation get in our way—to say nothing of the feelings we have brought with us, however hidden, from our early years. (p. 8)

This aspect of parenting the gifted has received little attention in the literature. It is not fashionable to speak of the hereditary component of giftedness. This is unfortunate, because the assumption that gifted children are randomly assigned to nongifted parents does a disservice to their parents, exacerbating their sense of inadequacy. Too many writers mistakenly assume that mismatches in intellectual power between parents and children occur regularly as in the stereotypical portrayal of the mother in the movie, *Little Man Tate*. Most parents of the gifted *are* intellectually equipped to raise their children effectively. The children will probably outdistance their parents in knowledge of a specific field, but parents and children are usually well matched intellectually.

It often comes as a surprise to parents to learn that they are as bright as their children. For example, during a parent interview, a father of a highly gifted boy recognized that when he was a child he had the same characteristics his son demonstrated, but his parents ignored those signs. He grew up thinking he was just strange. After having their children tested, some parents have had radically altered self-perceptions, resulting in new career aspirations, going back to school, and applying for scholarships.

Many mothers flatly deny any possibility of their own giftedness: "She gets it from her father." They may have gifted parents, spouses, siblings, and children and still see themselves as not gifted—as if the phenomenon just skipped over them. They suffer from the conception that giftedness equals achievement, so they have no basis for recognizing themselves as gifted. When they identify with the characteristics of giftedness in children this perception slowly begins to change. As their daughter's major role model, it is imperative that mothers acknowledge their own abilities. Otherwise, their daughters come to believe, "If mommies can't be gifted, how can I be?" Counseling groups have also been effective in helping women acknowledge their giftedness (Noble, 1989). Tolan (1992) reminds parents that "one of the best things about raising gifted children may be the selves we discover along the way" (p. 10).

CONCLUSION

Giftedness is a family affair. There are far-reaching implications of this phenomenon for every member of the family. Whether or not gifted children are recognized, labeled, or encouraged, there is no escape from the impact of giftedness on the family system: the characteristics and needs will still be there. Many of the normal attributes of giftedness are misjudged, and misinformation about the gifted continues to be propagated. Few counselors are aware of the unique concerns of gifted families or prepared to give them appropriate guidance. Without this knowledge base, counselors may prove more harmful than helpful to these families. Counselors need to be willing to explore their own biases and recognize and deal with their own feelings before they can be of help (Ross, 1964).

The literature about families of the gifted can also be counterproductive. Much of it paints an unattractive picture—assuming that parents label one child as the "star" for their own narcissistic ego needs (Cornell, 1984), teach their children they are superior, make invidious comparisons between their children, brag, have unrealistic expectations, are competitive and jealous, parentify their children, have weak role definitions, are overprotective or enmeshed, are incompetent in their parenting skills, and antagonize school districts with their unreasonable demands. The healthy, functional parents, who comprise the vast majority of the 1,700 families with whom I've worked, cannot even turn to the literature for guidance with their complex family and school problems. Contrary to these negative depictions, Mathews, West, and Hosie (1986) found that families of the gifted tend to have healthy interaction patterns and a higher level of psychological adjustment than the norm. But parents of gifted children feel abandoned within the field as well as outside of it.

A developmental counseling program recognizes that gifted children pose unique challenges to parents and includes ongoing work with families (Colangelo, 1991). Meckstroth (1991) offers a comprehensive guide for conducting parent workshops and seminars. Counselors can help parents understand the meaning of IQ tests, help family members become adjusted to labeling (Colangelo & Brower, 1987), and give parents instruction on how to interact effectively with schools (Dettman & Colangelo, 1980). Parents also can be helped to come to terms with the meaning of giftedness in their own lives. With appropriate counseling, myths can be dispelled, options presented, and support services obtained. Counselors are desperately needed who have special training in the area of giftedness, who understand the powerful emotional lives of their gifted clients, and who have a deep appreciation and respect for the difficult task involved in raising gifted children.

REFERENCES

Abelman, R. (1991). Parental communication style and its influence on exceptional children's television viewing. *Roeper Review, 14,* 23–27.

Albert, R. S. (1978). Observations and suggestions regarding giftedness, familial influence, and the achievement of eminence. *Gifted Child Quarterly, 22,* 201–211.

Albert, R. S. (1980). Exceptionally gifted boys and their parents. *Gifted Child Quarterly, 24,* 174–179.

Anderson, R. W., & Tollefson, N. (1991). Do parents of gifted students emphasize sex role orientations for their sons and daughters? *Roeper Review, 13,* 154–157.

Ballering, L. D., & Koch, A. (1984). Family relations when a child is gifted. *Gifted Child Quarterly, 28,* 140–143.

Baum, M. L. (1992). From parent to parent. *Understanding Our Gifted, 4*(4), 18.

Benbow, C. P. (1992). Everywhere but here! *The Gifted Child Today, 15*(2), 2–8.

Bloom, B. S. (Ed.). (1985). *Developing talent in young people.* New York: Ballantine.

Bloom, B. S., & Sosniak, L. A. (1981). Talent development vs. schooling. *Educational Leadership, 39*(2), 86–94.

Burks, B. S., Jensen, D. W., & Terman, L. M. (1930). *Genetic studies of genius, Vol. 3. The promise of youth: Follow-up of 1000 gifted children.* Stanford, CA: Stanford University Press.

Colangelo, N. (1991). Counseling gifted students. In N. Colangelo & G. A. Davis (Eds.), *Handbook of gifted education* (pp. 273–284). Needham Heights, MA: Allyn & Bacon.

Colangelo, N., & Brower, P. (1987). Labeling gifted youngsters: Long-term impact on families. *Gifted Child Quarterly, 31,* 75–78.

Colangelo, N., & Dettmann, D. F. (1983). A review of research on parents and families of gifted children. *Exceptional Children, 50,* 20–27.

Cornell, D. G. (1983). Gifted children: The impact of positive labeling on the family system. *American Journal of Orthopsychiatry, 53,* 322–336.

Cornell, D. G. (1984). *Families of gifted children.* Ann Arbor, MI: UMI Research Press.

Cox, J., Daniel, N., & Boston, B. O. (1985). *Educating able learners: Programs and promising practices.* Austin: University of Texas Press.

Culross, R. R. (1982). Developing the whole child: A developmental approach to guidance with the gifted. *Roeper Review, 5*(2), 24–26.

Dabrowski, K. (1964). *Positive disintegration.* London: Gryf.

Delisle, J. R. (1992). *Guiding the social and emotional development of gifted youth: A practical guide for educators and counselors.* New York: Longman.

Dettman, D. F., & Colangelo, N. (1980). A functional model for counseling parents of gifted students. *Gifted Child Quarterly, 24*(4), 158–161.

Dirks, J. (1979). Parent's reactions to identification of the gifted. *Roeper Review, 2*(2), 9–10.

Emerick, L. J. (1992). Academic underachievement among the gifted: students' perceptions of factors that reverse the pattern. *Gifted Child Quarterly, 36,* 140–146.

Feldhusen, J. F. (1992). Early admission and grade advancement for young gifted learners. *The Gifted Child Today, 15*(2), 45–49.

Feldhusen, J. F., & Moon, S. M. (1992). Grouping gifted students: Issues and concerns. *Gifted Child Quarterly, 36,* 62–66.

Feldhusen, J. F., Sayler, M. F., Nielsen, M. E., & Kolloff, P. B. (1990). Self-concepts of gifted children in enrichment programs. *Journal for the Education of the Gifted, 13,* 380–387.

Feldman, D. (1979). The mysterious case of extreme giftedness. In A. H. Passow (Ed.), *The gifted and talented: Their education and development* (pp. 335–351). The seventy-eighth yearbook of the National Society for the Study of Education, Part I. Chicago: University of Chicago Press.

Feldman, D. H., with L. T. Goldsmith. (1986). *Nature's gambit: Child prodigies and the development of human potential.* New York: Basic Books.

Fine, M. J. (1977). Facilitating parent-child relationships for creativity. *The Gifted Child Quarterly, 21,* 487–500.

Fine, M. J., & Pitts, R. (1980). Intervention with underachieving gifted children: Rationale and strategies. *Gifted Child Quarterly, 24,* 51–55.

Freed, J. N. (1990). Tutoring techniques for the gifted. *Understanding Our Gifted, 2*(6), 1, 11–13.

Freeman, J. (1979). *Gifted children.* Baltimore: University Park Press.

George, P. (1988). Tracking and ability grouping. *Middle School Journal, 20*(1), 21–28.

Gillespie, W. J. (1982). *A national survey of urban gifted educational programs.* Unpublished doctoral dissertation, University of Denver.

Gogel, E. M., McCumsey, J., & Hewett, G. (1985). *G/C/T,* Issue No. 41, 7–9.

Grenier, M. E. (1985). Gifted children and other siblings. *Gifted Child Quarterly, 29,* 164–167.

Gross, M. U. M. (1989). The pursuit of excellence or the search for intimacy? The forced-choice dilemma of gifted youth. *Roeper Review, 11,* 189–193.

Gross, M. U. M. (1992). The use of radical acceleration in cases of extreme intellectual precocity. *Gifted Child Quarterly, 36,* 91–99.

Hackney, H. (1981). The gifted child, the family, and the school. *Gifted Child Quarterly, 25,* 51–54.

Hall, E. G., & Skinner, N. (1980). *Somewhere to turn: Strategies for parents of gifted and talented children.* New York: Teachers College Press.

Hansen, J. B. (1992). Discovering highly gifted students. *Understanding Our Gifted, 4*(4), 1, 11–13.

Hanson, I. (1984). A comparison between parent identification of young bright children and subsequent testing. *Roeper Review, 7,* 44–45.

Higham, S. J., & Buescher, T. M. (1987). What young gifted adolescents understand about feeling "different." In T. M. Buescher (Ed.), *Understanding gifted and* talented adolescents: A resource guide for counselors, educators, and parents (pp. 77–91). Evanston, IL: The Center for Talent Development, Northwestern University.

Hollingworth, L. S. (1926). *Gifted children: Their nature and nurture*. New York: Macmillan.

Hollingworth, L. S. (1942). *Children above 180 IQ Stanford-Binet: Origin and development*. Yonkers-on-Hudson, NY: World Book.

Jacobs, J. (1971). Effectiveness of teacher and parent identification of gifted children as a function of school level. *Psychology in the Schools, 8*(2), 140–142.

Kaufman, A. S. (1992). Evaluation of the WISC-III and WPPSI-R for gifted children. *Roeper Review, 14*, 154–158.

Kaufmann, F. A., & Sexton, D. (1983). Some implications for home-school linkages. *Roeper Review, 6*, 49–51.

Kearney, K. (1989). Homeschooling gifted children. *Understanding Our Gifted, 1*(3), 1, 12–13, 15–16.

Kline, B. E., & Meckstroth, E. A. (1985). Understanding and encouraging the exceptionally gifted. *Roeper Review, 8*, 24–30.

Kolloff, P. B., & Moore, A. D. (1989). Effects of summer programs on the self-concepts of gifted children. *Journal for the Education of the Gifted, 12*, 268–276.

Kulieke, M. J., & Olszewski-Kubilius, P. (1989). The influence of family values and climate on the development of talent. In J. VanTassel-Baska & P. Olszewski-Kubilius (Eds.), *Patterns of influence on gifted learners: The home, the self, and the school* (pp. 40–59). New York: Teachers College Press.

Laffoon, K. S., Jenkins-Friedman, R., & Tollefson, N. (1989). Causal attributions of underachieving gifted, achieving gifted, and nongifted students. *Journal for the Education of the Gifted, 13*, 4–21.

Lewis, M., & Louis, B. (1991). Young gifted children. In N. Colangelo & G. A. Davis (Eds.), *Handbook of gifted education* (pp. 365–381). Needham Heights, MA: Allyn & Bacon.

Louis, B., & Lewis, M. (1992). Parental beliefs about giftedness in young children and their relation to actual ability level. *Gifted Child Quarterly, 36*, 27–31.

MacKinnon, D. W. (1962). The nature and nurture of creative talent. *American Psychologist, 17*, 484–495.

Mathews, F. N., West, J. D., & Hosie, T. W. (1986). Understanding families of academically gifted children. *Roeper Review, 9*, 40–42.

Meckstroth, E. (1989a). Guarding the gifted child. *Understanding Our Gifted, 1*(5), 1, 10–12.

Meckstroth, E. (1989b). On testing. *Understanding Our Gifted, 1*(5), 4.

Meckstroth, E. (1991). Guiding the parents of gifted children: The role of counselors and teachers. In R. M. Milgrim (Ed.), *Counseling gifted and talented children: A guide for teachers, counselors, and parents*. Norwood, NJ: Ablex.

Meisgeier, C., & Murphy, E. (1987). *Murphy-Meisgeier Type Indicator for Children*. Palo Alto, CA: Consulting Psychologists Press.

Montemayor, R. (1987). Parents and adolescents: Understanding the cycles of conflict and affection in relationships. In T. M. Buescher (Ed.), *Understanding gifted and talented adolescents: A resource guide for counselors, educators, and parents* (pp. 24–25). Evanston, IL: The Center for Talent Development, Northwestern University.

Munger, A. (1990). The parent's role in counseling the gifted: The balance between home and school. In J. VanTassel-Baska (Ed.), *A practical guide to counseling the gifted in a school setting* (2nd ed., pp. 57–65). Reston, VA: The Council for Exceptional Children.

Myers, I. B. (1962). *Manual for the Myers-Briggs Type Indicator.* Palo Alto, CA: Consulting Psychologists Press.

Noble, K. (1989). Living out the promise of high potential: Perceptions of 100 gifted women. *Advanced Development, 1,* 57–75.

Olenchak, F. R. (1991). Wearing their shoes: Role playing to reverse underachievement. *Understanding Our Gifted, 3*(4), 1, 8–11.

Olszewski-Kubilius, P. (1989). Development of academic talent: The role of summer programs. In J. VanTassel-Baska & P. Olszewski-Kubilius (Eds.), *Patterns of influence on gifted learners: The home, the self, and the school* (pp. 214–230). New York: Teachers College Press.

Parker, M., Ross, A., & Deutsch, R. (1980). Parenting the gifted adolescent. *Roeper Review, 2*(4), 40–42.

Pfouts, J. H. (1980). Birth order, age spacing, I.Q. differences and family relations. *Journal of Marriage and the Family, 42,* 517–531.

Piechowski, M. M. (1987). Family qualities and the emotional development of older gifted students. In T. M. Buescher (Ed.), *Understanding gifted and talented adolescents* (pp. 17–23). Evanston, IL: The Center for Talent Development, Northwestern University.

Piechowski, M. M. (1991). Emotional development and emotional giftedness. In. N. Colangelo & G. Davis (Eds.), *Handbook of gifted education* (pp. 285–306). Needham Heights, MA: Allyn & Bacon.

Reis, S. M. (1987). We can't change what we don't recognize: Understanding the special needs of gifted females. *Gifted Child Quarterly, 31,* 83–89.

Rimm, S. B., & Lovance, K. J. (1992). The use of subject and grade skipping for the prevention and reversal of underachievement. *Gifted Child Quarterly, 36,* 100–105.

Robinson, N. (1987). The early development of precocity. *Gifted Child Quarterly, 31,* 161–164.

Robinson, N. M., & Noble, K. D. (1991). Social-emotional development and adjustment of gifted children. In M. C. Wang, M. C. Reynolds, & H. J. Walberg (Eds.), *Handbook of special education: Research and practice, Volume 4: Emerging programs* (pp. 57–76). New York: Pergamon Press.

Roedell, W. C. (1985). Developing social competence in gifted preschool children. *Remedial and Special Education, 6*(4), 6–11.

Roedell, W. C. (1988). "I just want my child to be happy": Social development and young gifted children. *Understanding Our Gifted, 1*(1), 1, 7, 10–11.

Roedell, W. C. (1989). Early development of gifted children. In J. VanTassel-Baska & P. Olszewski-Kubilius (Eds.), *Patterns of influence on gifted learners: The home, the self, and the school* (pp. 13–28). New York: Teachers College Press.

Roeper, A. (1992). Whose problem is it? *Understanding Our Gifted, 4*(4), 5.

Ross, A. O. (1964). *The exceptional child in the family.* New York: Grune & Stratton.

Schecter, J. (1992). Comparing different measures of intelligence. *Understanding Our Gifted, 4*(4), 14–15.

Schetky, D. H. (1981). A psychiatrist looks at giftedness: The emotional and social development of the gifted child. *G/C/T*, Issue No. 18, 2–4.

Sebring, A. D. (1983). Parental factors in the social and emotional adjustment of the gifted. *Roeper Review, 6*(2), 97–99.

Shaw, M. C., & McCuen, J. T. (1960). The onset of academic underachievement in bright children. *Journal of Educational Psychology, 51,* 103–108.

Silverman, L. K. (1985). *Characteristics of Introversion in Children Scale.* Denver: Gifted Child Development Center.

Silverman, L. K. (1986). What happens to the gifted girl? In C. J. Maker (Ed.), *Critical issues in gifted education, Vol. 1: Defensible programs for the gifted* (pp. 43–89). Rockville, MD: Aspen.

Silverman, L. K. (1988, October). The second child syndrome. *Mensa Bulletin*, No. 320, pp. 18–20.

Silverman, L. K. (1989). Invisible gifts, invisible handicaps. *Roeper Review, 12,* 37–42.

Silverman, L. K. (1991). Help for the hidden handicapped. *Highly Gifted Children, 1*(2), 10–11.

Silverman, L. K., Chitwood, D. G., & Waters, J. L. (1986). Young gifted children: Can parents identify giftedness? *Topics in Early Childhood Special Education, 6*(1), 23–38.

Silverman, L. K., & Kearney, K. (1989). Parents of the extraordinarily gifted. *Advanced Development, 1,* 41–56.

Silverman, L. K., & Kearney, K. (1992). Don't throw away the old Binet. *Understanding Our Gifted, 4*(4), 1, 8–10.

Silverman, L. K., & Leviton, L. P. (1991). In search of the perfect program. *The Gifted Child Today, 14*(6), 31–34.

Singal, D. J. (1991). The other crisis in American education. *The Atlantic Monthly, 268*(5), 59–74.

Sloane, K. D. (1985). Home influences on talent development. In B. S. Bloom (Ed.), *Developing talent in young people* (pp. 439–476). New York: Ballantine Books.

Southern, W. T., & Jones, E. D. (Eds.). *The academic acceleration of gifted children.* New York: Teachers College Press.

Stanley, J. C. (1990). Leta Hollingworth's contributions to above-level testing of the gifted. *Roeper Review, 13,* 166–171.

Strom, R., Johnson, A., Strom, S., & Strom, P. (1992). Designing curriculum for parents of gifted children. *Journal for the Education of the Gifted, 15,* 182–200.

Sunderlin, A. (1981). Gifted children and their siblings. In B. S. Miller & M. Puce (Eds.), *The gifted child, the family, and the community.* New York: Walker.

Tannenbaum, A. J. (1992). Early signs of giftedness: Research and commentary. *Journal for the Education of the Gifted, 15,* 104–133.

Tolan, S. S. (1992). Only a parent: Three true stories. *Understanding Our Gifted, 4*(3), 1, 8–10.

VanTassel-Baska, J. (1989). The role of the family in the success of disadvantaged gifted learners. *Journal for the Education of the Gifted, 13,* 22–36.

Vernon, P. E. (1987). The demise of the Stanford-Binet scale. *Canadian Psychology, 28*(3), 251–258.

Whitmore, J. R. (1979). Discipline and the gifted child. *Roeper Review, 2*(2), 42–46.

Whitmore, J. R. (1980). *Giftedness, conflict, and underachievement.* Needham Heights, MA: Allyn & Bacon.

Whitmore, J. R. (1989). Re-examining the concept of underachievement. *Understanding Our Gifted, 2*(1), 1, 7–9.

Witty, P. A. (1958). Who are the gifted? In N. B. Henry (Ed.), *Education for the gifted* (pp. 42–63). The fifty-seventh yearbook of the National Society for the Study of Education, Part II. Chicago: University of Chicago Press.

Wright, L. (1990). The social and nonsocial behavior of precocious preschoolers during free play. *Roeper Review, 12,* 268–274.

Young, J., & Johnson, D. (1991). Up by our own bootstraps. *Understanding Our Gifted, 4*(1), 1, 13–15.

PART III

Counseling
in the Schools

The Roles of Educational Personnel in Counseling the Gifted

8

Joyce VanTassel-Baska and Lee Baska

One reason counseling tends to be ignored in the education of the gifted is the lack of trained personnel who feel they are adequately prepared to counsel gifted children. Trained counselors are in short supply in most educational institutions. When available, they usually work exclusively at the seventh to twelfth grade levels. Their responsibility to all students necessarily limits the services they are able to render to gifted students. In addition, few counselors have been trained in the special characteristics and needs of the gifted population, and therefore may not perceive the necessity of providing special services to this group. All of these reasons obviate against the likelihood that gifted students will receive appropriate counseling intervention from a counseling specialist in schools. Thus it is imperative that other personnel be responsible for a broad range of counseling needs. The two most critical individuals to provide support in this process are the teacher of the gifted and the school psychologist. Teachers with special training in gifted education are needed as much for the affective development of these students as for their cognitive development. The roles and functions of these professionals in enhancing the affective development of the gifted provide an important emphasis in gifted program evolution.

THE UNIQUE ROLE OF THE TEACHER OF THE GIFTED

The teacher of the gifted is uniquely qualified to meet some psychosocial counseling needs of these students. When the teacher acts as a teacher/counselor, there are multiple advantages to the student:

1. The gifted student can receive counseling assistance in the context of the regular classroom or specialized gifted setting, rather than being "taken out" for one more type of activity.
2. The gifted student can begin to perceive his or her program as holistic, not segmented by concerns for affective issues separate from cognitive ones.
3. The gifted student can discuss common interests and problems in a small group of gifted peers with an adult who knows the student in another context.
4. The gifted student can receive reinforcement and encouragement on an ongoing basis rather than postponing it until a special appointment has been made.

In reality, the teacher of the gifted spends more time with such students and therefore presumably knows them better than other educational personnel. Furthermore, the teacher of the gifted is trained in understanding and responding to the special characteristics and needs of this population. Thus, providing a counseling service to them merely extends and broadens the nature of services already being offered. Benefits to the student also benefit the teacher, especially in the case of "problem" students whose behavior needs some form of modification. The teacher, then, is a natural facilitator to implement small-group activities that address many of the unique counseling needs of the gifted.

Coping with Giftedness

Many counseling needs of gifted students can be met successfully by teachers who are aware of certain basic strategies. The special affective needs of gifted children include:

❑ Understanding one's differentness, yet recognizing one's similarities to others
❑ Understanding how to accept and give criticism
❑ Being tolerant of oneself and others
❑ Developing an understanding of one's strengths and weaknesses
❑ Developing skills in areas that will nurture both cognitive and affective development

Strategies that teachers may use include the following: role playing, tutorials, mentorships, internships, bibliotherapy, discussion groups, special projects, simulation, gaming, special interest clubs, skill development seminars, and career exploration. (Some of these strategies are discussed in greater detail in other chapters of this text; others are described here.)

Holding Discussion Groups

Counseling the gifted must begin with how each gifted student perceives his or her world. Development of healthy self-concept and self-esteem is predicated on self-understanding. The teacher of the gifted can use small-group activities to help foster in students a better sense of who they are in relation to others. Requisite to such activities, however, is opportunities for discussion among gifted students themselves, with the teacher acting as facilitator. (See chapter 5 for more information on conducting discussion groups.)

Modeling

Gifted students, particularly girls and individuals from disadvantaged backgrounds, can profit from exposure to good role models that provide impetus for mirroring gifted behaviors (Fox, Brody, & Tobin, 1980; Frazier, 1980). The teacher of the gifted has various avenues for providing students with role models. Mentorships and internships offer one context for modeling; however, time constraints often make it difficult for the teacher to set up such experiences. Alternative kinds of experiences may then be more appropriate.

Because gifted students enjoy reading and can easily become absorbed in the lives of characters, bibliotherapy is a natural way to access a variety of role models (Hollingworth, 1926). (Biographies, autobiographies, and novels featuring gifted children can be found in the Appendix.) Bibliotherapy can also be used as a successful strategy in other areas of counseling. Annotated book lists for such purposes are readily available (Baskin & Harris, 1980; Tway, 1980). (See chapter 4 for more information on bibliotherapy.)

Solving Unfamiliar Problems

The gifted student is frequently seen as one who takes tests well and has mastery over the kinds of content material they contain. It is reasonable to assume that gifted students do well on tests that are beneath their cognitive level, such as most in-grade, standardized achievement tests, but it cannot be assumed that they have the skills to cope with the more difficult tests to which they will be exposed as early as junior high age.

In fact, many gifted students are not good test-takers for several reasons, not the least of which is a lack of interest in or concern for what particular tests measure or what purpose they serve in a student's life (Renzulli, Reis, & Smith, 1981). Yet, if gifted students can begin to perceive tests as "problems to be solved" and as indicators of areas in which they excel, perhaps test-score information would more accurately reflect potential. Helping gifted students develop such a view is an important function teachers can perform. The carryover effect to curriculum that is "challenging" helps both gifted students and their teachers in estimating appropriate expectation levels for performance.

The Teacher as Advocate and Advisor

The activities described thus far reflect "direct intervention" approaches to counseling gifted students in classroom contexts. Teachers can be extremely effective in more indirect ways as well. Acting as an advocate for gifted students helps other educational personnel and parents understand these students' specific behaviors. Some teachers may expect them to be good in everything and may be unduly critical of their mistakes. As an advocate, the teacher of the gifted can explain the strengths and weaknesses of individual students and assist others in forming realistic appraisals of them.

Parents often express concern when their gifted child shows a clear preference for reading over more conventional "play" activities. Even educational personnel can become concerned by this pattern of behavior. A teacher advocate can assure parents and others that this behavior is typical, indeed "normal," for a gifted child, even though it seems unusual when viewed against the background of the preferences of less gifted children.

Acting as a good listener can also serve an important function. Too frequently, gifted students feel there is no one with whom they can share their feelings, particularly those that reflect negatively upon themselves, such as feelings of inadequacy and imperfection. For example, when entering a gifted program for the first time, gifted students frequently feel inadequate. Suddenly they are no longer the brightest in the class, and the "getting-by" behavior they have cultivated through their earlier years of schooling no longer works. Owning up to these feelings is an important part of a student's development and is necessary in order to shed old, inappropriate attitudes and behaviors. The teacher can create a setting in which children can reveal these feelings without fear of being exposed, thus providing them with an important outlet for expression and ultimate growth.

Acting as an informal advisor to gifted students is another important function. Many gifted students of junior high age, for example, have little idea of appropriate coursework to take as they enter secondary school, particularly as the decision relates to later college and career choices. Teachers can help them plan ahead in their educational experiences in order to maximize potential long-range benefits. The teacher of the gifted can recommend certain types of courses for which the student may be especially well suited, and can point out the importance of such courses, perhaps even based on personal experience. Only if teachers involve themselves in this way can gifted students get the "longer view" from someone who knows and understands their needs.

Certainly not all the counseling needs of gifted students can be met through the teacher in a classroom context, nor can individual and group activities meet every diverse and complex need. A knowledgeable and sensitive teacher working with the gifted in a group setting can, however, successfully address some of the significant affective needs of gifted students. In this way, counseling provisions for the gifted can become a part of standard program practice rather than a wished-for ideal.

THE ROLE OF THE ADMINISTRATOR IN COUNSELING

School administrators such as superintendents, principals, and central administrative staff members also have key roles to play in counseling gifted students. As primary decision-makers, they are able to effect both personal and institutional changes needed to ensure that these students have the educational and support services to flourish in the school setting. In addition, administrators' personal contact with students and their parents is important.

Administrators must serve as institutional advocates for these students. This involves keeping the interests of the gifted in mind when making decisions regarding program and curriculum, being willing to build flexibility into school programming and schedules, and allowing students to develop programs responsive to their individual needs. Administrators must also be certain that appropriate educational opportunities are available to students throughout their years in school.

Like the teacher, the administrator is often called upon to play a consulting role within the district, with parents, and with community members. Within the district, administrators should ensure that teachers and other personnel have received training in gifted education. This may be in the form of classes or professional development activities. By seeing to it that staff are trained, administrators help to ensure high-quality programming for gifted students.

The building principal plays a vital role in the lives of gifted children. He or she sets the tone within the school for either support or neglect of this group of children, and the staff follows suit. Gifted children not only flourish with a supportive principal, they blossom. Parents moving into a district often investigate which school does the most to develop talents. A principal who values excellence and strives for optimal development of *all* students will attract excellent students. Some principals even take time to work with gifted children in small groups or serve as mentors to students with leadership potential.

In the position of program leader or coordinator of the gifted program, the administrator plays a counseling role by making sure that programming options are in place, that counseling capabilities are available, and that excellence is a goal for all involved with the gifted education effort. When programs are in place, the administrator should take steps to see that they run smoothly and continuously.

Gifted students will approach administrators for counseling on personal and academic matters, as they do teachers. It is essential that administrators take time to listen and respond. This may mean making an appointment or just taking a focused moment in the hallway. Attending to the personal needs of gifted students should be considered an appropriate part of administrators' counseling roles.

THE ROLE OF THE SOCIAL WORKER

An important member of the pupil personnel team who has been under-utilized in serving the gifted is the social worker. The traditional task of the social worker has been defined as providing emergency or crisis service rather than as proactive involvement with the psychological needs of the child. Emergencies cannot be ignored; however, time could also be devoted to assisting gifted children who do not fit the traditional profile of the high achiever or who are at risk in other ways. Social workers have unique training in unraveling the familial patterns that contribute to atypical or idiosyncratic behavior in gifted children. Input from the social worker can strengthen the teacher's role in serving these children.

Knowledge of the family constellation enables the social worker to find those family members most able to contribute to the emotional nurturance of the child. In dysfunctional families a surrogate may need to be located who can perform a parenting role when the parent is incapable. This is critical for the development of all children, but the commonly observed pattern of height-ened emotional sensitivity in gifted children makes this role even more important for them.

For underachieving students, appropriate recognition needs to follow the student's first attempts at credible achievement. One function of the social worker can be finding the key to motivating underachievers and, in so doing, helping them build self-esteem. The most powerful tool schools have in reducing discipline problems and behavioral "emergencies" is the recogni-tion of student strengths. A proactive role for social workers can be helping teachers find specific strengths of students that can be used to design instruc-tional strategies. This should diminish the focus on the student's misbehavior and change the school climate for the child from negative to positive. (See chapter 12 for more information about working with gifted children at risk.)

The outreach nature of social work is perfect for finding mentors in the community who can help the atypical gifted child as well as provide more challenging experiences for others. Service clubs are another resource for providing scholarships, foreign exchange, and business experience, such as Junior Achievement programs.

Thus, social workers can provide an important role in counseling gifted students and their families. This role may be designed to include: work with dysfunctional and atypical family structures to ensure emotional maintenance for the child, serving as a child advocate in school settings, and locating community resources including mentors for the gifted child.

THE ROLE OF THE SCHOOL PSYCHOLOGIST

Another individual who needs to be involved in counseling gifted students is the school psychologist. Training in research and measurement gives that person a special place in the interpretation of children's behavior for a spectrum of abilities, including giftedness. Whereas gifted children usually have a remarkable resiliency which allows them to adapt to the demands of the classroom environment, this can be to the detriment of their own development. They become tutors, helpers, and assume various other roles which mask their boredom in a class that creates little challenge for them. The school psychologist/advocate needs to address the misuse of talent that parades as "good socialization skills for later life" by stressing the major role of the school—an appropriate education for every child. Suggesting a separate curriculum for children who have fewer legal imperatives attached to their needs may be unpopular in a financially stretched school district, but the special needs of the gifted are as varied and urgent for optimal development as the needs of children with disabilities. It is the school psychologist who may be best able to help others understand and address these needs in an appropriate fashion. The school psychologist is also the only one in the system who can identify gifted children with learning disabilities and explain their needs to the faculty.

The History of School Psychology

The role of the school psychologist became pivotal in facilitating educational decision-making for special education students in an earlier era. The "Great Society" legislation that gave us Headstart and other reforms in education in the mid-1960s also provided federal mandates for special education so that children previously excluded were guaranteed a "free and appropriate education in the least restrictive environment." Parents exercised their legal rights under these mandates and special education services grew dramatically in response to those demands. The rights of disabled students and due process procedures added a new dimension to schools that required training and hiring of new categories of specialists.

When the parents of disabled children mobilized to bring about the much needed reform for this part of our school population, it was difficult to anticipate the long-range consequences and impact on schools. The school psychologist often acquired the unfortunate role of psychometrician since an imprimatur is needed for special education placement. "Test and retest them until they qualify" has been a spin-off from pragmatist mentality that tried to recoup the investment made in special education services.

Whereas special classes for disabled children were first seen as beneficial, the trend now is to return such students to the "mainstream" or regular class as soon as practicable. It is feared that if children are isolated from other students by being placed in separate classes, this will be damaging to the children's self-perception. Although the research does not support these fears (Singal, 1991; Snyderman & Rothman, 1988), the benefits of small-group instruction may be outweighed by emotional concerns. Thus, the role of the psychologist has shifted more to a consultative model, assisting teachers and others who are working with disabled students day-to-day. It is in this type of role that the school psychologist can also assist in counseling gifted students.

The major trend, then, in the 1990s for school psychology is toward a consulting, therapeutic involvement, as opposed to psychometric placement tasks that assumed the infallibility of the test results. Gradually school personnel have come to rightfully question the decisions being made about children that did not take into account all relevant material and circumstances affecting the child's environment in and out of school. Staffing decisions that involve parents, a psychologist, social worker, and therapist(s) central to the child's presenting problem have become the norm for making placement decisions. Staffings can also be conducted for gifted students at the request of the school psychologist. Gifted students can be best served by school psychologists when the role of the psychologist is broadened beyond that of psychometrician.

New Roles for School Psychologists Working with the Gifted

The school psychologist has vital information about the meaning of giftedness which needs to be shared with the entire school community. It is essential that this individual be freed from other responsibilities so that this key role can be assumed. Overcoming the piecework mentality attached to special education testing may be the main obstacle to achieving this goal. The numbers of children tested and reports written by school psychologists become their primary preoccupation. These activities prohibit involvement of the school psychologist in a proactive role in serving gifted students. Some of the functions that a school psychologist might perform on behalf of gifted students follow.

Interpretation of Test Results to Various Publics

Key groups would include administrators, teachers, and parents.

Administrators. One important service that psychologists can provide is inspecting tests to be used for gifted populations with respect to issues of appropriateness, reliability, and validity. The school psychologist can anticipate typical problems of gifted students at early stages and develop strategies for improvement. He or she should develop student profile data that accurately represent the relationship among teaching, learning, and testing. This kind of information can enhance the instructional process for groups of teachers and aid a principal in promoting an emphasis on real learning in a school.

Teachers. An important part of an effective psychologist's function is providing constructive comments on weaknesses as well as praise or encouragement for the strengths of individual teachers. The cornerstone of this role is finding mutually acceptable approaches to instruction that will help teachers effectively grow and, thus, better serve students. Learning from teachers can obviously help the growth of psychologists as well.

Opening up the curriculum for gifted children beyond the field trip and term paper approach needs thoughtful exploration if the real abilities of these children are to be tapped. Interviews with children about their goals need to be conducted so the best match can be made for career planning. The assessment of personality traits can aid in this process, particularly looking at developmental growth over time through the succession of grades.

Parents. A critical translation task that school psychologists are trained to provide is assisting parents in understanding their child's strengths, weaknesses, and progress. Moreover, the school psychologist can promote effective school/home cooperation by helping parents ask appropriate questions about their child's progress. This empowers parents, improves the dialogue between home and school, and develops a good climate for educational support.

One of the confusing pieces of information offered parents is the periodic report of standardized testing. The grade level multiple choice test often obscures the real range of abilities within a group because of the ceiling (and floor) effects of the test. Gifted students do not get a chance to show the breadth or depth of their ability, and, conversely, low-functioning children can look good because of random guesses. The narrowing of both true abilities and disabilities may mask the real diversity in a school community and succeed in hiding talents and weaknesses for students to address. Thus, the purpose of testing becomes construed to be for assessing minimum standards of accountability rather than individual learning achievement and aptitude.

Low Incidence, Disabled, and Disadvantaged Gifted
Child-find processes are relatively well organized for the disabled, but there is no similar child-find attempt for the brightest children. And child-find personnel are not trained to recognize children who are both gifted and disabled. This is not to suggest neglecting the disabled but rather to recognize that low-incidence gifted children may have pressing needs that could be addressed in the same manner. A school psychologist might be charged with identification and program recommendations for all highly gifted and disadvantaged students in a given school context. As a districtwide advocate, psychologists can more easily discern the students in greatest need and plan appropriate services for them. Central coordination of such services is essential since individual schools can rarely provide all of the services required for such populations.

Community Networking
A major need of schools in the coming years will be developing abilities for high-tech jobs that are emerging in our society. Mentors who are involved in the work world can sometimes provide a better perspective on the demands of that future job and the accompanying preparation that schools cannot provide for students. They also act as role models for students who aspire to those fields of work.

Community resources, including service clubs such as Kiwanis, Rotary, Lions, Salvation Army, and others, can be an important part of the link to educational credibility within the community. Finding roles for willing volunteers within the schools and job/career opportunities for children in the work world can be a part of the process of networking on behalf of the gifted.

Organizing and monitoring mentors to work with the gifted will become an increasingly important task for schools that try to provide up-to-date training and experiences for the gifted. It is a role that school psychologists may assist in, particularly at the stage of matching students to individual mentors.

Developing IEPs for Gifted Students

The Individual Educational Plan (IEP) is one special education document that has given parents hope for an appropriate set of expectations for their child. Many of the parents of the gifted have no sense of the range of educational offerings and options that a highly gifted child could undertake. A planning document that makes the most of the child's aptitudes and abilities is absolutely necessary to begin the long-range view of schooling for that child. School psychologists have traditionally played a pivotal role in the development of IEPs for disabled students and would be an excellent resource in determining IEPs for gifted students.

Being a Resource for Test Review

School personnel are bombarded with publisher data that require intelligent review. An important task consistent with the psychologist's role is helping to organize the review process for schools so as to choose test materials that fit the goals of the school. Psychologists, then, can review diagnostic and achievement tests, can help teachers construct tests, and can assist in the interpretation of these tests.

School psychologists are in the position of performing a significant role in the faithful translation of testing data to curriculum intervention in the classroom. Work is currently underway at the College of William and Mary, for example, to develop profiles of interventions for special populations of gifted students based on test data. A two-step process that illustrates the conversions necessary to move from test data to classroom instruction is included in Tables 8.1 and 8.2.

TESTING AND ASSESSMENT

The traditional role for school psychologists has unarguably been that of testing, an arena with its own special history. The history of intelligence testing owes much to the nineteenth-century work of Binet and Simon leading to the first published scales in 1905, the initiation of a clinical norm group that exhibited identifiable characteristics for validation of predictive tests. Researchers such as Lewis Terman (1916) and all those involved in the testing of World War I draftees quickly increased the bank of test items to include most of the items we now accept as part of this process. Leta Hollingworth's work with gifted populations was unique and confirmatory of the process that emanated from Stanford (Hollingworth, 1926). What followed has been a refinement of the theory that supports testing and an improvement of statistical and methodological techniques. John Raven's nonverbal matrices (1938)

Table 8.1
INDIVIDUAL INSTRUCTIONAL PLAN (PART I)

To the assessor: After completing your psychological report for each student, please check the areas of strength and areas of weaknesses, based on the following list derived from the subsections of the testing battery. Thank you for your help.

Strengths	Weaknesses	
_____	_____	Freedom from distractibility (WISC-R)
_____	_____	Digit span
_____	_____	Arithmetic
_____	_____	Coding
_____	_____	Block design
_____	_____	Vocabulary (WISC-R & PIAT-R)
_____	_____	Reading comprehension (PIAT-R)
_____	_____	Math concepts (PIAT-R)
_____	_____	Spatial reasoning (WISC-R)
_____	_____	Block design
_____	_____	Mazes
_____	_____	Object assembly
_____	_____	Verbal reasoning (WISC-R)
_____	_____	Picture arrangement
_____	_____	Short-term memory (WISC-R)
_____	_____	Digit span
_____	_____	Arithmetic
_____	_____	Written expression (PIAT-R)
_____	_____	General information (WISC-R and PIAT-R)
_____	_____	Verbal creativity (Torrance)
_____	_____	Figural creativity (Torrance)
_____	_____	Social comprehension
_____	_____	Verbal analogistic reasoning
_____	_____	Similarities (WISC-R)
_____	_____	Visual closure (WISC-R)
_____	_____	Picture completion
_____	_____	Object assembly
_____	_____	Figural analogistic reasoning (MAT)

Is test performance within areas consistent across tests and/or subtests?
Yes_____ No_____ If no, please explain.

Are there any particular affective/behavioral issues to be considered with this child?
Yes_____ No_____ If yes, please explain.

Please forward this form to the person responsible for Individual Instructional Plan (IIP) development.

Source: From the Center for Gifted Education, College of William and Mary, Williamsburg, VA.

Table 8.2
INDIVIDUAL INSTRUCTIONAL PLAN (PART II)

To the IIP developer: After reviewing Part II of the plan, please check the areas of emphasis listed below under each category that correspond most closely to areas of strengths. Go back over the list a second time and star (*) those areas recommended for enhancement.

GENERAL GOALS
- ❑ Develop opportunities for creative/artistic expression
- ❑ Work on critical thinking skills of analysis, synthesis, and evaluation
- ❑ Enhance self-esteem

COGNITIVE/ACADEMIC
Verbal (Reading, Language Arts)
- ❑ Use an inquiry-based study of appropriate children's literature
- ❑ Use a writing program that encourages elaboration and incorporation of ideas from literature into stories
- ❑ Select biographies and books in the content areas (including subjects dealing with multicultural issues) for supplementary reading
- ❑ Include experiences in foreign language in the curriculum
- ❑ Emphasize the development and use of logic and critical thinking
- ❑ Use storytelling techniques
- ❑ Encourage and provide time to pursue free reading based on student interests
- ❑ Teach debate skills
- ❑ Stimulate broad reading patterns
- ❑ Develop expository writing skills
- ❑ Individualize a reading program that diagnoses reading level and prescribes reading material based on that level
- ❑ Form a literary group of similar students for discussions
- ❑ Focus on vocabulary building
- ❑ Develop word relationship skills (e.g., analogies, antonyms, homonyms)

Quantitative (Math)
- ❑ Focus on developing spatial skills and concepts through geometry and other media
- ❑ Focus on problem-solving skills with appropriately challenging problems
- ❑ Use of calculators and computers as tools in the problem-solving process
- ❑ Emphasize mathematical concepts more and computational skills less
- ❑ Focus on logic problems that require deductive thinking skills and inference
- ❑ Emphasize applications of mathematics in the real world through creation of special projects
- ❑ Emphasize algebraic manipulations
- ❑ Teach statistical techniques
- ❑ Focus on the use of probability

Nonverbal
- ❑ Teach visual spatialization techniques
- ❑ Teach mapping strategies
- ❑ Teach metacognition
- ❑ Use figural symbols to teach concepts
- ❑ Use puzzles and mazes

CREATIVE/AESTHETIC
- ❑ Practice skills of fluency, flexibility, elaboration, and originality

❑ Work on specific product development
❑ Prepare a skit or play for production
❑ Provide art appreciation opportunities
❑ Provide music opportunities
❑ Provide dramatic instruction
❑ Provide opportunities for dance and movement
❑ Teach role-playing
❑ Provide "collage" experience across art, music, literature
❑ Introduce various artistic forms
❑ Introduce various musical forms
❑ Use biographies of creative people
❑ Teach creative problem solving
❑ Use brainstorming

BEHAVIORAL/SOCIAL/AFFECTIVE
❑ Encourage independent work
❑ Encourage cooperative learning by interest area
❑ Encourage cooperative learning by instructional area
❑ Encourage a mentorship relationship
❑ Encourage tutorials
❑ Encourage internships
❑ Encourage use of long-term projects

Source: From the Center for Gifted Education, College of William and Mary, Williamsburg, VA.

added reasoning skills that have survived sixty years of research looking for tests less sensitive to cultural influence (Sattler, 1982).

More recently, independent publishers have found niches in the larger test market and claim to provide new ways of identifying gifted children. The "perfect test" has become a holy grail for the gifted education market besieged with fads and confusion within a well-developed tradition. Test development, printing, and validation costs require major publishers to focus on the total school population and sell their products as though they worked for all categories of students who require special treatment.

Common criticisms of testing and popular antitest reactions are often directed at the misuses of tests in the hands of inadequately qualified users. These misuses stem from a desire for quick answers and simple solutions to complex, real-life problems, and too often the decision-making responsibility is shifted to the test when this is only a tool to be used judiciously.

The interpretation of test scores calls for knowledge about the statistical properties of scores and the psychological characteristics being assessed. An understanding of percentiles, standard scores, deviation IQs, and caveats related to the standard error of measurement is critical to their proper use.

The 1985 publication of the Ninth Mental Measurements Yearbook (Mitchell, 1985) includes a table of frequencies for the fifty tests that had the largest number of reference citations. These tests probably represent a core of the most popular measures being used in today's market and in most cases the best tests available to measure a given construct.

General Principles of Testing

Many investigators in the field of gifted education have decried the use and abuse of intelligence tests (Renzulli, 1978; Sternberg, 1985). Others have found the use of any standardized testing procedure inappropriate for identifying the most talented (Alvino & Weiler, 1979; Bruch, 1971; Torrance, 1970), particularly for students from minority backgrounds. And most school districts continue to adopt identification procedures that attempt to balance testing with more observational data sources such as teacher recommendations and peer or parent inventories. Yet, no studies have refuted Martinson's claim (1974) that the individual Stanford-Binet (Form L-M) is still the single best measure to identify gifted children, and Richert, Alvino, and McDonnell (1982) still report it to be the best individual intelligence test available for identifying general intellectual ability. A comprehensive discussion of why and when to use the old Binet can be found in Silverman and Kearney (1992).

Talent Searches

One important development regarding the identification dilemma was proposed by Julian Stanley (Stanley, Keating, & Fox, 1974). The simple but elegant idea was to administer a more difficult test, one normed on older children, to a younger group. The idea originated with Leta Hollingworth (Stanley, 1990). Specifically, Stanley recommended using the Scholastic Aptitude Test (SAT) to find precocious seventh-grade students. The efficiency of this approach is now legend. Close to 100,000 students are now tested annually through this procedure both nationally and internationally.

The talent search model employs a two-step testing protocol. At step one, it seeks to find all students who are scoring at the 95th or 97th percentile on their in-grade standardized achievement test battery, either in mathematical or verbal areas. At step two, it discriminates within this academically able population by administering the Scholastic Aptitude Test, typically used at senior high school level to identify students who will do well in college. Because there is a dispersion of scores on the SAT such that there is virtually no ceiling effect, educators can better discern the potential of these junior high age students at this critical stage of development in major areas of academic aptitude. Furthermore, because these younger students usually have not had advanced coursework in mathematics or the verbal arts, the scores reflected are more representative of aptitude than achievement, thus countering the charge frequently made about the SAT when used with older populations—that it measures achievement rather than aptitude.

What important information does aptitude testing on the SAT provide educators as they institute local identification policies? The principles embodied in the talent search identification model have only recently begun to be employed within school districts to identify those students most in need of a differentiated program at the local level. Yet these principles translate very well to local program identification issues (VanTassel-Baska & Strykowski, 1985).

The Principle of Off-Level Testing

Because gifted children always score toward the top end of an in-grade standardized test, it is impossible to discriminate true potential based on scores from such tests. It also is unjustifiable to establish an arbitrary cutoff within the narrow band at the top of the test. True potential for specific academic work in mathematics and verbal areas can be discerned better by administering an off-level test, standardized on older populations. Many local school districts ignore this principle by arbitrarily using cutoff points within a narrow band of ability on in-grade measures. Consequently, many able learners are being overlooked in the process.

The Principle of Testing Specific Areas of Aptitude
Rather Than Global Intelligence

Current theoretical work in the field of gifted education involves a conception of multiple intelligences (Gardner, 1983), and current research on prodigies suggests that intelligence is displayed in domain-specific contexts (Feldman, 1980). Research on talent search students demonstrates the effectiveness of the Scholastic Aptitude Test measures in finding students who can profit from advanced coursework in specific aptitude areas (Keating, 1976; Stanley and Benbow, 1981; VanTassel-Baska, 1983). This method is particularly appropriate for identifying junior high school students. Global measures are less useful at this stage of development because of the ceiling effects on IQ tests and because most junior high students have begun to focus their intelligence in specific domains of knowledge.

But even if theory and research were not supportive of this direction, the talent search approach still represents a very reasonable identification course for local districts that program for gifted learners within a limited time frame, and therefore are frequently not prepared to meet all of the educational needs of this population. Furthermore, focusing on aptitudes allows a larger number of students to be identified and served, thus dispelling the notion that the gifted program is serving only the high-IQ student. Diversification of program options based on aptitude differences holds great potential particularly in higher socioeconomic suburban school districts where many bright students may be found.

The Principle of Providing a Specific Match Between
Tested Aptitude and Curriculum

If students are verbally able, they are best nurtured in that capacity by high-powered verbal programs that test their limits. And if students are mathematically precocious, a program should be geared to address that strength directly. The real beauty of aptitude testing is that school districts have important diagnostic information for curriculum planning. One could argue further that even a cursory content analysis of the test would provide a major sense of curricular inferences that might be made. Based on the type of items contained in the SAT-V, for example, one could begin to develop a strong verbal arts curriculum that focused strongly on certain test areas (see Table 8.3).

Types of Tests

Whereas general principles of testing are important, actual examples of appropriate tests for use with gifted populations may be of special interest. Examples of each type of useful test follow with some basic information about the instrument.

Individual Achievement Test
Example: Peabody Individual Achievement Test, Revised. The Peabody Individual Achievement Test, Revised (PIAT-R) is designed to assess levels of achievement on an individual basis. It can be used to measure children's ability from kindergarten through grade twelve. Standardization procedures meet the highest standards of current psychometric theory and include various disabled groups and cultural/linguistic minorities in the normative sample.

The PIAT-R is comprised of six subtests: General Information, Reading Recognition, Reading Comprehension, Mathematics, Spelling, and Written Language Composite. Grade equivalents and age equivalents with corresponding standard scores and percentiles are reported. The written expression subtest is a helpful addition to the scale revision but obviously dependent on motor/writing skills. As an untimed test it has particular value for testing disabled or atypical children and is used primarily in schools and clinical settings. It is not designed as a diagnostic test for any of the given subject areas but is meant to be a quick and useful device for generating hypotheses about the child's general performance skills.

Table 8.3
DEVELOPING CURRICULUM FROM TEST CATEGORIES

Sat-V Sections	Curriculum Inferences
Analogies	❏ Building analogy skills ❏ Discussion/writing about literary comparisons
Antonyms	❏ Vocabulary development ❏ Foreign language ❏ Word games
Reading Comprehension	❏ Critical reading skills such as analysis and interpretation ❏ Critical thinking skills, especially inference ❏ Discussion and critique of key passages in selected readings
Sentence Completions	❏ Study of semantics ❏ Analysis of reading passages across disciplines

Group Achievement Test

Example: Iowa Test of Basic Skills. The Iowa Test of Basic Skills is a well-respected and widely used test battery with a history of more than fifty years of development. The multilevel battery contains eleven subtests and is designed for use with grades three through nine. The secondary version of this test is the Iowa Test of Educational Development for grades nine to twelve. Internal consistency, validity, and reliability claims are well documented and the standardization procedures are exemplary. The test does an excellent job of providing information about the general performance of students in a variety of basic skill areas.

Group Aptitude Test

Example: Scholastic Aptitude Test (SAT). The Scholastic Aptitude Test is a test of verbal and mathematical reasoning ability normed on college-bound senior students, and used to predict success in college. Since 1975, it also has been used to identify verbally and mathematically precocious students of junior high age. It also can be used with highly gifted fifth- and sixth-grade students.

Individual Ability Test

Example: Wechsler Intelligence Scale for Children–III (WISC-III). The WISC-III is a very sound test of general intelligence with a long history of research and validation. No series of intelligence tests has yet equaled the success in research and practice of the Wechsler scales. Since the publication of the original WISC there have been over eleven hundred studies published, most pertaining to the WISC-R. Benefits of the WISC-III include its technical adequacy, the representativeness of norms, verbal and performance components, and recommendation for some at-risk groups.

The WISC-III was normed on a sample representative of the 1980 census. Two hundred children in eleven different age ranges from 6 years-6 months to 16 years-6 months years were included in the sample. Unlike the WISC, the WISC-III did include ethnic minorities in its sample.

The WISC-III has outstanding reliability. Each of the two IQ scales (Verbal, Performance) has reliabilities of .89 or higher, and the subscales all have average reliabilities of about .70. The test-retest reliabilities for the two IQ scales were .90 or above.

The WISC-III is individually administered, requiring approximately one hour of test time. It is intended for use with children age 6 years-9 months to 16 years-11 months, and the test administrator is required to have special training.

A major drawback of the WISC-III is its inordinate emphasis on speed in the Performance Section, which penalizes reflective children and children with poor motor coordination (Kaufman, 1992). An untimed test such as the Stanford-Binet (L-M) is preferable for students with observed weaknesses in motor speed. IQ scores in the gifted range are 5 to 6 points lower on average than those generated by the WISC-R. *Selection criteria for gifted programs need to be adjusted accordingly.* When children attain three subtest scores in the ceiling range of WISC-III scale scores (17, 18, or 19), the Stanford-Binet (Form L-M) should be used as a supplemental test as it has a higher range.

Group Ability Test

Example: Cognitive Abilities Test (CogAT). The CogAT is a measure of general intellectual functioning which was standardized on a carefully selected, stratified national sample of over 330,000 students. The standardization of this test is exemplary. The CogAT provides scores on three batteries: Verbal, Quantitative, and Nonverbal. The reliability information on the test is good with most estimates above .83. The CogAT is a group-administered test which requires one-and-a-half to three hours for administration and is appropriate for grades three through twelve. Whereas no special training is required, the length of administration time increases its accuracy. As a group test, it is still basically a screening device.

Nonverbal General Reasoning Test

Example: Raven's Coloured/Standard/Advanced Progressive Matrices. The Coloured and Standard Progressive Matrices provide a way to test children with severe language, auditory, or physical disabilities. Additionally, the test may be useful in assessing children with a limited command of English, since effects of culture are reduced for this test.

New norms were published for only the Coloured and Standard Progressive Matrices in 1986, by weighting cases from several studies performed on the tests. These norms are not representative of the United States, but may be an adequate sampling of school-aged children (Sattler, 1988). Reliability estimates for the Coloured and Standard tests fall mostly in the range for a screening test (test-retest reliabilities from .71 to .93; Sattler, 1988), with the lowest reliabilities for younger children.

Correlations of the tests with other intelligence tests (.50s and .80s) and achievement tests (.30s and .60s) indicate the validity of the tests. Studies have been done on populations of Caucasian, African-American, Hispanic, Native American, and deaf individuals.

Both of the tests can be administered individually or in groups and require fifteen to thirty minutes. The Coloured Progressive Matrices is used for children in the five to eleven age range; the Standard Progressive Matrices is used with those in the six to seventeen age range. The administrator requires no special training.

The Advanced Matrices has been utilized in conjunction with above-level achievement testing since 1982 as part of the Chicago Magnet High School admission procedure (Baska, 1986). Ninth-grade reading and math tests and the Advanced Matrices are administered to sixth-graders to select two hundred students from the more than seven hundred annual applicants for the seventh-grade magnet program. Findings from these data have shown that it is possible to incorporate a measure that was originally targeted for an adult population. The mean raw scores for the Advanced Matrices have been between 14 and 15 with a standard deviation of 5 points. The difficulty of this thirty-six-item measure allows for an adequate dispersion of scores without the common problem of ceiling effect when testing the gifted. Further, the item characteristic curves developed from the 1985 data also suggest the test is performing as demonstrated with an adult sample for England.

CONCLUSION

This chapter has addressed the role of important sources of counseling support for the gifted: teachers, administrators, social workers, and school psychologists. Each functions to meet different needs of gifted students in our schools, yet all can provide important psychosocial support to a group frequently overlooked in the context of school practices. School personnel and the guidance they provide special populations of gifted learners may be the most powerful influence these students experience in school. The power of one-on-one nurturance is unrivaled.

REFERENCES

Alvino, J. J., & Weiler, J. (1979). How standardized testing fails to identify the gifted and what teachers can do about it. *Phi Delta Kappan, 61*(2), 106.

Baska, L. K. (1986). The use of the Raven Advanced Matrices for junior high school gifted programs. *Roeper Review, 8,* 181–184.

Baskin, B., & Harris, K. (1980). *Books for the gifted child.* New York: R. R. Bowker.

Binet, A., et Simon, Th. (1905). Methods nouvelle pour le diagnostic due niveau intellectual des anormaux. *L'Annee Psychologique, 11,* 191–244.

Bruch, C. B. (1971). Modification of procedures for identification of the disadvantaged gifted. *Gifted Child Quarterly, 15,* 267–271.

Feldman, D. H. (1980). *Beyond universals in cognitive development.* Norwood, NJ: Ablex.

Fox, L., Brody, L., & Tobin, D. (Eds.). (1980). *Women and the mathematical mystique.* Baltimore: Johns Hopkins Press.

Frazier, M. (1980). Programming for the culturally diverse. In J. Jordan & J. Grossi (Eds.), *An administrator's handbook on designing programs for the gifted and talented.* Reston, VA: Council for Exceptional Children.

Gardner, J. (1983). *Frames of mind.* New York: Basic Books.

Hollingworth, L. S. (1926). *Gifted children: Their nature and nurture.* New York: Macmillan.

Kaufman, A. S. (1992). Evaluation of the WISC-III and WPPSI-R for gifted children. *Roeper Review, 14,* 154–158.

Keating, D. (1976). *Intellectual talent.* Baltimore: Johns Hopkins Press.

Martinson, R. (1974). *The identification of the gifted and talented.* Ventura, CA: Office of the Ventura County Superintendent of Schools.

Mitchell, J. V. (Ed.). (1985). *The ninth mental measurements yearbook.* Lincoln: University of Nebraska Press.

Raven, J. C. (1938). *Progressive matrices*. London: H. K. Lewis.

Renzulli, J. S. (1978). What makes giftedness: Re-examining a definition. *Phi Delta Kappan, 60,* 180–184.

Renzulli, J., Reis, S., & Smith, L. (1981). *The revolving door identification model*. Mansfield Center, CT: Creative Learning Press.

Richert, E. S., Alvino, J., & McDonnell, R. C. (1982). *National report on identification*. Sewell, NJ: Educational Improvement Center South.

Sattler, J. M. (1982). *Assessment of children's intelligence and special abilities* (2nd ed.). Needham Heights, MA: Allyn & Bacon.

Sattler, J. M. (1988). *Assessment of children's intelligence and special abilities* (3rd ed.). San Diego: Jerome Sattler.

Silverman, L. K., & Kearney, K. (1992). The case for the Stanford-Binet L-M as a supplemental test. *Roeper Review, 15,* 34–37.

Singal, D. J. (1991). The other crisis in American education. *The Atlantic Monthly, 268*(5), 59–74.

Snyderman, M., & Rothman, S. (1988). *The IQ controversy, the media and public policy*. New Brunswick, NJ: Transaction Books.

Stanley, J. C. (1990). Leta Hollingworth's contribution to above-level testing of the gifted. *Roeper Review, 12,* 166–171.

Stanley, J. C., & Benbow, C. P. (1981). Using the SAT to find intellectually talented seventh graders. *College Board Reviews, 122,* 2–15.

Stanley, J. C., Keating, D. P., & Fox, L. H. (Eds.). (1974). *Mathematical talent: Discovery, description, and development*. Baltimore: Johns Hopkins University Press.

Sternberg, R. J. (1985). *Beyond I.Q. A triarchic theory of intelligence*. New York:Cambridge University Press.

Terman, L. M. (1916). *The measurement of intelligence*. Boston: Houghton Mifflin.

Torrance, E. P. (1970). Broadening concepts of giftedness in the 70's. *Gifted Child Quarterly, 14,* 199–208.

Tway, E. (1980). The gifted child in literature. *Language Arts, 57*(1), 14–20.

VanTassel-Baska, J. (1983). Statewide replication of the Johns Hopkins study of mathematically precocious youth. In C. D. Benbow and J. D. Stanley (Eds.), *Academic precocity* (pp. 179–191). Baltimore: Johns Hopkins Press.

VanTassel-Baska, J., & Strykowski, B. (1985). *An identification resource guide on the gifted and talented*. Evanston, IL: Center for Talent Development, Northwestern University.

9 Academic Counseling for the Gifted

Joyce VanTassel-Baska

Academic counseling for the gifted should be an integral part of their program and services throughout the years that they are in school. Why is this service so important to their educational well-being? Because it provides an important template for overall educational planning K–12. Because the needs of many gifted children are not likely to be met only by the context of school programs, the role of academic counseling allows for parents to participate in the decision-making around particular options that may be appropriate for their child at a particular stage of development. And it sets the stage for an array of outside programs and services to be accessed by the family that may best respond to individual needs.

CURRENT TRENDS

In the school context, the status of counseling gifted students has not changed very much in the past decade (VanTassel-Baska, 1990). However, there have been important developments in the counseling literature, in clinical practice, and in other settings with the gifted that deserve commentary:

❏ Greater emphasis on counseling families and parents of the gifted (Silverman, 1991)
❏ Focus on the treatment of specific problems of the gifted such as underachievement and perfectionism (Whitmore, 1980)
❏ Recognition of counseling needs based on the developmental level of the gifted student under consideration; for example, a whole literature is evolving on counseling the gifted adolescent (Buescher, 1987)

❑ Counseling centers at universities that specialize in working with gifted children and their parents (Kerr & Colangelo, 1988)
❑ Self-help publications that guide students, parents, and teachers in providing assistance on coping with giftedness (Delisle & Galbraith, 1987; Galbraith, 1983; 1984)

Another prevalent phenomenon is that of teachers taking on the role of counselors with gifted learners at all stages of development by incorporating counseling strategies and activities into their curricular plans. This development has been cited in several publications (Berger, 1989; Parke, 1990; VanTassel-Baska, 1990). Whether this stems from the lack of a formal school counseling structure or from the individual initiative of teachers, it is an encouraging sign.

Although schools may not be incorporating extensive formal counseling programs for the gifted, informally they are providing information to parents regarding the need for counseling through selected parent education programs. Such information encourages many parents of the gifted to seek professional counseling, either from individuals in private practice or from universities offering counseling programs. The primary model used for family counseling is the family systems model (Hackney, 1981), which recognizes the gifted child as part of a larger social network.

In addition to family counseling on psychosocial issues in raising a gifted child, there has been real interest in counseling families regarding educational planning. Questions such as the following are routinely discussed with parents to help them choose an appropriate school for their child:

1. What is the philosophy of the school on self-pacing and flexibility regarding age/grade placement?
2. What is the policy of the school on grouping able learners together for special instruction, including multi-age opportunities, homogeneous grouping opportunities, and so forth?
3. What is the quality of the teaching staff of the school at current and subsequent grade levels from kindergarten through grade eight? How capable are they with respect to the following competencies:
   —Knowledge of subject matter
   —Flexible management style
   —Not intimidated by able students
4. Does the school value individualization as much as or more than socialization?
5. Is there a written curriculum guide and how is it used?
6. Are there adequate support services such as counseling, assessment, and tutorials geared to the needs of gifted learners?
7. Is the administrative staff flexible with respect to change of a teacher or program for a given child?
8. How is academic talent recognized and rewarded?

Special issues of the gifted such as underachievement and perfectionism have been dealt with effectively through counseling methods developed during the past several years. These concerns have been addressed separately in specific resources (Adderholdt-Elliott, 1987; Rimm, 1986; Whitmore, 1980) and have also spawned a fair amount of clinical work. Unfortunately, the empirical base regarding these areas is not much better defined than it was ten years ago except for promising work in the area of hidden disabilities, much of which is clinically based (Daniels, 1983; Fox, Brody, & Tobin, 1983; Silverman, 1989; Whitmore & Maker, 1985). And clinical practice has continued to observe and work on these areas as sources of difficulty for many gifted learners. Some schools have even established separate programs for gifted underachievers. Suggested interventions with this population include:

❑ One-on-one counseling
❑ Conducting activities to build self-esteem
❑ Analyzing major strengths and arranging participation in activities that build on them
❑ Helping the student set goals and initiate follow-through action
❑ Offering learning opportunities based solely on interest
❑ Providing college and career guidance
❑ Providing real-world experiences in an area of potential career interest
❑ Setting up tutorials in areas of the curriculum where the students need assistance

CRITICAL ISSUES IN ACADEMIC COUNSELING OF THE GIFTED

Yet, it is in the area of academic counseling that many needs of the gifted and their families may go unmet because of a lack of school-based services. Several critical issues are at stake.

Academic planning provides a blueprint for gifted students in negotiating a program of study that truly reflects their abilities and their interests. In that sense it offers a built-in opportunity for students assessing their academic profiles at key stages. They are then able to build on strengths and weaknesses in such a way that they can see progress and make changes or corrections in the planning process as needed based on good information.

Academic planning is the vehicle through which comprehensive curriculum and services can be made available to students and parents. Many times schools offer a wide array of opportunities, but these options are never fully presented and explained in such a way that gifted students can see them as important to their course of study. Some key examples include participation in the arts as important co-curricular areas of study that have a legitimate place in a gifted student's program. Or the inclusion of a course in architectural drafting as an option for pre-engineering students. Or chess club participation for students who demonstrate spatial abilities but lack a curricular outlet to display them. All of these examples are indicative of options that can enhance a comprehensive program for gifted learners.

Academic planning influences the extent of articulation in programming for gifted students. Without it, it would not be unusual to find a patchwork-quilt model of program delivery. With effective planning, students may put together an appropriate scope and sequence of offerings, thus eliminating the kind of fragmentation that is somewhat typical of the larger secondary school environment.

Academic planning provides a way to enhance personalized education for gifted students. This is particularly the case for students from special populations whose discrepant profiles and extraordinary needs may dictate an annual review of an individualized program of study in all major domains. For these students, then, academic planning becomes the vehicle that pulls together the information needed to provide a unique service delivery model to them at various stages of development. These special populations would include students from low-income and minority families where aspirations need concrete ideas to make them realities; gifted children with learning disabilities who can easily look average if special strengths are not recognized; and the highly gifted who require extraordinary services beyond the school program.

Early academic planning prevents the narrowing of options for gifted learners at important transition points in their program. In the secondary curriculum there are several classes that serve to separate students in courses of study at essential stages in their academic development. The most notable courses that meet this criterion are algebra and calculus in mathematics, and physics in science. Foreign language study, in general, is another area that functions in a similar way. If gifted students do not take these academic options at some point in their secondary experience, they could be penalized at the college level because these courses constitute important prerequisites for pursuing in any serious manner the areas of mathematics, science, and foreign language at advanced levels. Moreover, the absence of these courses also closes off important career options for gifted learners at a stage of development when career decisions have not yet been carefully deliberated.

A questionnaire used to assess counseling needs of middle school–age gifted students demonstrated parental concern about academic directions, particularly in choice of college and choice of secondary school (VanTassel-Baska, 1991). Thus, assistance with evaluating schools and programs is another area of needed provision.

What, then, are some important aspects of providing academic planning to gifted learners? The next section of this chapter deals with three areas of concern. One of them is who will provide the academic planning for the gifted in the schools? A second important consideration is the strategies and techniques to be used in the implementation of academic planning in a gifted program. And a third concern is related to organizational and administrative arrangements necessary to implement such an option effectively. The chapter concludes with ideas for integrating academic counseling into an overall program for gifted learners.

A PARTNERSHIP: COUNSELORS AND TEACHERS

School counselors, regular classroom teachers, and parents are often either unavailable or unskilled in counseling gifted students; therefore, one viable alternative for providing guidance to the gifted is the teacher of the gifted. In many settings, these individuals work with gifted children for varying amounts of time in the "pull-out" delivery system, and see the behavior of the gifted child from an objective stance and on an ongoing basis. They also have access to groups of gifted students at a given time. Frequently, these teachers are also knowledgeable about the nature and needs of gifted children, both cognitive and affective. Thus, the teacher of the gifted may be in the best position to provide the guidance so needed by gifted students who generally spend most of their time in the regular classroom. (See chapter 8.)

Teachers of gifted students present a reasonable alternative to meeting many counseling needs. A segment of time each week could be set aside to attend to specific academic counseling issues as well as those that arise in the classroom—for example, frustration at a less-than-perfect paper; disappointment over peers' lack of enthusiasm for a shared project; feelings of rejection at not being selected as the "best" student. Teachers of gifted students can frequently diagnose and effectively remedy such problems. In many instances such teacher interventions are quite successful.

Ideally, regular classroom teachers could provide fully for the special cognitive and affective needs of gifted children in their classrooms. This is not impossible in the light of advanced concepts of differentiation of curriculum and individualization of teaching materials and methods. We should certainly work continuously toward that goal. On the other hand, it is unlikely to occur on a large scale in the immediate future. Accordingly, we shall discuss what may be perhaps the most realistic compromise in implementing counseling programs for gifted students, that is, a partnership of school counselor and teachers of the gifted. If no teacher of the gifted is available, then a school district might consider training a regular classroom teacher in the requisite competencies. The following lists depict the strengths of each partner:

School Counselors
- ❑ Trained in general counseling and guidance techniques
- ❑ Sensitive to affective issues at various development stages
- ❑ Available to arrange mentorships, internships, and special programs
- ❑ Trained to administer and interpret special tests and inventories
- ❑ Familiarity with role-modeling techniques
- ❑ Capable of diagnosing problem areas in students' psychosocial development

Teachers of the Gifted
- ❏ Aware of the unique social and emotional needs of the gifted
- ❏ Trained in effective intervention techniques with gifted learners
- ❏ Sensitive to affective issues
- ❏ Available to handle psychosocial issues daily in the classroom
- ❏ Trained to translate assessment information into program options
- ❏ Familiar with gifted individuals who could serve as role models
- ❏ Capable of prescribing classroom activities and grouping that could assist in positive psychosocial development

Each role is critical to implementing a successful counseling program. A good general background in counseling and guidance provides a workable framework. Understanding the positive differences of a gifted population provides the specific translation needed to make such programs effective. Responsibility for the overall counseling program then might be divided according to the following job description:

Counselor for the Gifted (10% Time)
1. Work with individual cases as referred.
2. Provide small-group counseling sessions across grade levels once every two weeks (one hour each).
3. Establish mentorship/internship directories.
4. Develop a monthly lecture/discussion series on career areas of interest to gifted students.
5. Sponsor a high school trip to selected colleges and universities for gifted/talented students.
6. Hold semi-annual planning sessions for parents of the gifted.

Teacher of the Gifted (10% of Instructional Time)
1. Provide activities that promote positive psychosocial development among the gifted.
2. Implement an affective curriculum that focuses on the needs of the gifted.
3. Provide speakers who are good role models for the gifted.
4. Prepare bibliographies that focus on the best of biography and autobiography and/or on fiction that focuses on a gifted student as protagonist (see Appendix) and discuss these readings with the students.
5. Utilize small-group and individual consultation as strategies to promote social and self-understanding.
6. Use literature and art as tools to blend cognitive and affective issues.
7. Arrange for peer counseling or other assistance for students who are underachieving.

In this way, the responsibility is shared for meeting the academic counseling needs of the gifted, and the task does not become overwhelming to either counselors or teachers.

STRATEGIES AND TECHNIQUES

Given the partnership concept as the most viable for schools in providing counseling services to gifted students, what are the most important strategies and techniques that teachers and counselors can employ to work successfully with these students? Although the counselor or teacher may not be the individual to implement these strategies, it is important that all are considered and facilitated in school settings for the gifted.

One important technique to stress in a counseling program for the gifted is decision-making—the process of how to do it but also the major issues facing gifted individuals at various stages of development over the life span. For young adolescent gifted students, use of effective decision-making models is crucial to effective academic planning. Frequently, students are faced with choices between the arts and academics—should I sacrifice band for physics? This dilemma is fairly typical for students with talents and interests in multiple areas yet who lack time in their schedule. However, it represents a false choice. No gifted student should consider giving up an arts area that provides an important expressive outlet, potentially over a lifetime, for one academic subject at one point in time. The way one helps gifted students consider such a decision is critical.

Other issues that affect gifted students include decisions about majors and minors, making choices in foreign language course options, and how to decide if one is overscheduled in terms of academic work. Another related issue for consideration as well is whether an adolescent gifted student should be working during high school. Whereas many gifted students from disadvantaged backgrounds may have little choice in the matter, clearly for more advantaged teens, it does present a real decision. Is the "pocket money" from having a job at McDonald's worth the time and energy that go into a direction that is nonacademic at a critical point in their talent development process? Careful decision-making in this area seems warranted.

In addressing these academic planning issues, a model for decision-making that works well with gifted teens is some version of the creative problem-solving model (Parnes, 1975). One of the benefits of the model is its flexibility for different situations. In a counseling setting, one might create a scenario involving a student's facing one or more of the issues cited above. Students in small groups may then work through the following steps of the model to render a decision about the issue under study. The steps in the model that are most useful for this kind of exercise are:

1. *Problem Finding*
   Is there a problem? What is the problem? Provide examples of the problem. What are the implications of the problem over time? State the problem as a question.
2. *Solution Finding*
   What are possible solutions to the problem? Which solutions are most

feasible, given the specific situation? Can there be multiple solutions that work? Articulate a solution statement.

3. *Plan of Action*

   What strategies need to be employed to work out the solution? What are the barriers to a solution and how will they be overcome? What is the process for implementing the solution—who, what, when, and how will it occur? How will you know that the solution has been successful?

Another excellent technique for providing academic planning assistance to the gifted is to structure mentorship and internship experiences based on students' academic needs and interests. Given limited resources, the best candidates for such opportunities are gifted students in greatest need—the highly gifted, the disadvantaged, and the underachieving. These groups are most discrepant from the norm—many times in terms of overall needs as well as academic achievement—and can, therefore, profit from opportunities that provide variety in the learning context. For the highly gifted, a mentorship can provide advanced career preparation or practice in a potential career area that can challenge the student at a level beyond the school capability. For the disadvantaged student, such opportunities can provide important role models and the possibility of meaningful summer employment or even scholarships. For the underachieving gifted student, these opportunities can provide meaning in learning, since internships are very grounded in real-world work experiences and remove the student from the school context in which she is not succeeding.

Many college mentorship programs have been developed that link gifted high school students with university professors, graduate students, and community resources (Ellingson, Haeger, & Feldhusen, 1986; Prillaman & Richardson, 1989). These programs have provided an important stimulus for the involvement of mentors of various ages as well as roles. Universities as brokers for mentorships appear to be ideal institutions because they have access to a large talent pool that can provide such opportunities on an extremely cost efficient basis. (See chapter 10 for more on mentorships.)

Another academic planning strategy successfully used with gifted students is test-taking skills. There are four areas where students can benefit from such an emphasis. One is a review of the most useful knowledge in major areas of the curriculum. Review of basic grammar principles, for example, may be very useful in preparing to take the Test of Standard Written English, a thirty-minute subtest of the Scholastic Aptitude Test. Another benefit of emphasizing test-taking may come from the practice effect of doing tests in a safe environment that one will be required to take later. By providing test practice, counselors can ease the anxiety of students who have difficulty taking tests and therefore potentially enhance score results. It is also useful to help students focus on the metacognitive aspect of test-taking—planning out a strategy for handling certain sections of the test, managing time wisely, and pacing oneself through the test. The final area where assistance is required is in analyzing certain types of items commonly found on tests and deriving ways to approach such items. On the Scholastic Aptitude Test, for example, helping students understand how to handle analogies, vocabulary items, and reading comprehension passages can be essential to their manipulating these types of items on the test that is scored. A sample study sheet for analogies might include the following:

1. Establish a precise relationship between the two words that are given.
2. Make up a sentence using both words.
3. Locate the same relationship in the second pair of words.
4. Look for patterns in analogy pairs.

In the area of reading comprehension, students can be taught to use the following strategies:

1. Find the main idea.
2. Identify arguments that support a position.
3. Underline key words or phrases that provide clues to meaning.
4. Read for overall meaning: go back to the passage for specific details.
5. Determine the function of each paragraph in a passage.
6. Read questions first and key them to the passage.

Metacognitive coaching strategies at a broad level are also helpful to the gifted student. Many times these students fail precisely because of executive processing difficulties (Sternberg, 1985). Thus, special sessions that emphasize metacognitive skills are useful. The text, *Applied Intelligence*, by Robert Sternberg, has excellent activities to use in this realm. An outline of Sternberg's metacomponents in his taxonomy follows:

A. Recognizing a problem
B. Defining the problem
C. Steps for solving the problem
D. Ordering
E. Deciding on a form for information
F. Allocating resources
G. Monitoring
H. Using feedback

For some gifted students the most critical areas for emphasis will be in internalizing the process of how to study. Many of them never had to study until they reached junior high or high school where content expectations and homework increased significantly. Closely linked to the need for knowing how to study is the need for being taught time management skills and skills in setting priorities for doing work. Again, these are areas in which gifted students may fail because of a lack of preparation and failure to carefully consider alternatives.

Another academic counseling area to include in a program initiative would be using assessment data to plan and differentiate a student's program of study (see chapter 8). Careful assessment of individual student ability, aptitude, interests, and personal values may be useful in discriminating among options for students. Collecting profile data on each gifted student and then translating it into a workable format for planning can prove helpful. The author has developed a prototype model for program planning for learning disabled gifted students at the elementary level (VanTassel-Baska, 1992). The use of such prototypes may aid in reducing the paperwork for counselors, yet still remain sensitive to individual differences within the gifted population. The list of instruments reviewed in this book (see chapters 8 and 11) can provide the assessment basis for program building. Developing Individualized Educational Plans (IEPs) for each advisee can also provide a formal documentation of student program planning. Various IEP models have been used with gifted students, and most include the following components:

❑ Annual goals and objectives
❑ Benchmarks of progress
❑ Relevant assessment data
❑ Procedures and processes for implementing the plan
❑ Recommendations from staffing conferences

Another area of academic planning that warrants attention is in making students aware of in-school courses and out-of-school opportunities. Planning sessions with students and parents that link them to teachers in the high school program such as Advanced Placement instructors, special seminar lecturers, and independent study advisors allow students to preview potential academic options for themselves. Bringing in former graduates of a school system who are in college is another way to provide families with insights on academic opportunities from within. At the same time, counselors need to ensure that gifted students have adequate information about out-of-school programs as well. These special program opportunities at a national level include:

❑ Talent search testing and programming
❑ Odyssey of the Mind competitions
❑ Future Problem-Solving competitions
❑ University-based program opportunities on Saturdays and in the summer
❑ Specific content-based competitions such as Mathletes, Math Counts, JETS, and Young Authors contests

Other types of opportunities are also available in many areas on a regional basis. Contacts for procuring a specific list of these opportunities in a particular area would be the state consultant for gifted education or the office of the National Association of Gifted Children (NAGC) or the International Council for Exceptional Children, The Association for the Gifted (CEC-TAG).

A final strategy that should be noted is that of individual consultation. Whereas most of the techniques described above can be handled in small-group settings, the opportunity for one-on-one contact for many of these issues may be more appropriate. Such interviews can also link academic planning issues to other areas of counseling need so that the student is seen as a gifted individual whose academic needs are only a part of the total counseling process.

ORGANIZATIONAL AND ADMINISTRATIVE ARRANGEMENTS

Given the nature and extent of the school guidance strategies suggested, what arrangements might be made to implement them? What contexts would be workable in order to provide the expanse of services suggested? Some alternative ideas for implementation follow.

Use of Small Groups (Grades 5–11)

Most of the strategies suggested could be implemented in a small-group setting of six to twelve students. Prior work with group dynamics and building rapport typically strengthens the effectiveness of this approach. The advantage to it is the effectiveness of bringing students together to engage in relevant issues and discuss them and the efficiency of group rather than individual time allotment. The frequency of these sessions may vary, but they should be regular enough to constitute a provision. At least twice a month is recommended.

Seminar Model

The use of seminars for academic counseling can provide a consistent mode of delivery for important information. Built into the student schedule over the course of a semester, the seminar allows for careful articulation of several of the strategies suggested here. Its major advantage is systematic and predictable time with students in a group setting.

Classroom Delivery

In many schools, the only way academic planning for the gifted is likely to occur is in the regular classroom setting. Teachers of the gifted can address academic planning issues very well but will need to rethink the relationship of many of the topics to existing curricula. In most instances, much of the information would enhance academic preparation in any subject.

Individual Sessions

Whereas least cost effective in terms of resources used, scheduling individual sessions is still a viable way to provide academic planning, especially in small districts.

Computer Programmed Instruction/Self-Study

Some aspects of academic planning, like SAT preparation, can be handled through self-study and even computer programmed instruction. Making materials and space available to gifted students to pursue this delivery model is critical to its success, along with communication with students as to its availability.

Weekend Sessions

For topics that involve families, scheduling weekend sessions may be helpful. This mode of delivery is also useful for intensive sessions on topics of short duration. Test-taking sessions, for example, could be held over six weekends for three hours each.

Annual Academic Planning Conferences

Regardless of the predominant mode of delivery for academic planning services to gifted students, holding an annual conference for students and families is a basic service. Salient issues can be addressed by outside speakers and community people that cannot be drawn into the program at any other time. And the synergy of such an event is important to keep this program component of counseling evolving in a positive direction.

A sample model of an academic plan for a gifted learner is found in Table 9.1, articulated across grades five through twelve.

CONCLUSION

The role of academic counseling in a total spectrum of services to gifted learners and their families can be seen as fundamental in providing important information at a critical stage of development—the transition period from middle childhood to adolescence, and in school organization from elementary to middle or junior high school. The integration of academic counseling with other services to the gifted is also important since the counseling process provides the scaffolding on which students can take advantage of meaningful options and begin to build a multiyear program of study. Without such a scaffold, the secondary experience for many gifted learners can be disconnected and actually short-circuit future aspirations. Schools then need to find resources to ensure that this provision can be routinely a function of the secondary school experience.

REFERENCES

Adderholdt-Elliott, M. (1987). *Perfectionism: What's bad about being too good?* Minneapolis: Free Spirit.

Table 9.1
PROTOTYPE OF ACADEMIC PLAN FOR GIFTED LEARNERS GRADES 5–12

	GRADE 5	GRADE 6	GRADE 7	GRADE 8	GRADE 9	GRADE 10	GRADE 11	GRADE 12
English/L.A.	Critical reading, writing, & oral presentation	Literature w/ analysis & debate	Grammar & composition	Literature & composition	Literature & composition	American & British Lit. composition	AP Comp.	World Literature (AP Lit. test option)
Social Studies	MACOS	Facing history	Study of American culture	Study of cultures	Science technology & society	AP American history	European history	
Science	Concept-based (GEMS)	Concept-based (GEMS)	IPS	BSCS	Science technology & society	Chemistry	AP Biology/ AP Chemistry	Physics
Mathematics	Challenge of the unknown math	CSMP	Unified Mathematics	Algebra	Advanced Algebra	Geometry (plane & solid)	Math analysis	Calculus AP
		Algebra sequence option			Precalculus sequence		College coursework	
Foreign Languages	Exploratory (vocabulary & idioms)	Exploratory (vocabulary & idioms)	1 year (Latin I)	1 year (Latin II)	1 year (French/ Spanish/ German, etc.)	1 year (II)	1 year (III)	1 year (IV)
Special Acad. Counseling Seminars	X	X	X	X	X	X	X	X
Mentorships			X	X			X	
Internships								X
Independent Study				X			X	
Contests & Competitions			X	X	X	X	X	
Test-taking Skills			X			X	X	
Metacognitive Skills	X		X		X			
Decision-making				X				X
Testing and Assessment			X		X		X	
Individual Consultation	X	X	X	X	X	X	X	X

Berger, S. (1989). *College planning for gifted students.* Reston, VA: The Council for Exceptional Children.

Buescher, T. M. (Ed.). (1987). *Understanding gifted and talented adolescents: A resource guide for counselors, educators, and parents.* Evanston, IL: Center for Talent Development, Northwestern University.

Daniels, P. (1983). *Teaching the gifted/learning disabled child.* Rockville, MD: Aspen.

Delisle, J., & Galbraith, J. (1987). *The gifted kids survival guide II.* Minneapolis: Free Spirit.

Ellingson, M., Haeger, W., & Feldhusen, J. (1986). The Purdue mentor program. *GCT, 9*(2), 2–5.

Fox, L., Brody, L., & Tobin, D. (1983). *Learning disabled gifted children.* Baltimore: University Park Press.

Galbraith, J. (1983). *The gifted kids survival guide, for ages 11–18.* Minneapolis: Free Spirit.

Galbraith, J. (1984). *The gifted kids survival guide, for ages 10 and under.* Minneapolis: Free Spirit.

Hackney, H. (1981). The gifted child, the family, and the school. *Gifted Child Quarterly, 25,* 51–54.

Kerr, B., & Colangelo, N. (1988). The college plans of academically talented students. *Journal of Counseling and Development, 67,* 42–47.

Parke, B. (1990). Who should counsel the gifted? The role of educational personnel. In J. VanTassel-Baska (Ed.), *A practical guide to counseling the gifted in a school setting* (2nd Ed., pp. 31–39). Reston, VA: The Council for Exceptional Children.

Parnes, S. J. (1975). *Aha! Insights into creative behavior.* Buffalo, NY: DOK.

Prillaman, D., & Richardson, R. (1989). The William and Mary mentorship model: College students as a resource for the gifted. *Roeper Review, 12*(2), 114–118.

Rimm, S. (1986). *Underachievement syndrome: Causes and cures.* Watertown, WI: Apple.

Silverman, L. K. (1989). Invisible gifts, invisible handicaps. *Roeper Review, 22,* 34–42.

Silverman, L. K. (1991). Family counseling. In N. Colangelo & G. Davis (Eds.), *Handbook of gifted education* (pp. 307–328). Needham Heights, MA: Allyn & Bacon.

Sternberg, R. (1985). *Applied intelligence.* New York: Harcourt Brace Jovanovich.

VanTassel-Baska, J. (Ed.). (1990). *A practical guide to counseling the gifted in a school setting* (2nd ed.). Reston, VA: The Council for Exceptional Children.

VanTassel-Baska, J. (1992). *Planning effective curriculum for the gifted.* Denver: Love.

VanTassel-Baska, J. (1991). Teachers as counselors for gifted students. In R. M. Milgram (Ed.), *Counseling gifted and talented children: A guide for teachers, counselors, and parents* (pp. 34–52). Norwood, NJ: Ablex.

Whitmore, J. R. (1980). *Giftedness, conflict, and underachievement.* Needham Heights, MA: Allyn & Bacon.

Whitmore, J., & Maker, J. (1985). *Intellectual giftedness in disabled persons.* Rockville, MD: Aspen.

10

Career Counseling

Linda Kreger Silverman

Counseling gifted students about careers, like other facets of counseling discussed in this book, is highly complex and requires knowledge of the unique issues faced by this population. For the gifted, career development is a lifelong process, beginning with the values and attitudes in the home in early childhood and continuing throughout adulthood. These children need career guidance early in life to help them recognize their capabilities, clarify their interests, and expose them to the range of possibilities that await them. Career selection, however, may occur later than for other students because the broad spectrum of career opportunities increases the complexity of decision making (Milne, 1979).

The gifted are often multitalented—they have potential for success in many fields. Therefore, the typical aptitude tests used for career guidance are not particularly helpful. When one is capable in many areas, aptitude is an insufficient criterion for selecting a career. Financial security and career stability, two determining factors for their parents and grandparents, play less significant roles today in young people's career choices (Yankelovich, 1972). Questions gifted students raise are, "What career would be most interesting for me to pursue?" "Which field would offer the most opportunity for me to develop my potential?" "Where do I sense the greatest need?" "In what area can I be of most service?" These are value-laden questions, all of which can be explored through carefully designed experiences.

Effective career counseling programs provide opportunities for students to explore their own interests, personality types, beliefs about their abilities, and aspirations. Students are introduced to various fields, to successful adults who have made a variety of career and lifestyle choices, and to real-life experiences in the work world. Biographical research is included to help gifted students identify with those who have made great contributions in spite of

215

obstacles (Hollingworth, 1926). Students are exposed to various options and envision themselves in different lifestyles. They wrestle with existential issues, such as how different careers fit into the larger picture of constructing meaning for their lives. Societal and self-imposed limitations are challenged. The program enhances the aspirations of those who have not had much encouragement (e.g., many economically disadvantaged students) and deals with such issues as sex-role stereotyping and how both sexes can manage a career and a family. It also involves others in the young people's lives who influence their career choices.

Ideally, a comprehensive program of career development begins with parent education in the preschool and primary years and then provides seminars for parents throughout the child's school career. Career awareness activities and biographical studies can begin in the upper elementary grades. By junior high, career education for the gifted should incorporate such components as self-exploration, time management, study skills, planning for college, decision-making, participation in national talent searches (Berger, 1989), and job studies (Willings, 1986). Kelly and Cobb (1991) found that gifted junior high school students (eleven to fourteen years old) had career awareness typical of students several years older than themselves and were ready for more specifics. Senior high school students need detailed information about selecting colleges, obtaining scholarships, accelerated coursework, balancing extracurricular activities, entry requirements for different fields, and lifestyles related to different careers. If they have had opportunities to complete their coursework at a more rapid rate, they can plan in-depth investigations of careers through internships and mentorships. Gifted girls need differentiated career counseling to help them overcome internal and external barriers to success (Hollinger, 1991b) and to explore self-perceptions, aspirations, and role conflicts in a supportive environment. Disadvantaged students profit from college planning and mentorships. Career counseling is needed during the college years as well and is valuable at turning points in adult life.

PARENT EDUCATION

Career planning begins with the parents. Perhaps the best way to help gifted students select careers is to educate their parents. Parents play a critical role in shaping their children's aspirations; they are their children's first role models, and parental encouragement or discouragement has lasting effects. Parents need to understand that their children's multipotentiality affects the timing of career decisions. Because they have to pay for their children's advanced education, parents need information about financial aid. In some families, it is expected that the child will follow in the parent's footsteps, and all other career options are foreclosed. This has been the tradition in most parts of the world for centuries, and it is still quite common in certain geographical regions and cultural groups. Given the family dynamics involved, parent education should be a component of the career development program.

There is a difference between designing children's futures and enabling them to design their own futures with parental support. Parents sometimes need guidance in making this distinction so that they do not become overbearing. Schools play an important role by helping parents learn the art of responsive parenting through parent education seminars. A curriculum to enhance the parents' role in career guidance from the primary grades through high school might include the following topics:

- ❏ "Creator parents" vs. responsive parenting
- ❏ Family activities to develop interests
- ❏ Holding high expectations for daughters as well as sons
- ❏ Purchasing toys, games, and books that are not sex-typed
- ❏ Recognizing and nurturing mathematical talent at home
- ❏ Avoiding overprotectiveness—especially with daughters
- ❏ Critical periods in the development of special talents
- ❏ How to find expert instruction
- ❏ How many lessons? How much free time?
- ❏ Exposing children to various types of role models
- ❏ Introducing children to biographies
- ❏ Considerations regarding acceleration
- ❏ The importance of advanced mathematics in all careers
- ❏ Early emergers and late decision-makers
- ❏ The dangers of premature career selection
- ❏ Reversible career decisions: Preparing children for multiple careers
- ❏ College planning
- ❏ Obtaining scholarships and financial aid

Two currents simultaneously flow through modern thinking regarding parenting practices. One position holds that parents are their children's best teachers and that the most important years of childhood should not be wasted (Engelmann & Engelmann, 1980). Infant education is recommended—even education in the womb. The other position advocates allowing children to have full, rich childhoods without pressuring them to learn too much too soon. Some writers warn that the "hurried child" is a candidate for all kinds of stress-related symptoms (Elkind, 1981). Parents of the gifted have a particularly difficult time sifting through these disparate views. They recognize their children's abilities early in life (Kaufmann & Sexton, 1983), but do not know whether to teach their toddlers to read or to hide all the books and slow them down.

Early exposure and expert instruction provided by the family often determine gifted children's future career paths. Research by Bloom and his associates (1982, 1985) revealed that individuals who achieve world-class recognition in their fields before the age of thirty-five were groomed for their success while still in preschool. Concert pianists, for example, came from musically oriented families, in which all members of the family were expected to play musical instruments and were given early instruction. Bloom and Sosniak (1981) found the home to be far more important than the school in developing the talents of their subjects. In many cases, school was found to be counterproductive to talent development. This research has important child-rearing implications, but it must be balanced with the question: Is this what the child wants or what the parents want for the child?

"Creator parents" is a term given to parents who discount the role of heredity and believe that they can cultivate genius in an ordinary baby (Montour, 1977). They try to give their children an edge in the competition of life by enrolling them in classes in infancy and by constantly bombarding them with enrichment. Creator parents treat their children like moldable clay to be shaped as the parents' desire, instead of respecting them as unique human beings with their own desires. The dangers of usurping the child's sense of self to enhance the parents' egos are poignantly described by Miller (1981) and Montour (1977).

Fortunately, most gifted children have responsive parents who discover that their children are advanced and then wonder how they should respond to this advancement (Silverman, 1986a; Silverman & Kearney, 1989). When their child shows interest or talent in an area, responsive parents provide to the best of their ability the necessary tools, instruction, and support for the child to make continuous progress. However, they are not bent on their child's attaining a certain level of success. Both types of parents may engage their children in similar activities but for entirely different reasons. The same enrichment can be nurturing or harmful depending on whether it is an outgrowth of the child's needs or a forced experience to serve the parent.

The importance of avoiding sex-role stereotyping in the home cannot be overemphasized. Many gifted and creative children tend to be more androgynous, exhibiting some of the characteristics and interests of both sexes (Dellas, 1969; Wolleat, 1979). Boys display sensitivity usually thought of as feminine, and girls may show independence and aggressiveness associated with masculinity. Creative boys tend to have unusual career aspirations (Torrance, 1980), and gifted girls who have high career aspirations are thought of as unconventional. Traditional feminine stereotypes are limiting to achievement in women (Hollinger, 1991a); these attitudes are well-ingrained by the time the child reaches school age (Fox & Tobin, 1978).

Children need their parents' support, guidance, and nurturing of their talents, but they do not want to become carbon copies of their parents. They need the emotional freedom to determine their own life paths. Gifted children are often at risk for becoming what their parents want them to be, at the expense of their own needs and desires (Miller, 1981). Through parent education, counselors can help release both parents and children from taking too much responsibility for each other's happiness. When young people feel in the driver's seat of their future, instead of passengers in their parents' plans, then career education with the students can begin.

EARLY DECISION-MAKERS

Timing of career decisions tends to be either earlier or later for the gifted than for their age-mates (Milne, 1979). Because of their developmental advancement, gifted children begin to be concerned about vocational choice much earlier than their peers. A child who is mentally three years ahead may begin setting career goals in elementary school. Willings (1986) indicates that most gifted students are thinking seriously about career choices by the age of nine, and that they find conventional career search programs designed for high school students to be "boring and trivial" (p. 95).

Some gifted children become thoroughly engrossed in their interests early in life, and commit themselves to careers in those areas before they have had an opportunity to explore other options. The six-year-old "expert" on constellations announces for all time that he is going to become an astronomer. No amount of coaxing apparently can make him change his mind. When his interest in the stars wanes, he attaches to his chemistry set and is staunchly determined to pursue chemistry for the rest of his life. These young specialists may feel a sense of security in mapping out their life goals at an early age. Sometimes these goals change as their interests change, and sometimes they remain steadfast into maturity.

Children who determine their paths in the primary grades or whose parents have defined their career goals for them foreclose many options. Much has been written about the potential problems of premature career selection (Delisle & Squires, 1989; Fredrickson, 1986; Howley, 1989; Kerr, 1986; Kerr & Ghrist-Priebe, 1988), including the danger of narrow, constricted lifestyles (Marshall, 1981). When students feel locked into early career decisions, especially those that are externally imposed, they often lose their love of learning and higher education becomes merely a means to an end (Katchadourian & Boli, 1985). However, sometimes children have a better perspective of their futures than either their teachers or counselors. Willings (1986) provides the example of a fourteen-year-old gifted girl who wanted to be a race car driver and fashion model, despite the ridicule of her classmates. Her counselor told her she was immature, and her mother told her she'd outgrow these desires. But at twenty-six, she was working as a fashion model during the week and racing in a team on weekends.

Some children develop an early affinity with a certain life path; for them it is a vocation in the true sense of the term—a "calling" (Howley, 1989). Exceptionally talented children often show an early, intense interest in one field (Bloom, 1985; Cox, Daniel, & Boston, 1985). For example, musical prodigies who set their sights on the concert stage, or ballet dancers who aspire to greatness, show passionate dedication to their fields when they are very young (Feldman, 1986). They seem intuitively to realize that they must block out all distractions and forego other potentialities in order to achieve their goals (Fredrickson, 1986; Tannenbaum, 1984). There are also some gifted children who arbitrarily select careers at a young age simply to avoid dealing with the overwhelming multitude of career options available to them. Too many choices can be threatening.

LATE DECISION-MAKERS

Although some children decide their future careers before they enter school, many gifted youth complete high school without knowing what they will be when they grow up. Most multitalented gifted students suffer "an embarrassment of riches" (Gowan, 1980, p. 67), making the problem of selection difficult. The anxiety created by too many options reaches the attention of counselors much more often than the problem of foreclosure described above. Early bloomers may be held up as the ideal, and students who cannot decide what they want to do with their lives feel ashamed by comparison.

Coping with multiple talents and interests is a serious problem for most gifted students (Delisle & Squires, 1989) and has been addressed by several writers (Kerr, 1986; Kerr & Ghrist-Priebe, 1988; Marshall, 1981; Sanborn, 1979). Generalists find all aspects of life fascinating, and don't want to miss any of it. They need assurance that their multipotentiality is an asset rather than a liability and that lack of early specialization does not mark them as washouts for life.

> Multipotential young adults are equally brilliant across diverse subject areas and have multiple career interests. A straight-A student who edits the school newspaper, sings lead in the musical, and is captain of the volleyball team is probably multipotential....
> Traditional career counseling techniques which emphasize matching clients' abilities and interests with job characteristics may be of little use to the young gifted adult. Instead, an approach based on identifying the most deeply held values and planning life goals which actualize those values, may be the treatment of choice. Career development then becomes the search for meaning rather than the search for a job.... Sometimes, the talented adult must create for himself or herself the job which will be most fulfilling. (Kerr & Claiborn, 1991, p. 76)

Betsy is an example of multipotentiality. As a high school senior she had boundless enthusiasm for everything, and an endless supply of energy. Her interests included psychology, creative writing, language, physics, chemistry, jewelry making, fencing, bicycling, nature, science fiction, and "people." The lead cross-country runner in her senior class, she also topped the class in college aptitude tests and the Advanced Placement English examination. She had a strong desire to be of service to humanity, and she wanted to master twelve languages before she turned forty (Silverman, 1982). Vocational preference tests had little value for Betsy because they could not tell her what she was *unable* to do (Hoyt, 1978). How would she begin to make a career choice?

Students like Betsy experience vocational selection as an existential dilemma. They are as concerned about the road not taken as they are with finding the "right" path (Sanborn, 1979). Choosing to be a linguist means giving up a career as a physicist. Giving up dreams is not easy for any child, but most children learn that they must temper their dreams with the reality of their limitations. Not so for the gifted. They learn early that they can direct their abilities successfully in most pursuits. Any door to their future is closed by choice, and what if they make the wrong choice? What would their lives be like if they had made another choice? Is it better to become really good in one area or to know about a lot of areas? And if they try to hang onto all their interests, won't they become dilettantes, masters of none?

Career counseling for the gifted needs to be sensitive to their multiple interests, the existential dilemmas they face in making choices, their fear of making an error, their fear of being less than their ideal or not living up to their potential, the depth of their sadness over the road not taken, and their fear that if they try to nurture all of their potentials, they will end up second-rate at everything. "Both multipotential individuals and early emergers need differential career guidance" (Kerr, 1986, p. 602). Both types are described in Ursula LeGuin's (1976) enchanting novel, *Very Far Away from Anywhere Else*. This moving love story of two gifted high school students is guaranteed to stimulate insightful discussion among students and adults.

CAREER GUIDANCE FOR MULTIPOTENTIALITY

Through a well-planned career counseling program, Betsy, and others like her, can be assisted with their dilemma in many ways:

- ❑ Preparing them for many options
- ❑ Exploring with them careers in which they would have the opportunity to synthesize interests in many fields
- ❑ Allowing them to delay decision-making until college
- ❑ Giving them real-life experiences in some of their avenues of interest
- ❑ Discussing the possibility of serial or concurrent careers
- ❑ Helping them determine which of their interests they could maintain as avocations
- ❑ Suggesting the possibility of creating new careers
- ❑ Exploring life themes as a basis for career choice

The counselor can guide multipotential students in planning as rich a program as possible, one that will prepare them to enter any of several fields. It is particularly important for girls to be counseled to take advanced mathematics and science courses, so that they do not close these doors prematurely (Hollinger, 1991a; Kerr, 1991). In high school (ninth through twelfth grade), a good college preparatory program should include at least four years of English, four years of mathematics, four years of science, three years of a foreign

language, and three years of social science. These are basic minimum requirements for gifted students. With appropriate planning, it is useful to take an
accelerated program (Fredrickson, 1986; Howley, 1989), beginning algebra in
seventh grade, taking several Advanced Placement (AP) courses, and creating
room for internship or mentorship experiences.

The first two years of college may be well spent gaining a solid liberal
arts background. College is not simply a place to gain vocational training. For
the gifted, in particular, it is a time to gain an education—to open their minds to
philosophy, history, literature, psychology, mathematics, art, music, and science. This rich background will serve them in any field. During this time
students can take exploratory coursework and perhaps do part-time work or
observe in areas of interest. Of course, this plan can only be implemented with
the consent of parents, because parents are usually the ones to absorb the
financial costs of their children's education. Many parents are concerned with
their children's inability to decide on a career, and they may be reluctant to
invest thousands of dollars on their children's higher education while they are
still "floundering." Parents need to be educated about how to deal with their
children's indecision. If no parent education program is available, the counselor can assist the parents in understanding the student's dilemma, and may
be called upon to mediate between parent and child.

Exposure to interdisciplinary coursework enables students to see how
several fields can be blended together in one's life's work. The counselor can
expand this vision by introducing students to real-life models of generalists in
the work world and to books on figures who used knowledge in one field to
further knowledge in another (e.g., Bell's inventing the telephone after observing the membrane of the inner ear) (Gordon, 1961). Brainstorming sessions can be conducted on ways to combine several interests into existing or
new careers.

There are several excellent career education models for the gifted and
talented that deal with multipotentiality and decision-making: for example,
Hoyt and Hebeler's *Career Education for Gifted and Talented Students* (1976);
Keyes's *Exploring Careers for the Gifted* (1985); Kerr's *Career Education for
the Gifted and Talented* (1981); VanTassel-Baska's "A Comprehensive Model
of Career Education for Gifted and Talented" (1981); Willings's "Enriched
Career Search" (1986); and Moore, Feldhusen, and Owings's *The Professional Career Exploration Program for Minority and/or Low Income Gifted
and Talented High School Students* (1978). See also Berger's excellent manual
for college preparation: *College Planning for Gifted Students* (1989).

DIFFERENT PATHS FOR GIFTED ADULTS

Not all gifted individuals decide what to do with their lives in high school and
college. Some do not find their calling until mid-life. Gifted adults may move
from job to job within a profession or have several careers in their lives.

Voltaire's (1759) apt observation that anything is better than boredom is a creed for the gifted. In order for them to be happy with their work, they must be constantly stimulated, challenged, and learning. When they have learned all they can in a position, it is time to move on to new challenges. This may take them to higher echelons of management within a business, more demanding research projects in science, new schools of thought in mathematics, music, and art, or perhaps to new careers. If high school students and their parents are informed of the possibility of late blooming, and helped to understand that career decisions are not irreversible, some of the struggle around career choices can be lessened.

A former dentist, who rued the decision he had made in junior high school to study dentistry as a career, remarked, "What gives a 14-year-old the right to decide what a 40-year-old should do with the rest of his life?" In many cases, when we press adolescents to make decisions about their careers, we are recreating this dilemma. The mobility of our society may be making obsolete the ideal of a single career throughout life (Dunham & Russo, 1983). Gifted students "will likely pursue more than one career path during their lives" (Delisle & Squires, 1989, p. 102) and, therefore, should be prepared to deal with this possibility. Frequently, adults return to school to pursue training in another field. An elementary teacher becomes a college professor; a microbiologist becomes a psychologist; a lawyer decides to become an educator. Students can be introduced to individuals in the community who have made mid-career changes and successfully maintain several careers (Delisle & Squires, 1989).

There are several ways in which adults maintain interests in more than one field. It is possible to have concurrent careers, as did the famous Russian composer Borodin, who was also an internationally renowned chemist. One's career is not necessarily one's livelihood. Most musicians find that they cannot make a living with their music, and so they gain skills in other fields. Music, however, remains as their major life's work, while their other work supplies the money for them to survive. They sometimes refer to their two simultaneous careers as their "day job" and their "night job." Many gifted adults put a great deal of time and energy into avocations—major interests from which they do not attempt to derive their livelihood: coin collecting, classical guitar, watercolor, writing science fiction stories, research projects, and so forth.

The counselor can help students determine which interests would most likely supply them with an acceptable income and which to pursue as avocations. When gifted students find it difficult to determine which path to follow, it is wise to allow them extra time in which to make their career choices, and to give them a broad enough educational base so that later they can move in several different directions.

REAL-LIFE EXPERIENCES

The heart of a career counseling program is the opportunity it provides students to work with individuals in various fields. Career choices are often made on the basis of the lifestyles students see that correspond with various occupations, as well as the personalities of professionals they have met (Perrone, 1991). The adage, "Experience is the best teacher" is most appropriate in conjunction with selecting a career. Even at the elementary level, students can be engaged in "prementorships" (Delisle & Squires, 1989, p. 101) in which they interview community members and visit various work sites after school or on weekends. There are several ways for older students to gain experience in a field while they are still in school: shadowing, internships, mentorships, community service, job studies, work/study programs, and part-time employment.

Shadowing

In career week programs, junior high school students shadow a professional for an entire week to see what a particular career entails. The students participate in a different career experience each year. They are advised to keep a journal of their impressions of each occupation. One year, a would-be psychologist followed me around to all of my university courses and was able to observe many facets of my professional career—all but my private counseling sessions. This gifted fourteen-year-old boy outshone most of my graduate students in a discussion of myelinization of neural tissues. His immediate grasp of all the topics I covered made me wonder why he was still in junior high school!

At High School Redirection in Denver, Colorado, shadowing is one of the first phases in a career exploration "passage" students complete as part of their graduation requirements. (Other passages include global projects and creative expression.) After completing a survey and learning about available resources, advisors help students reflect upon a particular career they would like to learn about. The advisor makes arrangements for the student to shadow a professional. The student keeps a journal and writes an evaluation of the experience. Next, internships are arranged which are also carefully documented in a daily journal. A more in-depth career exploration follows that involves interviews and research to determine (a) education or training required and costs entailed, (b) salary potential, (c) constraints, (d) employee organizations, (e) future trends, and (f) related careers (describing at least five other careers that could be entered with minimal retraining). This exploration is similar to Willings's (1986) "Job Studies," which is described further on.

Internships

Apprenticeships are an interesting way to gain information about careers and to learn from role models (Kelly & Cobb, 1991). In an internship, the student works as an apprentice in a professional setting for at least one semester, and usually receives high school credit for the experience, but no reimbursement. It may be full-time or several hours a week. Many high schools arrange for internships in the community through the Executive High School Internship Program (Duperrault, 1992), which has trained 10,000 gifted and talented seniors in eighteen states since 1971. The intern works for one semester as an administrative assistant to upper level management, directors, and professionals in a variety of fields such as law, journalism, government, and television. To qualify, students must have completed most or all of their college preparatory requirements. Interns take English during their first period, then go to internship sites for the rest of the day. The Experienced Based Community Education (EBCE) programs also have proved to be a profitable source of internships for gifted students. Many of these programs have developed materials specifically geared for gifted and talented youth. There is an excellent report available from ERIC entitled, "Community-Based Mentorships for the Gifted and Talented" (National Commission on Resources for Youth, 1977) containing information on eleven model projects. Although this publication appears to be about "mentorships," it actually describes internships. Internships give the student a view of the system within which the professional works.

Mentorships

A mentorship is another type of apprenticeship, in which the student works directly with an individual on a one-on-one basis. A mentor is a guide, advisor, role model, counselor, and friend (Beck, 1989) who helps to advance the student's knowledge of a particular field. Internships frequently involve a type of mentor relationship because the student is usually assigned to one professional for his or her entire time with the organization. But mentorships differ from internships in that they are not confined to specific tasks or agencies (Swassing & Fichter, 1991). The mentor and protégé can discuss the mentor's profession in the park or at the soda fountain.

Mentorships may be the most fruitful form of career education for the gifted because the mentor is often the chief factor in a successful person's career (Feldhusen, 1980; Merriam, 1983). Studies and program evaluations report consistently positive results (Beck, 1989; Cox, Daniel, & Boston, 1985; Ellingson, Haeger, & Feldhusen, 1986; Hamilton & Hamilton, 1992; Hollinger, 1991a; Prillaman & Richardson, 1989; Swassing & Fichter, 1991; Wright & Borland, 1992). Mentorships are highly recommended for gifted students from economically disadvantaged backgrounds (Olszewski-Kubilius & Scott, 1992; Wright & Borland, 1992) and for gifted girls (Beck, 1989; Hollinger, 1991b), preferably with female mentors. In one innovative project disadvantaged adolescents tutor young able children from extremely disadvantaged backgrounds (Wright & Borland, 1992).

Mentorships appear to work best with students who are highly motivated and have focused interests (Swassing & Fichter, 1991). Energetic, talented program leadership and quality training for mentors appear to be two keys to success (Ellingson, Haeger, & Feldhusen, 1986). Howley (1989) cautions that mentorships require students to take time away from their studies; therefore, "they make the most sense for students who have been permitted to accelerate their academic progress in previous years" (p. 213). Runions (1980) maintains that mentors should be an integral part of the program for all gifted students.

Community Service/Volunteer Work

Active participation in community service prepares students to create a more caring, humane society (Fantini, 1981). Community service projects encourage the development of gifted students' natural capacity to care, their intense interest in justice, and their tendency toward moral, ethical behavior (Munger, 1990). There are endless ways to be of service—as guides, coaches, tutors, advocates, fund-raisers, researchers (Kahn, 1986), assistants for the disabled and elderly, directors of community improvement campaigns, and so forth. Service opportunities can develop a wide range of skills and enable students to use these skills to benefit others (Kahn, 1986). Gifted students in a number of schools are involved in community service as part of their course requirements, in key clubs, or as volunteer work after school. All of the tenth- and eleventh-grade students at the North Carolina School of Science and Mathematics participate in community service, and the twelfth-graders have internships and mentorships. Students in the Program for Exceptionally Gifted Girls (PEG), a five-year, combined high school/college program at Mary Baldwin College in Staunton, Virginia, construct a plan for community service for six hours each month. The recommended sites include hospitals, day care centers, fine arts associations, historical preservation agencies, nursing homes, public libraries, and schools. The De La Salle Academy in New York City "promotes a strong sense of community among its students and encourages them to believe that they can be agents of change. Pursuant to this, students are required to engage in community service" (Wright & Borland, 1992, p. 125). This is the school that provides gifted adolescent mentors for young gifted children from more severely disadvantaged families.

> Acts of service help us to experience and recognize the unity and connections between one another and feel the joy of reaching out to contribute time and effort to another's needs or successes. And in doing so, the returns may include a sense of accomplishment, confidence, and capability. (Shannon, 1989, p. 184)

Job Studies

A coordinated career education program can enhance the value of all of these experiences by helping students know what to look for and what kinds of questions to ask to gain the most from their career exploration. For example, students can inquire about educational background needed, salary ranges, opportunities for advancement, and opportunities for creativity. They can observe if there are equal opportunities for both sexes and people from different racial backgrounds. They can see if people seem happy and excited about their jobs, or weary and unenthusiastic. Most of all, they can get a feel for whether the profession matches their interests and abilities, and captures their enthusiasm.

Willings (1986) includes Job Study as a module in his Enriched Career Search Program in Norfolk, England. The two-year program, meeting once a week, consists of seven modules: (1) Your Career and You, (2) Self-Evaluation, (3) Job Study, (4) The Adult World, (5) Group Roles, (6) Ethical Considerations in Work, (7) Career Strategies and Strategies for Creative Growth. In the first module, "Your Career and You," students engage in fantasizing their futures and evaluating the possibilities. The "Self-Evaluation" module contains nine exercises, in which students write:

> (a) details of their career search to date; (b) their life goals; (c) their occupational priorities; (d) their non-occupational priorities; (e) the extent to which they believe that their goals and priorities will be met in their work; (f) details of the person who has influenced them most in their career choices to date; (g) the strengths they believe they have and the strengths they would like to have; (h) details of times when they felt exceptionally fulfilled; and (i) their aspirations for the future. (Willings, 1986, p. 96)

In the "Job Study" module, students are helped to distinguish between idealized images of careers (such as those on television) and the experiences of real human beings engaged in various professions. They learn interview techniques, construct a very detailed series of questions, rehearse some of their interviews in class, and compile charts of responses. Then they find individuals who are happy with their jobs and ask them 150 questions. These questions are designed to reveal the hidden aspects of a particular job, the key skills and the complementary skills, the physical skills required, job features, requirement for entry, problems of training, difficulties and distastes, and sources of reward.

Part-Time Employment and Work/Study

A student who is interested in becoming a veterinarian can sometimes obtain work after school and in the summer at an animal hospital. He can watch animal surgery, observe how the doctor spends most of her time, and assist her in a number of tasks. Several months of close association with someone in the profession should give him a realistic perspective of the nature of the work. He can envision himself spending his life at the same tasks, and ask himself if this is what he really wants to do. Students who complete their course requirements early may be able to arrange an opportunity like this during school hours. In work/study programs, students receive high school credit for the work they do in the world.

DESIGNING A CAREER

Typically, career counseling consists of assessing student aptitudes and interests, exploring existing careers, and attempting to find an appropriate match. One of the unique aspects of counseling the gifted is that they have the potential to create their own careers (Garrison, Stronge, & Smith, 1986; Kerr & Claiborn, 1991; Milne, 1979; Perrone, 1991; Sanborn, 1979). Fredrickson (1986) warns that these individuals probably will not find occupations that make full use of their abilities, but suggests that the gifted may be able to modify careers to fit their abilities and interests. According to Garrison, Stronge, and Smith (1986),

> Another way to handle multiple abilities and interests in career choice is to focus on creating careers rather than choosing among existing careers.... Creating a new career can be accomplished by sensing emerging roles based on current trends...or by creating new roles in anticipation of future trends.... (p. 103)

New careers are often created by people who can envision a better world. Innovative ideas come from observations of discrepancies between the way things are and the way they could be (Dabrowski, 1964). Gifted children are skilled at noting these discrepancies. Many of our current careers did not exist in the past: city planners, ecologists, educators of the gifted, word processing specialists, video dealers. Some predict that 70 percent of today's students will enter careers that do not currently exist (Anderson, 1986).

Counselors can guide gifted students in clarifying their values and interests, and in custom designing their futures (Hoyt, 1978). Students could explore how some modern careers began; envision careers of the future; spend time observing their environment for things that could be improved; and imagine themselves in careers in which they would have an opportunity to improve some facet of life. Creative problem-solving techniques and creative visualization can both be used effectively to help students set future goals. By including this facet of career counseling in a program for the gifted, students can be helped to see that they are the shapers of tomorrow.

EXPLORING LIFE THEMES

Gifted young people are concerned about reducing the amount of suffering in the world (Boehm, 1962; Martinson, 1961), improving the quality of life, and ending war and pollution (Roeper, 1991). Because of their increased sensitivity, they have experienced—either directly or vicariously—some share of the pain in the world. Their future career goals can be drawn from their sensitivity and moral concern. Some guidance for doing so can be derived from an intriguing study conducted by Csikszentmihalyi and Beattie (1979).

Thirty men from poor immigrant backgrounds were interviewed: half were successful intellectuals and the other half blue-collar workers. T study sought to determine the factors that differentiated the life paths of these two groups from similar backgrounds. Early in their lives (between the ages of eight and eighteen), each of these men developed a life theme around a particular problem he had experienced. For one, the problem was labeled poverty, and his solution was to work hard and be thrifty. For another, the problem was seen as injustice, and his solution was to do his part to prevent injustice. All of those who became professionals had been read to as young children, or, if their parents were illiterate, they had been told elaborate stories. Reading became an important part of their lives, an activity that occupied a considerable amount of their free time. Through their reading, at some point they discovered that they were not alone in their problem—that there were others in the world who had suffered similarly. The reading linked them with a community that had felt as they had, thus enabling them to abstract from their experience a cause involving others and envision potential solutions. This eventually led to their setting professional goals and undergirded their striving for success. In contrast, none of those subjects who remained in the blue-collar working class generalized their own experience to others.

As part of career counseling with the gifted, time could profitably be spent exploring the experiences that have had the greatest impact on them. Did any of these experiences lead to the formation of life goals? Were there films, plays, television programs, or books that deeply affected them? What impact might these have on their career goals? Have they ever thought about what their purpose in life might be? What events led them to believe they had this purpose?

Gifted young people may be helped to identify their own life themes, the critical issues they have faced, and the means by which they personally can resolve these issues for themselves and others. They can be exposed to role models in real life and in books who have faced similar issues and who have devoted their lives to dealing with them in some way. Career counseling from this perspective takes on a much deeper meaning. Instead of merely enabling students to select professions in which they might be successful and happy, such counseling could lead to gifted students forging a personal commitment to contribute to society.

SPECIAL PROBLEMS OF GIFTED GIRLS

In addition to the existential dilemmas faced by all gifted students, gifted girls must deal with a unique set of challenges. Talented young women face a number of internal and external barriers to success, including underrepresentation in nontraditional careers, inequities in salaries, and lack of affordable childcare, to name but a few (Hollinger, 1991b). They must overcome societal programming that the career world and femininity are somehow antithetical (Horner, 1972). They need to determine if they wish to have both a family and a career, and, if so, how to balance these desires. They need encouragement to explore career possibilities that traditionally have been for men only. And they need assistance in risk-taking and in overcoming counterproductive beliefs about their own abilities. Women have much more complex career patterns than men (Hollinger, 1991b), and their relation to the work world is not as clear. For these reasons, differential career counseling is needed for gifted young women.

In a career counseling program, gifted girls should be exposed to the research on different paths taken by gifted women. They need role models of women who successfully combine marriage, raising children, and a career. For example, Rodenstein and Glickauf-Hughes (1979) found that women who combined child-rearing with careers derived a great deal of personal satisfaction from both. They also need to meet women who have chosen to have marriage and a career but no children. And they need to meet successful, happy women who have made the decision not to marry. Despite the double standard of the debonair bachelor and the unmarriageable spinster, the follow-up studies of Terman's subjects (Sears & Barbee, 1977) indicated that gifted women who were single heads of households felt more fulfilled at mid-life than gifted women who had become housewives at the expense of their careers. They should also be introduced to women who have made more traditional choices, and learn about their lifestyles.

Most gifted young women plan on combining a full-time career with marriage and a family (Fleming & Hollinger, 1986), but they are unsure about timing. They need "information and skills essential for coping successfully with multiple role demands" (Hollinger, 1991b, p. 137). How to juggle marriage and a career looms large in the minds of many gifted young women, and career guidance programs should provide ample time for its exploration. Life planning can minimize the impact of interruptions in their careers (Garrison, Stronge, & Smith, 1986). The following list presents some options young women may not have seen in their homes or in the media:

How to be a Woman and Have a Successful Career
❑ Be the first-born in an all-girl family
❑ Have an adoring father and a working mother
❑ Enter school early and accelerate whenever possible
❑ Stay a tomboy until late teens
❑ Idolize Katharine Hepburn or a reasonable facsimile
❑ Take every math course possible
❑ Decide not to marry—or not to have children
❑ Marry late after your career is in place
❑ Start a career before a family
❑ Be rich enough to afford live-in help
❑ Have a role-reversal with spouse
❑ Share a position
❑ Work in a setting with childcare facilities
❑ Live close to adoring grandparents who babysit
❑ Stay at home for awhile and write feverishly

This, almost light-hearted, set of recommendations can be used as a jumping-off point for research and class discussions on how each factor would enhance one's career potential. For example, young women can explore how the opportunities in many fields are different for those who have not yet had families and for those who have waited to begin their careers until their children were older. They can discuss how acceleration buys them extra time to fit in two full-time occupations: child-rearing and a career. They can discuss the feasibility of various new options, such as role reversals (in which the husband is the primary caretaker and the wife is the breadwinner) or sharing a position with a spouse. Case studies can be presented, or students can scour the community for individuals who either are currently engaged in these strategies or have tried them at one time. Their strengths and weaknesses can be debated. Young women can work on prioritizing their goals and weighing the pros and cons of various timing patterns (Hollinger, 1991b).

Although some young women would prefer to be full-time homemakers, they need to know that the cost of living and divorce rates both make it necessary for most women to work while they raise their families (Verheyden-Hilliard, 1976). They also need to become aware of the differences in pay scales in various occupations. A few years ago, I asked a panel of gifted college freshmen about their career choices. All of the young women were heading for low-paying service occupations, whereas all of the young men were preparing for high-paying, executive positions. Similar results have been found in empirical investigations (Kelly & Cobb, 1991; Leroux, 1986). Leroux (1986) found that service to others was of paramount importance to twelfth-grade gifted young women, whereas job stability and autonomy were more important to boys. Kelly and Cobb (1991) report that junior high aged gifted boys showed greater preference than girls for high-paying occupations. Perrone (1991) explains differences such as these in terms of masculine and feminine identity formation: "Van den Daele...discussed finding a striking difference in the career motivation of males and females, with *achievement* being more congruent with a masculine identity and *morality* more congruent with a feminine identity" (p. 323).

Exposure to role models is also essential (Beck, 1989; Phelps, 1991). If the mother of a gifted young women has been a full-time homemaker, or has held a low-paying clerical position while trying to raise her family, her daughter may have little conception of what else might be possible for her. Role models may be professional women who come to a career development class, to a career day on campus, or to a special course designed for gifted girls. Arrangements can be made to work directly with women in their fields of interest. Mentorships are particularly valuable to gifted women in the early stages of their career, and have been shown to produce higher earnings for women (Kaufmann, Harrel, Milam, Woolverton, & Miller, 1986).

Gifted women need to be challenged to think about and plan for a way of life which is compatible with their interests, personalities, and values. The development of purpose should not be simply choosing a career. It needs to be choosing a lifestyle which can provide meaning and direction in their lives. Mentors and role models can be powerful influences and instrumental in the development of purpose. (Phelps, 1991, p. 141)

Many resources are available today to assist gifted young women in career planning. Some recommended materials include: *Smart Girls, Gifted Women* (Kerr, 1985); *Project CHOICE* (Fleming & Hollinger, 1979); *The Gifted Girl: Helping Her Be the Best She Can Be* (Addison, 1983); *Girls Can Be Anything They Want* (Foote, 1980); *Women and the Mathematical Mystique* (Fox, Brody, & Tobin, 1980); *Journal for the Education of the Gifted* Special Issue on Gifted Girls and Gifted Women (Winter, 1989); *Roeper Review* Gender Equity: Meeting the Special Needs of Gifted Females (April, 1991); and "What Happens to the Gifted Girl?" (Silverman, 1986b).

THE DISADVANTAGED GIFTED

Career education is especially needed for children from poor families. "Gifted children from economically disadvantaged backgrounds require early intervention to reduce the limiting effects of a lower social class background and to raise their typically lower levels of career expectations" (Perrone, 1991, p. 326). Dunham and Russo (1983) contend that all programs for disadvantaged gifted children should be integrated with career education so that the students can see how education is relevant to the work world. They also recommend that disadvantaged students be prepared for necessary career shifts in a mobile society.

Middle-class families begin early to convey expectations to their children that they will attend college (Olszewski-Kubilius & Scott, 1992). Economically disadvantaged children usually do not receive such messages, even when they are intellectually capable of succeeding in higher education. Disadvantaged students also do not have the continuous support of role models of achievement in their environment. They are less likely than middle-class students to gain access to information about college entrance procedures and how to apply for scholarships. Even in supportive families of talented disadvantaged youth, VanTassel-Baska (1989) found that there was insufficient understanding of the application processes and lack of planning which could deprive these students of college opportunities for which they were qualified.

Olszewski-Kubilius and Scott (1992) conducted a study of ninety-two high school sophomores enrolled in gifted programs at Northwestern University. One of the groups was composed of economically disadvantaged gifted students. According to academic records and test scores, both groups were very promising candidates for college. The researchers found that the disadvantaged students were as highly motivated to attend college as the middle-class group and that they had received a great deal of support from teachers and parents. However, they felt "somewhat less prepared to go to college and less confident about being admitted" (p. 146). They also felt less informed about the steps necessary to make career decisions.

The value systems of the two groups of students were quite different. The disadvantaged youth demonstrated greater social concern and desire to retain close relationships with their families. They placed much more significance on family and community responsibilities. These findings are echoed by Dunham and Russo (1983): "Community involvement seems to be one of the best methods for allowing students to envision their own future, and to integrate and apply the skills they acquire in an academic setting" (p. 27). Counselors need to be aware of the influence of close family ties and extended families on college placement and career decisions. Disadvantaged students may opt for colleges close to home even if they are accepted at prestigious universities that are farther away. The researchers recommended mentoring experiences with individuals who have attained advanced degrees: "To compensate disadvantaged youngsters will need early exposure to careers through mentorships and internships and early contact with adult professionals" (Olszewski-Kubilius & Scott, 1992, p. 147). The importance of supplying students from disadvantaged families with early encouragement, exposure to role models, and access to information is found repeatedly in the literature (Delisle & Squires, 1989).

CONCLUSION

Career development is a lifelong pursuit, with room for exploration and side roads throughout the journey. Decisions are affected by one's values and dreams, and opportunities are created, not just sought. Career counseling needs to be an integral part of the gifted program, involving real-life experiences and parent education as part of the process. It is imperative that early college and career preparation opportunities be made available to disadvantaged children of high ability. These students face the greatest risks of curtailing their education and underemployment unless they receive support and guidance throughout their school programs. Gifted young women also need differentiated counseling, but this is insufficient; boys need to receive information about the consequences of sex-role stereotyping as well (Hollinger, 1991a). The question of combining family and career is not just an issue for gifted young women. With more women entering the work force, divorce rates, and men gaining custody of their children, men have a much greater responsibility for childcare today than ever before. Career development programs must take this into account, asking young men as well as young women how they plan to combine work, family, and community involvements (Perrone, 1986).

As societal values change, many gifted young people are no longer willing to make work the central focus of their lives (Miner, 1973). These changes mean that both sexes need to examine careers within the context of their life plans. What are their hopes, dreams, aspirations? How will a specific career choice enhance the quality of their lives or the lives of others? According to Getzels (1972), attitudes toward work have changed dramatically in the last century. In the past, people were motivated to work to gain security and money and to fulfill obligations. Today, personal growth and self-satisfaction play major roles in career choices. Getzels sees a trend in which future generations may be motivated to work for selfless commitment to society. If this trend should materialize, career exploration will also undergo changes. Young people will still be receiving parental messages about finding a job in which they can earn a good living, but this may conflict with their desire to be of service.

Perrone (1991) suggests that gifted adolescents may make career plans and decisions from the reference point of Van den Daele's (1968) highest levels of cognitive development: creativity, striving for personal/social good, and striving for transcendent good (self-actualization). "A world view is superordinate to self-interest; emphasis is on becoming; means are construed as coequal with ends; and the individual engages in poetic, dialectical thinking" (Perrone, 1991, p. 323). From his thirty years of studying gifted students' career development, Perrone concludes that the gifted have greater awareness, "a more worldly view," a greater sense of social responsibility, a sense of exhilaration when pursuing a goal, and "a strong desire, seemingly an innate need, to make an *impact* on society" (p. 326). Gifted young women and youth from disadvantaged backgrounds, in particular, appear to value service to the community more than monetary gain. Career development, then, would be better named "Life Planning," since we are moving away from a work-defined society and toward a globally defined perspective. The gifted seek careers that will enable them to create meaningful lives and contribute to the whole. In future generations, service and social responsibility may become the entire focus of career counseling programs.

REFERENCES

Addison, L. B. (1983). *The gifted girl: Helping her be the best she can be. Inservice resource handbook.* Bethesda, MD: The Equity Institute.

Anderson, J. (1986, November 4). Luncheon address, National Association for Gifted Children Thirty-third Annual Convention, Las Vegas.

Beck, L. (1989). Mentorships: Benefits and effects on career development. *Gifted Child Quarterly, 33,* 22–28.

Berger, S. L. (1989). *College planning for gifted students.* Reston, VA: The Council for Exceptional Children.

Bloom, B. S. (1982). The role of gifts and markers in the development of talent. *Exceptional Children, 48,* 510–521.

Bloom, B. S. (Ed.). (1985). *Developing talent in young people.* New York: Ballantine Books.

Bloom, B. S., & Sosniak, L. A. (1981). Talent development vs. schooling. *Educational Leadership, 39*(2), 86–94.

Boehm, L. (1962). The development of conscience: A comparison of American children of different mental and socioeconomic levels. *Child Development, 33,* 575–590.

Cox, J., Daniel, N., & Boston, B. O. (1985). *Educating able learners: Programs and promising practices.* Austin: University of Texas Press.

Csikszentmihalyi, M., & Beattie, O. V. (1979). Life themes: A theoretical and empirical exploration of their origins and effects. *Journal of Humanistic Psychology, 19,* 45–63.

Dabrowski, K. (1964). *Positive disintegration.* Boston: Little, Brown.

Delisle, J., & Squires, S. (1989). Career development for gifted and talented youth: Position statement. Division on Career Development (DCD) and The Association for the Gifted (TAG). *Journal of the Education of the Gifted, 13,* 97–104.

Dellas, M. (1969). Counselor role and function in counseling the creative student. *The School Counselor, 17,* 34–39.

Dunham, G., & Russo, T. (1983). Career education for the disadvantaged gifted: Some thoughts for educators. *Roeper Review, 5*(3), 26–28.

Duperrault, J. H. (1992). The Executive High School Internship Program. *The Gifted Child Today, 15*(1), 35–37.

Elkind, D. (1981). *The hurried child: Growing up too fast too soon.* Reading, MA: Addison-Wesley.

Ellingson, M. K., Haeger, W. W., & Feldhusen, J. F. (1986). The Purdue mentor program. *G/C/T, 9*(2), 2–5.

Engelmann, S., & Engelmann, T. (1980). *Give your child a superior mind.* New York: Cornerstone.

Fantini, M. D. (1981). A caring curriculum for gifted children. *Roeper Review, 3*(4), 3–4.

Feldhusen, J. (1980, October 30). Luncheon address, National Association for Gifted Children Twenty-seventh Annual Convention, Minneapolis.

Feldman, D. H., with Goldsmith, L. T. (1986). *Nature's gambit: Child prodigies and the development of human potential.* New York: Basic Books.

Fleming, E., & Hollinger, C. L. (1979). *Project CHOICE: Creating her options in career exploration.* Boston: Educational Development Corporation.

Fleming, E., & Hollinger, C. L. (1986, April). *Gifted and talented female adolescents: A six-year longitudinal study of life choices.* Paper presented at the annual meeting of the American Educational Research Association, San Francisco.

Foote, P. (1980). *Girls can be anything they want.* Englewood Cliffs, NJ: Julian Messner.

Fox, L. H., Brody, L., & Tobin, D. (1980). *Women and the mathematical mystique.* Baltimore: Johns Hopkins University Press.

Fox, L., & Tobin, D. (1978). Broadening career horizons for gifted girls. *G/C/T, 4,* 19–22, 45.

Fredrickson, R. H. (1986). Preparing gifted and talented students for the world of work. *Journal of Counseling and Development, 64,* 556–557.

Garrison, V. S., Stronge, J. H., & Smith, C. R. (1986). Are gifted girls encouraged to achieve their occupational potential? *Roeper Review, 9,* 101–104.

Getzels, J. W. (1972). On the transformation of values: A decade after Port Huron. *School Review, 80,* 505–519.

Gordon, W. J. J. (1961). *Synectics.* New York: Harper & Row.

Gowan, J. C. (1980). Issues on the guidance of gifted and creative children. In J. C. Gowan, G. D. Demos, & C. J. Kokaska (Eds.), *The guidance of exceptional children: A book of readings* (2nd ed., pp. 66–70). New York: Longman.

Hamilton, S. F., & Hamilton, M. A. (1992). Mentoring programs: Promise and paradox. *Phi Delta Kappan, 73,* 546–550.

Hollinger, C. L. (1991a). Career choices for gifted adolescents: Overcoming stereotypes. In M. Birely & J. Genschaft (Eds.), *Understanding the gifted adolescent: Educational, developmental, and multicultural issues* (pp. 201–214). New York: Teachers College Press.

Hollinger, C. L. (1991b). Facilitating the career development of gifted young women. *Roeper Review, 13,* 135–139.

Hollingworth, L. S. (1926). *Gifted children: Their nature and nurture.* New York: Macmillan.

Horner, M. (1972). Toward an understanding of achievement-related conflicts in women. *Journal of Social Issues, 28,* 157–175.

Howley, C. B. (1989). Career education for able students. *Journal for the Education of the Gifted, 12,* 205–217.

Hoyt, K. B. (1978). Career education for gifted and talented persons. *Roeper Review, 1*(1), 9–10.

Hoyt, K., & Hebeler, J. (1976). *Career education for gifted and talented students.* Salt Lake City: Olympus.

Kahn, J. (1986). Volunteering: A new way for your child to learn by doing. *G/C/T, 9*(1), 15–17.

Katchadourian, H., & Boli, J. (1985). *Careerism and intellectualism among college students.* San Francisco: Jossey-Bass.

Kaufmann, F. A., Harrel, G., Milam, C. P., Woolverton, N., & Miller, J. (1986). The nature, role, and influence of mentors in the lives of gifted adults. *Journal of Counseling and Development, 64,* 576–578.

Kaufmann, F. A., & Sexton, D. (1983). Some implications for home-school linkages. *Roeper Review, 6,* 49–51.

Kelly, K. R., & Cobb, S. J. (1991). A profile of the career development characteristics of young gifted adolescents: Examining gender and multicultural differences. Roeper *Review, 13,* 202–206.

Kerr, B. A. (1981). *Career education for the gifted and talented.* Columbus, OH: ERIC Clearinghouse on Adult Vocational and Career Information (ERIC Information Series No. 230).

Kerr, B. A. (1985). *Smart girls, gifted women.* Columbus: Ohio Psychology.

Kerr, B. A. (1986). Career counseling for the gifted: Assessments and interventions. *Journal of Counseling and Development, 64,* 602–603.

Kerr, B. A. (1991). *A handbook for counseling the gifted and talented.* Alexandria, VA: American Counseling Association.

Kerr, B. A., & Claiborn, C. D. (1991). Counseling talented adults. *Advanced Development, 3,* 75–83.

Kerr, B. A., & Ghrist-Priebe, S. L. (1988). Intervention for multipotentiality: Effects of a career counseling laboratory for gifted high school students. *Journal of Counseling and Development, 66,* 366–370.

Keyes, F. (1985). *Exploring careers for the gifted* (Rev. ed.). New York: Richard Rosen Press.

LeGuin, U. (1976). *Very far away from anywhere else*. New York: Bantam.

Leroux, J. A. (1986, April). *Sex differences influencing gifted adolescents: An ethnographic study*. Paper presented at the annual meeting of the American Educational Research Association, San Francisco (ERIC Document No. ED 271 934).

Marshall, B. C. (1981). Career decision-making patterns of gifted and talented adolescents: Implications for career education. *Journal of Career Education, 7,* 305–311.

Martinson, R. A. (1961). *Educational programs for gifted pupils*. Sacramento: California State Department of Education.

Merriam, S. (1983). Mentors and proteges: A critical review of the literature. *Adult Education Quarterly, 33,* 161–173.

Miller, A. (1981). *The drama of the gifted child*. New York: Basic Books.

Milne, B. G. (1979). Career education. In A. H. Passow (Ed.), *The gifted and talented: Their education and development* (pp. 246–254). The seventy-eighth yearbook of the National Society for the Study of Education. Chicago: University of Chicago Press.

Miner, J. B. (1973). *The management process*. New York: Macmillan.

Montour, K. (1977). William James Sidis, the broken twig. *American Psychologist, 32,* 265–279.

Moore, B. A., Feldhusen, J. F., & Owings, J. (1978). *The professional career exploration program for minority and/or low income gifted and talented high school students*. (Tech. Rep. No. 770103-15821) West Lafayette, IN: Department of Education, Purdue University.

Munger, A. (1990). The parent's role in counseling the gifted: The balance between home and school. In J. VanTassel-Baska (Ed.), *A practical guide to counseling the gifted in a school setting* (2nd ed., pp. 57–65). Reston, VA: The Council for Exceptional Children.

National Commission on Resources for Youth, Inc. (1977). *New roles for youth in the school and community*. New York: Citation Press.

Olszewski-Kubilius, P., & Scott, J. M. (1992). An investigation of the college and career counseling needs of economically disadvantaged minority gifted students. *Roeper Review, 14,* 141–148.

Perrone, P. A. (1986). Guidance needs of gifted children, adolescents, and adults. *Journal of Counseling and Development, 64,* 564–566.

Perrone, P. A. (1991). Career development. In N. Colangelo & G. A. Davis (Eds.), *Handbook of gifted education* (pp. 321–327). Needham Heights, MA: Allyn & Bacon.

Phelps, C. R. (1991). Identity formation in career development for gifted women. *Roeper Review, 13,* 140–141.

Prillaman, D., & Richardson, R. (1989). The William and Mary mentorship model: College students as a resource for the gifted. *Roeper Review, 12,* 114–118.

Rodenstein, J. M., & Glickauf-Hughes, C. (1979). Career and lifestyle determinants of gifted women. In N. Colangelo & R. T. Zaffrann (Eds.), *New voices in counseling the gifted* (pp. 370–381). Dubuque, IA: Kendall/Hunt.

Roeper, A. (1991). Focus on global awareness. *World Gifted, 12*(4), 19–21.

Runions, T. (1980). The mentor academy program: Educating the gifted and talented for the 80's. *Gifted Child Quarterly, 24,* 152–157.

Sanborn, M. P. (1979). Career development: Problems of gifted and talented students. In N. Colangelo & R. T. Zaffrann (Eds.), *New voices in counseling the gifted* (pp. 284–300). Dubuque, IA: Kendall/Hunt.

Sears, P. S., & Barbee, A. H. (1977). Career and life satisfactions among Terman's women. In J. C. Stanley, W. C. George, & C. H. Solano (Eds.), *The gifted and the creative: A fifty-year perspective* (pp. 28–65). Baltimore: Johns Hopkins University Press.

Shannon, C. K. (1989). In the service of children: An open letter to global educators. *Roeper Review, 11*, 184–185.

Silverman, L. K. (1982). Giftedness. In E. L. Meyen (Ed.), *Exceptional children and youth in today's schools*. Denver: Love.

Silverman, L. K. (1986a). Parenting young gifted children. *Journal of Children in Contemporary Society, 18*, 73–87.

Silverman, L. K. (1986b). What happens to the gifted girl? In C. J. Maker (Ed.), *Critical issues in gifted education: Vol. 1. Defensible programs for the gifted* (pp. 43–89). Rockville, MD: Aspen.

Silverman, L. K., & Kearney, K. (1989). Parents of the extraordinarily gifted. *Advanced Development, 1*, 41–56.

Swassing, R. H., & Fichter, G. R. (1991). University and community-based programs for the gifted adolescent. In M. Bireley & J. Genshaft (Eds.), *Understanding the gifted adolescent: Educational, developmental, and multicultural issues* (pp. 176–185). New York: Teachers College Press.

Tannenbaum, A. J. (1984, March 1). Keynote address, Louisiana Conference on the Gifted, Baton Rouge, LA.

Torrance, E. P. (1980). Understanding creativity in talented students. In J. C. Gowan, G. D. Demos, & C. J. Kokaska (Eds.), *The guidance of exceptional children: A book of readings* (2nd ed., pp. 70–77). New York: Longman.

Van den Daele, L. (1968). A developmental study of the ego-ideal. *Genetic Psychology Monographs, 78*, 191–256.

VanTassel-Baska, J. (1981). A comprehensive model of career education for gifted and talented. *Journal of Career Education*, 325–331.

VanTassel-Baska, J. (1989). The role of the family in the success of disadvantaged gifted learners. *Journal for the Education of the Gifted, 13*, 22–36.

Verheyden-Hilliard, M. E. (1976). *A handbook for workshops on sex equality in education*. Alexandria, VA: American Personnel and Guidance Association.

Voltaire. (1759). *Candide*. In H. M. Block (Ed.), *Candide and other writings* (1956). New York: Modern Library.

Willings, D. (1986). Enriched career search. *Roeper Review, 9*, 95–100.

Wolleat, P. L. (1979). Building the career development of gifted females. In N. Colangelo & R. T. Zaffrann (Eds.), *New voices in counseling the gifted* (pp. 331–345). Dubuque, IA: Kendall/Hunt.

Wright, L., & Borland, J. H. (1992). A special friend: Adolescent mentors for young, economically disadvantaged, potentially gifted students. *Roeper Review, 14*, 124–129.

Yankelovich, D. (1972). *The changing values on campus*. New York: Washington Square Press.

11

Assessment Tools for Counselors

John F. Feldhusen, Fathi Jarwan, and Dan Holt

Tests provide systematic analysis of students' abilities, aptitudes, achievements, personal-social adjustment, self-concepts, self-esteem, values, attitudes, career aspirations, study methods and habits, and other psycho-educational characteristics. The instruments we call "tests" may be limited to those measures that assess students' maximum capability under high motivation. Those we call "scales," "inventories," "rating scales," "questionnaires," and "checklists" are measures of typical performance under normal, day-by-day motivational conditions. The latter depend upon insight and veracity of respondents for reliability, whereas tests require explicit directions to assure standardization, careful monitoring to assure that examinees do not cheat, and the development of rapport to encourage optimum motivation of examinees.

Tests and rating scales do not replace counselor, teacher, or clinician judgment. They provide reliable and valid (hopefully) information which serves as the basis for sound judgments and good decision-making regarding groups and individuals. For the gifted and talented, the decisions involve admission to programs, assignment to services, delineation of abilities and/or needs for which service will be provided, retention in programs, selection for special classes, and receipt of awards. Judgments may also be made concerning appropriate future experiences such as what summer program to attend, which college or university for higher education, career goals, and so forth. Tests and rating scales provide information to assist teachers, counselors, and gifted students themselves in making these decisions.

Gifted and talented children, especially the highly gifted, may experience social-emotional difficulties that are associated with or caused by their giftedness, or they may have need for specialized counseling services. Silverman (1989) lists the following as problem areas for the gifted and talented:

❑ Underachievement
❑ Depression (often masked as boredom)
❑ Hiding abilities
❑ Understanding their introversion
❑ Uneven development
❑ Excessive competitiveness
❑ Hostilities of others toward their abilities
❑ Feeling overly responsible for others
❑ Being overshadowed in the family by the eldest sibling
❑ Hidden disabilities
❑ Lack of true peers

Robinson and Noble (1991) suggest that 20 to 25 percent of highly gifted children may suffer serious maladjustment, which is double the rate in the "normal" population. Some of the problems they report to be associated with this group include:

❑ Social isolation
❑ Bullying by older classmates
❑ Play interests that cannot be shared
❑ Few peers with whom to share interests
❑ Great dependence on parents for companionship
❑ Poor school environment
❑ High expectations from others
❑ Awareness of parental concern about their giftedness

It seems clear that gifted children experience the world of school and home in ways that are different from the experience of other children. They have difficulty sometimes in relating to age peers because of their precocity in interests, abilities, and achievements. They may lack friends, suffer boredom in unchallenging school programs, and be the target of negative peer pressures. Thus, counselors should be aware of these problems and, through their own direct interviews with and observations of gifted students, see the need for more intensive diagnostic procedures afforded by tests and self-report inventories.

A well-structured counseling program for the gifted should include three major components: (1) academic counseling, (2) personal and social adjustment, and (3) vocational development and career counseling.

To cover these areas we present next descriptions of selected tests, inventories, and scales that are particularly useful in work with gifted and talented students. Our selections include the following instruments: the Myers-Briggs Type Indicator; the Self-Perception Profile for Children; the Piers-

Harris Children's Self-Concept Scale; the Sixteen Personality Factor Questionnaire; the California Psychological Inventory; the Kuder Preference Record—Vocational (Form C); the Strong Interest Inventory; and the Differential Aptitude Tests.

A large number of research studies and several reviews have been conducted on each of these instruments. Also, they have been used or recommended in gifted programs (Cornell, Callahan, & Loyd, 1991; French, 1959; Karnes & Wherry, 1981; Mills & Eiserer, 1982; Richert, Alvino, & McDonnel, 1982; Whitmore, 1980). However, we caution that counselors who use these instruments should have training in theories of human ability and personality as well as explicit education in the administration and interpretation of tests. Such training should include attention to the various types of validity (face-content, construct, and predictive) and to reliability analysis. It is especially important to know the psychometric strengths and limitations of tests, how to interpret test manuals, how to use various test evaluation resources, and the ethical limitations of test usage. It is also important to know the limitations or strengths of specific tests when used with gifted and talented youth—appropriateness of normative samples, ceiling potential, possible regression effects, and so forth. Test results are often used in making decisions that may have profound effects on the lives of gifted and talented children, so it is crucial that counselors have a sound knowledge of test theory, administration, and interpretation.

      Title: Myers-Briggs Type Indicator
   Authors: K. C. Briggs and I. B. Myers
  Publisher: Consulting Psychologists Press, Inc.
                3803 East Bayshore Road
                Palo Alto, California 94303

The Myers-Briggs Type Indicator (MBTI) is designed to help people determine which psychological types, as described by Carl Jung (1971), are dominant in their personality. The MBTI is basically concerned with the "valuable differences in people that result from where they like to focus their attention, the way they like to take in information, the way they like to decide, and the kind of lifestyle they adopt" (Myers, 1987, p. 4). With the information provided by the MBTI, a person can be helped to better understand reactions to various circumstances in life, such as personal relationships, career preference, and ability to function within a group or as an individual.

The MBTI is an objective self-report questionnaire which consists of forced-choice items. There are no right/wrong or good/bad responses, but rather choices between reactions to sets of circumstances. Depending on orientation, an individual will choose the most personally desirable courses of action.

There are six forms of the MBTI: Form F, Form G, Form AV (abbreviated version), Form G (self-scorable), Form K, and Form J (for discussion see catalog). Form G consists of 126 items whereas Form AV consists of only 50 items. Form AV may be used when time is limited and the added accuracy of Form G is not crucial. Form F has 166 items and is used when those administering the MBTI are prepared to share the results with the authors of the inventory for the purposes of ongoing research.

The MBTI, based on Jung's theory of psychological types (1971), provides personality preferences on four scales with two opposite preferences for each: extroversion–introversion (EI), sensing–intuition (SN), thinking–feeling (TF), and judgment–perception (JP). The combination and interaction of preferences is what determines a person's psychological type. For example, the four dominant preferences ISTJ mean that the person is an introvert (I) who likes to process information with sensing (S), uses thinking (T) to make decisions, and takes a judging (J) attitude toward the outer world. The purpose of the MBTI is to provide information about the choices between these preferences. "Every person is assumed to use both poles of each of the four preferences, but to respond first or most often with the preferred function or attitudes" (Myers & McCaulley, 1986, p. 3).

Adults and high school students are the target population for the MBTI. Younger children, with sixth-grade reading levels, can be evaluated, but more caution should be exercised in interpreting results. Even though Jung's theory is directed toward a universal human mental process, interpretation of the MBTI for non-English-speaking people should also be carried out cautiously.

Internal consistency reliabilities range from .75 to .85. A substantial amount of validity data is presented in the MBTI manual, which consists mainly of concurrent studies. The MBTI manual states that about 75 percent of those taking the MBTI agree with their reported type preferences. The person administering the MBTI is responsible for dealing with each individual to help interpret the results. Exploration of why the type preferences shown do not match the person's own experiences can lead to more in-depth counseling. The authors of the MBTI point out that the attitude of the person answering the questions on the MBTI makes a substantial difference in the results. Scores indicate the degree of consistency in choosing one preference over its opposite. High scores generally mean a clear preference. In younger people low scores are quite common. However, the scores should be viewed as signs that guide individuals to better understand their way of perceiving and responding to society.

The MBTI is a valuable tool, meant to assist either professional counselors or teachers who wish to help individuals gain insights about themselves and about how they interact with their personal-social sphere and professional environment. The MBTI will be helpful in starting the process of interacting with an individual in a counseling setting. It should be nonthreatening and, while providing insights, also be a point of departure for exploration of various problem areas. This, depending on the circumstances, can lead to in-depth discussions and counseling.

Title:	Self-Perception Profile for Children
Author:	Susan Harter
Publisher:	Dr. Susan Harter
	University of Denver
	2040 South York Street
	Denver, Colorado 80208

The Self-Perception Profile for Children is a recently revised edition of the Perceived Competence Scale for Children. The purpose for constructing the original scale, as stated by the author (Harter, 1981, p. 120), "was two-fold: (1) to provide an instrument which would be sensitive to domain-specific perceptions of competence, yet (2) to allow for a determination of one's global self-esteem, over and above one's perception of competence." The scale is based on the assumption that children in grades three through ten can make clear distinctions among their cognitive, social, and physical competence, as well as general self-worth. It is different from the majority of self-concept scales in that it does not attempt to assess global self-worth by summing responses to a wide variety of self-descriptions. Rather, it taps one's feelings of worth directly and independently of domain-specific judgments.

The Self-Perception Profile for Children has two other versions: one for young children and one for adolescents. The pictorial version for children four to seven years old does not include a general self-worth scale because the author (Harter, 1981) assumed that "young children do not have a sense of the self, in general" (p. 122). However, despite Harter's concerns, gifted children do seem to develop a generalized self-concept younger than others. The Self-Perception Profile for Children has been used with 7-year-old gifted children because they find the pictorial scales much too simplistic (L. Silverman, personal communication, January 12, 1991).

The Self-Perception Profile for Children contains six subscales, each of which includes six items, constituting a total of thirty-six items. According to the Manual (Harter, 1985, p. 6), the specific and general domains tapped by the subscales are:

1. *Scholastic Competence*: This scale taps the child's perception of his/her competence or ability within the realm of scholastic performance.
2. *Social Acceptance*: This scale taps the degree to which a child has friends, feels he/she is popular, and feels that most kids like him/her.
3. *Athletic Competence*: The items of this scale tap content relevant to sports and outdoor games.
4. *Physical Appearance*: This scale taps the degree to which a child is happy with the way he/she looks; likes his/her height, weight, body, face, hair; and feels that he/she is good-looking.

5. *Behavioral Conduct*: This scale was added to the original version to tap the degree to which children like the way they behave, do the right thing, act the way they are supposed to, and avoid getting into trouble.

6. *Global Self-Worth*: This scale taps the extent to which a child likes him- or herself as a person, is happy with the way she/he is leading life, and is generally happy with the way she/he is. The scale constitutes a global judgment of the self-worth as a person.

Within each subscale three items are worded with the first part of a statement reflecting high competence or adequacy and three items with the first part of a statement reflecting low competence or adequacy. The child is first asked to decide which kind of child is most like him or her, and then asked to indicate whether this likeness is only sort of true or really true. The scales may be administered individually or in groups. There is no time limit for administration. A scoring key master list is provided in the manual. A data coding sheet is available so that scores from a child's protocol can be transferred and grouped for each subscale. The six subscale means are plotted on a special form reflecting a given child's profile. There is an abbreviated form of the scale for use by teachers.

Statistics on the current revision of the scale are based on data collected from samples of boys and girls enrolled in third through eighth grades in Colorado schools. Sample sizes range from 178 to 748 students. Internal consistency reliabilities for all subscales and samples range between .71 and .86. Means fluctuate around the value of 3.0. Most standard deviations fall between .50 and .85. There are significant differences between boys' and girls' scores. Generally speaking, boys see themselves as more athletically competent than do girls. In contrast, girls view themselves as better behaved than boys.

Intercorrelations among subscales indicate that Scholastic Competence tends to be related to Behavioral Conduct and that Physical Appearance is consistently related to Self-Worth. Social Acceptance, Athletic Competence, and Physical Appearance also appear to form a cluster.

The Self-Perception Profile for Children is appropriate for normal children from third through sixth grades. It is designed to provide a rich and differentiated picture of a child's self-concept. Additional information can be obtained by conducting a structured interview after administering the scale.

The research results with gifted children using the Harter scales are interesting. For example, the brighter the child, the more likely there is to be a significant discrepancy between cognitive and social self-concept. If students are tested immediately after entering a gifted program, their cognitive self-concepts usually go down whereas their social self-concepts often go up. Later in the school year the scores stabilize. Also, the usefulness of self-concept or self-esteem inventories with gifted children is frequently reported in the literature (Feldhusen & Kolloff, 1981; Kolloff & Feldhusen, 1984; Nielsen, 1984; Thompson, 1981; Tidwell, 1980).

Title: Piers-Harris Children's Self-Concept Scale
(The Way I Feel About Myself)
Authors: E. V. Piers, & D. B. Harris
Publisher: Western Psychological Services
12031 Wilshire Boulevard
Los Angeles, California 90025

The Piers-Harris Children's Self-Concept Scale is a brief self-report measure consisting of eighty first-person declarative statements to which the child responds "yes" or "no." It is intended for use with children and adolescents, aged eight to eighteen, to assess self-concept. It was originally developed as a research instrument and as an aid to clinical and educational evaluation in applied settings. Self-concept, as measured by this instrument, is defined as a relatively stable set of self-attitudes reflecting both a description and an evaluation of one's own behavior and attributes. It is interchangeable with the terms self-esteem and self-regard.

The Piers-Harris was standardized on 1,183 children in grades four through twelve in one Pennsylvania school district (Piers, 1989). It has not been re-normed since the first publication in 1969. Although subsequent research has generally provided continuous support for use of the instrument as it was originally intended, the authors caution against using original norms with different populations. The Revised Manual 1984 provides complete information regarding scale development, rationale, standardization procedures, administration and scoring, purpose and uses, guidelines for interpretation, and recent reliability and validity studies. Extensive discussion and description of its use with specific ethnic, minority, and exceptional populations, including the gifted, is also presented.

The Piers-Harris Scale may be administered either individually or to small groups of eight to ten. The respondent is required to circle either "yes," indicating that the statement describes the way he or she feels about self, or "no," indicating that the statement does not describe the way he or she feels about self. Approximately half the items are positively worded (e.g., "I am a happy person") and half are worded in the negative direction (e.g., "I behave badly at home"). There are no time limits, but it usually takes 15 to 20 minutes to complete. In addition to hand-scoring, computer programs and mail-in services are available for accurate scoring and generating individual or group interpretation reports. The raw score is the total number of responses marked in the positive direction. The higher the raw score, the more positive the child's assessed self-concept. Raw scores can be converted to percentiles, stanines, and T-scores on a profile form. Two new measures have been designed to facilitate judgments regarding the validity of a child's protocol: Response Bias Index (assesses acquiescence or negative response sets) and Inconsistency Index (detects random response patterns).

In addition to an overall self-concept score, the Piers-Harris Scale provides six "cluster scales" derived empirically through factor analysis. The use of these scales is based on the assumption that self-concept is not a unitary structure. They may be used to assess an individual's sense of strengths and weaknesses. The cluster scales are:

1. *Behavior* (16 items): Reflects the extent to which the child admits or denies problematic behaviors.
2. *Intellectual and School Status* (17 items): Reflects the child's self-assessment of his/her abilities with respect to intellectual and academic tasks, including general satisfaction with school and future expectations.
3. *Physical Appearance and Attributes* (13 items): This scale is more sensitive than the others to sex differences. It reflects the child's attitudes concerning his/her other physical characteristics and attributes such as leadership and the ability to express ideas.
4. *Anxiety* (14 items): Reflects general emotional disturbance and dysphoric mood such as worry, nervousness, shyness, sadness, and fear. A low score on this scale suggests the need for further psychological evaluation or referral.
5. *Popularity* (12 items): Reflects the child's evaluation of his/her popularity with classmates and ability to make friends.
6. *Happiness and Satisfaction* (10 items): Reflects a general feeling of being satisfied with life.

The Piers-Harris Scale can be used as a screening device in special education and regular classroom settings to identify children who might benefit from further psychological evaluation. In addition, it can be used as an aid to individual assessment in a variety of clinical and counseling settings. Although the major function of the scale is to provide a global index of self-concept, it is considered a clinical tool that helps generate hypotheses and opens up areas for further clinical exploration and in-depth testing. However, as indicated in the 1984 Manual, the Piers-Harris Scale should never be used as the sole method for assessing self-concept if important decisions are to be made about a child, because it is designed to enhance and supplement skilled clinical judgment, not to replace it. Careful attention should be given to the extremely low scores (false positives) or the extremely high scores (false negatives). Only very low scores of the 16th percentile or below should be considered significant, and even these should be interpreted cautiously. Also the use and interpretation of the scale should be done by professionals with advanced training in psychological testing and with good knowledge of the scale. Potential users include psychologists, counselors, teachers, and school officials. In summary, the usefulness of the Piers-Harris has been documented as a screening instrument, as a component in individual assessment, and as a research instrument (Epstein, 1985; Jeske, 1985).

Title: Sixteen Personality Factor Questionnaire
Author: Raymond Cattell
Publisher: The Institute for Personality and Ability Testing, Inc.
P.O. Box 188
Champaign, Illinois 61824-0188

The Sixteen Personality Factor Questionnaire (16PF) was developed by Raymond Cattell as a multipurpose measure of primary personality traits based on his general theory of personality and extensive factor analytic research. Five major revisions have been done (and a sixth is in progress) since the first publication of the test in 1949 by the Institute for Personality and Ability Testing, Inc.

The 16PF has five forms: Forms A and B each contain 187 items and require 45–60 minutes for administration. Forms C and D are short forms of 105 items each and require 25–35 minutes for administration. The target populations for these four forms is high school level through adult, and a three-choice response format is employed throughout. Form E is designed for use with individuals whose reading level is equivalent to grades three through four. It contains 128 items and requires about one hour for administration.

The sixteen personality factors that the author calls "source traits" are: warmth, intelligence, emotional stability, dominance, impulsivity, conformity, boldness, sensitivity, suspiciousness, imagination, shrewdness, insecurity, radicalism, self-sufficiency, self-discipline, and tension (see Table 11.1 for brief descriptions). The sixteen factors are independent but correlate slightly with each other. In addition to the sixteen primary factors, the test can be used to measure five secondary dimensions derived by analysis of factor loadings. These broader factors are identified as follows: extraversion, anxiety, tough poise, independence, and behavior control.

Form A also includes three supplementary validity scales (Faking Good, Faking Bad, Random Response) as a built-in protection against distortion. Forms C and D contain a single motivational distortion scale. Whether administered individually or in groups, it is the responsibility of the examiner to establish good rapport and to have clients realize that careful and truthful responses produce accurate, beneficial results.

Scoring may be done by hand or machine. Raw scores are easily converted to sten scores with the norm tables for any of the sixteen personality factors. Norm tables are provided for high school students, university and college undergraduates, and general adult populations for males and females, separately and collectively. The final norm samples include data from thirty-six states for Forms A and B, and thirty states for Forms C and D. Translations into twenty-four languages and adaptations for five English-speaking cultures are available from the publisher.

A handbook and a brief administrator's manual are provided by the publisher. These include full details concerning design and construction of the

Table 11.1
THE PRIMARY SOURCE TRAITS COVERED BY THE 16PF TEST

Factor	Low Sten Score Description (1-3)	High Sten Score Description (8-10)
A	*Cool*, reserved, impersonal, detached, formal, aloof Sizothymia*	*Warm*, outgoing, kindly, easygoing, participating, likes people Affectothymia
B	*Concrete-thinking*, less intelligent Lower scholastic mental capacity	*Abstract-thinking*, more intelligent, bright Higher scholastic mental capacity
C	*Affected by feelings*, emotionally less stable, easily annoyed Lower ego strength	*Emotionally stable*, mature, faces reality, calm Higher ego strength
E	*Submissive*, humble, mild, easily led, accommodating Submissiveness	*Dominant*, assertive, aggressive, stubborn, competitive, bossy Dominance
F	*Sober*, restrained, prudent, taciturn, serious Desurgency	*Enthusiastic*, spontaneous, heedless, expressive, cheerful Surgency
G	*Expedient*, disregards rules, self-indulgent Weaker superego strength	*Conscientious*, conforming, moralistic, staid, rule-bound Stronger superego strength
H	*Shy*, threat-sensitive, timid, hesitant, intimidated Threctia	*Bold*, venturesome, uninhibited, can take stress Parmia
I	*Tough-minded*, self-reliant, no-nonsense, rough, realistic Harria	*Tender-minded*, sensitive, overprotected, intuitive, refined Premsia
L	*Trusting*, accepting conditions, easy to get on with Alaxia	*Suspicious*, hard to fool, distrustful, skeptical Protension
M	*Practical*, concerned with "down-to-earth" issues, steady Praxernia	*Imaginative*, absent-minded, absorbed in thought, impractical Autia
N	*Forthright*, unpretentious, open, genuine, artless Artlessness	*Shrewd*, polished, socially aware, diplomatic, calculating Shrewdness

O   *Self-assured*, secure, feels free of guilt, untroubled, self-satisfied
Untroubled adequacy

    Apprehensive, self-blaming, guilt-prone, insecure, worrying
Guilt proneness

Q₁   *Conservative*, respecting traditional ideas
Conservatism of temperament

    Experimenting, liberal, critical, open to change
Radicalism

Q₂   *Group-oriented*, a "joiner" and sound follower, listens to others
Group adherence

    Self-sufficient, resourceful, prefers own decisions
Self-sufficiency

Q₃   *Undisciplined self-conflict*, lax, careless of social rules
Low integration

    Following self-image, socially precise, compulsive
High self-concept control

Q₄   *Relaxed*, tranquil, composed, has low drive, unfrustrated
Low ergic tension

    Tense, frustrated, overwrought, has high drive
High ergic tension

*Titles in roman type are the technical names for the factors and are explained more fully in the Handbook.

---

tests, instructions for administering and scoring, reliability and validity estimates, and interpretation of the primary factors. Although the range of applications and uses is not clearly defined in these resources, the 16PF has been used in a wide variety of settings. It is most valuable in personnel selection, guidance and counseling, personality assessment, and personality research.

Clinical use of the test may be appropriate, but the publisher recommends the Clinical Analysis Questionnaire, which incorporates the 16PF, for this purpose. Normative scores are provided for high school, college, and general populations. Computer scoring generates a number of interpretive reports such as the Personal Career Development Profile, the Marriage Counseling Report, and a single-page report of the 16PF scores. Forms C and D are frequently used in occupational selection. For maximum precision, the use of at least two forms (A+B or C+D), if possible, is suggested by the authors (Cattell, Eber, & Tatsuoka, 1985, pp. 24–25; *Administrator's Manual*, 1979, p. 9).

To help interpret a personality profile, the handbook provides short, nontechnical definitions and interpretations of low and high scores on each of the sixteen primary factors. However, selection of the most appropriate norm group is a critical step in the interpretation process. Therefore, it should be done with much care.

Title: California Psychological Inventory
Author: Harrison G. Gough
Publisher: Consulting Psychologists Press
           3803 East Bayshore Road
           Palo Alto, California 94303

The California Psychological Inventory (CPI) is designed to assess personality characteristics and variables that are used to understand and predict individual behavior in a social context. The latest version of 1987 includes 462 items, 199 of which are taken from the Minnesota Multiphasic Personality Inventory. There are twenty scales focusing on interpersonal behavior or social interaction: Dominance, Capacity for Status, Sociability, Social Presence, Self-acceptance, Independence, Empathy, Responsibility, Socialization, Self-control, Good Impression, Communality, Well-being, Tolerance, Achievement via Conformance, Achievement via Independence, Intellectual Efficiency, Psychological-mindedness, Flexibility, and Femininity/Masculinity. The scales of Well-being, Communality, and Good Impression were developed to serve as validity controls. They measure self-underestimation, randomization of responses, and self-desirability, respectively. There is only one form of the CPI.

The CPI has been derived from the everyday life behaviors and processes of interpersonal and social functioning. They are not related to a specific personality theory. The *Administrator's Guide* (Gough, 1987) discusses the methods used in developing and validating the CPI scales. The basic CPI scales (1987 edition) yield twenty raw scores. Raw scores are plotted on a profile sheet and can be converted to standard scores with means of 50 and standard deviations of 10. Scores of all scales, except the last one for femininity/masculinity interests, are simply interpreted so that higher values suggest favored standing on the variable and lower values suggest less favored status. In other words, high scores indicate areas of strength and low scores, areas of weakness. Norms and profiles are given for males and females based on data from normative samples (1,000 subjects of each sex) which include a variety of educational, occupational, and clinical groups.

Accurate diagnosis and interpretation of a particular profile requires special skill and training, especially in regard to the additional three structural scales which were developed through factor and item analysis and added to the latest edition of 1987 to address factors of self-realization, norm-favoring, and internality.

The CPI is a self-report inventory and thus requires minimal involvement of the examiner when administering. But involvement for interpretation is needed. It can be done at home or by mail or under formal or informal conditions. According to the *Administrator's Guide* (Gough, 1987), administration conditions do not affect the accuracy of results. It is untimed, but administration usually takes 45–60 minutes. The raw score for each scale is obtained by counting the number of answers that agree with the designated responses on the scoring template. Computer scoring, profiling, and narrative interpretation services are available from the publisher.

The CPI has been developed to provide a comprehensive multidimensional assessment of normal persons in a variety of settings. It is a counseling tool to make certain predictions or to understand and assist normal clients in educational institutions and other settings as well. It has been used in a wide range of studies and applications including academic achievement in high school and college, social maturity, occupational counseling, psychiatric residency, marital adjustment, creativity, estimation of locus of control, drug abuse, and smoking cessation. Its ultimate use is for case evaluation and diagnosis. Gough (1987) compares CPI with the Strong-Campbell Interest Inventory in terms of the classificatory and predictive nature of the scales.

The CPI may be given beginning at grade seven, or at age thirteen to fourteen, but it is more appropriate for the high school and college level. It has been used in many studies with gifted students (Cornell et al., 1991; Keasey & Smith-Winberry, 1983). Overall, many experts consider the CPI one of the best instruments for personality analysis and evaluation (Domino, 1984).

> Title: Kuder Preference Record—Vocational (Form C̃)
> Author: F. Kuder
> Publisher: Science Research Associates, Inc.
> 155 North Wacker Drive
> Chicago, Illinois 60606

The Kuder Preference Record—Vocational (Form C) was developed by Frederick Kuder in the 1930s as a way to provide initial vocational career guidance to students in school. The Kuder "avoids the use of concepts about which a child's knowledge may change materially—for example, occupational titles— and vocabulary has been kept to the sixth-grade level" (Kuder, 1971, p. 3). The Kuder is intended to be a helpful tool for students, especially at the junior high school level, in making educational and vocational plans at various "choice points" in their development. The survey is both forced-choice in format and partially "ipsative" in character. It measures preferences in ten broad areas: Outdoor, Mechanical, Computational, Scientific, Persuasive, Artistic, Literacy, Musical, Social Service, and Clerical.

Although there is no time limit for the Kuder, students usually complete it in 45 to 60 minutes. It is straightforward in format and can be scored by hand. A pin is used to punch holes in the answer sheet. Students can score their own answer sheet by looking at the patterns produced by the holes in the answer sheet which has circles and lines on it. Although it can be scored by the student, professional guidance is still highly recommended in interpreting the scores. The survey should not be used to guide students to make definite career decisions, but rather to point out patterns and directions, verify areas of interest, and stimulate questions about previously unknown career possibilities.

Because of its low cost, ease of administration and scoring, and relevance for use with a wide range of age groups, the Kuder, Form C has maintained its popularity for over fifty years. It has quite often been compared to the Strong Vocational Interest Blanks (SVIB). Although it is reasonable to compare the two, they were designed with different objectives in mind. The Strong was created by constructing scales employing empirical methodology to be an efficient instrument for industry; the Kuder was developed simply as a career planning guide for students. The Kuder (Form C) was "constructed using the rational approach without any empirical check. Instead, homogeneity was the basis for each of the scales developed for the preference record" (Shertzer & Linden, 1979, p. 286). One of the main concerns regarding completely homogeneous interest inventories is that a desired result can be easily obtained by the examinee. Even so, for persons who are sincerely interested in gaining some insight into their patterns of interest, the homogeneous inventory is useful. Also, some people answer carelessly or without understanding. To combat some of these problems, Kuder introduced a verification scale intended to help counselors determine if a person is sincere in responding.

Zytowski (1974, p. 123) presented substantial evidence of predictive validity regarding the Kuder. In fact, according to Harmon (1978, p. 1011), "There is more evidence of predictive validity for the Kuder inventories than for any of the other more recent entries into the field of interest measurement which utilize homogeneous scales." The Kuder has a long history as a valuable tool when used within the setting for which it is intended. The results, though, should be seen as only a point of departure, not the destination, for the counselor and student.

Title:	Strong Interest Inventory
Authors:	Edward K. Strong and Jo-Ida C. Hansen
Publishers:	Stanford University Press
	Stanford, California 94305
Distributor:	Consulting Psychologists Press, Inc.
	3803 East Bayshore Road
	Palo Alto, California 94303

The Strong Interest Inventory (the Strong, Form T325) is the latest edition of the Strong Vocational Interest Blank which was initially published in 1927 by Stanford University (Campbell & Hansen, 1981). The Strong is intended to measure a respondent's interest in a wide range of occupations, occupational activities, hobbies, leisure activities, school subjects, and types of people

(Hansen & Campbell, 1985). The respondent is asked to indicate his or her interest as either "like," "indifferent," or "dislike" in response to the items. The answers are analyzed by computer (hand-scoring is impossible) to derive scores on 264 scales. Results are reported in a profile format which offers interpretive information.

The theoretical foundation for the development and application of the Strong is based on two assumptions: (1) personality interests and characteristics are relatively stable, and (2) workers in each occupation share common interests and characteristics. Accordingly, when an individual's interests and traits match the interest patterns of an occupation, the probability of entering that occupation and succeeding in it is high.

Prior to 1974 the Strong was published in two forms—one for men and one for women. In 1974 the two forms were merged into a single booklet (Form 325T) which contains 325 items grouped under seven domains:

1. *Occupations* (131 items): These items are names of occupations. Respondents indicate how they feel about doing particular kinds of work by marking each occupation "L" (Like), "I" (Indifferent), or "D" (Dislike).
2. *School Subjects* (36 items): Respondents indicate their interest in a wide range of school subjects.
3. *Activities* (51 items): This is a diverse collection of activities that include individual behaviors, social interactions, and work-related functions, such as repairing electrical wiring, cooking, and making statistical charts.
4. *Leisure Activities* (39 items): These items cover a sample of spare-time activities, hobbies, games, and other entertainments.
5. *Types of People* (24 items): Respondents are asked to indicate how they feel about working day-to-day with various types of people.
6. *Preference between Two Activities* (30 items): This part contains several pairs of activities or occupations, such as a taxicab driver vs. police officer or outside work vs. inside work. The respondent is asked to contrast and decide which is the more appealing, or whether the two should be seen as equally attractive or unattractive.
7. *Your Characteristics* (14 items): Respondents indicate what kind of person they are, based on whether or not various statements describe them, by responding to each item as either "Y" if it does, "N" if it doesn't, or "?" if they are undecided.

Computer analysis of responses yields a profile that contains four types of scales in addition to the Administrative Indexes Scales:

1. *General Occupational Themes Scales* (6 scales): Based on Holland's occupational theory, six main groupings of scales are produced: Realistic, Investigative, Artistic, Social, Enterprising, and Conven-

tional. Each theme is measured by 20 items. The raw score of each scale is a simple summation of the item scores. Raw scores are transformed to T-scores to facilitate comparisons with the general norming samples.

2. *Basic Interest Scales* (23 scales): These scales, with 5 to 24 items for each, have been identified by the analysis of inter-item correlations across all items. They are clustered into six categories corresponding to their relationships to the general occupational themes. Scores are reported in the same format as in the General Occupational Themes.

3. *Occupational Scales* (207 scales): These scales include 101 common occupations for both sexes, four occupations represented only by female-normed scales (Dental Assistant, Dental Hygienist, Home Economists Teacher, and Secretary), and one occupation represented only by a male-normed scale (Agribusiness Manager). For each scale, the respondent's answers are checked against the sex-norm keys. A high score indicates that the respondent's interests are similar to the interests of the criterion group.

4. *Special Scales* (2 scales): The Academic Comfort scales indicate the degree of comfort in academic settings and degree of interest and persistence in intellectual tasks. Ph.D.'s score higher on this scale than other professional degree holders. The Introversion/Extroversion Scale is designed to discriminate between people-oriented and non-people-oriented occupational interests.

The Strong Interest Inventory serves two main functions in career counseling: (1) it provides individuals with useful information about themselves and their relationship to the working world, and (2) it provides decision-makers with information to facilitate judging the unique characteristics of each individual. The more common applications, according to Tzeng (1985), include (a) counseling students or employees "for such purposes as high school and college curriculum planning, mid-career evaluation and change, occupational rehabilitation, and leisure counseling" (p. 743); and (b) conducting basic and field research to investigate the nature and process of career development, the impact of similar interests on human relationships, and cross-cultural influences. The manual and user's guide have chapters describing procedures that facilitate interpreting the Strong results. Many case studies are included to help counselors understand and explain the results.

The Strong can be administered by any qualified counselor or personnel worker and can be given individually or in groups. It takes about 25 to 35 minutes to complete the whole test. It is not recommended for use below the high school level. However, gifted students aged thirteen to sixteen can benefit from the inventory as a means for early career planning. A number of studies of reliability, concurrent validity, and predictive validity of the Strong have been conducted in various settings and times with a variety of populations. Results indicate that it can be used with confidence as an interest inventory in career counseling.

   Title: Differential Aptitude Tests
   Authors: G. K. Bennett, H. G. Seashore, and A. G. Wesman
   Publisher: The Psychological Corporation
   Harcourt Brace Jovanovich, Inc.
   555 Academic Court
   San Antonio, Texas 78204-2498

The Differential Aptitude Tests (DAT) were developed as a multiple integrated aptitude battery to meet the needs of teachers and counselors for more in-depth information, beyond the boundaries of single-score tests, and as a reflection of emerging trends in mental measurement. According to the *Administrator's Handbook* of 1982, the DAT "represents an attempt to measure abilities from a multifaceted point of view" (p. 5). The DAT is primarily intended for use with students in educational and vocational counseling (Pennock-Roman, 1985) in order to assist them in formulating academic and career goals.

   The Fifth Edition of 1990 (Form C) has two levels of both the DAT and the accompanying Career Interest Inventory; one for grades seven through nine and adults, and the other for grades ten through twelve and adults. The previous editions include Forms V and W (1980), Forms S and T (1972), Forms L and M (1962), and Forms A and B (1947). The essential nature of the DAT remains unchanged. In large testing sessions and retesting, the authors suggest using alternate forms.

   Each form of the DAT consists of eight tests. Each test can be administered and interpreted independently. The DAT provides nine scores, one of which is a combined score for Verbal Reasoning and Numerical Reasoning as a scholastic aptitude indicator. The Verbal Reasoning and Abstract Reasoning tests are classified as group intelligence tests in the *Eighth Mental Measurements Yearbook* (Buros, 1978). The eight tests included in the DAT Fifth Edition (Form C, 1990) are:

1. *Verbal Reasoning*: Consists of 40 verbal analogy items measuring the ability to see relationships among words. Each analogy has two missing words. The subject is asked to choose from among five pairs of words the one pair that best fits the first and the last terms of the analogy. According to the manual, the test may be useful in predicting academic success in fields where verbal relationships and concepts are important (e.g., law, journalism, education).
2. *Numerical Reasoning*: Consists of 40 problems that require some arithmetic computation and knowledge of basic algebraic concepts. The test measures "the student's ability to reason with numbers, to manipulate numerical relationships, and to handle quantitative mate-

rials" (Bennett, Seashore, & Wesman, 1974, p. 7). A combination of Numerical Reasoning and Verbal Reasoning tests measures general learning ability and serves the same purpose as scholastic aptitude tests. The combined score indicates potential for success in school.

3. *Abstract Reasoning*: Consists of 40 nonverbal items measuring ability to understand ideas that are not framed in words or numbers and to discover relationships using geometric shapes or figures. Elements of each item change according to rules the subject is asked to infer. The test completes the general intelligence component measured by the Verbal and Numerical tests. It is classified with the Verbal Reasoning test as a group intelligence test.

4. *Perceptual Speed and Accuracy*: Consists of two parts of 100 items each. This test is intended to measure the student's speed and accuracy in comparing and marking written sets of numbers and letters in a series of situations which approximate clerical tasks.

5. *Mechanical Reasoning*: Consists of 60 items presented as pictures of mechanical devices or persons working with tools. The ability measured by this test is required in mechanical or engineering occupations.

6. *Space Relations*: Consists of 50 items measuring the ability to think in spatial terms or to deal with concrete materials through visualization. The tasks require mental manipulation of objects in three-dimensional space from a two-dimensional pattern. These items measure skills important in occupations such as architecture, drafting, and art.

7. *Spelling*: Consists of 40 items presented in a four-option format that includes three correctly spelled words and one misspelled word. Students are asked to identify the misspelled words.

8. *Language Usage*: Consists of 40 items designed to measure students' ability to detect errors in grammar, punctuation, and capitalization.

The Spelling and Language Usage tests are achievement-oriented. They are not highly correlated; thus, two separate scores are reported.

In addition, a Career Interest Inventory to assess students' interests and career goals may be used in conjunction with the DAT. New norms for the DAT are provided to compare the performance of students in grades seven through twelve to that of nationally representative samples. A Counselor's Manual and a Technical Manual also are available. The Counselor's Manual includes a collection of actual case studies involving the use of the DAT in counseling. The manuals and the Directions for Administering provide clear instructions and information concerning the battery development, administration and scoring, norms and profiles, reliability, and validity estimates.

The format of the test booklets allows for flexible testing schedules (e.g., 2, 4, or 6 sessions), according to the local situation. The two-session program takes about three hours and may be held on two days. Proper training and familiarity with administration directions are needed for examiners. Scoring is done by hand or machine. The raw score for each test is the total number of right answers. The nine raw scores yielded by the DAT are converted to percentile ranks and plotted on a profile chart which is easily read and understood. A student's score on each test should be interpreted relative to the appropriate national normative sample and with his or her own performance on the other tests of the battery. Separate norms are given in percentiles and stanines by semester (spring and fall), sex (male and female), and grade (7–12) for junior and senior high school, and post–high school students. The norming samples for all forms are very large (approximately 170,000 students were tested in spring and fall for the Fifth Edition) and well-chosen.

The primary use of the DAT has been in counseling, selection, and placement. It may be used, as suggested by Stanley (1984), in testing gifted students at the end of the seventh grade to provide a basis for identifying "the combination of aptitudes on which the individual excels..." (p. 177). Stanley also suggested the use of Verbal Reasoning, Numerical Reasoning, Language Usage, and perhaps Spelling tests as a screening method for intellectually talented students. The DAT has been used in many studies in the field of gifted education (Benbow & Minor, 1990; Cramond, 1983; Mills & Eiserer, 1982; Weiner & Robinson, 1986). Overall, the DAT is considered by many researchers (Hambleton, 1985) to be the best available aptitude battery for use in schools.

REFERENCES

Administrator's Manual for the 16PF. (1979). Champaign, IL: Institute for Personality and Ability Testing.

Benbow, C. P., & Minor, L. L. (1990). Cognitive profiles of verbally and mathematically precocious students: Implications for identification of the gifted. *Gifted Child Quarterly, 34*, 21-26.

Bennett, G. K., Seashore, H. G., & Wesman, A. G. (1974). *Fifth edition manual for the differential aptitude tests, Forms S and T*. New York: Psychological Corporation.

Buros, O. K. (Ed.). (1978). *The eighth mental measurements yearbook* (Vol. I). Highland Park, NJ: Gryphon Press.

Campbell, D. P., & Hansen, J.-I. C. (1981). *Manual for the SVIB-SCII. Strong-Campbell interest inventory, Form T 325 of the Strong Vocational Interest Blank* (3rd ed.). Stanford, CA: Stanford University Press.

Cattell, R. B., Eber, H. W., & Tatsuoka, M. M. (1985). *Handbook for the Sixteen Personality Factor Questionnaire (16PF)*. Champaign, IL: Institute for Personality and Ability Testing.

Cornell, D. G., Callahan, C. M., & Loyd, B. H. (1991). Personality growth of female early college entrants: A controlled prospective study. *Gifted Child Quarterly, 35*, 58–66.

Cramond, B. L. (1983). Predicting mathematics achievement of gifted adolescent females. *Dissertation Abstracts International, 43*, 2281A. (University Microfilms No. 82-28677)

Domino, G. (1984). California Psychological Inventory. In D. J. Keyser & R. C. Sweetland (Eds.), *Test critiques* (Vol. 1, pp. 146–157). Kansas City, MO: Test Corporation of America.

Epstein, J. H. (1985). Review of Piers-Harris Children's Self-Concept Scale. In J. V. Mitchell, Jr. (Ed.), *The ninth mental measurements yearbook* (Vol. II, pp. 1167–1169). Lincoln: The Buros Institute of Mental Measurements of the University of Nebraska.

Feldhusen, J. F., & Kolloff, M. B. (1981). A self-concept scale for gifted students. *Perceptual and Motor Skills, 53,* 319–323.

French, J. L. (1959). *Educating the gifted: A book of readings.* New York: Holt.

Gough, H. G. (1987). *California psychological inventory: Administrator's guide.* Palo Alto, CA: Consulting Psychologists Press.

Hambleton, R. K. (1985). Review of Differential Aptitude Tests, Forms V and W. In J. V. Mitchell, Jr. (Ed.), *The ninth mental measurements yearbook* (Vol. 1., pp. 504–505). Lincoln: The Buros Institute of Mental Measurements of the University of Nebraska.

Hansen, J.-I. C., & Campbell, D. P. (1985). *Manual for the Strong Interest Inventory, Form T325 of the Strong Interest Blanks* (4th ed.). Stanford, CA: Stanford University Press.

Harmon, L. W. (1978). Review of the Kuder Preference Record. In O. K. Buros (Ed.), *The eighth mental measurements yearbook* (Vol. II, pp. 1011–1012). Highland Park, NJ: Gryphon Press.

Harter, S. (1981). Developmental perspectives on the self-system [Transcript]. Denver: University of Denver.

Harter, S. (1985). *Manual for the self-perception profile for children.* Denver: University of Denver.

Jeske, P. J. (1985). Review of Piers-Harris Children's Self-Concept Scale. In J. V. Mitchell, Jr. (Ed.), *The ninth mental measurements yearbook* (Vol. II, pp. 1169–1170). Lincoln: The Buros Institute of Mental Measurements of the University of Nebraska.

Jung, C. G. (1971). *Psychological types* (H. G. Baynes, Trans., rev. by R. F. C. Hull). Vol. 6 of *The collected works of C. G. Jung.* Princeton, NJ: Princeton University Press. (Original work published 1921)

Karnes, F. A., & Wherry, J. N. (1981). Self-concept of gifted students as measured by the Piers-Harris Children's Self-Concept Scale. *Psychological Reports, 49,* 903–906.

Keasey, C. T., & Smith-Winberry, C. (1983). Educational strategies and personality outcomes of gifted and nongifted college students. *Gifted Child Quarterly, 27,* 35–41.

Kolloff, P. B., & Feldhusen, J. F. (1984). The effects of enrichment on self-concept and creative thinking. *Gifted Child Quarterly, 28,* 53–57.

Kuder, F. (1971). *General interest survey manual.* Chicago: Science Research Associates.

Mills, C. J., & Eiserer, L. A. (1982). Evaluation of a college program for gifted adolescents. *Gifted Child Quarterly, 26,* 185–189.

Myers, I. B. (1987). *Introduction to type: A description of the theory and applications of the Myers-Briggs Type Indicator.* Palo Alto, CA: Consulting Psychologists Press.

Myers, I. B., & McCaulley, M. H. (1986). *Manual: A guide to the development and use of the Myers-Briggs Type Indicator* (2nd ed.). Palo Alto, CA: Consulting Psychologists Press.

Nielsen, M. E. (1984). *Evaluation of a rural gifted program: Assessment of attitudes, self-concept, and critical thinking of high ability students in grades 3 through 12.* Unpublished doctoral dissertation, Purdue University, West Lafayette, IN.

Pennock-Roman, M. (1985). Differential Aptitude Tests. In D. J. Keyser, & R. C. Sweetland (Eds.), *Test critiques* (Vol. II, pp. 226–245). Kansas City, MO: Test Corporation of America.

Piers, E. V. (1989). *Piers-Harris Children's Self-Concept Scale: Revised manual 1984.* Los Angeles, CA: Western Psychological Services.

Richert, E. S., with Alvino, J., & McDonnel, R. (1982). *The national report on identification of gifted and talented youth.* Sewell, NJ: Educational Improvement Center–South.

Robinson, N. M., & Noble, K. D. (1991). Social-emotional development and adjustment of gifted children. In M. C. Wang, M. C. Reynolds, & H. J. Walberg (Eds.), *Handbook of special education: Research and practice* (pp. 57–76). New York: Pergamon Press.

Shertzer, B., & Linden, J. (1979). *Fundamentals of individual appraisal—assessment techniques for counselors.* Boston: Houghton Mifflin.

Silverman, L. K. (1989). Affective curriculum for the gifted. In J. VanTassel-Baska, J. Feldhusen, K. Seeley, G. Wheatley, L. Silverman, & W. Foster (Eds.), *Comprehensive curriculum for gifted learners* (pp. 335–355). Needham Heights, MA: Allyn & Bacon.

Stanley, J. C. (1984). Use of general and specific aptitude measures in identification: Some principles and certain cautions. *Gifted Child Quarterly, 28,* 177–180.

Thompson, L. B. (1981). The prediction of academic achievement and self-concept in gifted children. *Dissertation Abstracts International, 41,* 3947A-3948A. (University Microfilms No. 80-26320)

Tidwell, R. (1980). A psycho-educational profile of 1,593 gifted high school students. *Gifted Child Quarterly, 24,* 63–68.

Tzeng, O. (1985). Strong-Campbell Interest Inventory. In J. V. Mitchell, Jr. (Ed.), *The ninth mental measurements yearbook* (Vol. II, pp. 737–749). Highland Park, NJ: The Buros Institute of Mental Measurements.

Weiner, N. C., & Robinson, S. E. (1986). Cognitive abilities, personality, and gender differences in math achievement of gifted adolescents. *Gifted Child Quarterly, 30,* 83–87.

Whitmore, J. R. (1980). *Giftedness, conflict, and underachievement.* Needham Heights, MA: Allyn & Bacon.

Zytowski, D. (1974). Predictive validity of the Kuder preference record, form B, over a 25-year span. *Measurement and evaluation guide, 7*(2), 122–129.

PART IV

Special Issues

12 Gifted Students at Risk

Ken Seeley

UNDERACHIEVEMENT AND "AT-RISK" STUDENTS

The issue of underachievement among the gifted has captured the interest of educators sporadically over the past thirty years. In the most basic definition, an underachiever is a student who does not achieve in the academic areas at a level consistent with his or her capability. When underachievement is applied to the gifted, it becomes a more complex issue which calls for a new conceptualization.

Students "at-risk" is relatively recent terminology which was borrowed from the field of health and wellness and applied to school problems. The question that often arises when the at-risk term is used is, "At risk for what?" The answer may be drug abuse, sexually transmitted disease, school dropout, delinquency, out-of-home placement, or underachievement—to name only a few of the potential dangers. The advantage of casting concerns about gifted problem students in terms of their being at-risk, rather than merely underachieving, is that it broadens the net for identification and prevention. Both of these conceptualizations form the basis for this chapter.

The conceptualization of underachievement in education has gone through many iterations in the last three decades. The whole field of learning disabilities grew from an attempt to explain underachievement as a disabling condition with causes attributed to one or more of the following: brain damage, emotional disorders, early language deprivation, poor acquisition of English for speakers of other languages, economically deprived home situations, poor nutrition, and physical or medical disabilities. Intervention programs have been designed to address these causes, some with more success than others. Clearly, these causes can contribute to underachievement among gifted students. This group is usually referred to as "learning disabled gifted"; they comprise a significant portion of the population of gifted underachievers. (See chapter 6 for more information about group counseling with this population.)

Most gifted underachievers appear to educators as "unmotivated," "lazy," or having behavior problems. Whitmore (1989) urges us to view this population as a result of "underachieving schools" and "underserved groups." This conceptualization helps us to move away from blaming the students and their families for underachievement. The blaming mode has been in place for too long and allows educators to avoid responsibility for teaching a group whom they have labeled "capable of doing much better." Given Whitmore's notion, it is the schools that are capable of doing much better because they fail to create appropriate learning environments for children with various learning styles.

Schools are also "underserving" special populations of gifted students, resulting in underachievement that goes largely unnoticed. When schools do not actively identify giftedness among young children, culturally different students, gifted girls, or special populations, they "underserve" these students who consequently underachieve in relation to their potential.

A change in conceptualization of underachievement allows us to look at this population as an "at-risk" group of learners. The semantics are important if we expect schools to take on the task of seeking out and serving under-achieving gifted students. The gifted are within at-risk groups that are receiving attention in public education. These groups include dropouts, minority groups, low-income groups, and preschool children. School reform efforts are focused on many of these at-risk groups. Even the highly gifted are included in the concerns about math and science achievement.

Inappropriate school environments also put gifted children at risk. In a study of 2,000 middle school students in the upper intellectual quartile, this author found that 37 percent were averaging "C" or worse in grade point average (Seeley, 1988). Over half of these students were at risk for dropping out of school due to behavior problems, low grade point average, and poor attendance. Part of the study included a factor analysis to look for causes of the problems that put these students at risk. A reciprocal relationship was found between behavior and grade point average. That is, by lowering students' grades (who are "capable of doing better") the schools inadvertently prompted the students to act out and become behavior problems. Students with behavior problems automatically got lower grades regardless of their ability. This vicious cycle of grading on behavior and behavior producing grades works against high-risk gifted students and results in a push-out program.

Another advantage of considering special populations of gifted students at risk is that preventive steps can be taken before underachievement occurs. By actively looking for giftedness in special populations early in the elementary school years, we can identify this potential and adjust the educational program to the needs of the child. Preventive strategies are discussed later in this chapter.

In summary, it is important to conceptualize the problem of gifted underachievers as students who are at risk for underachievement or school failure. By viewing the problem as students at risk we remove the blaming factors historically assigned to this group and can focus on preventive approaches.

RISK FACTORS

Disabilities

The first area to be considered which puts gifted children at risk is disabilities. Those with congenital disabilities such as blindness, deafness, and cerebral palsy are often overlooked and are at risk for not having their giftedness identified because of stereotyped thinking that physical disabilities are associated with mental retardation. Among the deaf and blind, for instance, the incidence of giftedness is the same as in the normal population. Indeed, the population of gifted with physical handicaps has made significant contributions. Maker (1978) interviewed over ninety disabled scientists who not only overcame their disabilities but achieved academic and career success in spite of the educational system that largely treated them as less capable because of their disabilities.

Gifted children with learning disabilities also are overlooked in the typical identification schemes. By definition, these children may look slow or "normal" but be capable of much greater achievement than is demonstrated by their performance. Their potential often goes unnoticed by teachers who see them as average or "lazy." Because learning disabilities have a variety of causes and manifestations it is fruitful to look for gifted students in this population through less traditional testing formats. Discrepancies between strengths and weaknesses can be used to determine children with dual exceptionalities. Parents and peers are often reliable in identifying potential giftedness among the learning disabled. Nonacademic interests and products are also good indicators of giftedness.

Low Income and Cultural Diversity

Poverty is a major risk factor affecting school success because of its effects on family life. Intergenerational poverty contributes to lower parental expectations of children, lower educational level of family members, and poorer general health and nutrition. However, many potentially gifted children come from low-income families and require different approaches to identification and programming than children from upper-income groups.

Because of the greater number of minority groups at the low-income level, minority family status has been mistakenly identified as a risk factor. *The underachievement and higher dropout rate for minority group students is a function of poverty, not race or ethnicity.* Unfortunately, schools often believe in this false stereotype and create underachievement among minority students through lower expectations. (See chapter 13.)

A recent survey of "disadvantaged"/gifted programs in the United States was completed by a research team at the College of William and Mary (VanTassel-Baska, Patton, & Prillaman, 1989). These authors found that the majority of states do not attend to low socioeconomic status as a factor for special consideration in identification, programming, or definitions. Many states (32.7%) assume that cultural difference accounts for low-income groups. They also report that a majority of the states (78.8%) do not differentiate programs or services for disadvantaged gifted, nor do they use special assessment techniques to identify this special needs group. One recommendation from this survey was to drop the term *disadvantaged* to describe culturally diverse or low-income groups because of the negative connotation. It will take a concerted effort to dispel the stereotype that cultural difference implies low income and poor achievement. A demand for appropriate identification and programming will help raise consciousness of these issues and, hopefully, will result in better service to this population of at-risk gifted youth.

Delinquency

There has been much speculation about the relationship of giftedness and juvenile delinquency, with two opposing theories at work. One notion is that gifted youth are more vulnerable to delinquency because of their heightened sensibilities and intellectual characteristics which make them feel different from other children. They often do not feel they fit in well in their environment. Thus, the gifted are more likely to be adversely affected by problems at home or school. The opposing theory is that giftedness is a protection against proneness to delinquency. Because of higher ability, youths have a greater insight into their own actions and those of others, and can see the long-range consequences of their behavior. As a result, they are more able to understand and cope with environmental conditions and are not as likely to be at risk for delinquency. The protection theory suggests that environmental conditions must become extremely unfavorable to cause a gifted child to become delinquent (Mahoney, 1980).

A careful review of the research reveals that both theories are true depending upon the cognitive style of the gifted child (Seeley, 1984). If the young person's abilities are largely creative and divergent, she or he is probably more vulnerable to delinquency. In contrast, a convergent thinking style with strong achievement motivation usually provides protection from risk of delinquency. The home and school environments, of course, are major influences for either type of cognitive style and affect the degree of risk.

In a study of 300 youths in a juvenile justice system, an interdisciplinary team from the University of Denver found a disproportionately larger number of gifted subjects than would be expected (Mahoney & Seeley, 1982). Most of these youths were the vulnerable types discussed previously, who demonstrated high levels of fluid ability rather than crystallized abilities. Horn (1978) describes *fluid ability* as an intelligence that is not taught, but is characterized by a quick perceptiveness and intuitive ability used to process information and solve problems. Conversely, *crystallized ability* is a type of intelligence that takes in and uses information from the environment to solve problems and understand phenomena. Convergent thinkers are high in crystallized abilities, and are usually achievers because they meet teacher expectations. Gifted students with high levels of fluid ability seem to be at greater risk for delinquency and poor school performance. As with other types of gifted students at risk, they have abilities that may not be identified with existing procedures or addressed in the classroom. In determining levels of risk it is important to differentiate the cognitive style of the individual and to further specify the types of abilities shown.

School Environment

School does seem to play a role in promoting underachievement in certain types of students whom educators view as less desirable; this is clearly suggested by the middle school study of dropouts reported earlier (Seeley, 1988). The self-fulfilling prophecy moves forward from this point. Giftedness compounds this dynamic, particularly for those fluid ability students who are smart but not achieving. Add to these factors contentious relationships at the onset of adolescence and we have the perfect formula for frustration, alienation, school failure, and school dropout.

In a companion study, 128 gifted high school dropouts were interviewed to determine some of the factors that these former students attributed to their choice to leave school (Seeley, 1988). The following list is a summary of school environment risk factors which emerged from the study:

- ❏ Attendance rules tended to push out students
- ❏ Academic work was seen as too easy, boring, and repetitive
- ❏ School size was reported as too big, impersonal
- ❏ School supported cliques were alienating (e.g., athletes, honor students)
- ❏ Uneven academic performance led to the school focusing on weaknesses
- ❏ School starting time was seen as too early
- ❏ There was lack of flexibility in daily school schedule
- ❏ Frequency of school changes was a major factor
- ❏ Conflicts with teachers began at junior high school (not in elementary grades)
- ❏ Teacher/counselor attitude was "shape up or ship out"
- ❏ Teacher indifference or hostility was a major factor
- ❏ Teachers who did not like what they were teaching was an obvious problem

❏ Students wanted respect and responsibility
❏ Assignments were often seen as busywork
❏ There was too little experiential learning

It is interesting that almost all of the dropouts assumed full responsibility for their decision. They did not externalize or blame the school, but rather indicated *their choice to leave was an adaptive response to a poor situation that did not fit for them.* Most indicated that they would go back to a different educational program and continue their education at a community college or an alternative school if that were available. This is important to keep in mind when solutions are discussed later.

ADOLESCENCE

Normal developmental periods can put young people at risk if the home or school does not adapt to developmental changes in their behavior. This is amplified for gifted children who often appear to be more mature than they really are. Because of advanced verbal reasoning, they are expected to act older than their chronological age. Many parents or teachers wonder why a young person so smart can do such dumb things sometimes. But adolescence is marked with inconsistencies between thought and action.

Gifted adolescents often labor under an externally imposed set of goals—aspirations that are not theirs, but rather their parents' or teachers'. During the middle school years many gifted youth begin to challenge these external standards. It is precarious to have an adult thinker in the body of an adolescent and be expected to act "gifted" in order to meet the requirements of others for high performance. The imposition of external standards combined with the normal adolescent needs for separation and search for identity may result in stress and alienation expressed in underachievement, antisocial behavior, or indifference. Educators and parents must allow adolescents to take time to explore options, develop their own vision, and understand their own developmental stages. Adults also need to encourage input from young persons about decisions affecting their lives. This promotes independence and acknowledges the adult mind of the gifted adolescent. Gifted youth should be taught the stages of normal development so they can gain insights and develop healthy responses to thoughts and feelings they might otherwise regard as strange or disturbing. (More about the specific issues of adolescents can be found in chapters 5, 7, 10, and 14.)

MOTIVATION

Recent research and theoretical development on the various facets of motivation were reviewed by Nicholls and Miller (1984) and Ackerman, Sternberg, and Glaser (1989). This literature sheds light on the relationships between levels of ability and underachievement. One major influence in underachievement is the level of motivation of the student. This multifaceted concept is usually discussed in education circles as a unitary quality over which the student is expected to exercise control. When motivation is perceived as an inherent characteristic of the student, underachievement is explained simplistically as "lack of motivation," and the subtle message is to blame the student. This distorted cause-and-effect relationship may help educators feel better but does little to solve the problem for the student.

In discussing adolescents and motivation, Csikszentmihalyi and Larsen (1984) state,

> Both negative feelings and passivity relate to a...process that can block the efficient use of attention: loss of motivation. When something stands in the way of a person's goals, when goals become confused, or when external goals are imposed by adults, adolescents become disinterested and have a hard time investing psychic energy in their pursuits. This is a state in which thoughts and actions are in conflict. (p. 21)

Apparent lack of motivation springs from inner conflict involving the student's goals which affects interest level. The dynamic expressed so well by these authors helps define the basics of motivation and attribution. At a minimum, this definition provides the broad parameters for analysis of the relationship between underachievement and motivational factors. When we see underachievement and think motivational problem, we need to ask the following questions as educators:

- ❏ What are my goals and expectations for this student?
- ❏ What are the student's goals and expectations relative to this learning task?
- ❏ Are the goals unclear for either me or the student?
- ❏ Are the goals in conflict?
- ❏ What are the barriers to our respective and collective goals?
- ❏ What is the student's interest level in this learning task?
- ❏ If goals are different, how can I bring them into concert?
- ❏ If the interest level is not high, how can I increase it?
  (Csikszentmihalyi & Larsen, 1984)

The answers to these questions provide both an assessment of the problem and the teaching strategy. We avoid labeling the student as unmotivated by engaging the student in a thoughtful discussion about goals, interests, and barriers.

In examining motivation and learning strategies, Ames and Archer (1988) studied academically advanced students as to their goal orientation and perceptions of classroom experiences. Goal orientations were described as either performance goals or mastery goals. Performance goals relate to being judged able; students believe that successful performance defines their level of ability. Mastery goals, on the other hand, focus on developing new skills and indicate that the learning process and effort are valued. Findings revealed that when students perceived mastery goals they preferred tasks that were challenging and used more effective learning strategies (Dweck, 1986). In other words, they appeared to be more highly motivated in an environment that valued learning over pure performance. This is particularly important in an age when outcome-based education is in vogue. It would be easy for educators to create a performance goal environment where success is the performance, not learning or effort. Further, Ames and Archer (1988) suggest that

> [a] mastery, but not a performance structure provides a context that is likely to foster long-term use of learning strategies and a belief that success is related to one's effort...modifying the goal structure of a classroom in such a way that mastery goals are salient and are adopted by students may also be necessary to elicit adaptive motivation patterns. (p. 265)

The linkages between goals, learning, and motivation are clear and form the basis for understanding the causes of underachievement. Self-esteem of the learner is also affected by this interaction of goals, learning strategies, and motivation and as such is at the root of the solution.

TOWARD SOLUTIONS

As indicated at the beginning of the chapter, we have moved away from blaming at-risk children and their families for lack of achievement. This is not to say that schools are unilaterally responsible for solutions. Parents and gifted children need to be heavily involved in the educational decision-making process in order to invest in the solution.

Special approaches are needed for gifted underachievers whose alienation becomes overwhelming. They need to overcome both the fear of success and the fear of failure that entrap them. When these feelings of alienation become great enough, they contribute to putting students at risk when the students try to reconcile their identity crises in maladaptive ways. It is incumbent upon us as educators and counselors to provide appropriate support to these students. Special tutoring and peer counseling programs can be effective solutions.

In order to address the feelings of alienation and isolation among at-risk students, a sense of community needs to be developed at school. Many students in the mainstream of school life experience this feeling of community, of belonging, of counting in someone else's life. At-risk students, on the other hand, are outside of the community and feel like aliens in a strange and distant place. Alternatives are needed that foster community to different groups of students. One important option is community service. Like other students, at-risk students want to find a caring environment at school, but also they need to be caring and giving about something important to them. School-sponsored community service options can be an excellent way to involve these students who might not choose pep club, football, or chorus as a vehicle for feeling a part of the school community. (See chapters 10 and 14 for more information about community service.)

The final section of this chapter is an outline of activities suggested by students and educational leaders who were assembled at a workshop designed to develop solutions to the problems of underachievement and school dropout (Seeley, 1988). Five areas were identified as targets of intervention: *peer/ social relationships, home and family, minority status of students, teacher issues, and school environment issues*. This section is presented as a blueprint for local counselors or educators to use as a framework for discussion and planning at the school level. Each solution presents an objective and a set of strategies. This is merely a beginning for local initiatives to address the complex problems of underachievement.

I. PEER AND SOCIAL RELATIONSHIPS

OBJECTIVE 1.1: *Provide more flexibility in schools to foster peer and social relationships among students*

EXPLANATION: The major reason most students come to school is for the social interaction with other students. Instead of trying to deny the social learning of interpersonal relationships, educators should maximize this motivational factor and structure learning in teams, groups, dyads, peer tutorials, etc.

STRATEGIES:
- ❑ Allow students to do more teaching of others
- ❑ Organize K–8 schools for the gifted
- ❑ Promote student planning of space utilization
- ❑ Organize multi-age groups across grade levels

OBJECTIVE 1.2: *Assist students with successful transitions*

EXPLANATION: What we know of human development for all ages is that transitions are difficult emotionally, logistically, intellectually, and developmentally. We also know that transitions are important growth experiences out of which come rich and enduring life skills. We can do much to capitalize on these periods in schooling.

STRATEGIES:
- ❑ Develop adoption program of younger students by older students
- ❑ Offer transition "survival courses" when changing grade levels/schools
- ❑ Arrange summer jobs for students based at schools
- ❑ Offer longer-term orientation programs at transition points
- ❑ Provide parent education programs about transitions
- ❑ Allow parent–student input for selection of teachers for next level

OBJECTIVE 1.3: *Provide an effective counseling/advisement program*

EXPLANATION: School counseling has never been a strength of public education. This is largely because the counselors are usually expected to do too much with too many students. Advisement expands the reach of counselors, and meets important goals for guiding students and building advocates for them.

STRATEGIES:
- ❑ Use all school personnel as advisors after training them
- ❑ Provide elementary counselors for preventive services
- ❑ Develop peer counseling programs
- ❑ Promote small-group meetings for problem solving
- ❑ Provide small-group topical meetings (e.g., divorce, transitions, etc.)
- ❑ Develop family–school support systems with meaningful family involvement
- ❑ Provide screened referrals for students and families with special needs

OBJECTIVE 1.4: *Promote empowerment and autonomy for students*

EXPLANATION: Students need greater control over their own learning if they are to be responsible for and invested in their education. Teachers who share power and control usually earn the respect of their students and find more motivated learners in their classes.

STRATEGIES:
- ❑ Solicit student input for teacher planning of learning activities
- ❑ Implement a self-paced/mastery learning curriculum
- ❑ Solicit student input into school policies and personnel hiring
- ❑ Promote recognition and awards for achievement and effort
- ❑ Provide leadership training and school outlets for leadership
- ❑ Involve students in evaluating the school and solutions for improvement
- ❑ Develop community service/school service opportunities

II. MINORITY STUDENT INVOLVEMENT

OBJECTIVE 2.1: *Promote cultural competence in all students*

EXPLANATION: The concept of cultural competence implies a set of generic skills that can be applied to developing sensitivity to ethnic, racial, or language differences in people. This sensitivity and awareness does not promote stereotypic characteristics of cultural groups, but rather aims to value difference with an openness and comfort to explore the meaning of the cultures between and among those involved.

STRATEGIES:
- ❏ Celebrate the rich cultural heritage and language diversity of students
- ❏ Develop programs that aim to be competent in their understanding of the cultural context in which students and their families live, work, and learn
- ❏ Provide staff development to gain knowledge and respect for cultural differences among the students and their families and the staff

OBJECTIVE 2.2: *Develop gifted programs that are sensitive to diversity*

EXPLANATION: Historically, gifted programs have been associated with an overrepresentation of white students. Identification procedures and program design and content should invite cultural diversity while maintaining high standards and fast pace.

STRATEGIES:
- ❏ Involve minority staff and students in the identification process
- ❏ Actively recruit minority teachers/mentors for gifted programs
- ❏ Define giftedness in the cultural context of each minority group in the community
- ❏ Use community-based organizations as change agents in school reform and to assist in educational staff development

III. APPROPRIATE TEACHER/COUNSELOR ROLES

OBJECTIVE 3.1: *Improve communication between teachers and counselors as to underachievers*

EXPLANATION: Team planning between teachers and counselors for underachieving students is essential in addressing their needs. Communication needs to be valued, scheduled regularly, and follow an agreed-upon protocol that is efficient.

STRATEGIES:
- ❏ Create a teacher-advisement program with counselor supervision
- ❏ Use the advisement program to find underachievers and develop a plan
- ❏ Give release time to effective advisors to work with underachievers
- ❏ Develop IEP approaches and monitor carefully
- ❏ Allow counselors sufficient time to support teacher-advisors through training, group problem solving, identification of resources, and referrals as needed

OBJECTIVE 3.2: *Incorporate self-esteem development as a legitimate curriculum concern for teachers and their students*

EXPLANATION: Much lip service is paid to the importance of developing good self-esteem as a precursor to learning, but it is still regarded by many educators as a frill or "touchy-feely nonsense." Teacher time and self-esteem curriculum need to be endorsed by administrators and curriculum leaders as important and expected as routine classroom activities along with the traditional curriculum topics.

STRATEGIES:
- ❏ Use a homeroom system with small group meetings and periodic debriefings with students
- ❏ Develop and monitor a community mentorship program
- ❏ Use goal-setting and decision-making activities with students in planning for learning

OBJECTIVE 3.3: *Improve the learning environment for students*

EXPLANATION: Generally, school reform efforts suggest creating an "inviting" learning environment for all students. This is essential for underachievers who need an extra measure of teacher caring and attention to their individual strengths and needs.

STRATEGIES:
- ❏ Expand learning beyond the classroom into the community
- ❏ Allow students to participate in governance
- ❏ Use flexible instructional groups based on needs
- ❏ Promote year-round learning opportunities
- ❏ Support the development of alternative schools at all levels
- ❏ Promote pass/fail/incomplete system of grading
- ❏ Encourage positive confrontation and conflict resolution

CONCLUSION

Giftedness and underachievement is a complex, multiproblem phenomenon which has been grossly oversimplified in cause, concept, and approach. This chapter has moved from a simple base definition through a network of risk factors, potential causes, and approaches that make learning more accessible and possible for large numbers of at-risk students. The restructuring of education may result in many of the reforms mentioned in the blueprint above. However, individual professional caring and persistence must be applied with structural change. Understanding the role of motivation and planning realistic goals with students can build on strengths and interests and move the gifted underachiever out of risk. Surely we cannot afford to lose this important potential talent. Counselors and teachers can make an important difference to avoid this loss for student, school, and society.

REFERENCES

Ackerman, P. L., Sternberg, R. J., & Glaser, R. (1989). *Learning and individual differences.* New York: W. H. Freeman.

Ames, C., & Archer, J. (1988). Achievement goals in the classroom: Students' learning strategies and motivation processes. *Journal of Educational Psychology, 80,* 260–267.

Csikszentmihalyi, M., & Larsen, R. (1984). *Being adolescent: Conflict and growth in the teenage years.* New York: Basic Books.

Dweck, C. S. (1986). Motivational processes affecting learning. *American Psychologist, 41,* 1040–1048.

Horn, J. (1978). The nature and development of intellectual abilities. In R. T. Osborne, L. E. Noble, & N. Weyl (Eds.), *Human variation* (pp. 107–136). New York: Academic Press.

Mahoney, A. R. (1980). Gifted delinquents. *Children and Youth Services Review, 2,* 315–330.

Mahoney, A. R., & Seeley, K. R. (1982). *A study of juveniles in a suburban court.* Technical report. Washington, DC: U. S. Dept. of Justice, OJDPP.

Maker, J. (1978). *Handicapped gifted scientists.* A special report to the Council for Exceptional Children. Reston, VA: CEC.

Nicholls, J. G., & Miller, A. T. (1984). Development and its discontents: The differentiation of the concept of ability. In J. G. Nicholls & M. L. Maeher (Eds.), *Advances in Motivation and Achievement* (Vol. 3, pp. 185–218). Greenwich, CN: JAI Press.

Seeley, K. R. (1984). Giftedness and juvenile delinquency in perspective. *Journal for the Education of the Gifted, 8,* 59–72.

Seeley, K. R. (1988). *High ability students at risk.* Technical report. Denver: Colorado Department of Education.

VanTassel-Baska, J., Patton, J., & Prillaman, D. (1989). The disadvantaged gifted: At-risk for educational attention. *Focus on Exceptional Children, 22*(3), 1–15.

Whitmore, J. R. (1989). Re-examining the concept of underachievement. *Understanding Our Gifted, 2*(1), 1, 7-9.

13 Multicultural Counseling

Kathy Evans

Gifted children, like all other children, come in all shapes and sizes, races, and cultural groups. As the diversity of the U.S. population grows, so does the diversity of the gifted student population. It is important for counselors to be as effective with children who are racially and culturally different from themselves as they are with children who are similar. Although the populations of Hispanics, African-Americans, Asian-Americans, and Native Americans are increasing, these groups are still underrepresented among the ranks of trained psychologists, counselors, and mental health workers. It is likely, therefore, that Caucasian counselors will, with growing frequency, be called upon to work with children who are racially and culturally different from themselves.

It is believed by many that it is unethical for counselors who have not been trained in multicultural counseling to provide mental health services to clients who are racially and culturally different from themselves (Cayleff, 1986; Pedersen & Marsella, 1982). Counselors of culturally diverse children need to have an awareness of cultural differences, knowledge of specific racial and cultural groups, and the skills to work effectively with them. In this chapter, the terms *racially and culturally different*, *racially and culturally diverse*, and *children of color* are used interchangeably. These terms refer to children who differ from the white middle-class norm for giftedness and include children of African-American, Asian-American, Native American, and Hispanic descent.

SHORTCOMINGS OF CURRENT THEORIES

The biggest problem with existing counseling theories is the reliance on Anglo-American, or Western value systems. Contained in these theories are assumptions about people based on the Western ideal of what is normal. Almost all of these theories fail to recognize that what is normal in Western culture may not be normal in other cultures. Sue (1981) and Pedersen (1988) point out several limitations to Western theories and of Western thought in working with culturally diverse groups. Table 13.1 summarizes their ideas.

The first four issues described by Sue (1981) focus on Western expectations of communication in a counseling setting. Counseling effectiveness can be severely limited when the client's cultural group discourages communication in the way the counselor expects (e.g., expectations of openness and disclosure of intimate details). The monolingual orientation of counselors

Table 13.1
WESTERN ASSUMPTIONS REGARDING COUNSELING

Sue:

1. Expectations of openness, psychological mindedness, or sophistication
2. Disclosure of intimate aspects of their lives, or they are resistant
3. Expectations of patterns of communication
4. Monolingual orientation
5. Emphasis on long-range goals
6. Distinction between physical and mental well-being
7. Emphasis on cause-and-effect relationships
   (Sue, 1981)

Pedersen:

1. That people all share a common measure of normal behavior
2. That individuals are the basic building blocks of society
3. Based on Western culture's dependence on abstract words and the assumption of counselors in the U. S. that others will understand these abstractions in the same way they intend
4. That independence is valuable and dependencies are undesirable
5. That the natural support system is not important to the client
6. That counselors need to change individuals to fit the system and are not intended to change the system to fit the individual
7. That everyone depends on linear thinking—wherein each cause has an effect and each effect is tied to a cause—to understand the world around them
8. That history is not important in understanding contemporary events
9. That counselors already know all of their assumptions
10. That problems are defined by using a framework limited by academic discipline boundaries
    (Pedersen, 1988)

Sources: Adapted from *Counseling the Culturally Different: Theory and Practice* (p. 29) edited by D. W. Sue, 1981, New York: Wiley; and *A Handbook for Developing Multicultural Awareness* (pp. 39–44) by P. Pedersen, 1988, Alexandria, VA: American Counseling Association.

limits the counselor significantly when dealing with a client whose first language is not English. The next three issues point to the pitfalls of other judgmental behavior on the part of the counselor. If a client is not interested in long-range planning or cause-and-effect relationships, or is more interested in interaction between physical and mental well-being, the counselor is likely to label this as pathological behavior.

Pedersen's (1988) list of assumptions of Western psychology heightens the awareness that there may be cultures whose values differ significantly from Western values. There are cultures in which the group is much more important than the individual, and this focus conflicts completely with the assumptions of individuality, independence, natural support, and history. The counselor proceeding under these assumptions will not understand her or his client's resistance to interventions. The other assumptions that could be disputed are those that assume that there is a common definition of what is normal. They include the assumptions that abstractions are interpreted the same way by everyone and that linear thinking is the preferred mode of thinking for everyone. People from different cultures have different language patterns and learn to interpret language according to those language patterns. The same could be said about thinking patterns and problem solving.

All of these assumptions have the potential to harm the client, but none is so dangerous as the last, the assumption that counselors know all their assumptions. The counselor who stops questioning the effects of his and her beliefs and values is certain to do more harm than good when working with clients. It is for these reasons that Western theories and models of counseling may not apply for the racially and culturally different client. There is a need, therefore, for counselors to learn other ways to be effective.

ISSUES FOR CULTURALLY DIFFERENT CHILDREN

Silverman (1990) listed twelve frequently occurring problems for gifted children. They range from personal to interpersonal to academic. Some of those problems that may be especially troublesome to children of color include: (a) the difficulty gifted students have in accepting criticism (which could be linked with self-identity and self-esteem); (b) their nonconforming behavior and resistance to authority (which may be linked with motivation); (c) isolation from peers; and (d) hiding talents to fit in with peers. In addition to the problems listed above, the racially and culturally different gifted child must also cope with racism and prejudice and other developmental issues common to children of color. This complex mix of issues is further complicated by the interaction of the factors. This creates an even greater challenge for the gifted child.

Racism and the Deficit Model

Racism has been defined by Katz (1976) as "whatever acts or institutional procedures help create or perpetuate sets of advantages or privileges for whites and exclusions or deprivations for minority groups" (p. 22). Although the United States was founded on the premise that every person is equal, that ideal has yet to be realized. Racism is alive and well in the United States of America. Originally, American society fostered the notion of the melting pot. People would come from different cultures, races, and religions and all become "American." Unfortunately what that meant was that everyone had to conform to the white middle-class idea of "an American." Anyone who differed substantially from what society deemed "American" was not acceptable.

"Non-American" included anyone who was not a white Anglo-Saxon Protestant or anyone who did not, at least, try to assimilate in order to closely resemble that description. Anyone who was obviously different was considered substandard and inferior (Copeland, 1983). Individuals who belong to visibly different racial groups were never able to appear the same as the white culture. Therefore, they were always considered inferior. Stereotypes developed to perpetuate the inferiority concept. Legal measures excluded people who were racially and culturally different. Over the years, though, the laws have changed, and open racism and discrimination have become illegal.

Legal restrictions did not stop institutionalized efforts to prove that being different still meant being inferior. These efforts have manifested themselves in many different forms. The most recent and harmful result of these racist beliefs and actions has been the institutionalization of the deficit model. The cultural deficit model, according to Smith (1981), uses the inferiority assumption; but rather than attribute the inferiority to the race of the group, the model attributes it to the deficits in the culture. People of cultures different from white middle-class culture were considered culturally deprived, disadvantaged, or impoverished. As Sue (1981) indicated, this concept (1) implies that the racial groups have no culture, (2) causes confusion that could affect educational research and planning, (3) assumes the superiority of the white middle class, and (4) becomes equated with pathology.

The deficit model, as it applies to the gifted child in the school system, results in (1) lack of identification of the child as being gifted; (2) lack of encouragement to develop gifts and talents; and (3) identification of the child as a discipline or behavior problem when she or he acts defiantly, resulting in referrals for placement in special education. The society has done such a good job at this inferiority concept that there are groups of people, including people of color, who have internalized and accepted the model as fact.

Racism and prejudice affect the child of color as an individual as well. According to Allport (1954), children are targets on three levels—verbal rejection, discrimination, and physical attack. Bombarded with these realities of his or her uniqueness, the child learns some real lessons about what it means to be different in American society. Gifted children, because of their heightened sensitivities, "may experience the pain of discrimination more intensely than their peers who are of average ability" (Lindstrom & Van Sant, 1986, p.

584). This creates all the more work for the child and the adult support system.

The racially or culturally different gifted child must find ways to overcome labels of inferiority and to selectively internalize the information received about his or her people. The child who is able to accomplish this task effectively can have a positive self-concept (Gibbs, Huang, & Assoc., 1989).

Another aspect of the issue of inferiority can be seen in the attempts to change norms for identifying gifted children in order to include more culturally different students in gifted programs. Because many assessment instruments have been criticized as being culturally biased (Gallagher & Kinney, 1974; Jones, 1988; Ogbu, 1988), alternatives to traditional assessment are needed to correctly assess culturally different children (Baldwin, 1985; Zappia, 1989). People with racial and cultural biases see the changing of assessments as changing standards, and they see these changes as equivalent to lowering rather than broadening standards. The majority group assumption of inferiority may confuse the gifted child of color, who may wonder whether she or he is actually gifted (Colangelo, 1985). It is believed that most gifted children underestimate their abilities and that children of color are even less likely to correctly assess their giftedness (McIntosh & Greenlaw, 1986). The added doubt that they are really qualified for a gifted program can affect self-esteem and motivation.

Fitting In

Racially and culturally different children must move in and out of two different cultures. Often these cultures have conflicting values and expectations of the children. Failure to understand the culture of students may lead to counselor expectations of the child that conflict completely with parental expectations. This confuses the child even more. Also, the counselor who does not respect the child's culture (thinks it is inferior, needs to be shed) hurts the child in terms of his or her own identity development. Although there is a great deal of stress in straddling two cultures, it has been found that children with competence in more than one culture have higher self-esteem, greater understanding, and higher achievement than others (Ramirez, 1983).

Often the families of children of color lack enthusiasm for the special treatment given their gifted children. Some families like to maintain a normal relationship with schools, which cannot be done with a child in a gifted program. Often parents are concerned that they may lose control over their gifted child, or they may worry that the child is so smart he or she may want to usurp parental authority (McIntosh & Greenlaw, 1986). The child, aware of parental feelings, is caught between pleasing school officials, teachers, and counselors and pleasing the family. Once gifted children reach adolescence, the conflict becomes a three-way pull: they are then discouraged by less able peers from succeeding by the dominant culture's rules (Lindstrom & Van Sant, 1986). In other words, they are warned not to sell out their culture to become more like the dominant culture.

Socioeconomic Status

In the preceding discussion, "cultural difference" is defined in terms of racial and ethnic dissimilarities. *Culturally different* is a term used to describe people who differ from the white majority in the United States. Similarities within these culturally different groups and differences between them are assumed. Nevertheless, there are important differences within groups that influence the work of the multicultural counselor.

The challenge of multicultural counseling is compounded by the effects of economic status. Economic status transcends racial and ethnic barriers and lies in the nature of the system through which resources of the society are distributed and used. Steady, well-paying employment, adequate housing, and abundant opportunities may produce middle- and upper-income (class) groups. This middle-class group (whose socialization reflects the nature and values of the greater society) is seen, is treated, and feels like "winners."

Conversely, high unemployment, limited opportunity, substandard housing, and low wages lead to the development of a culture of poverty (Lewis, 1965). Characteristics of those in this group influence their perception of and response to the system. The group develops its own self-contained social system which provides identity and protection for its members. Members of the poverty group are often seen and treated (by themselves and others) as inadequate and deficient—"losers."

The children who grow up under conditions of poverty are socialized into a culture of poverty. They are seldom exposed to the nature and values of the greater society. Lewis (1965) listed, among others, the following culture-of-poverty characteristics: (a) a present rather than future time focus, (b) an inability to delay gratification, (c) a tendency toward action, (d) an inability to trust others, (e) manifestations of helplessness and dependency, and (f) expressed feelings of inferiority.

Many children of color are products of the culture of poverty. Some counselors confuse this culture of poverty with the child's racial or ethnic culture. Smith (1977) identified several errors counselors often make based on stereotypes about minority clients, including the belief that they come from disorganized families and broken homes. There is also the mistaken belief that all racially and culturally different individuals are poor. Contrary to that belief, many culturally different children are represented in the economic strata that range from lower to middle to upper income. Children of color are linked with poverty because they are overrepresented among the poor. In 1986 (U. S. Bureau of the Census, 1990), the distribution of families living below the poverty level for children under eighteen was reported as follows:

- ❑ African-American—42%
- ❑ Puerto Rican—42%
- ❑ Native American—23.7%

❑ Mexican-American—24%
❑ Chinese-American—12%

Whereas differences among socioeconomic strata may not be clearly defined, individuals within a stratum have more in common with each other than they do with individuals in another stratum. For example, a Puerto Rican child from an upper-income family may have more in common with a white person from the same income group than with a Puerto Rican child who is poor. Nicholas and Anderson (1973) found that IQ differences in favor of whites over African-Americans was reduced by 10 points when the socioeconomic status of the two groups was similar.

Two types of cultural differences need to be distinguished—those that are related to race and ethnicity and those that are influenced by socioeconomic factors. The client's perception of the professional's motivation and behavior in this distinction is the embodiment of the multicultural counseling challenge. Given the nature of poverty, it seems reasonable to assume that, for people of color, perceived negative behavior in white/nonwhite counselor/client dyads is racial or cultural intolerance.

Often, families with low-income levels have had negative experiences with counselors and the social service system which have made them suspicious of all institutional intrusions. The reception of the parent to counseling interventions with the gifted child could be cold and distant. Counselors are faced with the challenge of turning around the suspicion so that parents see the benefits for their gifted learner. The gifted, impoverished child is one who is hurt most by the assumption of some educators and parents that the gifted (because of their abilities) will do better than other children even without assistance or special programs (Marland, 1972).

Without the support structure of gifted education in the school, gifted children of color who are poor may risk never achieving their academic potential. Given the temptations of their environment, they may be inclined to use their gifts in ways that are detrimental to themselves and to society. According to VanTassel-Baska, Patton, and Prillaman (1989),

> It is this population of learners that is in the greatest need of programs and services to help optimize their human potential. And it is this population that is at greatest risk of being forgotten in the context of both gifted and general education. (p. 3)

THE EFFECTS OF BIAS ON THE COUNSELOR AND THE CHILD

Effects on the Counselor

Counselors who are not willing to change or to be flexible regarding the treatment of clients, who refuse to look at their inappropriate assumptions or who feel they have nothing else to explore, can be characterized as *culturally encapsulated* (Pedersen, 1988; Sue, 1981). Such counselors are trapped in their own culture, their own way of thinking or believing.

Those counselors who get training in multicultural counseling often find themselves dealing with a great many emotions as well as a wealth of information. Therefore, a single seminar or course is insufficient to adequately qualify a counselor to work with a specific population. Training programs, however, can raise counselors' awareness levels. Raising awareness levels tends to set into motion the development of a white racial identity. Hardiman (1982), Helms (1990), and Ponterotto (1988) have each contributed to the theoretical development of the stages of white racial identity. Hardiman focused on the sociological aspects of racial identity, Helms concentrated on black–white interaction, and Ponterotto applied it to counselor trainees. Ponterotto (1988) stated that he could see the students in his multicultural counseling course progressing through several stages of racial awareness. The stages were refined and broadened by Sabnani, Ponterotto, and Borodovsky (1991). They include:

1. Lack of awareness of self as a racial being.
2. Interaction with members of other cultures.
3. Breakdown of former knowledge regarding racial matters and conflict.
4. Pro-minority stance.
5. Pro-white, anti-minority stance.
6. Internalization.

Whereas the stages may seem linear, counselors may or may not follow a linear pattern in their development. Often individuals will loop back to an earlier stage at critical decision points of their development.

Stage 1. Lack of Awareness of Self as a Racial Being

In this stage, the counselor trainee has had little or no exposure to other cultural groups and is likely to use the Western standards of counseling. It is believed that if clients are treated equally, they will be appropriately served. The trainees see no reason for special training in multicultural counseling when everyone is treated as an individual. Counselors at this stage also believe they hold no prejudices or biases against others.

Stage 2. Interaction with Other Cultures

Sabnani, Ponterotto, and Borodovsky (1991) stated that it could be argued that Stage 2 is more of an event than a stage. The counselors in this stage find that there are people who are different from themselves and recognize that the differences can be substantial and meaningful. The interaction "forces a person to acknowledge his or her whiteness and examine his or her own cultural values" (p. 79). For example, the first time a counselor witnessed a bilingual child translating for his parents, she suddenly realized that there were some family dynamics that she hadn't considered.

Stage 3. Breakdown
In this stage the counselor starts to question the values he or she once held and acknowledges his or her whiteness and accompanying privileges. This stage is characterized by conflict between wanting to conform to majority norms and wishing to uphold humanistic nonracist values.

Stage 4. Pro-Minority
In this stage the counselor, feeling guilty about the oppression of minority groups in general, and his or her participation in that oppression specifically, compensates by over-identifying with racially and culturally different clients. This person may become overprotective of their different clients or may want to be "the good guy," different from the other white counselors.

Stage 5. Pro-White
Some counselors react differently to guilt and shame over oppression. Some become angry, and those that do enter the defensive stage of their racial identity development—a retreat into white culture. This counselor has heard just about enough of this multicultural stuff and feels that special treatment for racially and culturally different children deprives white children. He or she prefers not to see children of color and makes referrals whenever possible. This counselor is likely to be angry about what has been termed *reverse discrimination*.

Stage 6. Internalization
This counselor begins to incorporate a positive white identity into the self. These counselors are comfortable with their white identity and have begun to adopt a more flexible world view.

Effects on the Child
The racially or culturally different children who work with the Stage 1 counselor are denied a sense of their cultural identity, get mixed messages because they *are* treated differently because of race or culture, and get the message that it is inappropriate to talk about being different. This counselor is also likely to try to get the client to assimilate to American norms, thereby rejecting familial and cultural norms. The counselor may see the child who finds this difficult to do as pathological.

The Stage 3 counselor starts to doubt his or her ability to work with racially and culturally different clients. These counselors may be anxious to refer such clients or may second-guess their interventions, which may or may not be appropriate. Confused counselors often seek more information and more training.

The Stage 4 counselor over-identifies with the racially and culturally different client. Often this is done in a paternalistic way. The counselor is overprotective of the client or is eager to show the client how sympathetic he or she can be. This counselor is likely to attack when she or he believes others are acting in a racist manner. This counselor is also not able to see pathology in children of color—instead attributing all problems children may have as due to racism and prejudice or the client's poor living conditions (Ridley, 1989). A focus on being "the good guy" does not help the client grow.

When gifted students encounter a counselor with these kinds of cultural biases, they find that the very person who is trained to help them can hurt them the most. The counselor who sees the child as a rare exception to the stereotype of children in their group is operating on the deficit model and does the child a disservice. Children who are racially and culturally different and who are gifted are aware of the inferiority stereotypes about their racial or cultural groups. The counselor who conveys such attitudes alienates the children from their culture and could contribute to the children's loss of respect for their own community, culture, or family.

In Stage 5, the counselor will try to avoid working with racially and culturally different clients. If unable to refer clients, there is a great likelihood that she or he will misdiagnose children of diverse backgrounds because of stringent adherence to culturally biased norms, standards, and procedures. This may result in a child's not being identified as gifted or even being referred to special education for behavior problems.

The counselor at Stage 6 has a more multicultural approach to clients, and clients sense their appreciation and respect for their culture. The clients, too, are helped to see positive aspects of all cultures. They help to build self-esteem, motivation, and exploration on the part of the client.

THE MULTICULTURAL COUNSELOR

Sue's (1981) description of characteristics of the culturally skilled counselor is one that is heavily used in the field. It encompasses the need for awareness, knowledge, and skill. Table 13.2 summarizes his key points. Awareness and knowledge are the key elements. When counselors are aware of their biases, they have a place to begin further work through supervision or other training. Consciousness raising is the first priority of most training programs in multicultural counseling. Multicultural skills build on the awareness and knowledge of the counselor and they cannot be performed effectively without them. The more uncomfortable a counselor is with the client's differences, the more likely the client will suffer.

The ideal multicultural counselor would have progressed through all the stages of racial identity to internalization. To stop training before reaching the sixth stage would limit the counselor's effectiveness in working with racially and culturally different clients. All stages prior to the internalization stage include elements of potential bias which would be harmful to the culturally different client.

Knowledge of the specific cultural groups and their unique qualities is a key component of multicultural counseling. However, caution is always war-

Table 13.2
THE CULTURALLY SKILLED COUNSELOR

Awareness of Assumptions, Values, and Biases
1. Is one who has moved from being culturally unaware to being aware and sensitive to his or her own cultural baggage.
2. Is aware of his or her own values and biases and how they may affect minority clients.
3. Is one who is comfortable with differences that exist between the counselor and client in terms of race and beliefs.
4. Is sensitive to circumstances (personal biases, stage of ethnic identity, sociopolitical influences) that may dictate referral of the minority client to a member of his or her own race or culture.
5. Acknowledges and is aware of his or her own racist attitudes, beliefs, and feelings.

Knowledge and Understanding of Client's World View
1. Must possess specific knowledge and information about the particular group he or she is working with.
2. Will have a good understanding of the sociopolitical system's operation in the United States with respect to its treatment of minorities.
3. Must have a clear and explicit knowledge and understanding of the generic characteristics of counseling and therapy.
4. Is aware of institutional barriers that prevent minorities from using mental health services.

Techniques
1. Must be able to generate a wide variety of verbal and nonverbal responses.
2. Must be able to send and receive both verbal and nonverbal messages accurately and "appropriately."
3. Is able to exercise institutional intervention skills on behalf of his or her client when appropriate.
4. Is aware of his or her helping style, recognizes the limitations he or she possesses, and can anticipate the impact upon the culturally different client.

Source: Adapted from *Counseling the Culturally Different: Theory and Practice* (2nd ed., pp. 167–171) by D. W. Sue and D. Sue, 1990, New York: Wiley.

ranted when this information is shared. Counselors need to be careful not to misuse the information they have learned by developing new stereotypes about different races and cultures. There are a great many within-group differences that make gross generalizations about any one group counterproductive. Gibbs, Huang, and Associates (1989) and Sue and Sue (1990) suggest that both group and individual factors are necessary to consider when counseling individuals of color. They suggest that counselors take note of their clients' culture (from the group perspective—e.g., language, customs) as well as their socioeconomic status, level of acculturation, racial identity, educational background, immigration history, attitudes, and belief systems. All of these factors influence the client's culture.

The list of specific skills or techniques to be used with the culturally different client is not very long. Counselors may use many of the skills they have always used, but in a culturally specific context.

Pedersen (1988) outlined four skill areas that emerged from his experience in training counselors to work across cultures. The areas are:

> (1) articulating the problem from the client's cultural perspective; (2) recognizing resistance from a culturally different client in specific rather than general terms; (3) being less defensive in a culturally ambiguous relationship; and (4) learning recovery skills for getting out of trouble when making mistakes in counseling culturally different clients. (p. 343)

He found that each of these areas can be addressed effectively by adapting the microcounseling skills developed by Ivey (1980) for use with the culturally different client. Again, in order to adapt these skills, there must be a firm knowledge of the culturally different group, its language, values, and behaviors. That kind of knowledge comes from learning their history, the current sociopolitical climate for the specific groups, and from experience in working with them.

CONCLUSION

The counselor of the racially or culturally different gifted child must keep in mind that this child is special in a great many ways. To think of the child only as a gifted child who "happens to be" African American, Native American, Asian American, or Hispanic is doing the child a great disservice. To think of a child *only* in terms of race, culture, or ethnicity is equally harmful. The effective multicultural counselor of the gifted child must be sensitive to all the child's needs, potential problems, and desires. These include aspects of race, culture, and identity as well as gifts and talents.

Gifted children of color are often overlooked when it comes to gifted programs and are seriously under-represented in those programs (Baldwin, 1985; VanTassel-Baska, Patton, & Prillaman, 1989). Racially and culturally different children are, however, over-represented in special education classes for emotional and behavioral disorders and mental retardation (Jones, 1988). It is important that counselors do what they can to eliminate bias which contributes to this imbalance. Conquering personal bias against various groups and the practices that institutionalize biases will go far to remedy this phenomenon. Multicultural counseling is complex, and it takes great effort and skill to do it well. It is dynamic and requires that the counselor continuously engage in learning about new cultures and in experimenting with techniques which may be effective with each group. As long as the counselor remains open to learning more about other cultures and is willing to explore his or her own prejudices and biases, he or she has the essence of what is needed to be an effective multicultural counselor.

REFERENCES

Allport, G. W. (1954). *The nature of prejudice*. Reading, MA: Addison-Wesley.

Baldwin, A. (1985). I'm Black but look at me, I am also gifted. *Gifted Child Quarterly, 31,* 180–185.

Cayleff, S. E. (1986). Ethical issues in counseling gender, race, and culturally distinct groups. *Journal of Counseling and Development, 64,* 345–347.

Colangelo, N. (1985). Counseling needs of culturally diverse gifted students. *Roeper Review, 8,* 33–35.

Copeland, E. J. (1983). Cross-cultural counseling and psychotherapy: A historical perspective, implications for research and training. *Personnel & Guidance Journal, 62,* 10–15.

Gallagher, J., & Kinney, L. (Eds.). (1974). *Talent delayed–talent denied: A conference report*. Reston, VA: Foundation for Exceptional Children.

Gibbs, J. T., Huang, L.N., & Associates. (1989). *Children of color: Psychological interventions with minority youth*. San Francisco: Jossey-Bass.

Hardiman, R. (1982). White identity development: A process oriented model for describing the racial consciousness of White Americans. *Dissertation Abstracts International, 43,* 104A. (University microfilms No. 82-10330)

Helms, J. E. (1990). *Black and white racial identity: Theory, research and practice*. New York: Greenwood.

Ivey, A. (1980). *Counseling and psychotherapy: Skills, theories and practice*. Englewood Cliffs, NJ: Prentice-Hall.

Jones, R. L. (Ed.). (1988). *Psychoeducational assessment of minority group children: A casebook*. Berkeley, CA: Cobb & Henry.

Katz, P. A. (1976). *Towards the elimination of racism*. New York: Pergamon Press.

Lewis, O. (1965). *La Vida: A Puerto Rican family in the culture of poverty—San Juan and New York*. New York: Vintage Books.

Lindstrom, R. R., & Van Sant, S. (1986). Special issues in working with gifted minority adolescents. *Journal of Counseling and Development, 64,* 583–586.

Marland, S. P. (1972). *Education of the gifted and talented: Vol. I. Report to the Congress of the United States by the U. S. Commissioner of Education*. Washington, DC: U.S. Government Printing Office.

McIntosh, M. E., & Greenlaw, M. J. (1986). Fostering the postsecondary aspirations of gifted and urban minority students. *Roeper Review, 9,* 104–107.

Nicholas, P., & Anderson, E. (1973). Intellectual performance, race, and socioeconomic status. *Social Biology, 20,* 367–374.

Ogbu, J. U. (1988). Human intelligence testing: A cultural-ecological perspective. *Phi Kappa Phi Journal, 68,* 23–29.

Pedersen, P. (1988). *A handbook for developing multicultural awareness*. Alexandria, VA: American Counseling Association.

Pedersen, P. B., & Marsella, A. J. (1982). The ethical crisis for cross-cultural counseling and therapy. *Professional Psychology, 13,* 492–500.

Ponterotto, J. G. (1988). Racial consciousness development among white counselor trainees: A stage model. *Journal of Multicultural Counseling and Development, 16,* 146–156.

Ramirez, M. (1983). *Psychology of the Americas: Mestizo perspectives on personality and mental health*. New York: Academic Press.

Ridley, C. R. (1989). Racism in counseling as an adversive behavioral process. In P. B. Pedersen, J. G. Draguns, W. J. Lonner, & J. E. Trimble (Eds.), *Counseling across cultures* (3rd ed., pp. 55–77). Honolulu: University of Hawaii Press.

Sabnani, H. B., Ponterotto, J. G., & Borodovsky, L. G. (1991). White racial identity developments and cross-cultural counselor training: A stage model. *The Counseling Psychologist, 19,* 17–102.

Silverman, L. K. (1990). Issues in affective development of the gifted. In J. VanTassel-Baska (Ed.), *A practical guide to counseling the gifted in a school setting* (2nd ed., pp. 15–30). Reston, VA: ERIC Clearinghouse for the Gifted.

Smith, E. J. (1977). Counseling Black individuals: Some stereotypes. *Personnel and Guidance Journal, 55,* 390–396.

Smith, E. J. (1981). Cultural and historical perspective in counseling Blacks. In D. W. Sue (Ed.), *Counseling the culturally different* (pp. 141–185). New York: Wiley.

Sue, D. W. (Ed.). (1981). *Counseling the culturally different: Theory and practice.* New York: Wiley.

Sue, D. W., & Sue, D. (1990). *Counseling the culturally different: Theory and practice* (2nd ed.). New York: Wiley.

U. S. Bureau of the Census. (1990). *Statistical abstract of the United States: 1990* (110th ed.). Washington, DC: U. S. Department of Commerce.

VanTassel-Baska, J., Patton, J., & Prillaman, D. (1989). Disadvantaged gifted learners at risk for educational attention. *Focus on Exceptional Children, 22,* 1–15.

Zappia, I. A. (1989). Identification of gifted Hispanic students: A multidimensional view. In C. J. Maker & S. W. Schiever (Eds.), *Critical issues in gifted education: Defensible programs for cultural and ethnic minorities* (pp. 19–26). Austin, TX: Pro-Ed.

14

Social Development, Leadership, and Gender Issues

Linda Kreger Silverman

The social development of the gifted is paradoxical. On the one hand, the research unequivocally indicates that gifted children have excellent social adjustment (Janos & N. Robinson, 1985; N. Robinson & Noble, 1991). On the other hand, clinical experience reveals that many of these well-adjusted young people suffer great loneliness and endure inner conflicts between their desire to fit in and their ideals. Although the conflict between social acceptance and achievement in adolescent girls has been well documented (Reis & Callahan, 1989), as has their progressive loss in self-esteem (AAUW Educational Foundation, 1992; Gilligan, 1991), the vulnerability of gifted children generally is not reflected in the wealth of social adjustment research. Perhaps this is because the questions addressed in these studies center on how well gifted children relate to other children (a Level II concern: adapting to group norms). Gifted students—particularly girls—frequently have superb social skills, which may be practiced at the expense of their inner lives (a Level III concern: striving to attain inner ideals). (See chapter 1 for more information about levels.) The road toward self-actualization (Level IV) may actually require choosing solitude over popularity (Dabrowski, 1972; Kerr, 1985; Maslow, 1968). It may come as a surprise that the full flowering of leadership ability also involves "a capacity for solitude"—the development of "an active inner life which is often refreshed by retreating from the world..." (Ramey, 1991, p. 17).

Developmentally advanced children tend to be socially mature, able to take the needs of others into account, and able to solve social problems. Because of these traits, they are valued by their peers and often chosen as leaders. Leadership ability appears to be a natural component of giftedness, although it may express itself only under the appropriate social circumstances, as in a community of equals. For example, a quiet child who has few friends in his or her early years may emerge as an expert leader among a group of art critics or research physicists in adult life. Popularity in childhood predicts adult leadership in some arenas but not others. Also, boys and girls do not have equal opportunity to develop their potential for leadership: boys' leadership talent is likely to be recognized and nurtured, whereas similar abilities in girls tend to be unconsciously stifled.

Good leaders have highly developed ethical judgment and responsibility; they are people of integrity. Such leaders combine high intelligence with deep feelings of emotional connectedness with others. They understand the complexities of the human condition and devote their lives to helping others. Many gifted children have the developmental potential to become this type of humanitarian leader (Dabrowski, 1972; Piechowski, 1986, 1991). The aim of social development of the gifted should not be fitting in with age peers; this is a short-sighted goal. To serve society in the long run, the goals should be *wholeness* of the individual, humanitarian values, and moral integrity. With these broader aims in mind, many of our current socialization practices can be understood as obsolete. We must recognize our need for moral leaders, and begin to create environments in which potential for moral leadership can be actualized.

SOCIAL ADJUSTMENT OF THE GIFTED

Social adjustment of the gifted has always been more of a concern to our society than these children's self-concept, academic progress, or inner development. In the nineteenth and early twentieth century, it was believed that brilliant children were doomed to social isolation and alienation (Alger, 1867; Hirsch, 1931).

A passion for perfection will make its subject solitary as nothing else can. At every step he leaves a group behind. And, when, at last, he reaches the goal, alas! where are his early comrades? (Alger, 1867, p. 144)

The genius is constantly forced to solitude, for he early learns from experience that his kind can expect no reciprocation of their generous feelings.... Solitude can best be defined as the state in which friends are lacking or absent, rather than as the opposite of sociability.... Solitude is but a refuge of genius, not its goal. Time after time one detects, from the lives or writings of genius, that solitude is not its destiny but only a retreat; not the normal fruition of its being, but an empty harbor sheltering it from the tortures, griefs, and calumnies of the world. (Hirsch, 1931, pp. 303–304)

The sad prophecy of inevitable solitude for persons of genius was not accepted by Terman (1925) and Hollingworth (1926). Indeed, many researchers worked diligently in the first half of the century to reverse this prediction and counter the myths that the gifted were awkward misfits (e.g., Burks, Jensen, & Terman, 1930; Cox, 1926; Hollingworth, 1931; W. Lewis, 1943; Witty, 1930). In his longitudinal study of over 1,500 children above 140 IQ, Terman (1925) established that the gifted are above average in many respects, including emotional stability, social adjustment, and moral character.

Research in the second half of the century has consistently confirmed these earlier findings. A host of studies of elementary aged gifted children, conducted during the Sputnik era, found them to enjoy a high degree of popularity among their gifted and nongifted peers alike (M. Bell, 1958; J. Gallagher & Crowder, 1957; Grace & Booth, 1958; Grupe, 1961; Miller, 1956). Purkey (1966) reported that high school students in the superior range of intelligence were better adjusted and possessed more favorable personality characteristics than students in the average range.

In more recent studies, when gifted young people are compared with average students, the research indicates that they have more positive self-concepts, more maturity in interactions with others, and better social relations (Lehman & Erdwins, 1981); more positive personality characteristics, values, and interests (Pollin, 1983); greater social competence and less delinquency (Ludwig & Cullinan, 1984); more sophisticated play interests (Wright, 1990); lower levels of anxiety (Davis & Connell, 1985; Schlowinski & Reynolds, 1985); more independence, intrinsic motivation, flexibility, and self-acceptance, as well as early psychological maturity (Olszewski-Kubilius & Kulieke, 1989); and better adjustment with fewer indications of psychological problems (Monks & Ferguson, 1983; Olszewski-Kubilius, Kulieke, & Krasney, 1988).

On combined assessments of social and emotional adjustment, a highly favorable portrait of gifted elementary students emerges:

> Perusal of a large group of studies of preadolescent children revealed [that]... as a group, gifted children were seen as more trustworthy, honest, socially competent, assured and comfortable with self, courteous, cooperative, stable, and humorous, while they were also seen as showing diminished tendencies to boast, to engage in delinquent activity, to aggress or withdraw, to be domineering, and so on. (N. Robinson & Noble, 1991, p. 62)

The rose loses some of its luster in adolescence, particularly in relation to girls, many of whom begin to doubt their abilities or feel that they pay too high a social price for their giftedness (L. Bell, 1989; Buescher & Higham, 1989; Kelly & Colangelo, 1984; Reis & Callahan, 1989). Culturally diverse students, whose adjustment is rarely studied, have a unique set of issues with which to contend. Cultural values differ, such as time concepts, feelings about competition, and peer acceptance of achievement (N. Robinson & Noble, 1991).

There is also some evidence that exceptionally gifted children experience greater difficulties with social adjustment than their more moderately able peers. The greater the difference between the child's abilities and the abilities of others in his or her social group, the greater the potential for loneliness and problems in social adjustment (Dauber & Benbow, 1990; Hollingworth, 1939; Kerr, 1991a; Kline & Meckstroth, 1985; Roedell, 1985). Studies conducted at the Gifted Child Development Center reveal that the discrepancy between cognitive and social self-concept on Harter's (1985) *Self-Perception Profile for Children* increases with IQ (Silverman, Chitwood, & Waters, 1986). Moderately and highly gifted children (above 132 and 148 IQ, respectively) had significantly less social than academic self-confidence, whereas less capable children showed no discrepancies between these domains. Similar findings were reported by Freeman (1979), Ross and Parker (1980), and Katz (1981).

The plight of the extremely gifted child was noted by Hollingworth (1942) over a half-century ago. She indicated that children with Binet IQs above 180 tended to be solitary, not by choice, but because they lacked available companions with similar interests or language abilities. "The more intelligent a person is, regardless of age, the less often he can find a truly congenial companion" (p. 263). Terman (1925) found elementary and junior high school students with Binet IQs above 170 more solitary than children with Binet IQs in the 140 range. One-fourth of J. Gallagher and Crowder's (1957) sample of children with IQs above 165 experienced some social or emotional problems. But even children in the highest IQ ranges are "ordinarily friendly and gregarious by nature" (Hollingworth, 1939, p. 588) and have good social adjustment when they find others like themselves. The composite of studies reviewed by N. Robinson and Noble (1991) indicates that the majority of highly gifted children are well adjusted, with only 20 to 25 percent appearing to suffer from adjustment problems of various kinds.

Given the extensiveness of the findings on the positive social adjustment of gifted students, it is remarkable that the justification for cooperative learning for the gifted rests on the erroneous assumption that most gifted children are socially maladjusted! Ann Robinson (1990b) advises concerned parents and educators to

> speak plainly on the issue of cooperative learning as therapy for socially maladjusted, talented students. The assumption that gifted children are more likely than others to have a variety of personal and social problems is not supported in the literature. Thus, the pill of cooperative learning may be prescribed for a perfectly healthy patient. (p. 35)

This is excellent advice, since at least half of these children—gifted girls— are *overly* socialized at the expense of the development of their abilities (Kerr, 1985). Girls often prefer to help others rather than take on new challenges in learning, which eventually undermines their self-confidence (Dweck, 1986). But gender equity and gifted children are both low priorities in the school reform movement. "Gender equity is still not a part of the national debate on educational reform" (AAUW Educational Foundation, 1992, p. 1). A review of 183 articles on school reform revealed that only one author discussed issues related to gender (Sadker, Sadker, & Steindam, 1989), and only 3 of 295 articles on cooperative learning mentioned the gifted (A. Robinson, 1990a). The gifted girl has no place in the new crusade; in fact, she faces even greater pressures to conform.

Although the "problem" of socializing able children may exist more in our minds than in reality, many parents and school officials are convinced that the most important lesson a gifted child must learn is how to get along successfully with others. The misguided conviction that the gifted are destined to become social misfits leads to prescriptions that often cause the very problem they are attempting to prevent. The lay and professional communities are united on the panacea: educate children of different abilities in a melting pot that boils away the differences and they will all learn to get along with each other. In the many cases where this panacea fails, the children are perceived as maladjusted, with their family stability held in question, but rarely is the prescription itself questioned.

GENDER ISSUES

The overwhelming evidence of the social competence of preadolescent gifted children is stunning, especially upon closer examination of what is required of the child. When gifted children are asked to adapt to children who are mentally or developmentally much younger than themselves, as is typically the case in a heterogeneous class, an atypical set of social skills must be developed. This exercise is a way of helping teachers understand the enormity of the assignment:

> *Imagine that you live on another planet in another solar system in which everyone is convinced that in order for children to have appropriate social adjustment they must be grouped with children who are of similar height. That way no one feels bigger or smaller than anyone else and it is easier to play team sports. You happen to be extremely short. In fact, you are in the bottom two percentile in height, so you have been grouped with children three years younger than you who are the same height. You are nine years old and they are six. You will be with this group for the next twelve years. There is no way out of the situation because everyone on the planet agrees that this is best for your social adjustment. What does this feel like to you? What do you do to survive?*

The situation is actually worse than this for gifted children, because the intellectual differences between them and their age-mates *increase* with age: a five-year-old with an eight-year-old mind will become a ten-year-old with a sixteen-year-old mind! After groups have had a chance to respond to the questions at the end of the fantasy, I pose another question: "Suppose you were the teacher responsible for helping this nine-year-old learn the social skills to fit in with six-year-olds. What would you teach the child?"

The more mature child would have to learn (a) how to explain ideas in simpler terms that others can understand; (b) how to wait patiently while others struggle with concepts he or she has known for some time; (c) how to delay the gratification of answering all the teacher's questions so that others have an opportunity to participate; (d) how to fit in socially with children whose games are uninteresting and play by rules that seem crude and unfair; and, hardest of all, (e) how to live without any real friends or understanding from others. Obviously, these are not age-appropriate social expectations for all children; they are unique social demands placed on the gifted. The complexity of these tasks is rarely understood. To reiterate the quotation in chapter 1, "such a child has to have an exceptionally well-balanced personality and be well nigh a social genius. The higher the IQ, the more acute the problem" (Terman, 1931, p. 579). One cannot help but wonder what price the individual pays internally for accomplishing this feat—a cost that may later result in self-alienation.

Gifted girls generally have an easier time than gifted boys mastering the complex social skills required of advanced children. Because of their enhanced ability to perceive social cues (Levy, 1982) and their early conditioning about the critical importance of social acceptance, gifted girls are much more adept than gifted boys at imitation. They fit in by pretending to be less capable than they really are, disappearing into the crowd. Young gifted girls are rewarded for their compliance and subtly taught to dull their sensibilities and intellectual acumen in the service of social acceptance. Gifted boys, on the other hand, either lack the requisite social skills or rebel against the task—and rightly so! They guard their individuality, but appear socially inept in the bargain.

Girls' aptitude for social adaptation often prevents the detection of their giftedness, which, in turn, inhibits the development of their talents. This adaptability of gifted girls has been noted as a barrier to their achievement (Kerr, 1985), but it has not been recognized as a special strength. However, when we compare the developmental patterns of young gifted girls to those of gifted boys, we begin to wonder whether gifted boys are socially deficient or if girls are "social geniuses." Instead of recognizing the incredible social talent being demonstrated by gifted girls, their behavior is assumed to be an appropriate expectation for both genders, and boys are called "immature" and punished for not accomplishing this difficult social agenda. The irony is that what passes for social maturity is the falsification of the Self.

The So-Called Immature Gifted Boy

Gifted boys are *not* skillful at hiding their abilities. Following is a typical scenario. The gifted five-year-old bursts into the classroom on his first day of school ready to master this new frontier. He has been eagerly anticipating going to school, excited to share what he knows and enthusiastic about all the new things he is going to learn. Five, going on eight, he has already devoured a great deal of information about astronomy, so at recess he takes his new friends on a space adventure, telling them all about planets, asteroids, and mysterious black holes.

> *By three-and-a-half, [M] had taught himself the solar system [and made up daily quizzes for his parents such as] "What's the difference between meteors, meteorites, and asteroids?"...He knew the planets in order from the sun, he knew their features, understood a solar system and a galaxy. He knew other solar systems existed. He read about black holes and features of the stars. M. often borrowed a video from the library—"Conquest." It ran four hours and he'd watch it over and over. It detailed the development of space exploration. He redesigned the interior of the space shuttle, made drawings for NASA, modified delta wings and designed space stations. At three years, eight months, M's babysitter, a junior in high school, informed us M. knew more about space than she did and she had just learned most of her information in her sophomore year of school.*

But this space voyage is unsuccessful. One by one, the boy's classmates disappear because they have no idea what he's talking about. Soon he is alone—a leader with no followers. Undaunted, he returns to the classroom looking for someone intelligent to talk to, so he monopolizes his teacher. Eventually, even the most patient teacher must remind such a student that he is not the only one in the room and that she needs to pay attention to the others as well. What is he to do to keep his active mind occupied? He glances at the other children's activities and wonders why anyone would want to play such silly games. He may remark offhandedly, "That's stupid. What are you doing that for?" This doesn't win him too many close friends. When he tries to play games with his classmates, he becomes upset that the others do not follow the rules; he says, "He *cheats!*" He is unable to grasp that his age-mates are not mentally ready to comprehend the meaning of rules.

If the teacher pushes him into joining the other children in their activities, the student is likely to engage in some acting-out behavior. He will invent ingenious ways to annoy his classmates, and if he gets into enough trouble, eventually he may withdraw and play by himself. One kindergartner spent every recess playing alone in the sandbox. The "readiness" examiner was quite concerned that the boy was displaying signs of "social immaturity" and recommended that he be held back in school. When his mother asked him why he was spending all his time in the sandbox, he replied, "Oh, I'm categorizing all the crystals. You should see them, Mom!"

Hollingworth (1930) provides another poignant example of the misreading of a child's behavior:

A case in point is that of a six-year-old boy of IQ 187, who was reported as too immature for the work of first grade, because he would "go off by himself, lie down on his back, and look up at the ceiling." This child's *mental age* was twelve. He could read as well as any sixth-grade children ordinarily can, according to standard tests. He could perform all the fundamental processes of arithmetic, could square numbers and could read numbers to the billions. Bored with the material being presented to beginners, yet not knowing how to formulate his difficulty, he simply drifted away from the teacher and the group, as his childish solution to the situation. When asked what he did lying on the floor, he said, "Oh, mostly mathematical calculation, or my imaginary land." (p. 443)

Sadly, over sixty years later, with all of our educational progress, this story is uncomfortably familiar. Roedell (1989) provides a modern version:

"Bill needs socialization—he's already so far ahead academically, he doesn't need anything in that area." There are two major problems with this rationale. First, educators are essentially telling such students that there is no need for them to learn anything in school. There is even an element of penalty: "We're not going to teach you any more—you already know too much." Teachers who have to deal with that child later on in school will wonder why the child remains unmotivated and seems to be "turned off" to school. Usually they blame the child or the parents; rarely do they attribute this lack of motivation to the educational process that slammed the door on the child's early enthusiasm for learning. (p. 15)

Instead of advancing such children or providing special programs for them so that they can find true peers, many teachers believe that intellectually precocious boys should be held back in school so that they "have time to develop socially." A five-year-old boy with an eight-year-old mind can play chess, Scrabble, and board games with rules, but he has a difficult time relating to five-year-old boys with five-year-old minds who do not yet understand the meaning of rules. How could anyone think that the solution to this problem is retaining the child so that he will be a six-year-old with a nine-year-old mind trying to adjust to five-year-olds!

The melting pot can easily become a hostile environment for gifted children. Numerous children's books portray the cruelty and ostracism faced by the most capable children (e.g., *A Wrinkle in Time*, by Madeleine L'Engle)—from teachers as well as other students. A gifted little boy who thinks and talks differently from his classmates is likely to be called "weird" or worse. If he is laughed at or rejected, he concludes that there must be something wrong with him (Janos, Fung, & N. Robinson, 1985). As a gifted boy, he is unusually sensitive (Lovecky, 1991); he takes the teasing and criticism of others to heart and may begin to develop a "protective" veneer. This thin layer doesn't really protect him—underneath he is as vulnerable as ever—but it manages to place some distance between himself and other children in hopes that they can't hurt him as easily.

If a child is perpetually exposed to hostility, he will withdraw more and more from social interaction. He will come to see himself as awkward and unlovable, incapable of making friends. He will distrust not only the children who make fun of him, but most other children as well. He will expect to be laughed at and rejected, even by strangers. A child who has had too many early negative experiences with others may become an alienated adult. However, if the child has *early contact* with others like himself, he does not come to see himself as different or strange. He is able to make friends easily with others who think and feel as he does, who communicate on his level, and share his interests.

The Disappearing Gifted Girl

Gifted girls and gifted boys start out life in equal numbers. They remain equal for about the first decade of life (Silverman, 1986b). Girls even have an edge over boys in verbal intelligence, grade point averages, and achievement tests throughout grade school (Kerr, 1985, 1991a; Reis & Callahan, 1989). But as they get older, gifted girls mysteriously disappear; there is a gradual, relentless decline in the number of gifted girls and women identified on all indices. Although some theorize that boys' abilities are more real than girls because they correlate with adult achievement, there is strong reason to believe that the progressive loss of talent in girls can be traced to socialization practices that steadily erode gifted girls' self-confidence and undermine their aspirations.

Part of the problem is the built-in sex biases in our conceptions of giftedness, our methods of measurement, and our interpretations of test data. Giftedness defined as eminence or the potential for eminence is gender biased (and racially and socioeconomically biased as well) because women, minorities, and the poor have less opportunity in our society for the attainment of lasting fame (Hollingworth, 1926). Women often focus their abilities on nurturing others, as in teaching and parenting, goals that are antithetical to the attainment of eminence (Eccles, 1985; Reis, 1987). This automatically excludes them from the ranks of gifted adults according to current conceptions of giftedness. The definition proposed in chapter 1 of giftedness as *asynchronous development* corrects this inequity.

Group intelligence, aptitude, and achievement tests are competitive and timed—two strikes against girls. Girls who have excellent grades often lower their aspirations after receiving their Scholastic Aptitude Test (SAT) scores, despite the fact that they have greater potential for success in college than male peers with similar scores (AAUW Educational Foundation, 1992; Rosser, 1989). Gender differences on the SAT often can be traced to disparities in *speed* of performance rather than competence (Dreyden & S. Gallagher, 1989; Kelly-Benjamin, 1990).

The new emphasis on speed in individual IQ tests (Kaufman, 1992) adds another barrier to finding gifted girls. On the original *Stanford-Binet Intelligence Scale*, an untimed test of verbal abstract reasoning abilities, girls surpassed the boys at every age level until adolescence (Terman, 1916). But from the time Wechsler first studied men who could not qualify on the Army Alpha to serve in the armed forces (Matarazzo, 1981), we have moved steadily toward more spatial conceptions of intelligence. "Intelligence tests that deemphasize verbal skills and emphasize performance, that is, spatial-visual activities, may also be biased against girls who receive much less practice than boys at puzzles and assembly" (Kerr, 1991a, p. 408). With all the efforts on behalf of gender equity over the last seventy-five years, how could we have moved toward more sexist methods of measuring intelligence? New theories of intelligence offer no solution to these problems because they have "little or nothing to say about gender" (Kerr, 1991a, p. 402).

Perhaps the most insidious form of sex discrimination is the wholesale discounting of early indicators of giftedness: for example, rapid advancement through the developmental milestones, high IQ scores achieved during the preschool years and early reading ability. Recently, an assistant principal told a parent of a gifted/dyslexic girl whose IQ score had dropped 30 points, "I can explain it perfectly well. Caitlin *has finally grown into her TRUE IQ.* The only reason her IQ was higher three years ago was because she had early childhood enrichment in the home." (as quoted in Silverman, 1992, p. 2). It is this type of fallacious reasoning—not considering that older children have had more "enrichment" than younger children—that leads us to ignore the early signs of giftedness in girls. The majority of individuals who "used to be gifted" are female (Silverman, 1986b).

There appear to be three critical periods in gifted girls' development when their giftedness is at particular risk: preschool/kindergarten, third/fourth grade, and seventh/eighth grade.

Preschool/Kindergarten

Gifted girls are chameleons. From the time they enter preschool, they learn how to *blend in* with their peer group so that they are "just like" all the other girls. If a girl's social group is developmentally much younger than she is, she will frequently don the mental attire of her friends, and soon will be imperceptible from them in thought, manner, and achievement. Here is an excerpt from a letter I received from a parent:

> I have a daughter who is in public school in kindergarten.... At the first parent/ teacher conference I was informed that she was working at or below grade level. She was in a low pre-reading group and a low math group. (She has been reading since three years old and has done basic addition and math since four.)
>
> I urged them to please look more closely. At another conference at semester end the teacher informed me of something strange which she had discovered. When my daughter worked with her best friend she worked below grade level (as did her friend—she is below grade level). In fact *their work was almost identical.* With more advanced children she worked at their level. *The quality of her work seemed to depend almost entirely on her association.*
>
> When asked about this, she thought about it for awhile and then told me she wanted the other kids to like her. I am unable to convince her that she doesn't have to do this to be liked. *To her, being friends is to be just like each other. She is extremely adaptable.*
>
> The school is becoming aware, but is not willing to help very much. They gave

her a reading test two weeks ago and she reads fourth-grade level. They are unprepared to do anything. She continues in a pre-reading group. (S. Perry, personal communication, February 7, 1986, emphasis added)

Unfortunately, this is not an isolated case. Gifted girls quite commonly hide their abilities for fear of being rejected by their peers. Whereas gifted boys tend to reject age-mates who are less capable, gifted girls modify their behavior according to the social norms of the group. Able boys stand out from their classmates in a variety of ways—through leadership or achievement or attempts to gain teacher attention or annoyance of other students or withdrawal from social interaction. Each of these adaptive mechanisms is *highly visible*. Able girls, however, use their talents to gain social acceptance; they simply blend into the group and become *invisible*. A knowledgeable preschool director has said that she has no difficulty picking out the gifted boys at her school, but she cannot find the gifted girls. By the age of four they have gone into hiding.

Parents frequently report with frustration that their daughters are very different at home and at school. At home, the girl draws beautiful, complex pictures that her parents display with pride; at school, however, she sees that the girl sitting next to her scribbles with an orange crayon so she copies the scribble. She shows her work to the teacher timidly, who gives her considerable praise, because the teacher is unaware that she is capable of more advanced work. At home, she demonstrates a large vocabulary with excellent articulation; at school, she talks baby talk and has a limited vocabulary. At home, she can tie her shoes; at school she requests assistance zipping her jacket. Several cases have been reported of girls who have two styles of reading—"home reading" (fluidly) and "school reading" (stammering)! School becomes a place to show only a fraction of a girl's capabilities.

A question frequently raised is, "How much of the differences in gifted boys' and girls' behavior can be traced to sex-role stereotyping in the home?" The literature is replete with examples of the differential socialization of girls and boys in early childhood (Astin, 1984; Callahan, 1991; Kline & Short, 1991; Schwartz, 1991), beginning with girls' dresses that button in the back (boys' clothes *always* button and zip in the front), and reinforced by the active boy/passive girl content of cartoons and commercials (Kerr, 1991a).

Only one indicator of gender bias in the family has caught my attention at the Gifted Child Development Center, but it occurs with discomforting regularity. When asked if their children show signs of leadership, parents tend to respond differently for their young sons and daughters: "He is a leader with his friends." "He likes to be the boss." "He's the director of activities—even with older children." "He likes to suggest a game and then he assigns roles." "He decides what game to play, who should be what character, what toys to use." "She's *bossy*." "She's so bossy I'm afraid she isn't going to have any friends." Preschool and primary teachers respond similarly, even asking for advice as to how to correct the "bossiness" they observe in gifted girls.

Do young boys really lead in a different manner from girls, or is it simply expected that boys will tell others what to do but unacceptable for girls to do the same? In almost every case in which the term *bossy* has been used to describe a child, that child has been female. It seems unlikely that this would occur by chance among 1,700 families! "Bossy" shows up in the literature also—only in relation to girls (Lutfig & Nichols, 1990; Olszewski-Kubilius & Kulieke, 1989). Apparently the same quality is perceived positively and encouraged in young boys but frowned upon and discouraged in young girls. The message conveyed is that it is inappropriate for a girl to be "the boss"; she should be a follower instead. The long-range impact of having one's "bossiness" curbed early in life may be a tragic loss of initiative and confidence in one's ability to lead.

Third/Fourth Grades

The second critical period is around the age of eight or nine (third or fourth grade). This is the age at which children typically enter the concrete operational stage (Piaget & Inhelder, 1969), during which their lives are governed by rigid rules. Because the concept of rules represents a completely new mental facility for children, they tend to overuse rules and apply them to all facets of their lives. They see everything in terms of black and white—right and wrong—and there is no room for deviation. There is only one way to sing a song, play a game, dress, talk, think, and act. The social group determines "right" behavior and exerts considerable peer pressure on its members to conform.

Boys' peer groups appear to tolerate much more individuality than do girls' peer groups. As long as a boy participates in team activities, he can read Shakespeare in his spare time, if he wishes. Boys seem to have only one airtight demand that they place on each other—athletic competence. If a boy is athletic, he is forgiven for being intelligent (Tannenbaum, 1983). If he is not athletic, a boy can still get by if he has a good sense of humor (Lutfig & Nichols, 1990; Ziv & Gadish, 1990); his sense of humor is often used to hide his intellect. A boy with neither of these qualities is likely to be spurned—even by his teachers (Cramond & Martin, 1987).

For girls the picture is more confining. Girls demand thorough conformity of their peers, and woe to the girl who is "different" in any way, shape, or form. If the group turns on her, she becomes "poison." No one will play with her, invite her to parties, look at her, acknowledge her. They will make fun of her, tell rumors about her, and find other ways to humiliate her. Anyone who dares to be nice to her will find that they are "poison" too. This is a very effective method of squelching giftedness. "The pre-adolescent peer group tends to reject a girl who appears to be too smart or too successful" (Noble, 1987, p. 371).

> Girls who exhibit outstanding academic ability, intense commitment to their chosen interests, leadership and critical judgment are at risk in public schools

today.... By fourth grade, they begin to lose self-confidence, become extremely self-critical, and often lower their effort and aspirations in order to conform to gender stereotyped social expectations.... Underachievement among girls with high potential begins to emerge by fourth or fifth grade and becomes widespread by junior high school.... (L. Bell, 1989, p. 119)

Boys apparently will leave their peer groups behind at any point in their school career to take advantage of opportunities to accelerate to higher grades, whereas girls usually will not leave their peer groups from grades three through nine. Boys of any age usually try to do their best on assessments of intellectual ability, but girls eight or over may or may not show what they know. Many only answer questions they are absolutely certain they will get right. More boys than girls risk guessing the answers to questions they are uncertain about, and this willingness to guess makes a difference in a student's IQ (or SAT) score. In some cases, girls have purposely made mistakes or refused to answer questions so that they would not be identified as gifted. Girls intuit the societal message early that it is smart not to be too smart—especially if you are a girl.

Seventh/Eighth Grades

If giftedness survives the middle years, the worst test is yet to come. Junior high school has proved to be the most vulnerable period for gifted girls (L. Bell, 1989; Buescher, Olszewski, & Higham, 1987; Kerr, 1991a) initiating a downward spiral in self-esteem (AAUW Educational Foundation, 1992; Buescher & Higham, 1989; Kline & Short, 1991). Adolescence is precarious for most girls: "Girls are pressed at adolescence to take on images of perfection as the model of the pure or perfectly good woman; the woman whom everyone will promote and value and want to be with" (Gilligan, 1991, p. 24). Gifted girls, in addition, face torment from both boys and girls if they choose achievement over conformity. Buescher, Olszewski, and Higham (1987) found that in their early teens gifted girls often sacrifice their gifted friends to gain the acceptance of their less capable classmates. They are also at greater risk than their male counterparts for denying, camouflaging, or abandoning their talents (Buescher & Higham, 1989). Highly capable junior high school girls will not leave their friends for the opportunity of acceleration (Fox, 1977). In later adolescence, girls see many disadvantages in being gifted and are concerned about the impact of their giftedness on others (Kerr, Colangelo, & Gaeth, 1988).

Even more disturbing are the findings from the research on self-concept and achievement. Locksley and Douvan (1980) discovered that girls with high grade point averages were significantly more depressed and had more psychosomatic symptoms and lower self-esteem than boys with high grade point averages. Petersen (1988) found that self-image scores in high-achieving junior high school girls increase as their grades decrease, whereas the opposite is true for boys. A recent, large-scale study of 3,000 students documents an alarming loss in self-confidence and achievement in girls as they move from childhood to adolescence (AAUW Educational Foundation, 1992). These losses are not matched in boys.

One factor that clearly undermines gifted adolescent girls' self-esteem is their belief that high ability means achieving good grades effortlessly. "The mere exertion of effort calls ability into question" (Dweck, 1986, p. 1043). Girls who were used to sliding by performing what they already knew for the first six years of school are suddenly thrust into mathematics classes where they encounter a considerable amount of new material. For the first time since they began school, they have to stretch themselves intellectually. They have had so little experience doing so that they have no idea if they can. "Continued success on personally easy tasks...is ineffective in producing stable confidence, challenge seeking, and persistence.... Indeed, such procedures have sometimes been found to backfire by producing lower confidence in ability" (Dweck, 1986, p. 1046).

It is exactly at this stage of development, when girls are most vulnerable and uncertain about their abilities, that the term "overachiever" creeps into educators' vocabularies. When conference participants are asked to visualize an underachiever, then visualize an overachiever, the results are predictable. Most underachievers are male, whereas most overachievers are female. The meaning of "underachiever" is clear—a person who does not achieve to his or her level of ability. But what on earth is an "overachiever"? How can anyone achieve more than she is capable of achieving? "Overachiever" conveys the belief that the student works hard to make up for her lack of ability. It is a subtle, unconscious attack against girls' intelligence.

Fennama (1990) reports that teachers attribute the mathematical success of their best male students to capability and the success of their best female students to effort. If this is how we think of gifted girls, it is no wonder they get the impression that working hard means they aren't smart. It should come as no surprise, then, that girls believe boys have ability whereas girls only work hard (L. Bell, 1989; Cramer, 1989; Reis & Callahan, 1989; N. Robinson & Noble, 1991). Like "bossy," "overachiever" is a sexist term; it has dealt the death blow to the confidence of countless gifted girls and women and remains in their belief systems throughout life. It should be banned.

What Can Be Done to Preserve Giftedness in Girls?

Without the encouragement of family, teachers, and an appropriate social group to develop their talents, much of gifted girls' talents may be permanently lost (Borland, 1986; Buescher, 1991). The tragic waste of high potential in girls and women can be avoided if we care enough about the plight of gifted girls to implement the necessary interventions. Because life goals and attitudes toward achievement are usually forged before school age (N. Robinson & Noble, 1991), the earlier positive intervention occurs the more likely that girls will value and develop their intellectual capabilities.

Astin (1984) has outlined a number of differences in the early-childhood gender socialization that lead to diminished productivity in talented women. She indicates that the amount of outdoor play, types of games, degree of independence allowed, types of household chores, and types of early paid work of boys and girls all set different expectations of the world of work. These barriers can be lifted through an active program of parent education and counseling (Higham & Navarre, 1984).

Gifted girls need "a secure emotional base" and "warm, nurturing parents who encourage exploration,...independent thinking, independent behavior and tolerance for change" (Noble, 1987, p. 373). They also profit from direct academic support from their families. Girls apparently do better in accelerated math classes when their parents provide one-on-one instruction (Olszewski-Kubilius, Kulieke, Shaw, Willis, & Krasney, 1990). It is important for parents to hold high expectations for their daughters as well as their sons. Fathers play a vital role in the formation of their daughters' aspirations (Lemkau, 1983).

Early identification of giftedness, between the ages of three and seven, is highly recommended, before gifted girls go underground (Silverman, 1986b). These early scores *need to be taken seriously*, not discounted. Our performance is always *less* than our competence, because no test can assess all that we know. Information about their superior abilities should be shared with girls very early in life (Kerr, 1991a), because it affects their confidence and aspirations. Whenever possible, early admission to kindergarten should be sought. Research on the positive impact of early entrance is solid, particularly for gifted girls (Daurio, 1979; Proctor, Black, & Feldhusen, 1986; N. Robinson & Weimer, 1991). Early entrance increases the chances of an "optimal match" (N. Robinson & Weimer, 1991, p. 29) between the child's learning rate and the level of challenge provided by the school curriculum. "When schools are locked into an age-in-grade format, early admission to kindergarten may be the *only* window of opportunity available to gifted girls" (Kerr, 1991a, p. 408).

Gifted girls can strive for achievement and gain social acceptance simultaneously when they have the support of others like themselves. Casserly's (1979) interviews with achievement-oriented gifted girls revealed "the importance of girlfriends who shared 'common school experiences and similar interests on similar levels' in dealing with the teasing and disapproval of the boys, which 'peaked in ninth grade'..." (p. 356). Whenever possible, capable girls should be grouped together for instruction; they should be given opportunities to interact with mental peers in preschool and primary grades before they learn to hide their abilities.

Counselors are needed, particularly at the middle, junior, and senior high school levels, who are sensitive to the vulnerabilities of preadolescent and adolescent gifted girls and who are committed to preserving their talents. It is essential that girls be guided into taking the most challenging courses available to them in high school. Although gifted young women may underestimate their abilities (Higham & Navarre, 1984), they appear to be happiest when they are intellectually challenged (Kerr, 1991a). Girls need to understand that college admissions officials carefully scrutinize the coursework taken and place more value on a difficult courseload than on high grades in easy courses. *Four years of mathematics is a must.*

> Few gifted girls are aware of the absolute importance of mathematics to their future goals. Frequently, gifted girls drop out of math and science courses for superficial reasons, not realizing that most college majors leading to high-level careers and professions require 4 years of high school preparation in math and science. (Kerr, 1991a, p. 411)

Salary differentials between men and women are substantially decreased when young women continue their mathematics education in college (AAUW Educational Foundation, 1992). It would be wise for girls to accelerate in mathematics, so that algebra and possibly geometry are mastered before girls are bombarded with the junior high message, "Girls aren't good at math."

Noble (1987) recommends *psychological education* be made available to gifted girls from an early age to assist them in making choices and resisting self-defeating myths. Counselors need to encourage risk taking (Kerr, 1991a) and inoculate elementary aged girls against the intense social pressures they are likely to encounter in junior high school and beyond (L. Bell, 1989). "Waiting until seventh grade when the problems of female underachievement become more apparent may be too late" (L. Bell, 1989, p. 119).

One area in which gifted girls need special assistance is in goal setting. Boys set goals for themselves early in life, but girls less frequently either set goals or strive to reach their goals. Therefore, an important part of programs to reach gifted girls involves raising their aspirations and teaching them the strategies they need to achieve them. Fox and Turner (1981) recommend career and life planning counseling as a top priority for gifted girls from middle school on. Girls should be exposed to female role models who have chosen varied life paths (Phelps, 1991). Internships and mentorships, classroom speakers, career days, shadowing professionals, biographical studies, and films are all valuable ways to enhance girls' awareness of their own potential. (See chapter 10.) Same-sex schools should be seriously considered for high school or undergraduate work because they promote leadership and higher achievement in girls (Callahan, 1991; Higham & Navarre, 1984; Kerr, 1991a; Lee & Bryk, 1986; Riordan, 1990; Schwartz, 1991; Tidball, 1986).

Socialization is not an appropriate goal for gifted girls. Kerr (1985) suggests that the reason gifted women are not counted among the eminent is that they are *too* socialized. Their advanced intelligence enables them to be more sensitive to what other people want. They are eager to please their teachers, parents, and peers, and they receive so much reward for being what others want them to be that they learn to be content using only a small portion of their potential (Conarton & Silverman, 1989). In studying eminent women who escaped the feminine role stereotype, Kerr (1985) found that these women spent a great deal of time alone as children and were not popular as adolescents. She recommends that we de-emphasize the pursuit of popularity for gifted girls (Kerr, 1991a).

Societal support for the development of gifted girls' talents must become a priority. All practices that denigrate girls' abilities should be resisted—for example, use of sexist terms, such as "bossy" and "overachiever" and disparaging or disregarding girls' early achievements (reading or IQ scores), good grades, and social talents. Conceptions of giftedness need to be carefully examined for gender bias; nurturance cannot be devalued in favor of the pursuit of eminence. The emphasis on processing speed in standardized tests needs to be removed. Linguistic awareness is imperative: inclusive language should replace sexist language in every classroom. Funding should be allocated for assistance with mathematics for adolescent girls in similar proportions to the allocations for remedial reading instruction that primarily targets boys (Callahan, 1991). Parent counseling, nonsexist childrearing and teaching practices, early identification of abilities, opportunities for early entrance and acceleration, grouping gifted girls for instruction and counseling, tutorial assistance with mathematics, untimed standardized tests, and special counseling assistance to build self-esteem and guide girls in life planning are all needed if we are to gain equity for gifted girls. Other recommendations can be found in Silverman (1986b; 1991) and Kerr (1985).

Materials useful in counseling gifted girls—particularly in the area of goal setting—include *Choices* (Bingham, Edmondson, & Stryker, 1983); *The Gifted Girl Inservice Resource Handbook* (Addison, 1983); *Girls Are Equal Too* (Carlson, 1973); *Barriers between Women* (Caplan, 1981); *The Cinderella Complex* (Dowling, 1981); *Smart Girls, Gifted Women* (Kerr, 1985); and *What Color Is Your Parachute?* (Bolles, 1981). See also the annotated bibliography of curricular materials to encourage gifted females (Reis & Dobyns, 1991) and the bibliography for gifted girls (in Kerr, 1991b, pp. 184–187). (Additional materials are listed in chapter 10.)

PROMOTING POSITIVE SOCIAL DEVELOPMENT

It has been apparent ever since gifted children were first studied that they select friends who are their *mental age* rather than their chronological age (Gross, 1989; Hollingworth, 1931; Mann, 1957; O'Shea, 1960; N. Robinson & Noble, 1991; Terman, 1925). Roedell (1985) found that gifted children develop social skills more easily when they interact with their true peers.

> The term "peer" does not, in essence, mean people of the same age, but refers to individuals who can interact at an equal level around issues of common interest.... The more highly gifted a child, the less likely that child is to find developmentally defined, true peers among age-mates.
> For children whose development is highly uneven, true peers may vary depending on the activity. A child with extraordinary intellectual but average physical

skills might have one set of peers for reading and discussing books and another set for riding tricycles and playing tag.

Special efforts are needed to help gifted children find companions with similar interests and abilities. Without such efforts, gifted children run the risk of being labeled different and strange by their age-mates. They may internalize these labels and become socially alienated at an early age.... Gifted children can learn the skills necessary to interact successfully with many different types of children.

There is no substitute, however, for the social and cognitive growth that occurs through the interaction of peers of similar developmental stages. (p. 8)

With true peers, gifted children can be themselves, laugh at the same jokes, play games at the same level, share the depth of their sensitivity, and develop more-complex values. In relationships there is more opportunity for equal give and take. And through interaction with others with similar capabilities they quickly learn that they cannot be the best at everything or always have their own way. Boys and girls alike are happier and better adjusted when they have opportunities to relate to other gifted children.

According to a series of older studies, children choose leaders who are slightly above the average intelligence of their group (Finch & Carroll, 1932; Hollingworth, 1926; McCuen, 1929; Pasternak & Silvey, 1969; Warner, 1923). If there is too great a discrepancy between the intelligence of the group and the intellectual level of the child, communication becomes a major barrier (Stogdill, 1974). Therefore, leadership, too, develops best in gifted students when they are placed with other students of comparable ability.

Many researchers have found that gifted students enrolled in special programs experience enhanced self-esteem (Coleman & Fults, 1982; Feldhusen, Sayler, Nielsen, & Kolloff, 1990; Karnes & Wherry, 1981; Kolloff & Feldhusen, 1984; Maddux, Scheiber, & Bass, 1982), primarily because of the opportunities these special classes provide for social interaction with true peers. The benefits of summer programs for the gifted have been well documented also (Higham & Buescher, 1987; Kolloff & Moore, 1989; Olszewski-Kubilius, 1989; VanTassel-Baska, Landau, & Olszewski, 1984), with some unexpected bonuses.

Systematic studies at the larger regional university programs have reported significant gains in academic performance and skill competence, strengthened self-esteem and self-image....More interesting in some ways than these measured gains are the unanticipated benefits specialized summer programs appear to induce. Parents, in particular, and secondary school teachers as well, comment in letters, telephone conversations, and direct contacts with program directors across the country about startling changes occurring with an adolescent son or daughter... changes in responsible behavior, self-discipline, confidence in challenging or stressful situations, and willingness to seek out opportunities that stretch and mold identified talents.... Some teenagers, for example, report that for the first time in years they were able to meet, enjoy, and interact deeply with a peer. (Buescher, 1989, p. 17)

The best news is that there is a ripple effect from these positive social experiences: "Many adolescents report that the 'effect' carries over to their regular schools when they return home; they are able to feel comfortable and socially adept in a peer group which is more diversely composed" (Higham & Buescher, 1987, p. 88).

If a solid base of self-esteem is developed in early childhood, gifted students are better equipped to branch out and make friends with others who are unlike themselves. Adolescence is developmentally the most appropriate stage for these widening horizons of social interaction. Gifted adolescents select their closest friends from among their mental peers, but they can also participate in team sports, band, extracurricular clubs, church and community activities, and social events in which they have opportunities to interact with students who have a wide range of abilities. With a support system of gifted friends and classmates, they can join in other groups without fear of rejection, and they are more likely to gain respect and assume leadership positions.

Materials to Enhance Social Development

To relate effectively with others requires self-knowledge. Only in recent years have books become available to help these students understand their gifted-ness. The following books can be used in the classroom, in small-group counseling, and at home: the three *Gifted Kids' Survival Guides* (Delisle & Galbraith, 1987; Galbraith, 1983, 1984); *Giftedness: Living with It and Liking It* (Perry, 1987); *Gifted Children Speak Out* and *Gifted Kids Speak Out* (Delisle, 1984, 1987); and *On Being Gifted* (American Association for Gifted Children, 1978). The following are some resources for assisting social adjust-ment: *A Kid's Guide to Making Friends* (Wilt, 1980); *SAGE: Self-Awareness Growth Experiences, Grades 7-12* (Kehayan, 1983); *Awareness and Change* (Kline, Kline, & Overholt, 1990); *Reading Ladders for Human Relations* (6th ed.) (Tway, 1981); *Self-Esteem, Communication and High Level Thinking Skills: A Facilitator's Handbook* (Greenlee, 1992); and *The Bookfinder 4: When Kids Need Books* (Spredemann-Dreyer, 1989).

Bibliotherapy is an excellent way to help gifted children deal with problems of self-esteem and developing friendships. *The Bookfinder* (Spredemann-Dreyer, 1989) is useful in locating children's books related to specific issues. In addition, certain children's writers feature gifted children in their books. The following are some recommended authors: Helen Cresswell, Maria Gripe, Virginia Hamilton, Mollie Hunter, E. L. Konigsburg, Joseph Krumgold, Madeleine L'Engle, Ursula LeGuin, Sonia Levitin, Zibby O'Neal, Katherine Paterson, K. M. Peyton, Mary Rodgers, William Sleator, Stephanie Tolan, and Cynthia Voigt. A list of specific books about gifted children appears in the Appendix. (More on bibliotherapy can be found in chapter 4.)

SOCIAL LEADERSHIP

Social leadership denotes interpersonal, psychosocial, and human relations abilities. It involves natural talents and personality traits as well as a set of learned skills. Gardner's (1983) theory of interpersonal intelligence is the basis for including leadership ability as a type of giftedness.

> *Interpersonal intelligence* entails the ability to understand other individuals—their actions and their motivations. In addition, it includes the ability to act productively based on that knowledge.... In more developed forms, this intelligence can be seen in teachers, therapists, and salespersons as well as religious and political leaders. Children skilled in this domain can be perceived as leaders and organizers in the classroom, as cognizant of how and where other children spend their time, and as sensitive to the needs and feelings of others. (Ramos-Ford & Gardner, 1991, pp. 57–58)

Interpersonal intelligence incorporates emotional components essential to the development of leaders who *serve* rather than manipulate the individuals they lead. Evidence of the sensitivity of student leaders was provided by Karnes, Chauvin, and Trant (1984):

> Teachers of the gifted should note that tendermindedness and sensitivity figured prominently in the profiles of gifted leaders. Coupled with tenseness and the tendency to be driven the picture emerges of a very vulnerable individual who may put unrealistic expectations on his/herself. (p. 48)

The emotional sensitivity, intensity, perfectionism, and vulnerability found in student leaders match the personality traits of the gifted described in chapters 1 and 3, and suggests that the gifted population as a whole may have leadership potential.

The debate as to whether leaders are born or made is still not settled (Foster, 1981); however, because there is a strong positive correlation between giftedness and intelligence (Stogdill, 1974), leadership development programs appear to be beneficial to most gifted students. Intelligence and emotional sensitivity may come with the territory, but leadership education can help students learn to use those qualities wisely in the service of others. A leadership curriculum for the gifted should include becoming aware of one's own strengths; becoming aware of the needs of others; problem finding and exploring real problems; becoming aware of global issues; learning about the positive qualities of good leaders and the negative qualities of poor leaders; and analyzing group processes and practicing cooperative communication skills.

Leadership skills are often taught to gifted students during adolescence (Feldhusen & Kennedy, 1988), and many of the leadership development programs have been designed as short-term summer institutes. Evaluations of these experiences indicate that even a one- or two-week intensive program produces gains in leadership ability (Follis & Feldhusen, 1983; Karnes, Meriweather & D'Ilio, 1987; M. Myers, Slavin, & Southern, 1990; Sisk, 1988; Smith, Smith, & Barnette, 1991). Although most groups initially are dominated by the student with the most forceful personality, the most effective leaders are those who encourage involvement of the entire group and who listen to all members (M. Myers, Slavin, & Southern, 1990). These "interpersonal leaders" (p. 259) produce the highest-quality results and promote the most group cohesiveness. Authoritarian leaders, on the other hand, usually invite antagonism from members of the group who feel discounted. Lamb and Busse (1983) suggest that good leadership is a combination of a high concern for task coupled with a high concern for people. This type of leader elicits the best that each member can contribute to the whole.

Introversion and Leadership

Understanding leadership in gifted children is made somewhat more complicated by the high incidence of introversion in the gifted (Hoehn & Bireley, 1988; I. Myers & McCaulley, 1985; M. Rogers, 1986; Silverman, 1986a). Isabelle Myers described a considerable number of studies with the *Myers-Briggs Type Indicator* involving gifted junior high school students, National Merit Finalists, creative adults, and students at colleges such as CalTech and Stanford. Introverts outnumbered extraverts in all groups. The highest achievers were Introverted Intuitives. This combination of personality variables is associated with scholastic potential, as measured by the SAT, IQ scores on Terman's *Concept Mastery Test*, and higher grade point averages at prestigious colleges. And the proportion of introverts increases with educational level (Myers & McCaulley, 1985).

Leaders are generally thought of as extraverts (Richardson & Feldhusen, 1988). There are, however, many introverts who are leaders in their adult lives. Extraverts attain leadership in public domains such as the political arena and business, but introverts dominate the theoretical and aesthetic fields (I. Myers & McCaulley, 1985). The personality profile of introversion, less focused on the values and attitudes of the mainstream, allows for creative introspection. Those giant figures who created new fields of thought or who rearranged existing knowledge often spent long periods in solitude (Albert, 1978), a classic characteristic of introversion. For example, Descartes moved his residence frequently so that no one could disturb him in his work, and Darwin used psychosomatic illness as a means of isolating himself (Boring, 1950).

Leadership is not just the charisma to lead groups; it also occurs in more solitary forms in scientific breakthroughs, the creation of philosophy, and the writing of profound books. Richardson and Feldhusen (1988) indicate that leaders have superior skill, quality of knowledge, and personal position. Introverts are as likely as extraverts to have these qualities. Scholastically achieving introverts frequently gain prestigious positions at universities and research institutes, are valued for their knowledge and skills, and have excellent opportunities to rise to positions of leadership through scholarly efforts and creative contributions to their fields.

This information has bearing on our search for gifted children with "leadership potential." It is easy to overlook introverted gifted children because they do not exhibit the people-moving qualities we generally look for in young leaders. Leadership education can be made more relevant for gifted students when we interpret leadership to include the potential for major contribution or exemplary moral values in adult life.

Materials for Developing Leadership

Some materials for developing leadership skills in gifted students include: *Leadership Education: Developing Skills for Youth* (Richardson & Feldhusen, 1988); *Skills for Leaders* (Gray & Pfeiffer, 1987); *Developing Student Leaders: Exemplary School Activities Programs* (Leatt, 1987); *Leadership Skills Development Program* (Karnes & Chauvin, 1985); *Leadership: A Skills Training Program: Ages 8–18* (Roets, 1981); *Leadership Series* (House, 1980); *A Handbook of Structured Experiences for Human Relations* (Pfeiffer, 1985); *Leadership: Making Things Happen* (Sisk & Shalcross, 1986); and *A Leadership Unit* (J. Gallagher, 1982).

MORAL LEADERSHIP

Leadership education must be conjoined with the study of ethics in order to educate future leaders toward moral excellence:

> The relativism of our time is pernicious; it eats away at the very core of our culture, catalyzing all the various moral fibre into a rather gelatinous soup from which everyone sips sanctimoniously, smiling, nodding, excusing, apologizing.... For years the schools have, for myriad reasons, struggled to educate the nation's children in a relatively value-free environment. Now it becomes evident that we must establish moral education at the core of the curriculum, particularly for students gifted in leadership. If we are to regain our national conscience, our sense of propriety, our hunger for excellence in every endeavor, we must begin with the design of a curriculum in moral education that will provide our future leaders with the appropriate models and methodologies for re-establishing these values at the center of our consciousness. (Lindsay, 1988, p. 9)

Leadership ability without ethics leads to manipulation and corruption; leadership ability with ethics leads to service to humanity. In preparing gifted students to assume leadership positions in society, we must keep in mind the importance of their ethical development. Popularity is not enough.

Moral leaders characteristically choose ethical rather than expedient alternatives when faced with a dilemma; go against the group rather than compromise their values; are committed to principles and causes; identify with humanity, not just their own group; feel compassion and forgiveness; admit to their shortcomings; and hold their own personal ideals, transcending societal norms (Getzels & Jackson, 1962; Lindsay, 1988). These values characterize Dabrowski's (1972) "multilevel" individuals (Levels III, IV, and V) and are essential to the path of self-actualization (Maslow, 1968).

By means of contrast, a Level II orientation, with a heavy reliance on group norms, appears to be more typical. Carl Rogers (1969) maintained that most individuals have

> relinquished the locus of evaluation to others, and... [feel] profoundly insecure and easily threatened in [their] values.... Values [are] mostly introjected, held as fixed concepts, rarely examined or tested.... By taking over the conceptions of others as our own, we lose contact with the potential wisdom of our own functioning, and lose confidence in ourselves. (p. 85)

Again and again we see gifted children demonstrate moral concerns at an earlier age and in a more intensified manner than their peers (Boehm, 1962; Hollingworth, 1942; Martinson, 1961; Passow, 1988; Roeper, 1988; Terman, 1925). Eighty percent of the more than four hundred gifted children whom Galbraith (1985) polled reported that they worry a great deal more about world problems than their peers—problems such as world hunger, nuclear war, pollution, and international relations. These findings were confirmed by Clark and Hankins's (1985) comparative study which found that young gifted students read the newspapers more often than nongifted students, paid more attention to world news items, and were more concerned about war.

> One of the well-known characteristics of the gifted is their acute sense of justice. Gifted children are questioners, keen observers, logical thinkers. They will notice inequities, unfairness, double standards, and will question instances and experiences of that sort with passion. Often they feel helpless and powerless to make an impact, and they suffer deeply from this. They worry about the injustices of the world. They worry about peace, about the bomb, about their futures, about the environment, about all the problems that they encounter. (Roeper, 1988, p. 12)

At two-and-a-half years old, Sara Jane observed the news report of the earthquake that hit Russia, leaving countless people homeless. With tears in her eyes, she brought her piggy bank to her mother and said, "Mama, send my money." The following Christmas, at the age of three, Sara requested that her presents be given to needy children: "I have everything I need. I wish you would give my presents to some little girl or boy who won't get any." Her family obliged, giving her a few and then wrapping presents to take to a shelter.

Martin Rogers (1986) asked parents of gifted and average third-graders to rate their children's concerns about morality and justice on a 5-point scale from "always" to "never." Whereas 36 percent of the gifted children were described as having deep concerns about morality and justice, only 8 percent of the average children were characterized in this manner. Janos, N. Robinson, and Lunneborg (1989) found accelerated gifted adolescents to be advanced in moral reasoning on Rest's *Defining Issues Test* (Rest, 1979), attaining levels similar to those achieved by graduate students.

These findings are consistent with Dabrowski's (1972) hypothesis that the gifted are endowed with greater developmental potential for higher level moral development. (See chapter 1.) Other researchers also suggest that the unique ethical sensitivity of the gifted indicates a special potential for high moral development (Drews, 1972; Vare, 1979). This is probably because of the complexity of moral issues and the intellectual demands involved in ethical judgments. However, this potential cannot develop in a vacuum. Tannenbaum (1972) reminds us that, without training, the gifted are no better equipped to grapple with the value dimensions of their studies than they are to solve problems in non-Euclidean geometry. Rarely has moral awareness or potential been used as a basis for program planning or counseling for the gifted.

Kohlberg (1984) suggested that moral levels can be raised or lowered through environmental influences. He advocated a type of moral education in which students participate in discussions involving moral choices in order to understand other viewpoints and the bases used by others to determine what is just. Exposure to higher levels of moral judgment provides the cognitive dissonance that motivates the student to strive toward more comprehensive principles of justice. Actual experiences involving moral choices can also further development.

However, higher level moral judgment may require more than the intellectual capability to comprehend abstract principles of justice. A factor that has been overlooked until recently is the capacity to care. The role of compassion, caring, and responsibility to oneself and others is illumined by Gilligan (1982) in her analysis of the development of moral judgments in women. At the highest levels there is an interplay between justice and mercy, rights and responsibilities, and a recognition of the interconnectedness of all life.

> The moral imperative that emerges repeatedly in interviews with women is an injunction to care, a responsibility to discern and alleviate the "real and recognizable trouble" of this world. For men, the moral imperative appears rather as an injunction to respect the rights of others and thus to protect from interference the rights to life and self-fulfillment.... Development for both sexes would therefore seem to entail an integration of rights and responsibilities through the discovery of the complementarity of these disparate views. (Gilligan, 1982, p. 100)

The theme of caring is echoed in Fantini's (1981) plea that all learning be subordinated to the main function of preparing students to create "a humane, *caring* society" (p. 3). To internalize caring values, Fantini recommends that students actively participate in community service as part of their education. He suggests that the curriculum be redesigned to include a section on the desirability of caring values and behaviors as they apply to the self, toward others, and toward nature and the environment. The section might include psychology, health, ecology, contemporary social issues, and ethics. Gifted students could examine social issues from the perspective of humaneness (Passow, 1988); in addition, they could be asked to devise ways to complement their cognitive learning with practical experience that would allow them to demonstrate caring behaviors (Shannon, 1989).

Activities to Enhance the Development
of Moral Leaders

1. Expose students to the theories of Dabrowski, Kohlberg, and Gilligan as well as similar literature that would help them form ideals of leadership toward which they could strive (Dana & Lynch-Brown, 1991; Leroux, 1986).

2. Have students examine values, ethical principles, and philosophical systems (Feldhusen & Kennedy, 1988).

3. Give them opportunities to discuss ethical issues and come to their own decisions (e.g., Blatt & Kohlberg, 1975; Maker, 1982). A good guide for selecting books that explore moral dilemmas is *Values in Selected Children's Books of Fiction and Fantasy* (Field & Weiss, 1987).

4. Offer them the opportunity to construct their own moral dilemmas (Colangelo, 1991; Weber, 1981).

5. Provide opportunities for them to internalize caring values by making community service a part of their curriculum or extracurricular activities (e.g., in hospitals, day care centers, nursing homes). Encourage students to "recognize service opportunities in the classroom, school, home, and community" (Shannon, 1989, p. 185).

6. Encourage emotional sensitivity in gifted young men and women through counseling seminars and discussion groups. (See chapter 5.)

7. Believe in their ideals. Don't try to talk them out of their "unrealistic" expectations.

8. Help them learn how to set priorities so that they discover which are their most important goals.

9. Support their courage to stand up for their convictions, despite the blows to self-esteem they might sustain from others.

10. Give them books to read and films to watch to familiarize themselves with moral leaders so that they have appropriate role models. Explore with them humanitarian values and the lives of individuals dedicated to service (Nelson, 1981).

11. Assist them in designing projects related to social and moral issues (e.g., writing research papers; developing films, videotapes, or plays; conducting panel discussions; using an art medium such as painting or sculpting to represent a contemporary social ill; planning strategies for raising the consciousness of their community with respect to a particular concern) (Weber, 1981).

12. Help them critically examine the historical development of philosophies and the effects of these values on the development of societies (Ward, 1980).

13. Introduce them to the contributions of the inconspicuous and unsung who show admirable qualities and lead worthwhile lives (e.g., parents who sacrifice for their children; disabled individuals who lead pro-

ductive lives; VISTA and Peace Corps volunteers who leave comfort and security in order to help others) (Christenson, 1976).

14. Examine with them moral issues shown on television, seen in the newspapers, or found in the community (Drews, 1972).

15. Encourage them to attempt to solve some of the problems confronting society and share these alternatives with civic leaders (Weber, 1981).

16. Employ simulations, role play, or perspective-taking exercises. Focus on different viewpoints in everyday interactions; have the teacher and students share their feelings about interactions, events, or activities (Hensel, 1991).

17. Involve them in group dynamics activities in which children learn to interact cooperatively with each other, respect each other's rights, and gain a sense of social responsibility (Leroux, 1986; Sisk, 1982).

18. Have students establish their own code of rules for behavior (Leroux, 1986).

19. Conduct philosophy seminars in which students explore the principles of moral reasoning and discuss how individual values influence society in positive ways (Leroux, 1986).

20. Have students participate on an equal footing with faculty members in decision making (Leroux, 1986; Roeper, 1990).

21. Model caring behaviors (Hensel, 1991; Doescher & Sugawara, 1989; Roeper, 1991).

22. Help students become activists by engaging them in the study and solution of real-life problems (Galbraith, 1985; B. Lewis, 1991; Passow, 1988).

23. Encourage students to read newspapers so they can begin to see how they and their communities are not isolated from the outside world; provide opportunities for them to share their perceptions and questions with others on a regular basis (Clark & Hankins, 1985; Passow, 1988).

24. Network students with gifted children from various countries (Passow, 1988).

25. Encourage gifted students to think about the moral and ethical dimensions of the subjects they study and to raise questions of conscience regarding content (Passow, 1988).

26. "Allow students to develop and discuss their own images of service and reflect on the consequences and benefits for themselves, others, and communities" (Shannon, 1989, p. 185).

27. Give students opportunities to think about their role in the world. "What impact could they make? What impact do they want to make? What impact does the world have on their lives? They need the tools to make an impact on their own destiny and the ever expanding interrelatedness of the destiny of everybody on the planet." (Roeper, 1988, p. 12)

CONCLUSION

Ramey (1991) suggests that the traditional pursuit of achievement is an insufficient goal for society's leaders. He contends that gifted leaders have a "commitment to a higher purpose" (p. 17). Dabrowski maintained that most political leaders are operating at the lowest level of development, motivated by self-interest rather than a desire to serve. If we want ethical leaders, we need to openly discuss ethical issues and foster this moral leadership in our programs. Perhaps the clearest direction for those of us who guide tomorrow's leaders is the one offered in an impassioned essay by Passow (1988):

> We have a sound enough base for gifted education that we can—no, we must—attend to another dimension of giftedness: the development of caring, concerned, compassionate, committed individuals who develop and use their giftedness for society's benefit as well as for self-fulfillment.
>
> As an integral part of their education, we must sensitize gifted children and youth to the major problems our world societies face—among them, poverty, famine, war and nuclear annihilation,...depletion of resources, environmental pollution, cultural conflict,...employment, and quality of life. We must sensitize gifted and talented children and youth to be concerned about these problems not because they are going to resolve them as students, but because we want them to care enough to devote themselves to developing their specialized gifts and talents to contributing to the resolution of the problems which beset the world... (p. 13)
>
> There is research which suggests that gifted children have the potential for greater and more profound social, moral, and ethical concerns. We need to nurture this potential. We talk of the gifted exercising future leadership but seldom design educational programs that will help them develop the skills, the motivation, and the values of leadership. We enhance our gifted students' knowledge but avoid helping them think about the morality of that knowledge.... We reward competitive behavior which results in winners and losers but do not teach or encourage the skills of cooperation.... (p. 14)
>
> Self-actualization is but one goal of gifted education: self-actualization in service to humankind is the twin goal. To achieve these goals, we need persons who are caring, compassionate, conscientious, committed, and involved. (p. 15)

REFERENCES

AAUW Educational Foundation. (1992). *The AAUW Report: How schools short-change girls*. Executive summary. Washington, DC: American Association of University Women Educational Foundation.

Addison, L. B. (1983). *The gifted girl: Helping her be the best she can be. Inservice resource handbook*. Bethesda, MD: The Equity Institute.

Albert, R. S. (1978). Observations and suggestions regarding giftedness, familial influence, and the achievement of eminence. *Gifted Child Quarterly, 22,* 201–211.

Alger, W. K. (1867). *The solitudes of nature and of man: Or the loneliness of human life*. Boston: Roberts Bros.

American Association for Gifted Children. (1978). *On being gifted*. New York: Walker.

Astin, H. S. (1984). The meaning of work in women's lives: A sociopsychological model of career choice and work behavior. *The Counseling Psychologist, 12,* 117–126.

Bell, L. A. (1989). Something's wrong here and it's not me: Challenging the dilemmas that block girls' success. *Journal for the Education of the Gifted, 12,* 118–130.

Bell, M. E. (1958). *A comparative study of mentally gifted children heterogeneously and homogeneously grouped.* Unpublished doctoral dissertation, Indiana University, Bloomington.

Bingham, M., Edmondson, J., & Stryker, S. (1983). *Choices: A teen woman's journal for self-awareness and personal planning.* Santa Barbara, CA: Advocacy Press.

Blatt, M., & Kohlberg, L. (1975). The effects of classroom moral discussion upon children's level of moral judgment. *Journal of Moral Education, 4,* 129–161.

Boehm, L. (1962). The development of conscience: A comparison of American children of different mental and socioeconomic levels. *Child Development, 33,* 575–590.

Bolles, R. N. (1981). *What color is your parachute?* Berkeley, CA: Ten Speed Press.

Boring, E. G. (1950). *A history of experimental psychology* (2nd ed.). Englewood Cliffs, NJ: Prentice-Hall.

Borland, J. H. (1986). What happens to them all? In C. J. Maker (Ed.), *Critical issues in gifted education: Vol. 1. Defensible programs for the gifted* (pp. 91–106). Rockville, MD: Aspen.

Buescher, T. M. (1989). Adolescent passages: The benefits of summer programs. *Understanding Our Gifted, 2*(2), 17.

Buescher, T. M. (1991). Gifted adolescents. In N. Colangelo & G. A. Davis (Eds.), *The handbook of gifted education* (pp. 382–401). Needham Heights, MA: Allyn & Bacon.

Buescher, T. M., & Higham, S. J. (1989). A developmental study of adjustment among gifted adolescents. In J. VanTassel-Baska & P. Olszewski-Kubilius (Eds.), *Patterns of influence on gifted learners: The home, the self, and the school* (pp. 102–124). New York: Teachers College Press.

Buescher, T. M., Olszewski, P., & Higham, S. J. (1987, April). *Influences on strategies gifted adolescents use to cope with their own recognized talents.* Paper presented at the 1987 biennial meeting of the Society for Research in Child Development, Baltimore.

Burks, B. S., Jensen, D. W., & Terman, L. M. (1930). *Genetic studies of genius: Vol. 3. The promise of youth: Follow-up of 1000 gifted children.* Stanford, CA: Stanford University Press.

Callahan, C M. (1991). An update on gifted females. *Journal for the Education of the Gifted, 14,* 284–311.

Caplan, P. (1981). *Barriers between women.* New York: Spectrum.

Carlson, D. (1973). *Girls are equal too: The women's movement for teenagers.* New York: Atheneum.

Casserly, P. L. (1979). Helping able young women take math and science seriously in school. In N. Colangelo & R. T. Zaffrann (Eds.), *New voices in counseling the gifted* (pp. 346–369). Dubuque, IA: Kendall/Hunt.

Christenson, R. M. (1976). McGuffy's ghost and moral education today. *Phi Delta Kappan, 58,* 737–742.

ark, W. H., & Hankins, N. E. (1985). Giftedness and conflict. *Roeper Review, 8,* 50–53.

Colangelo, N. (1991). Counseling gifted students. In N. Colangelo & G. A. Davis (Eds.), *Handbook of gifted education* (pp. 271–284). Needham Heights, MA: Allyn & Bacon.

Coleman, J. M., & Fults, B. A. (1982). Self-concept and the gifted classroom: The role of social comparisons. *Gifted Child Quarterly, 26,* 116–120.

Conarton, S., & Silverman, L. K. (1989). Feminine development through the life cycle. In M. A. Douglas & L. E. Walker (Eds.), *Feminist psychotherapies* (pp. 37–67). Norwood, NJ: Ablex.

Cox, C. (1926). The early mental traits of three hundred geniuses. In L. M. Terman (Ed.), *Genetic studies of genius* (Vol. 2). Stanford, CA: Stanford University Press.

Cramer, R. H. (1989). Attitudes of gifted boys and girls toward math: A qualitative study. *Roeper Review, 11,* 128–130.

Cramond, B., & Martin, C. E. (1987). Inservice and preservice teachers' attitudes toward the academically brilliant. *Gifted Child Quarterly, 31,* 15–19.

Dabrowski, K. (1972). *Psychoneurosis is not an illness.* London: Gryf.

Dana, N. F., & Lynch-Brown, C. (1991). Moral development of the gifted: Making a case for children's literature. *Roeper Review, 14,* 13–16.

Dauber, S. L., & Benbow, C. P. (1990). Aspects of personality and peer relations of extremely talented adolescents. *Gifted Child Quarterly, 34,* 10–15.

Daurio, S. P. (1979). Educational enrichment versus acceleration: A review of the literature. In W. C. George, S. J. Cohn, & J. Stanley (Eds.), *Educating the gifted: Acceleration and enrichment* (pp. 13–63). Baltimore: Johns Hopkins University Press.

Davis, H. B., & Connell, J. P. (1985). The effect of aptitude and achievement status on the self-system. *Gifted Child Quarterly, 29,* 131–135.

Delisle, J. R. (1984). *Gifted children speak out.* New York: Walker.

Delisle, J. R. (1987). *Gifted kids speak out.* Minneapolis: Free Spirit.

Delisle, J., & Galbraith, J. (1987). *The gifted kids' survival guide II.* Minneapolis: Free Spirit.

Doescher, S. M., & Sugawara, A. I. (1989). Encouraging prosocial behavior in young children. *Childhood Education, 65,* 213–215.

Dowling, C. (1981). *The Cinderella complex.* New York: Summit Books.

Drews, E. M. (1972). *Learning together.* Englewood Cliffs, NJ: Prentice-Hall.

Dreyden, J. I., & Gallagher, S. A. (1989). The effects of time and direction: Changes on the SAT performance of academically talented adolescents. *Journal for the Education of the Gifted, 12,* 187–204.

Dweck, C. S. (1986). Motivational processes affecting learning. *American Psychologist, 41,* 1040–1048.

Eccles, J. S. (1985). Why doesn't Jane run? Sex differences in educational and occupational patterns. In F. D. Horowitz & M. O'Brien (Eds.), *The gifted and talented: Developmental perspectives* (pp. 251–295). Washington, DC: American Psychological Association.

Fantini, M. D. (1981). A caring curriculum for gifted children. *Roeper Review, 3*(4), 3–4.

Feldhusen, J. F., & Kennedy, D. M. (1988). Preparing gifted youth for leadership roles in a rapidly changing society. *Roeper Review, 10,* 226–230.

Feldhusen, J. F., Sayler, M. F., Nielsen, M. E., & Kolloff, P. B. (1990). Self-concepts of gifted children in enrichment programs. *Journal for the Education of the Gifted, 13,* 380–387.

Fennama, E. (1990). Teachers' beliefs and gender differences in mathematics. In E. Fennama & G. Leder (Eds.), *Mathematics and gender* (pp. 169–187). New York: Teachers College Press.

Field, C. W., & Weiss, J. S. (1987). *Values in selected children's books of fiction and fantasy.* Hamden, CN: Shoe String Press.

Finch, F. H., & Carroll, H. A. (1932). Gifted children as high school leaders. *Pedagogical Seminary, 41,* 476–481.

Follis, H., & Feldhusen, J. F. (1983). Design and evaluation of a summer academic leadership program. *Roeper Review, 6,* 92–96.

Foster, W. (1981). Leadership: A conceptual framework for recognizing and educating. *Gifted Child Quarterly, 25,* 17–25.

Fox, L. H. (1977). Sex differences: Implications for program planning for the academically gifted. In J. C. Stanley, W. C. George, & C. H. Solano (Eds.), *The gifted and the creative: A fifty year perspective* (pp. 113–138). Baltimore: Johns Hopkins University Press.

Fox, L. H., & Turner, L. D. (1981). Gifted and creative females: In the middle school years. *American Middle School Education, 4*(1), 17–23.

Freeman, J. (1979). *Gifted children.* Baltimore: University Park Press.

Galbraith, J. (1983). *The gifted kids' survival guide.* Minneapolis: Free Spirit.

Galbraith, J. (1984). *The gifted kids' survival guide for ages 10 and under.* Minneapolis: Free Spirit.

Galbraith, J. (1985). The eight great gripes of gifted kids: Responding to special needs. *Roeper Review, 8,* 15–18.

Gallagher, J. J. (1982). *A leadership unit.* New York: Trillium Press.

Gallagher, J. J., & Crowder, T. (1957). The adjustment of gifted children in the classroom. *Exceptional Children, 23,* 306–319.

Gardner, H. (1983). *Frames of mind: The theory of multiple intelligences.* New York: Basic Books.

Getzels, J. W., & Jackson, P. W. (1962). *Creativity and intelligence.* New York: Wiley.

Gilligan, C. (1982). *In a different voice: Psychological theory and women's development.* Cambridge, MA: Harvard University Press.

Gilligan, C. (1991). Women's psychological development: Implications for psychotherapy. In C. Gilligan, A. G. Rogers, & D. L. Tolman (Eds.), *Women, girls & psychotherapy: Reframing resistance* (pp. 5–31). New York: Haworth Press.

Grace, H. A., & Booth, N. L. (1958). Is the gifted child a social isolate? *Peabody Journal of Education, 35,* 195–196.

Gray, J. W., & Pfeiffer, A. L. (1987). *Skills for leaders.* Reston, VA: National Association of Secondary School Principals.

Greenlee, S. (1992). *Self-esteem, communication and high level thinking skills: A facilitator's handbook.* Needham Heights, MA: Allyn & Bacon.

Gross, M. U. M. (1989). The pursuit of excellence or the search for intimacy? The forced-choice dilemma of gifted youth. *Roeper Review, 11,* 189–193.

Grupe, A. J. (1961). *Adjustment and acceptance of mentally superior children in regular and special fifth grade classes in a public school system.* Unpublished doctoral dissertation, University of Illinois, Urbana.

Harter, S. (1985). *Self-perception profile for children*. Denver: University of Denver.

Hensel, N. H. (1991). Social leadership skills in young children. *Roeper Review, 14*, 4–6.

Higham, S. J., & Buescher, T. M. (1987). What young gifted adolescents understand about feeling "different." In T. M. Buescher (Ed.), *Understanding gifted and talented adolescents: A resource guide for counselors, educators, and parents* (pp. 77–91). Evanston, IL: The Center for Talent Development, Northwestern University.

Higham, S. J., & Navarre, J. (1984). Gifted adolescent females require differential treatment. *Journal for the Education of the Gifted, 8*, 43–58.

Hirsch, N. D. M. (1931). *Genius and creative intelligence*. Cambridge, MA: Sci-Art.

Hoehn, L., & Bireley, M. K. (1988). Mental processing preferences of gifted children. *Illinois Council for the Gifted Journal, 7*, 28–31.

Hollingworth, L. S. (1926). *Gifted children: Their nature and nurture*. New York: Macmillan.

Hollingworth, L. S. (1930). Personality development of special class children. *University of Pennsylvania Bulletin. Seventeenth Annual Schoolmen's Week Proceedings, 30*, 442–446.

Hollingworth, L. S. (1931). The child of very superior intelligence as a special problem in social adjustment. *Mental Hygiene, 15*(1), 1–16.

Hollingworth, L. S. (1939). What we know about the early selection and training of leaders. *Teachers College Record, 40*, 575–592.

Hollingworth, L. S. (1942). *Children above 180 IQ Stanford-Binet: Origin and development*. Yonkers-on-Hudson, NY: World Book.

House, C. (1980). *Leadership series*. Coeur d'Alene, ID: Listos.

Janos, P. M., Fung, H. C., & Robinson, N. M. (1985). Self-concept, self-esteem, and peer relations among gifted children who feel "different." *Gifted Child Quarterly, 29*, 78–82.

Janos, P. M., & Robinson, N. M. (1985). Psychosocial development in intellectually gifted children. In F. D. Horowitz & M. O'Brien (Eds.), *The gifted and talented: Developmental perspectives* (pp. 149–195). Washington, DC: American Psychological Association.

Janos, P. M., Robinson, N. M., & Lunneborg, C. E. (1989). Markedly early entrance to college: A multi-year comparative study of academic performance and psychological adjustment. *Journal of Higher Education, 60*, 496–518.

Karnes, F. A., & Chauvin, J. C. (1985). *Leadership skills development program*. East Aurora, NY: United D.O.K.

Karnes, F. A., Chauvin, J. C., & Trant, T. J. (1984). Leadership profiles as determined by the HSPQ of students identified as intellectually gifted. *Roeper Review, 7*, 46–48.

Karnes, F. A., Meriweather, S., & D'Ilio, V. (1987). The effectiveness of the leadership studies program. *Roeper Review, 9*, 238–241.

Karnes, F. A., & Wherry, G. N. (1981). Self-concepts of gifted students as measured by the Piers-Harris Children's Self-Concept Scale. *Psychological Reports, 49*, 903–906.

Katz, E. L. (1981). *Perceived competence in elementary level gifted children*. Unpublished doctoral dissertation, University of Denver.

Kaufman, A. S. (1992). Evaluation of the WISC-III and WPPSI-R for gifted children.

Roeper Review, 14, 154–158.

Kehayan, V. (1983). *SAGE: Self-awareness growth experiences, grades 7–12.* Rolling Hills Estates, CA: B. L. Winch.

Kelly, K., & Colangelo, N. (1984). Academic and social self-concepts of gifted, general, and special students. *Exceptional Children, 50,* 551–553.

Kelly-Benjamin, K. (1990, April). *Performance differences on SAT math questions.* Paper presented at the meeting of the American Educational Research Association, Boston.

Kerr, B. A. (1985). *Smart girls, gifted women.* Columbus: Ohio Psychology.

Kerr, B. A. (1991a). Educating gifted girls. In N. Colangelo & G. A. Davis (Eds.), *Handbook of gifted education* (pp. 402–415). Needham Heights, MA: Allyn & Bacon.

Kerr, B. A. (1991b). *A handbook for counseling the gifted and talented.* Alexandria, VA: American Counseling Association.

Kerr, B. A., Colangelo, N., & Gaeth, J. (1988). Gifted adolescents' attitudes toward their giftedness. *Gifted Child Quarterly, 32,* 245–248.

Kline, B. E., Kline, K., & Overholt, M. (1990). *Awareness and change.* McPherson, KS: McPherson Family Life Center.

Kline, B. E., & Meckstroth, E. A. (1985). Understanding and encouraging the exceptionally gifted. *Roeper Review, 8,* 24–30.

Kline, B. E., & Short, E. B. (1991). Changes in emotional resilience: Gifted adolescent females. *Roeper Review, 13,* 118–121.

Kohlberg, L. (1984). *The psychology of moral development.* New York: Harper & Row.

Kolloff, P. B., & Feldhusen, J. (1984). The effects of enrichment on self-concept and creative thinking. *Gifted Child Quarterly, 28,* 53–58.

Kolloff, P. B., & Moore, A. D. (1989). Effects of summer programs on the self-concepts of gifted children. *Journal for the Education of the Gifted, 12,* 268–276.

Lamb, R. A., & Busse, C. A. (1983). Leadership beyond lip service. *Roeper Review, 5*(3), 21–23.

Leatt, D. J. (1987). *Developing student leaders: Exemplary school activities programs.* Eugene: University of Oregon.

Lee, V., & Bryk, A. (1986). Effects of single sex secondary schools on student achievement and attitudes. *Journal of Educational Psychology, 78,* 381–395.

Lehman, E. B., & Erdwins, C. K. (1981). The social and emotional adjustment of young, intellectually-gifted children. *Gifted Child Quarterly, 25,* 134–137.

Lemkau, J. P. (1983). Women in male-dominated professions: Distinguishing personality and background characteristics. *Psychology of Women Quarterly, 8,* 144–165.

L'Engle, M. (1962). *A wrinkle in time.* New York: Farrar, Straus & Giroux.

Leroux, J. A. (1986). Making theory real: Developmental theory and implications for education of gifted adolescents. *Roeper Review, 9,* 72–77.

Levy, J. (1982, November). *Brain research: Myths and realities for the gifted male and female.* Paper presented at the Illinois Gifted Education Conference, Chicago.

Lewis, B. A. (1991). *The kid's guide to social action: How to solve the social problems you choose—and turn creative thinking into positive action.* Minneapolis: Free Spirit.

Lewis, W. D. (1943). Some characteristics of very superior children. *Journal of Genetic Psychology, 62,* 301–309.

Lindsay, B. (1988). A lamp for Diogenes: Leadership giftedness and moral education. *Roeper Review, 11,* 8–11.

Locksley, A., & Douvan, E. (1980). Stress on female and male high school students. In R. E. Muuss (Ed.), *Adolescent behavior and society: A book of readings* (3rd ed., pp. 275–291). New York: Random House.

Lovecky, D. (1991). The sensitive gifted boy. *Understanding Our Gifted, 3*(4), 3.

Ludwig, G., & Cullinan, D. (1984). Behavior problems of gifted and nongifted elementary school girls and boys. *Gifted Child Quarterly, 28,* 37–40.

Lutfig, R. L., & Nichols, M. L. (1990). Assessing the social status of gifted students by their age peers. *Gifted Child Quarterly, 34,* 111–115.

Maddux, C. D., Scheiber, L. M., & Bass, J. E. (1982). Self-concept and social distance in gifted children. *Gifted Child Quarterly, 26,* 77–81.

Maker, C. J. (1982). *Teaching models in education of the gifted.* Rockville, MD: Aspen.

Mann, H. (1957). How *real* are friendships of gifted and typical children in a program of partial segregation? *Exceptional Children, 23,* 199–206.

Martinson, R. A. (1961). *Educational programs for gifted pupils.* Sacramento: California State Department of Education.

Maslow, A. H. (1968). *Toward a psychology of being* (2nd ed.). New York: D. Van Nostrand.

Matarazzo, J. D. (1981). David Wechsler (1896-1981). *American Psychologist, 36,* 1542–1543.

McCuen, T. L. (1929). Leadership and intelligence. *Education, 50,* 89–95.

Miller, R. V. (1956). Social status and socioempathic differences among mentally superior, mentally typical, and mentally retarded children. *Exceptional Children, 22,* 199–206.

Monks, F., & Ferguson, T. (1983). Gifted adolescents: An analysis of their psychosocial development. *Journal of Youth and Adolescence, 12,* 1–18.

Myers, I. B., & McCaulley, M. H. (1985). *Manual: A guide to the development and use of the Myers-Briggs Type Indicator.* Palo Alto, CA: Consulting Psychologists Press.

Myers, M. R., Slavin, M. J., & Southern, W. T. (1990). Emergence and maintenance of leadership among gifted students in group problem solving. *Roeper Review, 12,* 256–261.

Nelson, R. G. (1981). Values education for gifted adolescents. *Roeper Review, 3*(4), 10–11.

Noble, K. D. (1987). The dilemma of the gifted woman. *Psychology of Women Quarterly, 11,* 367–378.

Olszewski-Kubilius, P. (1989). Development of academic talent: The role of summer programs. In J. VanTassel-Baska & P. Olszewski-Kubilius (Eds.), *Patterns of influence on gifted learners: The home, the self, and the school* (pp. 214–230). New York: Teachers College Press.

Olszewski-Kubilius, P. M., & Kulieke, M. J. (1989). Personality dimensions of gifted adolescents. In J. VanTassel-Baska & P. Olszewski-Kubilius (Eds.), *Patterns of influence on gifted learners: The home, the self, and the school* (pp. 125–145). New York: Teachers College Press.

Olszewski-Kubilius, P. M., Kulieke, M. J., & Krasney, N. (1988). Personality dimensions of gifted adolescents: A review of the empirical literature. *Gifted Child Quarterly, 32,* 347–352.

Olszewski-Kubilius, P. M., Kulieke, M. J., Shaw, B., Willis, G. B., & Krasney, N. (1990). Predictors of achievement in mathematics for gifted males and females. *Gifted Child Quarterly, 34,* 64–71.

O'Shea, H. E. (1960). Friendship and the intellectually gifted child. *Exceptional Children, 26,* 327–335.

Passow, A. H. (1988). Educating gifted persons who are caring and concerned. *Roeper Review, 11,* 13–15.

Pasternak, M., & Silvey, L. (1969). Leadership patterns in gifted peer groups. *The Gifted Child Quarterly, 13,* 126–128.

Perry, S. M. (1987). *Giftedness: Living with it and liking it.* Greeley, CO: ALPS (Autonomous Learner Publications).

Petersen, A. (1988). Adolescent development. *Annual Review of Psychology, 39,* 583–607.

Pfeiffer, J. (1985). *A handbook of structured experiences for human relations training, VXI.* San Diego: University Associates.

Phelps, C. R. (1991). Identity formation in career development for gifted women. *Roeper Review, 13,* 140–141.

Piaget, J., & Inhelder, B. (1969). *The psychology of the child.* New York: Basic Books.

Piechowski, M. M. (1986). The concept of developmental potential. *Roeper Review, 8,* 190–197.

Piechowski, M. M. (1991). Emotional development and emotional giftedness. In. N. Colangelo & G. Davis (Eds.), *A handbook of gifted education* (pp. 285–306). Needham Heights, MA: Allyn & Bacon.

Pollin, L. (1983). The effects of acceleration on the social and emotional development of gifted students. In C. Benbow & J. C. Stanley (Eds.), *Academic precocity: Aspects of its development* (pp. 160–179). Baltimore: Johns Hopkins University Press.

Proctor, T. B., Black, K. N., & Feldhusen, J. F. (1986). Early admission of selected children to elementary school. A review of the research literature. *Journal of Educational Research, 80,* 70–76.

Purkey, W. W. (1966). Measured and professed personality characteristics of gifted high-school students and an analysis of their congruence. *Journal of Educational Research, 60,* 99–103.

Ramey, D. A. (1991). Gifted leadership. *Roeper Review, 14,* 16–19.

Ramos-Ford, V., & Gardner, H. (1991). Giftedness from a multiple intelligence perspective. In N. Colangelo & G. A. Davis (Eds.), *Handbook of gifted education* (pp. 55–64). Needham Heights, MA: Allyn & Bacon.

Reis, S. M. (1987). We can't change what we don't recognize: Understanding the special needs of gifted females. *Gifted Child Quarterly, 31,* 83–89.

Reis, S. M., & Callahan, C. M. (1989). Gifted females: They've come a long way—or have they? *Journal for the Education of the Gifted, 12,* 99–117.

Reis, S. M., & Dobyns, S. M. (1991). An annotated bibliography of nonfictional books and curricular materials to encourage gifted females. *Roeper Review, 13,* 129–134.

Rest, J. (1979). *Manual for the Defining Issues Test.* Minneapolis: University of Minnesota.

Richardson, W. B., & Feldhusen, J. F. (1988). *Leadership education: Developing skills for youth* (2nd Ed.). Monroe, NY: Trillium Press.

Riordan, C. (1990). *Girls and boys in school: Together or separate?* New York: Teachers College Press.

Robinson, A. (1990a). Cooperation or exploitation? The argument against cooperative learning for talented students. *Journal for the Education of the Gifted, 14,* 9–27.

Robinson, A. (1990b). Response to Slavin: Cooperation, consistency, and challenge for academically talented youth. *Journal for the Education of the Gifted, 14,* 31–36.

Robinson, N. M., & Noble, K. D. (1991). Social-emotional development and adjustment of gifted children. In M. C. Wang, M. C. Reynolds, & H. J. Walberg (Eds.), *Handbook of special education. Research and practice: Vol. 4. Emerging programs* (pp. 57–76). New York: Pergamon Press.

Robinson, N. M., & Weimer, L. J. (1991). Selection of candidates for early admission to kindergarten and first grade. In W. T. Southern & E. D. Jones (Eds.), *The academic acceleration of gifted children* (pp. 29–50). New York: Teachers College Press.

Roedell, W. C. (1985). Developing social competence in gifted preschool children. *Remedial and Special Education, 6*(4), 6–11.

Roedell, W. C. (1989). Early development of gifted children. In J. VanTassel-Baska & P. Olszewski-Kubilius (Eds.), *Patterns of influence on gifted learners: The home, the self, and the school* (pp. 13–28). New York: Teachers College Press.

Roeper, A. (1988). Should educators of the gifted and talented be more concerned with world issues? *Roeper Review, 11,* 12–13.

Roeper, A. (1990). *Educating children for life: The modern learning community.* Monroe, NY: Trillium.

Roeper, A. (1991). Focus on global awareness. *World Gifted, 12*(4), 19–21.

Roets, L. S. (1981). *Leadership: A skills training program: Ages 8–18.* New Sharon, IA: Leadership.

Rogers, C. (1969). Toward a modern approach to values: The valuing process in the mature person. In P. Kutz (Ed.), *Moral problems in contemporary society.* Englewood Cliffs, NJ: Prentice-Hall.

Rogers, M. T. (1986). *A comparative study of developmental traits of gifted and average children.* Unpublished doctoral dissertation, University of Denver, Colorado.

Ross, A., & Parker, M. (1980). Academic and social self-concepts of the academically gifted. *Exceptional Children, 47,* 6–10.

Rosser, P. (1989). *Sex bias in college and admissions tests: Why women lose out.* Cambridge, MA: National Center for Fair and Open Testing.

Sadker, M., Sadker, D., & Steindam, S. (1989). Gender equity and educational reform. *Educational Leadership, 46*(6), 44–47.

Schlowinski, E., & Reynolds, C. R. (1985). Dimensions of anxiety among high IQ children. *Gifted Child Quarterly, 29*(3), 125–130.

Schwartz, L. L. (1991). Guiding gifted girls. In R. M. Milgram (Ed.), *Counseling gifted and talented children: A guide for teachers, counselors and parents* (pp. 143–160). Norwood, NJ: Ablex.

Shannon, C. K. (1989). In the service of children: An open letter to global educators. *Roeper Review, 11,* 184–185.

Silverman, L. K. (1986a). Parenting young gifted children. *Journal of Children in Contemporary Society, 18,* 73–87.

Silverman, L. K. (1986b). What happens to the gifted girl? In C. J. Maker (Ed.), *Critical issues in gifted education: Vol. 1. Defensible programs for the gifted* (pp. 43–89). Rockville, MD: Aspen.

Silverman, L. K. (1991). Helping gifted girls reach their potential. *Roeper Review, 13,* 122–123.

Silverman, L. K. (1992). Editorial. *Understanding Our Gifted, 4*(4), 2.

Silverman, L. K., Chitwood, D. G., & Waters, J. L. (1986). Young gifted children: Can parents identify giftedness? *Topics in Early Childhood Special Education, 6*(1), 23–38.

Sisk, D. A. (1982). Caring and sharing: Moral development of gifted students. *Elementary School Journal, 82,* 221–229.

Sisk, D. A. (1988). A case for leadership development to meet the need for excellence in teachers. *Roeper Review, 11,* 43–46.

Sisk, D. A., & Shalcross, D. J. (1986). *Leadership: Making things happen.* Buffalo, NY: Bearly Limited.

Smith, D. L., Smith, L., & Barnette, J. (1991). Exploring the development of leadership giftedness. *Roeper Review, 14,* 7–12.

Spredemann-Dreyer, S. S. (1989). *The bookfinder 4: When kids need books.* Circle Pines, MN: American Guidance Service.

Stogdill, R. M. (1974). *Handbook of leadership: A survey of theory and research.* New York: Free Press.

Tannenbaum, A. J. (1972). A backward and forward glance at the gifted. *National Elementary Principal, 51*(5), 14–23.

Tannenbaum, A. J. (1983). *Gifted children: Psychological and educational perspectives.* New York: Macmillan.

Terman, L. M. (1916). *The measurement of intelligence.* Boston: Houghton Mifflin.

Terman, L. M. (1925). *Genetic studies of genius: Vol. 1. Mental and physical traits of a thousand gifted children.* Stanford, CA: Stanford University Press.

Terman, L. M. (1931). The gifted child. In C. Murchison (Ed.), *A handbook of child psychology* (pp. 568–584). Worcester, MA: Clark University Press.

Tidball, M. E. (1986). Baccalaureate origins of recent natural science doctorates. *Journal of Higher Education, 57,* 606–620.

Tway, E. (1981). *Reading ladders for human relations* (6th ed.). Washington, DC: American Council on Education.

VanTassel-Baska, J., Landau, M., & Olszewski, P. (1984). The benefits of summer programming for gifted adolescents. *Journal for the Education of the Gifted, 8,* 73–82.

Vare, J. V. (1979). Moral education for the gifted: A confluent model. *The Gifted Child Quarterly, 24,* 63–71.

Ward, V. S. (1980). *Differential education for the gifted.* Ventura, CA: Ventura County Superintendent of Schools Office.

Warner, M. LaV. (1923). Influence of mental level in the formation of boys' gangs. *Journal of Applied Psychology, 7,* 224–236.

Weber, J. (1981). Moral dilemmas in the classroom. *Roeper Review, 3*(4), 11–13.

Wilt, J. (1980). *A kid's guide to making friends*. Waco, TX: Educational Product Division, Word.

Witty, P. (1930). A study of one hundred gifted children. *University of Kansas Bulletin of Education, 2*(7).

Wright, L. (1990). The social and nonsocial behavior of precocious preschoolers during free play. *Roeper Review, 12,* 268–274.

Ziv, A., & Gadish, O. (1990). Humor and giftedness. *Journal for the Education of the Gifted, 13,* 332–345.

Conclusion

Linda Kreger Silverman

Emotional development is clearly as important as cognitive development and deserves equal consideration as a goal in educating the gifted. If we really desire our gifted children to actualize their potential, we need to help them develop their inner lives, not just prepare them to enter the work force.

It is hoped that this book will become a catalyst for the development of counseling programs throughout public and private schools, that it will assist classroom teachers in becoming teacher/counselors, and that it will enhance the capacity of psychologists, social workers, counselors and psychotherapists to work effectively with their gifted clients. The chapters in this book serve as a blueprint for establishing a developmental counseling program for gifted students. Typically school counselors are limited to scheduling and advisement of large numbers of students and barely have time to respond to emotional crises when they occur. In this book, we have reframed the role of the counselor so that he or she can orchestrate a program of prevention rather than remediation. The main goals of a preventive counseling program are to promote emotional development and self-actualization in the students. Such a program can teach students how to establish positive relations with peers, develop leadership skills, make appropriate career choices and assist friends in trouble. World concerns can be discussed along with action plans for making a difference.

A book of this nature cannot teach a novice all that there is to know about counseling or help seasoned counselors deal with all the various problems than can arise for young people. Teachers who are drawn to the teacher/counselor aspect of their roles should seek further training in counseling techniques through local institutions of higher education. A developmental counseling program potentially can surface longstanding problems in need of attention.

This should not deter the teacher/counselor from establishing these kinds of services to students. Instead, support systems should be actively engaged in the initial planning and a comprehensive referral network should be established early on. Agencies and individuals specializing in family counseling, substance abuse, suicide prevention, sexual abuse and crisis intervention, should all be contacted in advance so that these services can be activated easily, should the need arise. It would be helpful to provide specific contact persons in these agencies with information about the developmental counseling program as well as about issues and personality traits of the gifted. The Appendix contains a guide for locating individuals who specialize in working with gifted children and their families. Many of these centers also provide consultations to schools.

There is a great need for research on the emotional development of the gifted. We still do not know if these students are at greater risk than the general population for suicide, although the evidence appears to point in that direction. While most gifted children have excellent social adjustment, we are not clear what internal price is paid for social acceptance. There is almost no information available on the social and emotional development of culturally diverse gifted students and gifted students from low socio-economic circumstances. It is imperative that we fill these holes in our knowledge base. Research is also needed on the effects of the school reform movement on gifted girls, since this group has been overlooked in these efforts. The particular issues of the highly gifted need to be investigated more thoroughly.

Longitudinal data should be collected on the emotional development of the gifted to determine if their developmental potential actualizes in higher moral values in adult life. We need to locate and study those children who show unusual emotional sensitivity in childhood to determine the kinds of support systems that would enable their sensitivity to blossom into moral leadership. Nourishing the emotional as well as the cognitive resources of our gifted young could change the moral fabric of society.

Appendix

Bibliography for Parents

Linda Kreger Silverman

Adderholdt-Elliott, M. (1987). *Perfectionism: What's bad about being too good?* Minneapolis: Free Spirit.

Alvino, J. (1985). *Parents' guide to raising a gifted child: Recognizing and developing your child's potential.* Boston: Little, Brown.

Alvino, J. (1989). *Parents' guide to raising a gifted toddler: Recognizing and developing the potential of your child from birth to five years.* Boston: Little, Brown.

American Association for Gifted Children. (1978). *On being gifted.* New York: Walker.

American Association for Gifted Children. (1980). *Reaching out: Advocacy for the gifted and talented.* New York: Teachers College Press.

American Association for Gifted Children. (1981). *The gifted child, the family, and the community.* New York: Walker.

Armstrong, T. (1991). *Awakening your child's natural genius: Enhancing curiosity, creativity, and learning ability.* Los Angeles: Jeremy P. Tarcher.

Berger, S. L. (1989). *College planning for gifted students.* Reston, VA: The Council for Exceptional Children.

Bireley, M., & Genschaft, J. (Eds.). (1991). *Understanding the gifted adolescent: Educational, developmental, and multicultural issues.* New York: Teachers College Press.

Bloom, B. S., (Ed.). (1985). *Developing talent in young people.* New York: Ballantine Books.

Buescher, T. M. (Ed.). (1987). *Understanding gifted and talented adolescents: A resource guide for counselors, educators, and parents.* Evanston, IL: Center for Talent Development, Northwestern University.

Clark, B. (1992). *Growing up gifted: Developing the potential of children at home and at school* (4th ed.). New York: Macmillan.

Coffey, K., Ginsburg, G., Lockhart, C., McCartney, D., Nathan, C., & Wood, K. (1976). *Parentspeak on gifted and talented children.* Ventura, CA: Ventura County Superintendent of Schools.

Colangelo, N., & Davis, G. (Eds.). (1991). *Handbook of gifted education.* Needham Heights, MA: Allyn & Bacon.

Cox, J., Daniel, N., & Boston, B. (1985). *Educating able learners: Programs and promising practices.* Austin, TX: University of Texas Press.

Delisle, J. R. (1987). *Gifted kids speak out.* Minneapolis: Free Spirit.

Delisle, J. R. (1992). *Guiding the social and emotional development of gifted youth: A practical guide for educators and counselors.* New York: Longman.

Delisle, J., & Galbraith, J. (1987). *The gifted kids survival guide II.* Minneapolis: Free Spirit.

Delp, J. L., & Martinson, R. A. (1977). *A handbook for parents of gifted and talented.* Ventura, CA: Ventura County Superintendent of Schools Office.

Eby, J. W., & Smutny., J. F. (1990). *A thoughtful overview of gifted education.* White Plains, NY: Longman.

Engel, J. (1987). *It's OK to be gifted or talented: A parent/child manual.* New York: St. Martin's Press.

Farris, D. (1991). *Type tales: Teaching type to children.* Palo Alto, CA: Consulting Psychologists Press.

Feldhusen, J., VanTassel-Baska, J., & Seeley, K. (Eds.). (1989). *Excellence in educating the gifted.* Denver: Love.

Flack, J. D. (1989). *Inventing, Inventions and Inventors.* Englewood, CO: Teacher Ideas Press.

Flowers, J. V., Horsman, J., & Schwartz, B. (1982). *Raising your gifted child.* Englewood Cliffs, NJ: Prentice-Hall

Freeman, J. (1991). *Gifted children growing up.* London: Cassell Educational Limited.

Galbraith, J. (1983, 1984). *The gifted kids survival guides, I & II.* Minneapolis: Free Spirit.

Ginsburg, G., & Harrison, C. H. (1977). *How to help your gifted child.* New York: Monarch.

Goertzel, V., & Goertzel, M. G. (1962). *Cradles of eminence.* Boston: Little, Brown.

Goertzel, M. G., Goertzel, V., & Goertzel, T. G. (1978). *Three hundred eminent personalities.* San Francisco: Jossey-Bass.

Golant, S. K. (1991). *The joys and challenges of raising a gifted child.* New York: Prentice-Hall.

Graue, E. B. (1982). *Is your child gifted? A handbook for parents of gifted preschoolers.* San Diego, CA: Oak Tree.

Hall, E. G., & Skinner, N. (1980). *Somewhere to turn: Strategies for parents of the gifted and talented.* New York: Teachers College Press.

Hollingworth, L. S. (1942). *Children above 180 IQ Stanford-Binet: Origin and development.* Yonkers-on-Hudson, NY: World Book.

Horowitz, F. D., & O'Brien, M. (1985). *The gifted and talented: Developmental perspectives.* Washington, DC: American Psychological Association.

Kanigher, H. (1977). *Everyday enrichment for gifted children at home and at school.* Ventura, CA: Ventura County Superintendent of Schools.

Kaufmann, F. (1976). *Your gifted child and you.* Reston, VA: The Council for Exceptional Children.

Keirsey, D., & Bates, M. (1978). *Please understand me: Character and temperament types.* Del Mar, CA: Prometheus Nemesis Books.

Kerr, B. A. (1985). *Smart girls, gifted women.* Columbus, OH: Ohio Psychology.

Kerr, B. (1991). *A handbook for counseling the gifted and talented.* Alexandria, VA: American Counseling Association.

Keyes, F. (1985). *Exploring careers for the gifted* (Rev. ed.). New York: Richard Rosen Press.

Khatena, J. (1978). *The creatively gifted child: Suggestions for parents and teachers.* New York: Vantage Press.

Kroeger, O., & Theusen, J. M. (1988). *Type talk: Or how to determine your personality type and change your life.* New York: Delacorte Press.

LeGuin, U. K. (1976). *Very far away from anywhere else.* New York: Bantam.

Levinson, H. N. (1984). *Smart but feeling dumb.* New York: Warner Books.

Lewis, B. A. *The kids guide to social action: How to solve the social problems you choose—and turn creative thinking into positive action.* Minneapolis: Free Spirit.

Maker, C. J. (1986). *Critical issues in gifted education: Vol. 1: Defensible programs for the gifted.* Austin, TX: Pro-Ed.

Marone, N. (1988). *How to father a successful daughter.* New York: McGraw-Hill.

Milgram, R. M. (Ed.). (1991). *Counseling gifted and talented children: A guide for teachers, counselors and parents.* Norwood, NJ: Ablex.

Miller, A. (1981). *The drama of the gifted child.* New York: Basic Books.

Moore, L. P. (1981). *Does this mean my kid's a genius?* New York: McGraw-Hill.

Papert, S. (1980). *Mindstorms: Children, computers, and powerful ideas.* New York: Basic Books.

Parenting your gifted child. (1985). *Roeper Review,* Symposia Series, No. 1 (October).

Perino, S. C., & Perino, J. (1981). *Parenting the gifted: Developing the promise.* New York: R. R. Bowker.

Perry, S. M. (1985). *Giftedness: Living with it and liking it.* Greeley, CO: ALPS (Autonomous Learner Publications).

Roedell, W., Jackson, N., & Robinson, H. (1980). *Gifted young children.* New York: Teachers College Press.

Roeper, A. (1990). *Educating children for life: The modern learning community.* Monroe, NY: Trillium Press.

Saunders, J., & Espeland, P. (1986). *Bringing out the best: A resource guide for parents of young gifted children.* Minneapolis: Free Spirit.

Silverman, L. K. (1988). *Parenting the gifted child* (3rd ed.). Denver: Gifted Child Development Center.

Smutny, J. F., Veenker, K., & Veenker, S. (1989). *Your gifted child: How to recognize and develop the special talents of your child from birth to age seven.* New York: Facts on File.

Southern, W. T., & Jones, E. D. (Eds.). (1991). *The academic acceleration of gifted children.* New York: Teachers College Press.

Stone, N. A. (1989). *"Gifted" is **not** a dirty word.* Irvine, CA: Technicom. (About adult giftedness.)

Takacs, C. A. (1986). *Enjoy your gifted child.* Syracuse, NY: Syracuse University Press.

Turecki, S., & Tonner, L. (1985). *The difficult child.* New York: Bantam.

Tuttle, F. B., & Becker, L. A. (1983). *Characteristics and identification of gifted and talented students* (2nd ed.). Washington, DC: National Education Association.

VanTassel-Baska, J. (Ed.) (1990). *A practical guide to counseling the gifted in a school setting* (2nd ed.). Reston, VA: Council for Exceptional Children.

VanTassel-Baska, J., & Olszewski-Kubilius, P. (Eds.). (1989). *Patterns of influence on gifted learners: The home, the self, and the school.* New York: Teachers College Press.

Walker, S. Y. (1991). *The survival guide for parents of gifted kids: How to understand, live with, and stick up for your gifted child.* Minneapolis: Free Spirit.

Webb, J. T., Meckstroth, E. A., & Tolan, S. S. (1982). *Guiding the gifted child: A practical source for parents and teachers.* Columbus: Ohio Psychology.

Wetherall, C. F. (1989). *The gifted kids' guide to creative thinking.* Minneapolis: Paradon.

Whitmore, J. R. (1980). *Giftedness, conflict and underachievement.* Needham Heights, MA: Allyn & Bacon.

Whitmore, J. R. (1986). *Intellectual giftedness in young children: Recognition and development.* New York: The Haworth Press.

Books for Children Featuring Gifted Children

Linda Kreger Silverman and Deirdre Lovecky

Arkin, A. (1976). *The Lemming Condition*. New York: Harper Collins.

Arthur, R. M. (1967). *Requiem for a Princess*. New York: Atheneum.

Auel, J. M. (1980). *The Clan of the Cave Bear*. New York: Crown. (Young Adult). (First of a three-part series.)

Avi. (1990). *The True Confessions of Charlotte Doyle*. New York: Orchard Books.

Avi. (1991). *Nothing But the Truth*. New York: Orchard Books. (Young Adult.)

Avi. (1992). *Blue Heron*. New York: Bradbury Press. (Young Adult.)

Babbitt, N. (1975). *Tuck Everlasting*. New York: Farrar, Straus & Giroux.

Bell, W. (1986). *Crabbe's Journey*. Boston: Little, Brown. (Young Adult).

Blume, J. (1970). *Are You There, God? It's Me, Margaret*. New York: Bradbury.

Blume, J. (1972). *Otherwise Known as Sheila the Great*. New York: Dutton.

Blume, J. (1972). *Tales of a Fourth Grade Nothing*. New York: Dutton.

Bonhan, F. (1968). *The Nitty Gritty*. New York: Dutton.

Boyd, C. D. *Charlie Pippin*. New York: Viking Penguin.

Brink, C. (1973). *Caddie Woodlawn*. New York: Macmillan.

Brittain, B. (1991). *Wings*. New York: Harper Collins.

Brooks, B. (1986). *Midnight Hour Encores*. New York: Harper & Row. (Young Adult.)

Brooks, J. (1992). *Knee Hold*. New York: Orchard Books. (Young Adult.)

Brown, I. (1981). *Morning Glory Afternoon*. Hillsboro, OR: Blue Heron.

Bryce, C. (1989). *The Power of One*. New York: Ballantine. (Young Adult.)

Bunting, E. (1990). *The Wall*. Boston: Clarion Books.

Burnett, F. (1987). *The Secret Garden*. New York: Scholastic.

Burnett, F. (1989). *The Little Princess*. New York: Putnam.

Burningham, J. (1978). *Time to Get Out of the Bath, Shirley*. New York: Crowell.

Calvert, P. (1980). *The Snowbird*. New York: Charles Scribner's Sons.

Cameron, E. (1971). *A Room Made of Windows*. Boston: Little, Brown. (First in a series.)

Castaneda, O. (1991). *Among the Volcanoes*. New York: Lodestar.

Cauvin, P. (1979). *A Little Romance*. New York: Dell. (Young Adult). (also, film/video from Warner Bros., 1979).

Clark, A. (1990). *A Ghost from the Grand Banks*. New York: Bantam. (Young Adult.)

Cleaver, V., & Cleaver, B. (1971). *I Would Rather Be a Turnip*. Philadelphia: Lippincott.

Cohen, B. (1991). *213 Valentines*. New York: Henry Holt.

Cole, B. (1989). *Celine*. New York: Farrar, Straus & Giroux. (Young Adult.)

Conford, E. (1977). *And This Is Laura*. Boston: Little, Brown.

Corcoran, B. (1986). *I Am the Universe*. New York: Atheneum.

Cresswell, H. (1977). *Ordinary Jack*. New York: Macmillan. ("The Bagthorpe Saga," Book 1)

Cresswell, H. (1978). *Absolute Zero*. New York: Macmillan. ("The Bagthorpe Saga," Book 2)

Cresswell, H. (1978). *Bagthorpes Unlimited*. New York: Macmillan.

Cresswell, H. (1979). *Bagthorpes vs. The World*. New York: Macmillan.

Cresswell, H. (1984). *Bagthorpes Abroad*. New York: Macmillan.

Cresswell, H. (1986). *Bagthorpes Haunted*. New York: Macmillan.

Cresswell, H. (1989). *Bagthorpes Liberated*. New York: Macmillan.

Cunningham, J. (1965). *Dorp Dead*. New York: Pantheon Books.

Dahl, R. (1982). *George's Marvelous Medicine*. New York: Bantam.

Dahl, R. (1988). *Matilda*. New York: Viking Penguin.

Danziger, P. (1974). *The Cat Ate My Gymsuit*. New York: Delacorte Press.

DeAngelo, M. (1974). *Fiddlestrings*. New York: Doubleday.

deTrevino, E. B. (1965). *I Juan de Pareja*. New York: Bell Books.

Dickinson, P. (1989). *Eva*. New York: Delacorte Press. (Young Adult.)

Duncan, L. (1971). *A Gift of Magic*. Boston: Little, Brown. (Young Adult.)

Dunlop, E. (1975). *Elizabeth*. New York: Holt, Rinehart & Winston.

Fenner, C. (1991). *Randall's Wall*. New York: McElderry Books.

Fisk, N. (1980). *A Rag, A Bone and a Hank of Hair*. New York: Crown.

Fitzgerald, J. D. (1967). *The Great Brain*. New York: Dial. (The first of an extensive series).

Fitzhugh, L. (1964). *Harriet, the Spy*. New York: Dell Yearling.

Fitzhugh, L. (1965). *The Long Secret: The Further Adventures of Harriet, the Spy*. New York: Dell Yearling.

Fitzhugh, L. (1974). *Nobody's Family is Going to Change*. New York: Farrar, Straus & Giroux.

Gardam, J. (1977). *Bilgewater*. New York: Greenwillow.

George, J. C. (1959). *My Side of the Mountain*. New York: E. P. Dutton.

Greene, B. (1973). *Summer of My German Soldier*. New York: Dial.

Greene, B. (1974). *Philip Hall Likes Me. I Reckon Maybe*. New York: Dial Press.

Greene, B. (1978). *Morning is a Long Time Coming*. New York: Dial.

Greene, C. (1969). *A Girl Called Al*. New York: Viking.

Greene, C. (1975). *I Know You, Al*. New York: Viking.

Greene, C. (1979). *Your Old Pal, Al*. New York: Viking.

Greene, C. (1982). *Al(exandra) the Great*. New York: Viking Press.

Greene, C. (1986). *Isabelle and Little Orphan Frannie*. New York: Viking Kestrel.

Greenwald, S. (1983). *Will the Real Gertrude Hollings Please Stand Up?* Boston: Little, Brown. (About Dyslexia.)

Greenwald, S. (1987). *Alvin Webster's Surefire Plan for Success (And How it Failed)*. Boston: Little, Brown.

Greenwald, S. (1991). *Here's Hermione. A Rosy Cole Production*. Boston: Little, Brown.

Gripe, M. (1969). *Hugo and Josephine*. New York: Dell.

Gripe, M. (1976). *In the Time of the Bells*. New York: Delacorte.

Hamilton, V. (1971). *The Planet of Junior Brown*. New York: Macmillan.

Hamilton, V. (1976). *Arilla Sun Down*. New York: Greenwillow Books. (Young Adult.)

Hamilton, V. (1979). *Justice and Her Brothers*. New York: Wm. Morrow. ("The Justice Cycle," Book 1.)

Hamilton, V. (1980). *Dustland*. New York: Wm. Morrow. ("The Justice Cycle," Book 2.)

Hamilton, V. (1981). *The Gathering*. New York: Wm. Morrow. ("The Justice Cycle," Book 3.)

Hassler, J. (1981). *Jemmy*. New York: Atheneum.

Hermes, P. (1990). *I Hate Being Gifted*. New York: Putnam.

Hersey, J. (1961). *The Child Buyer*. New York: Bantam. (Young Adult.)

Hodges, M. (1967). *The Hatching of Joshua Cobb*. New York: Farrar, Straus & Giroux.

Hoffman, M. (1991). *Amazing Grace*. New York: Dial.

Holmann, F. (1974). *Slake's Limbo*. New York: Scribner's.

Hoover, H. M. (1976). *Treasures of the Morrow*. New York: Four Winds Press (Young Adult.)

Howker, J. (1989). *Badger on the Barge and Other Stories*. New York: Greenwillow Books.

Hunt, I. (1978). *The Lottery Rose*. New York: Scribner's.

Hunter, M. (1972). *A Sound of Chariots*. New York: Harper & Row.

Hurwitz, J. (1988). *Teacher's Pet*. New York: Morrow.

Jarrell, R. (1963). *The Bat Poet*. New York: Macmillan.

Johnston, N. (1977). *A Mustard Seed of Magic*. New York: Atheneum.

Karr, K. (1990). *It Ain't Always Easy*. New York: Farrar, Straus & Giroux.

Kerr, J. (1971). *When Hitler Stole Pink Rabbit*. New York: Dell.

Kerr, J. (1975). *The Other Way Round*. New York: Coward, McCann & Geohagen.

Kerr, M. E. (1975). *Is that You, Miss Blue?* New York: Harper & Row. (Young Adult.)

Kerr, M. E. (1986). *Night Kites*. New York: Harper & Row. (Young Adult.)

Key, A. (1965). *The Forgotten Door*. Philadelphia: Westminster Press.

Keyes, D. (1966). *Flowers for Algernon*. New York: Harcourt Brace Jovanovich. (Young Adult.)

Knowles, J. (1960). *A Separate Peace*. New York: Macmillan. (Young Adult.)

Konecky, E. (1976). *Allegra Maud Goldman*. New York: Dell. (Young Adult.)

Konigsburg, E. L. (1967). *From the Mixed-Up Files of Mrs. Basil E. Frankweiler*. New York: Atheneum.

Konigsburg, E. L. (1968). *Jennifer, Hecate, Macbeth, William McKinley, and Me, Elizabeth*. New York: Atheneum.

Konigsburg, E. L. (1972). *(George)*. New York: Atheneum.

Konigsburg, E. L. (1976). *Father's Arcane Daughter*. New York: Atheneum.

Konigsburg, E. L. (1986). *Up from Jericho Tel*. New York: Atheneum.

Krumgold, J. (1967). *Henry 3*. New York: Atheneum.

Lasky, K. (1981). *The Night Journey*. New York: F. Warne.

Lasky, K. (1986). *Pageant*. New York: Four Winds.

LeGuin, U. (1968). *The Wizard of Earthsea*. Berkeley, CA: Parnassus Press. (Volume 1 in "The Earthsea Trilogy.")

LeGuin, U. (1971). *The Tombs of Atuan*. New York: Atheneum. (Volume 2 in "The Earthsea Trilogy.")

LeGuin, U. (1972). *The Farthest Shore*. New York: Atheneum. (Volume 3 in "The Earthsea Trilogy.")

LeGuin, U. (1990). *Tehanu: The Last Book of Earthsea*. New York: Atheneum.

LeGuin, U. (1976). *Very Far Away From Anywhere Else*. New York: Bantam. (Young Adult).

LeGuin, U. (1979). *Leese Webster*. New York: Atheneum.

L'Engle, M. (1962). *A Wrinkle in Time*. New York: Farrar, Straus, & Giroux. (Book 1 in series.)

L'Engle, M. (1973). *A Wind in the Door*. New York: Farrar, Straus & Giroux. (Book 2 in series.)

L'Engle, M. (1978). *A Swiftly Tilting Planet*. New York: Farrar, Straus & Giroux. (Book 3 in series.)

L'Engle, M. (1986). *Many Waters*. New York: Farrar, Straus & Giroux. (Book 4 in series.)

L'Engle, M. (1989). *An Acceptable Time*. New York: Farrar, Straus & Giroux. (Book 5 in series.)

L'Engle, M. (1968). *The Young Unicorns*. New York: Farrar, Straus & Giroux.

L'Engle, M. (1969). *Prelude*. New York: Vanguard Press.

L'Engle, M. (1983). *And Both Were Young*. New York: Delacorte Press.

Levitin, S. (1976). *The Mark of Conte*. New York: Macmillan. (Young Adult.)

Levitin, S. (1977). *Beyond Another Door*. New York: Atheneum.

Little, J. (1972). *From Anna*. New York: Harper Collins.

Little, J. (1977). *Listen for the Singing*. New York: Harper Collins.

Lord, B. (1984). *In the Year of the Boar and Jackie Robinson*. New York: Harper & Row.

Love, S. (1978). *Melissa's Medley*. New York: Harcourt, Brace, Jovanovich.

Lowry, L. (1979). *Anastasia Krupnik*. Boston: Houghton Mifflin.

Lowry, L. (1981). *Anastasia Again*. Boston: Houghton Mifflin.

Lowry, L. (1982). *Anastasia At Your Service*. Boston: Houghton Mifflin.

Lowry, L. (1984). *Anastasia, Ask Your Analyst*. Boston: Houghton Mifflin.

Lowry, L. (1985). *Anastasia on Her Own*. Boston: Houghton Mifflin.

Lowry, L. (1986). *Anastasia Has the Answers*. Boston: Houghton Mifflin.

Lowry, L. (1987). *Anastasia's Chosen Career*. Boston: Houghton Mifflin.

Lowry, L. (1988). *All About Sam*. Boston: Houghton Mifflin.

MacKinnon, B. (1984). *The Meantime*. Boston: Houghton Mifflin.

MacLachlan, P. (1988). *The Facts and Fictions of Minna Pratt*. New York: Harper & Row.

Mahy, M. (1986). *The Catalogue of the Universe*. New York: Atheneum. (Young Adult).

Mahy, M. (1987). *The Tricksters*. New York: Scholastic. (Young Adult.)

Martin, A. M. (1988). *Very Turly, Shirley*. New York: Holiday House. (About Giftedness and Dyslexia.)

Mathis, S. B. (1972). *Teacup Full of Roses*. New York: Viking. (Young Adult.)

McKinley, R. (1984). *The Hero and the Crown*. New York: Greenwillow Books.

Moser, D. (1975). *A Heart to the Hawks*. New York: Atheneum.

Murphy, S. R. (1974). *Poor Jenny, Bright as a Penny*. New York: Viking.

Murray, M. (1988). *Like Seabirds Flying Home*. (Young Adult).

Newman, R. (1967). *The Boy Who Could Fly*. New York: Atheneum.

Nostlinger, C. (1976). *Konrad*. New York: Avon.

O'Brien, R. C. (1971). *Mrs. Frisby and the Rats of Nimh*. New York: Atheneum.

O'Neal, Z. (1980). *The Language of Goldfish*. New York: Viking. (Young Adult.)

O'Neal, Z. (1985). *In Summer Light*. New York: Viking Kestrel. (Young Adult).

Paterson, K. (1974). *Of Nightingales that Weep*. New York: Thomas Y. Crowell.

Paterson, K. (1976). *The Master Puppeteer*. New York: Thomas Y. Crowell.

Paterson, K. (1977). *Bridge to Teribithia*. New York: Thomas Y. Crowell.

Paterson, K. (1978). *The Great Gilly Hopkins*. New York: Thomas Y. Crowell.

Paterson, K. (1980). *Jacob Have I Loved*. New York: Avon. (Young Adult.)

Paterson, K. (1985). *Come Sing, Jimmy Jo*. New York: E. P. Dutton.

Paterson, K. (1991). *Lyddie*. New York: Lodestar.

Paulsen, G. (1987). *Dogsong*. New York: Puffin. (Young Adult.)

Paulsen, G. (1989). *Hatchet*. New York: Puffin. (Young Adult.)

Peck, R. (1985). *Remembering the Good Times*. New York: Delacorte Press. (Young Adult).

Peyton, K. M. (1970). *Pennington's Last Term*. New York: Thomas Y. Crowell. (Young Adult).

Peyton, K. M. (1970). *Pennington's Seventeenth Summer*. New York: Thomas Y. Crowell. (Young Adult).

Peyton, K. M. (1972). *The Beethoven Medal*. New York: Thomas Y. Crowell. (Young Adult).

Peyton, K. M. (1973). *Pennington's Heir*. New York: Thomas Y. Crowell. (Young Adult).

Peyton, K. M. (1973). *A Pattern of Roses*. New York: Thomas Y. Crowell. (Young Adult.)

Peyton, K. M. (1977). *Prove Yourself a Hero*. London: Oxford University Press. (Young Adult).

Peyton, K. M. (1981). *Dear Fred*. New York: Philomel.

Pfeffer, S. (1989). *Dear Dad, Love Laurie*. New York: Scholastic.

Picard, B. L. (1966). *One is One*. New York: Holt, Rinehart, & Winston.

Pinkwater, J. (1989). *Buffalo Brenda*. New York: Macmillan.

Pinkwater, J. (1991). *Tails of the Bronx*. New York: Macmillan.

Potok, C. (1967). *The Chosen*. New York: Random House. (Young Adult.)

Potok, C. (1969). *The Promise*. New York: Random House. (Young Adult.)

Raskin, E. (1978). *The Westing Game*. New York: Avon Books.

Rodgers, M. (1972). *Freaky Friday*. New York: Harper & Row.

Rodgers, M. (1974). *Billions for Boris*. New York: Harper & Row.

Rogers, P. (1973). *The Rare One*. Nashville, TN: Thomas Nelson.

Roe, E. (1989). *Circle of Light*. New York: Harper & Row.

Ryan, M. (1991). *My Sister is Driving Me Crazy*. New York: Simon & Schuster.

Sachar, L. (1991). *Someday Angeline*. New York: Avon.

Sachar, L. (1991). *Dogs Don't Tell Jokes*. New York: Knopf.

Sachs, M. (1991). *Circles*. New York: Dutton.

Say, A. (1979). *The Ink-Keeper's Apprentice*. New York: Harper & Row. (Young Adult.)

Sebestzen, O. (1979). *Words by Heart*. Boston: Little, Brown.

Sebestzen, O. (1989). *The Girl in the Box.* Boston: Little, Brown.

Sefton, C. (1964). *In a Blue Velvet Dress.* New York: Harper & Row.

Shecter, B. (1967). *Conrad's Castle.* New York: Harper.

Shiras, W. H. (1953). *Children of the Atom.* New York: Gnome Press (available from Science Fiction Book Club).

Sleator, W. (1983). *Fingers.* New York: Atheneum. (Young Adult.)

Sleator, W. (1985). *Singularity.* New York: E. P. Dutton.

Sleator, W. (1986). *The Boy Who Reversed Himself.* New York: E. P. Dutton.

Sleator, W. (1988). *The Duplicate.* New York: E. P. Dutton.

Sleator, W. (1990). *Strange Attractors.* New York: E. P. Dutton.

Smith, B. (1943). *A Tree Grows in Brooklyn.* New York: Harper & Row. (Young Adult.)

Snyder, Z. (1987). *And Condors Danced.* New York: Delacorte.

Snyder, Z. (1990). *Libby on Wednesday.* New York: Delacorte Press.

Smith, D. B. (1978). *Dreams and Drummers.* New York: Thomas Y. Crowell.

Sobol, D. (1963). *Encyclopedia Brown, Boy Detective.* New York: Elsevier/ Nelson Books. (The first of an extensive series; some published by Bantam Skylark, Delacorte, Morrow, T. Nelson, and Four Winds Press.)

Stolz, M. (1973). *Lands End.* New York: Harper & Row.

Stone, B. (1988). *Been Clever, Forever.* New York: Harper & Row. (Young Adult.)

Sypher, L. (1991). *Cousins and Circuses.* New York: Puffin.

Sypher, L. (1991). *The Edge of Nowhere.* New York: Puffin.

Sypher, L. (1991). *The Spell of the Northern Lights.* New York: Puffin.

Sypher, L. (1991). *The Turnabout Year.* New York: Puffin.

Talbert, M. (1985). *Dead Birds Singing.* Boston: Little Brown. (Young Adult.)

Taylor, M. (1976). *Roll of Thunder, Hear My Cry.* New York: Dial.

Taylor, M. (1981). *Let the Circle Be Unbroken.* New York: Dial.

Taylor, M. (1990). *The Road to Memphis.* New York: Dial.

Terris, S. (1990). *Author, Author.* New York: Farrar, Straus & Giroux.

Thompson, J. F. (1987). *Simon Pure.* New York: Scholastic. (Young Adult.)

Tolan, S. (1980). *The Last of Eden.* New York: Frederick Warne. (Young Adult).

Tolan, S. (1981). *No Safe Harbors.* New York: Scribner's. (Young Adult).

Tolan, S. (1983). *A Time to Fly Free.* New York: Scribner's.

Tolan, S. (1983). *The Great Skinner Strike.* New York: Macmillan.

Tolan, S. (1986). *The Great Skinner Enterprises.* New York: Four Winds Press.

Tolan, S. (1987). *The Great Skinner Getaway.* New York: Four Winds Press.

Tolan, S. (1988). *The Great Skinner Homestead.* New York: Four Winds Press.

Tolan, S. (1986). *Pride of the Peacock.* New York: Scribner's. (Young Adult).

Tolan, S. (1988). *A Good Courage.* New York: Morrow Jr. Books. (Young Adult).

Tolan, S. (1990). *Plague Year*. New York: Morrow Jr. Books. (Young Adult).

Tolan, S. (1991). *Marcy Hooper and the Greatest Treasure in the World*. New York: William Morrow.

Tolan, S. (1992). *Sophie and the Sidewalk Man*. New York: Four Winds Press.

Towne, M. (1990). *Steve the Sure*. New York: Atheneum.

Ure, J. (1985). *The Most Important Thing*. New York: W. Morrow. (Young Adult).

Vinke, H. (1984). *The Short Life of Sophie Scholl*. New York: Harper & Row. (Young Adult).

Voigt, C. (1981). *The Homecoming*. New York: Atheneum. (Young Adult.)

Voigt, C. (1982). *Dicey's Song*. New York: Atheneum. (Young Adult.)

Voigt, C. (1987). *Come a Stranger*. New York: Ballantine. (Young Adult.)

Walsh, J. (1991). *A Chance Child*. New York: Farrar, Straus & Giroux.

Weiman, E. (1982). *It Takes Brains*. New York: Atheneum.

Wells, R. (1980). *When No One Was Looking*. New York: The Dial Press.

Whitaker, A. (1986). *Dream Sister*. New York: Dell.

Wilhelm, K. (1986). *Huysman's Pets*. New York: Ace. (Young Adult.)

Williams, B. W. (1983). *Mitzi's Honeymoon with Nana Potts*. New York: Dell.

Williams, V. B. (1986). *Cherries and Cherry Pits*. New York: Greenwillow Books.

Williams, J., & Abrashkin, R. (1968). *Danny Dunn and the Homework Machine*. New York: McGraw-Hill.

Wojciechowska, M. (1964). *Shadow of a Bull*. New York: Atheneum.

Wojciechowska, M. (1970). *Don't Play Dead Before You Have To*. New York: Harper & Row.

Wolff, V. (1991). *The Mozart Season*. New York: Holt. (Young Adult.)

Wood, M. (1988). *The Secret Life of Hilary Thorne*. New York: Macmillan.

Woodson, J. (1990). *The Last Summer with Maizon*. New York: Dell Yearling.

Wyndham, J. (1983). *The Chrysalids*. Guilford, CN: Ulverscroft.

Yep, L. (1977). *Child of the Owl*. New York: Harper & Row.

Yep, L. (1982). *Kind Hearts and Gentle Monsters*. New York: Harper & Row.

Yep, L. (1991). *The Star Fisher*. New York: Morrow.

Some of these books are no longer in print. However, they are well worth looking for in the library or ordering from interlibrary loan.

The following resources provide annotations of a number of these books. Some suggest age levels based on the ages of the main characters and the developmental issues faced; however, gifted readers often read advanced material. Some of the resources also provide instructional guidelines and sample lessons for use with gifted students.

Amerikaner, S., & Simon, S. (1988). *The gifted and talented catalogue*. New York: Price Stern Sloan.

Baskin, B. H., & Harris, K. H. (1980). *Books for the gifted child.* New York: R. R. Bowker.

Flack, J., & Lamb, P. (1984). Making use of gifted characters in literature. *G/C/T,* No. 34 (Sept/Oct), 3–11.

Halsted, J. (1988). *Guiding gifted readers from pre-school to high school: A handbook for parents, teachers, counselors and librarians.* Columbus, OH: Ohio Psychology.

Hauser, P., & Nelson, G. A. (1988). *Books for the gifted child.* New York: R. R. Bowker.

Karnes, F., & Collins, E. C. (1980). *Handbook of instructional resources and references for teaching the gifted.* Needham Heights, MA: Allyn & Bacon.

Polette, N. (1984). *Books and real life: A guide for gifted students and teachers.* Jefferson, NC: McFarland.

Polette, N., & Hamlin. M. (1980). *Exploring books with gifted children.* Littleton, CO: Libraries Unlimited.

Schroeder-Davis, S. (1991). Books for use in counseling gifted students. In B. Kerr. *A handbook for counseling the gifted and talented* (pp. 188–206). Alexandria, VA: American Counseling Association.

Sisk, D. (1982). Caring and sharing: Moral development of gifted students. *The Elementary School Journal, 82,* 221–229.

Spredemann-Dreyer, S. S. (1989). *The Bookfinder 4: When kids need books.* Circle Pines, MN: American Guidance Service.

Tolan, S. (1983). Novels for children and young adults which have exceptionally gifted characters. Unpublished paper.

Tolan, S. The Reading Room. Regular feature column in *Understanding Our Gifted.* Boulder, CO: Open Space Communications, Inc.

Tway, E. (1980). The gifted child in literature. *Language Arts, 57*(1), 14–20.

Biographies for Gifted Students

Jerry Flack and Deirdre Lovecky

Anderson, W. (1987). *Laura Ingalls Wilder: Pioneer and Author*. New York: Kipling Press.

Angelou, M. (1969). *I Know Why the Caged Bird Sings*. New York: Bantam. (Young Adult.)

Archer, J. (1968). *The Unpopular Ones*. New York: Crowell-Collier Press.

Asimov, I. (1979). *In Memory Yet Green*. New York: Avon Books. (Young Adult.)

Baker, R. (1982). *Growing Up*. New York: New American Library. (Young Adult.)

Bateson, M. C. (1985). *With a Daughter's Eye*. New York: Washington Square Press. (Young Adult.) (Biography of Margaret Mead.)

Berry, M. (1988). *Georgia O'Keeffe*. New York: Chelsea House Publishers.

Blos, J. W. (1991). *The Heroine of the Titanic*. New York: Morrow Junior Books.

Boslough, J. (1985). *Stephen Hawking's Universe*. New York: William Morrow.

Brower, K. (1978). *The Starship and the Canoe*. New York: Harper & Row. (Young Adult.)

Carpenter, H. (1985). *Tolkien: A Biography*. New York: Ballantine Books. (Young Adult.)

Cleary, B. (1988). *A Girl from Yamhill: A Memoir*. New York: Dell.

Cohen, D. (1987). *Carl Sagan: Superstar Scientist*. New York: Dodd, Mead.

Cousins, M. (1965). *The Story of Thomas Alva Edison*. New York: Random House.

Cremaschi, G. (1982). *Albert Schweitzer*. Englewood Cliffs, NJ: Silver Burdett.

Dash, J. (1991). *Triumph of Discovery: Women Scientists Who Won the Nobel Prize*. Englewood Cliffs, NJ: Julian Messner.

Delisle, J. (1991). *Kid Stories: Biographies of 20 Young People You'd Like to Know*. Minneapolis, MN: Free Spirit.

Dillard, A. (1987). *An American Childhood*. New York: Harper & Row. (Young Adult.)

Durwood, P. (1988). *Beatrix Potter: Creator of Peter Rabbit*. New York: The Kipling Press.

Faber, D. (1985). *Eleanor Roosevelt: First Lady to the World*. New York: Viking Penguin.

Ferris, J. (1991). *Native American Doctor: The Story of Susan LaFlesche Picotte*. Minneapolis, MN: Carolrhoda Books.

Fisher, A., & Rabe, O. (1968). *We Alcotts*. New York: Atheneum.

Fradin, D. (1987). *Remarkable Children*. Boston: Little, Brown.

Freedman, R. (1987). *Lincoln: A Photobiography*. New York: Clarion Books.

Fritz, J. (1982). *Homesick: My Own Story*. New York: G. P. Putnam's Sons.

Gies, M. (1987). *Anne Frank Remembered*. New York: Simon & Schuster.

Goertzel, V., & Goertzel, M. G. (1962). *Cradles of Eminence*. Boston: Little, Brown. (Young Adult.)

Graves, C. (1973). *John Muir*. New York: Thomas Y. Crowell.

Kerr, M. E. (1983). *ME, ME, ME, ME, ME*. New York: Harper & Row.

Kudlinski, K. (1988). *Rachel Carson, Pioneer of Ecology*. New York: Viking Kestrel.

Lepscky, I. (1982). *Albert Einstein*. New York: Barron's Educational Series.

Little, J. (1987). *Little by Little: A Writer's Education*. New York: Viking Kestrel.

Little, J. (1990). *Stars Come Out Within*. New York: Viking.

Lomask, M. (1988). *Great Lives: Exploration*. New York: Charles Scribner's Sons.

Markham, B. (1983). *West with the Night*. San Francisco: North Point Press. (Young Adult.)

McKissack, P. C. (1985). *Mary McLeod Bethune: A Great American Educator*. Chicago: Children's Press.

Meltzer, M. (1968). *Langston Hughes. A Biography*. New York: Thomas Y. Crowell.

Meltzer, M. (1985). *Dorothea Lange: Life Through the Camera*. New York: Viking Penguin.

McPherson, S. S. (1990). *Rooftop Astronomer: A Story of Maria Mitchell*. Minneapolis, MN: Carolrhoda Books.

Michener, J. A. (1991). *The World is My Home: A Memoir*. New York: Random House. (Young Adult.)

Miller, M. (1974). *Plain Speaking: An Oral Biography of Harry S. Truman*. New York: Berkley Books. (Young Adult.)

Milton, J. (1987). *Marching to Freedom. The Story of Martin Luther King, Jr.* New York: Dell.

Neimark, A. E. (1986). *One Man's Valor: Leo Baeck and the Holocaust*. New York: Lodestar Books (E. P. Dutton).

North, S. (1956). *Abe Lincoln. Log Cabin to White House*. New York: Random House.

Peavy, L. S. & Smith, U. (1983). *Women Who Changed Things*. New York: Scribners.

Sandburg, C. (1956). *Abe Lincoln Grows Up*. New York: Harcourt, Brace & World.

Sills, L. (1989). *Inspirations: Stories about Women Artists*. Niles, IL: Albert Whitman.

Sloat, S. (1990). *Amelia Earhart: Challenging the Skies*. New York: Ballantine.

Smith, S. (1985). *Journey to the Soviet Union*. Boston: Little, Brown.

Weidt, M. N. (1990). *Presenting Judy Blume*. New York: Laurel Leaf Books.

X., Malcolm. (1965). *The Autobiography of Malcolm X*. New York: Grove Press. (Young Adult.)

Zhensun, Z. & Low, A. (1991). *A Young Painter: The Life and Paintings of Wang Yani—China's Extraordinary Young Painter*. New York: Scholastic.

Periodicals in Gifted Education

Linda Kreger Silverman

Advanced Development
Institute for the Study of Advanced Development
777 Pearl Street
Denver, CO 80302

The first journal on adult giftedness from the viewpoint of inner development. Published annually, each issue of *Advanced Development* has a different theme and contains articles on a specific theorist, a moral exemplar, issues of gifted adults, therapeutic applications, giftedness in women, and poetry.

Challenge
Good Apple Publishers
Box 299
Carthage, IL 62321

A magazine published five times per year for parents and teachers of preschool through eighth grade gifted children. *Challenge* contains reproducible activities for gifted students, articles by leaders in gifted education, a calendar of upcoming events and helpful ideas for parents.

Gifted Child Quarterly
National Association for Gifted Children (NAGC)
1155 15th St. N.W.
Suite 1002
Washington, DC 20005

A scholarly journal, the official publication of NAGC, containing the latest research in the field. *Gifted Child Quarterly* is the oldest professional journal in gifted education and the most frequently cited in articles in education and psychology.

The Gifted Child Today
P. O. Box 637
100 Pine Avenue
Holmes, PA 19043-9937

A magazine for parents and teachers, originally known as *G/C/T*, designed to meet the needs of gifted, creative and talented youngsters. *The Gifted Child Today* is published bimonthly, often has thematic issues, and contains scholarly articles of value in academic settings as well.

Gifted Education Review
P. O. Box 2278
Evergreen, CO 80439-2278

A publication abstracting the latest articles from all of the leading journals and magazines in gifted education. *Gifted Education Review* is published quarterly and provides readers with an overview of the most recent information published.

Journal for the Education of the Gifted
Journals Department
University of North Carolina Press
P. O. Box 2288
Chapel Hill, NC 27515-2288

The official publication of The Association for the Gifted, a division of the Council for Exceptional Children. *The Journal for the Education of the Gifted* publishes quarterly original research, theoretical papers, historical perspectives, reviews of literature, and descriptions of innovative programming.

Roeper Review
P. O. Box 329
Bloomfield Hills, MI 48303

A quarterly professional journal, containing regular departments on family issues, global awareness, assessment issues, recent doctoral dissertations, book reviews, and professional development. *Roeper Review* is designed around themes, includes a wide variety of philosophical, theoretical, empirical and practical articles appealing to a broad audience.

Understanding Our Gifted
Open Space Communications, Inc.
P. O. Box 18268
Boulder, CO 80308-8268

A bimonthly publication for parents, teachers and counselors. *Understanding Our Gifted* is a mini-journal with short, scholarly articles on different themes and regular columns on parenting, instructional strategies, the highly gifted, creativity, current developments, reviews of children's books, hidden gifted learners and aspects of the gifted personality.

Resources for Counseling and Assessment

Linda Kreger Silverman

Association for the Education of Gifted Underachieving Students (AEGUS)
Dr. Susan Baum, Past President
College of New Rochelle
New Rochelle, NY 19805
(914) 654-5336
(203) 429-8117

short-term counseling on underachievement and gifted children with learning disabilities; referrals for assessment; strategies for helping children compensate

The Center for Creativity, Innovation and Leadership
Dr. Dorothy Sisk, Director
2111 Redbird Lane
Beaumont, TX 77710
(409) 880-8046

assessment; counseling of parents; enrichment seminars for parents and teachers

The Center for Gifted
Joan Franklin Smutny, Director
National Louis University
Evanston, IL 60201
(708) 256-1220
(708) 251-2661
(708) 256-5150, ext. 2144

counseling; referrals for assessment; programs for four-year-olds to eleventh graders, Sundays and summers throughout Chicago area; parent and teacher workshops; journal; publications; individual conferencing

Center for Gifted Education
Dr. Joyce VanTassel-Baska, Director
College of William and Mary
Jones Hall Room 304
Williamsburg, VA 23185
(804) 221-2362

assessment and counseling; parent workshops; academic year and summer programs; Governor's schools; newsletter; publications; specializing in disadvantaged and at-risk populations

Center for Talent Development
Dr. Paula Olszewski-Kubilius, Director
Dr. Barry Grant, Associate Director
Northwestern University
School of Education and Social Policy
2003 Sheridan Road
Evanston, IL 60208
(708) 491-3782

Talent Search; referrals for assessment and counseling; parent seminars; summer and academic year programs; newsletter for parents; publications; specializing in economically disadvantaged gifted students

The Center for Talented Youth
Dr. William Durden, Director
Dr. Linda Brody, Director of the Study of Exceptional Talent
Linda Barnett, Director of Talent Searches
The Johns Hopkins University
3400 North Charles St.
Baltimore, MD 21218
(410) 516-0337

assessment and research; Talent Searches: SAT, SSAT, and highly capable students in grades five, six, and seven; children under age thirteen with SAT scores of at least 630 V and 700 M; summer academic programs; publications; public policy

Child and Youth Development Center
Dr. Bruce E. Kline, Director
529 E. Stroop Road
Dayton, OH 45429
(513) 294-6004

intellectual, academic, personality and emotional assessment; individual and group counseling of children, youth, adults and families; school and educational consulting; publications; specializing in parent education, school advocacy and child and youth management

The Counseling Laboratory for Talent Development
Dr. Nicholas Colangelo, Director
Dr. Susan Assouline, Associate Director
Connie Belin National Center for Gifted Education
210 Lindquist Center
The University of Iowa
Iowa City, IA 52242
(319) 335-6148
1-800-336-6463

career counseling; family counseling; Talent Searches; school consultations; summer programs

Educational Consulting Services
Dr. Joan S. Wolf, President
1399 S. 700 East, Suite #16
Salt Lake City, UT 84105
(801) 487-5659

assessment and consultation of gifted children; parent/school consultation; private school and alternative program placement

Excellence in Learning, Inc.
Dr. Marlin Languis, Director
Dr. Marlene Bireley, Chief Psychologist
4900 Reed Road
Upper Arlington, OH 43220
(614) 457-1119

assessment of gifted children with learning disabilities; brain mapping; short-term counseling; strategies for study skills

Family Achievement Clinic
Dr. Sylvia Rimm, Director
1227 Robruck Drive
Oconomowoc, WI 53066
(414) 567-4560

assessment; counseling; family counseling; newsletter; publications; specializing in underachievement, creativity and the highly gifted; creativity and underachievement assessment instruments

Dr. Esther Gelcer, Psychologist
687 Bloor Street East
Toronto, Ontario Canada M4W 1J3
(416) 928-3179   FAX (416) 928-1916

assessment; learning disabilities, neuropsychology, personality, and academic achievement; therapy with individuals, groups, and families; play and art therapy, intergenerational work; specializing in identification and treatment of gifted children, extended family therapy, and social skills training

Gifted Child Development Center
Dr. Linda Silverman, Director
Betty Maxwell, Associate Director
777 Pearl Street
Denver, CO 80303
(303) 837-8378

assessment; developmental counseling (focusing on self understanding and self-actualization) with children and adults; journals and publications; consulting; specializing in the gifted/learning disabled, the highly gifted, spatial learners, emotional development and giftedness in adults

Gifted/Talented Development Services
Elizabeth Meckstroth, Co-Director
2112 W. Cullom
Chicago, IL 60618
(312) 472-4164
intellectual and personality assessment; counseling; parenting workshops; consultations; specializing in highly gifted and adult giftedness

Dr. Miraca Gross
Senior Lecturer of Gifted Education
Faculty of Professional Studies
University of New South Wales
P. O. Box 1
Kensington, New South Wales
Australia 2033
(02) 697-4903

counseling; referrals for assessment; specializing in highly gifted and social and emotional development of gifted children and adolescents

Guidance Laboratory for Gifted and Talented
Dr. Collie Conoley
131 Bancroft Hall
University of Nebraska-Lincoln
Lincoln, NE 68510
(402) 472-6947

career counseling

The Hollingworth Center for Highly Gifted Children
Marcia Greason, Director
P. O. Box 464
South Casco, ME 04077
(207) 655-3767

referrals for counseling and assessment; newsletter; conferences; networking
for parents of highly gifted children

Institute for the Study of Child Development
Dr. Michael Lewis, Chief
Dr. Barbara Louis, Coordinator, Gifted Child Clinic
UMDNJ-RWJ Medical School
97 Paterson Street
New Brunswick, NJ 08903-0019
(908) 937-7700

assessment of preschool and school aged children; skill profiling; educational
counseling; parent counseling

The Laboratory for Gifted at the Counselor Training Center
Dr. Barbara Kerr, Director
401 Payne Hall
Arizona State University
Tempe, AZ 85287
(602) 965-5067

career counseling

The Leta Hollingworth Center for the Study and Education of the Gifted
Dr. Lisa Wright, Director
Teachers College, Columbia University
Box 170
New York, NY 10027
(212) 678-3851

referrals for assessment and counseling; consultations to schools; seminars for parents and workshops for educators; preschool program; week-end enrichment program; Saturday programs for two-year-olds and their parents; summer science camp

Dr. Deirdre Lovecky, Psychologist
11 Whiting Street
Providence, RI 02906
(401) 421-3426

assessment and counseling of gifted children and adults; children's groups; networking for parents; publications; specializing in highly gifted children and gifted children with attention deficits

Office for Precollegiate Programs for Talented and Gifted
Dr. Camilla Benbow, Director
Iowa State University
Ames, IA 50011
(515) 294-1772

educational and vocational counseling; Talent Searches; summer programs

Parents of GT/LD Children
6222 Broad Street
Bethesda, MD 20816
(301) 986-1422

referrals for assessment and counseling; parent networking

Dr. Mary L. Parkinson, Director
Potential Development
68 Risdon Road
New Town, Tasmania
Australia 7008
(002) 28-4068; 28-5480

assessment; counseling; programming; workshops for parents and teachers; camps; thinking and research skills; consulting

Dr. Joan Pinkus, Psychologist
314-2025 West 42nd Avenue
Vancouver, BC V6M 2B5
Canada
(604) 266-5354

assessment; counseling of gifted children and adolescents; family counseling

Halbert Robinson Center for the Study of Capable Youth
Dr. Nancy Robinson, Director
Dr. Kathleen Noble, Assistant Director
Guthrie Annex II, NI-20
University of Washington
Seattle, WA 98195
(206) 543-4160

assessment and short-term counseling; early entrance to college program; Talent Search; summer programs

Rocky Mountain Talent Search
Dr. Jill Burruss, Director
Dr. Karin Dittrick-Nathan, Coordinator
2135 E. Wesley Ave.
200 Wesley Hall
University of Denver
Denver, CO 80208
(303) 871-2983

counseling; Talent Search and summer institutes; referrals for assessment; consulting

Roeper Consultation Service
Dr. Annemarie Roeper
1200 Lakeshore Avenue, #24D
Oakland, CA 94606
(510) 763-3173

counseling with children and parents; consultations with school administrators and teachers; parent groups; publications

Supporting Emotional Needs of the Gifted (SENG)
Dr. James Webb, Director
Leona Gray, Coordinator
Wright State University
School of Professional Psychology
P. O. Box 2745
Dayton, OH 45401
(513) 873-4300

assessment and counseling services; publications; parent workshops; conferences; facilitator training; national referral service for assessment, counseling, consulting

Talent Identification Program
Dr. David Goldstein, Director
Box 40077
Duke University
Durham, NC 27706
(919) 684-1400

Talent Searches; summer programs

Teaching the Talented Program
Dr. Joseph Renzulli, Director
Dr. Sally Reis, Associate Director
362 Fairfield Road
U-7 Hall Building
University of Connecticut
Storrs, CN 06269
(203) 486-4826

educational advice; referrals for assessment and counseling; information packets; National Research Center for Gifted/Talented Newsletter; publications; Confratute; information about summer programs for students

Wisconsin Center for Academically Talented Youth
Dr. Ellie Schatz, Director
8017 Excelsior Drive, Suite 120
Madison, WI 53717
(608) 831-6144

referrals for assessment and counseling; parent seminars and consultations; residential summer programs and workshops for students

Contributors

Leland Baska, M.A., M.S., is a former school psychologist with the Chicago Public School Gifted Program. He has authored several chapters and articles in gifted education and currently serves as a consultant for educational programs and psychological services in Williamsburg, Virginia.

Nicholas Colangelo, Ph.D., is the Myron and Jacqueline Blank Professor of Gifted Education and Director of The Connie Belin National Center for Gifted Education at the University of Iowa. He has authored numerous research and theoretical articles on affective development and counseling needs of gifted students. He was awarded NAGC's 1991 Distinguished Scholar Award. His newest book is *Handbook of Gifted Education* (1991), edited with Gary Davis.

Kathy M. Evans, Ph.D., L.P.C., is an assistant professor of education in the counseling program at the College of William and Mary. She has been involved in counseling culturally different groups since the late 1970s. She is Chairperson of the Virginia Association of Black Psychologists and serves on the Multicultural Research Team for the Virginia Department of Education.

John F. Feldhusen, Ph.D., is the R. B. Kane Distinguished Professor of Education at Purdue University and Founder and Director of Purdue's Gifted Education Resource Institute. Listed in *Who's Who in America*, John is Editor of the *Gifted Child Quarterly* and Past President of the National Association for Gifted Children (NAGC). His latest book is *Talent Identification and Development in Education*.

Dan Holt is a doctoral candidate in educational psychology at Purdue University. His interests are in gifted education with current research in stress and humor as they relate to gifted children.

Fathi Jarwan received his doctorate in gifted education and measurement from Purdue University. His research interests include program development and special schools for gifted students.

Deirdre V. Lovecky, Ph.D., is a clinical psychologist in private practice in Providence, Rhode Island, specializing in the assessment and treatment of gifted children and adults. She is on the advisory board of the Hollingworth Center for Highly Gifted Children, a contributing editor for *Roeper Review*, and a regular columnist for *Understanding Our Gifted*.

Sal Mendaglio, Ph.D., is a counseling psychologist and associate professor in the counseling psychology program at the University of Calgary. He is actively involved in the Council for Exceptional Children and National Association for Gifted Children. He is Past President of TAG-Canada and past Editor of *Global Visions*.

Jean Sunde Peterson, M.A., M.A.T., is a doctoral student in counseling and human development at the University of Iowa. Named South Dakota Teacher of the Year in 1984, she has published several articles and teaching materials, including *Dealing with the Burdens of Capability* for counseling groups.

Kenneth Seeley, Ed.D., is special projects consultant for the Piton Foundation in Denver, Colorado, and adjunct professor at the University of Denver. Formerly the Coordinator of Graduate Education at the University of Denver, he initiated several special programs for gifted and creative students. His publications include co-editing *Excellence in Educating the Gifted* (Love, 1989) and *Comprehensive Curriculum for Gifted Learners*.

Linda Kreger Silverman, Ph.D., is a licensed psychologist and Director of the Gifted Child Development Center in Denver, Colorado. She edits *Advanced Development* and *Understanding Our Gifted* and directs the Institute for the Study of Advanced Development. For nine years, she served on the faculty of the University of Denver in gifted education and counseling psychology. She has published numerous articles and chapters on the emotional development and counseling needs of the gifted.

Joyce VanTassel-Baska, Ed.D., is the Jody and Layton Smith Professor of Education at The College of William and Mary in Virginia where she directs the Center for Gifted Education. She has published widely, including *A Practical Guide to Counseling the Gifted in a School Setting, Comprehensive Curriculum for Gifted Learners*, and *Patterns of Influence: The Home, The Self and The School*. Her most recent book is *Planning Effective Curriculum for Gifted Learners* (Love, 1992).

Index